MW00861352

On a Great Battlefield

On a Great Battlefield

The Making, Management, and Memory of Gettysburg National Military Park, 1933–2023

WITH A NEW PREFACE

Jennifer M. Murray

The University of Tennessee Press / Knoxville

Unless otherwise noted, the photographs are courtesy of Gettysburg National Military Park.

New preface copyright © 2023 by The University of Tennessee Press/ Knoxville.
Copyright © 2014 by The University of Tennessee Press / Knoxville.
All Rights Reserved. Manufactured in the United States of America.
First Edition.

Cloth: 1st printing, 2014.
Paper: 1st printing, 2017; 2nd printing, 2023.

An earlier version of chapter 2 first appeared as "'Far Above Our Poor Power to Add or Detract': National Park Service Administration of the Gettysburg Battlefield, 1933–1938," *Civil War History*, Volume 55, Number 1, March 2009, pp. 56–81. Copyright © 2009 by The Kent State University Press. Reprinted with permission.

The title of the original edition, published in 2014, was *On a Great Battlefield: The Making, Management, and Memory of Gettysburg National Military Park, 1933–2013*.

Library of Congress Cataloging-in-Publication Data
Murray, Jennifer M.
On a great battlefield: the making, management, and memory of Gettysburg National Military Park, 1933–2023 / Jennifer M. Murray. — First edition.
    pages cm
Includes bibliographical references and index.
ISBN 978-1-62190-844-9 (paperback)
1. Gettysburg National Military Park (Pa.)—History.
I. Title.

E475.56.M87 2014
974.8'43—dc23
2014004154

Fourscore and seven years ago our fathers brought forth on this continent, a new nation, conceived in Liberty, and dedicated to the proposition that all men are created equal.

Now we are engaged in a great civil war, testing whether that nation, or any nation so conceived and so dedicated, can long endure. We are met on a great battle-field of that war. We have come to dedicate a portion of that field, as a final resting place for those who here gave their lives that that nation might live. It is altogether fitting and proper that we should do this.

But, in a larger sense, we cannot dedicate—we can not consecrate—we can not hallow—this ground. The brave men, living and dead, who struggled here, have consecrated it, far above our poor power to add or detract. The world will little note, nor long remember what we say here, but it can never forget what they did here. It is for us the living, rather, to be dedicated here to the unfinished work which they who fought here have thus far so nobly advanced. It is rather for us to be here dedicated to the great task remaining before us—that from these honored dead we take increased devotion to that cause for which they gave the last full measure of devotion—that we here highly resolve that these dead shall not have died in vain—that this nation, under God, shall have a new birth of freedom—and that government of the people, by the people, for the people, shall not perish from the earth.

—President Abraham Lincoln, "Address Delivered at the Dedication of the Cemetery at Gettysburg, November 19, 1863 (Bliss version), *Collected Works of Abraham Lincoln,* vol. 7:22–23.

Contents

ILLUSTRATIONS

Figures

Maps

PREFACE TO THE 2023 EDITION: GETTYSBURG BEYOND THE SESQUICENTENNIAL, 2013–2023

The chapters that follow offer a comprehensive and detailed history of the Gettysburg battlefield from its establishment to the sesquicentennial of the battle in 2013. *On A Great Battlefield* is a story of preservation and interpretation at America's most iconic battlefield. It is a narrative that highlights the various ways that the Gettysburg battlefield has been used, sold, and maligned since the Army of the Potomac and the Army of Northern Virginia departed the fields in early July 1863. But, above all, it is a story of the National Park Service's successes and failures in preserving our nation's most "hallowed ground" since that agency assumed control in 1933. One might ask, however, what has happened on the Gettysburg battlefield since the publication of the first edition of *On a Great Battlefield* in 2014. As it turns out, quite a lot. And updating the story only adds to the list of successes and failures on those six thousand acres, further underscoring the battlefield as a landscape of constant transition. Perhaps more crucially, this period of the battlefield's history provides a clarion reminder of the ways in which contemporary events and politics influence not only the stories we tell at Gettysburg, but also our shifting understanding of courage, honor, loyalty, and sacrifice.

Fittingly, a good place to begin is on a relatively cloudy July day in Gettysburg, Pennsylvania, when approximately 40,000 people gathered to commemorate the 150th anniversary of Pickett's Charge, the climatic but unsuccessful frontal assault made by some 13,000 infantrymen of General Robert E. Lee's Army of Northern Virginia. National Park Service rangers conducted multiple walks on that day, July 3, 2013, providing battlefield visitors an opportunity to follow the route of nine Confederate brigades that participated in Pickett's Charge or learn more about the defense of Cemetery Ridge and the action of the men in Major General George G. Meade's Army of the Potomac. More people participated in that commemorative walk than had advanced in the assault 150 years earlier—a tangible sign that Americans' interest in the Battle of Gettysburg remains strong. Four months later, on November 19, 2013, distinguished Civil War scholar James McPherson delivered a keynote address commemorating the 150th anniversary of the day that President Abraham Lincoln came to Gettysburg to honor the Union dead and dedicate the newly established Soldiers' National Cemetery.[1]

The Gettysburg sesquicentennial reflected changes in the park and the country since a similar event fifty years earlier. The National Park Service began planning for the Civil War's sesquicentennial as early as 1998, when a group of superintendents from Civil War sites met in Nashville, Tennessee, to discuss expanding interpretive initiatives at their sites. The superintendents recognized the sesquicentennial as an opportunity not only to educate visitors about the significance and relevance of the Civil War but also to widen its interpretive framework in order to include historically marginalized voices—foremost among them four million enslaved peoples.[2] Decades earlier, the centennial commemoration of the Civil War had occurred amidst violent social and racial upheaval, and the official events overwhelmingly privileged a retelling of a story of the clash between equally noble white Federal and white Confederate soldiers. In preparation for the sesquicentennial and acknowledging the simultaneous anniversaries of both the Civil War and the Civil Rights Movement, the agency's steering committee changed the title of the commemorative events planned for 2011 through 2015 from "Civil War 150" to "Civil War to Civil Rights" (or in government shorthand CW2CR). This philosophical shift was debated within the agency itself, but supporters stressed that this theme better reflected the reality that the Civil War was not a singular event that resolved a myriad of questions centering on citizenship and equality. Defining the years 1861 (the outbreak of hostilities of the Civil War) to 1964 (the passage of the Civil Rights Act) as "critically important to understanding the history of our nation," the National Park Service seized the opportunity to provide better and broader educational opportunities to understand this era in our nation's past.[3]

Over fifty national park sites affiliated with the Civil War participated in the commemoration, but few could match the scope and grandeur of Gettysburg. Yet some observers found the impact and the magnitude of the Civil War sesquicentennial as a whole underwhelming. Rather than a coordinated federal effort to commemorate the war's 150th anniversary, as seen fifty years earlier during the centennial, state and local organizations often organized and executed the events. Distinguished Civil War historian Gary Gallagher quipped that the sesquicentennial was "anemic," while owners of Civil War memorabilia stores grumbled that the 150th did not generate the economic bump they had hoped for. Despite this critique, the sesquicentennial events at Gettysburg, while lacking in the extravagance of those of 1963, still were an impressive success.[4] National Park Service officials at Gettysburg declared that the sesquicentennial events in July and November "exceeded everyone's expectations."[5] Compared to the years leading up to the battle's 150th anniversary, Gettysburg National Military Park enjoyed a slight uptick in visitation recording 1,213,349 visitors in 2013.[6]

What no one could see at the time was that the events of the 150th anniversary of the Battle of Gettysburg lowered the curtain on what in many ways stood as the Park Service's "golden age at Gettysburg."[7] In the fifteen or so years leading up to the sesquicentennial, the battlefield witnessed some of the most sweeping and profound changes in its history, including the opening of a controversial new visitor center, widespread rehabilitation improvements to the historic landscape, and unsurpassed interpretive experiences, events that will be chronicled in later chapters. Yet, the grandeur of the accomplishments seen in the "golden age at Gettysburg" was the exception—not the rule—to the trends in the battlefield's history. At Gettysburg, moreover, the decade following the battle's 150th anniversary saw profound instability in the park's management and served as testimony to the subtle and overt ways that park management exercises its influence on matters of preservation, interpretation, and access. The post-sesquicentennial years brought smaller-scale achievements on the battlefield and some changes to the Park Service's interpretive programming, but nothing like what had come before.

Over the years, Gettysburg's superintendents wielded considerable influence in the management of the battlefield, its resources, and the interpretation of the three-day battle. A change in upper management came quickly upon the heels of the sesquicentennial when Bob Kirby, the park's eleventh superintendent, retired on January 3, 2014. As explained in the conclusion of the present volume, Kirby's brief tenure at Gettysburg, which began in March 2010, was highlighted by the events of 2013, as well as the final removal of the Gettysburg Cyclorama building and the opening phases of the rehabilitation of Ziegler's Grove.[8] On January 1, 2014, the National Park Service announced Ed W. Clark as the battlefield's new superintendent, the twelfth man to hold this post in the agency's history. Most recently serving as the superintendent of Manassas National Battlefield Park, Clark was, according to the NPS Regional Director, "the ideal candidate to lead one of the most significant battlefields in the nation, if not the world."[9]

Under Clark's tenure, the Park Service continued to work to rehabilite the battlefield to its 1863 condition and to implement management philosophies prescribed in the park's 1999 *General Management Plan.* With the removal of the visitor center (2009) and the cyclorama building (2013), the Park Service turned its attention to rehabilitating Cemetery Ridge and Ziegler's Grove, key features of the Army of the Potomac's battle line. That rehabilitation work took several forms. In 2014, for instance, the agency removed the large parking lot at the old visitor center and began restoring the terrain to its 1863 contours.[10] With financial contributions from the Gettysburg Foundation and the NPS Centennial Project in 2016, the National Park Service began a $1.5-million rehabilitation project that provided the resources to clear non-historic trees, alter and revise the cyclorama parking lot and walkways, and re-establish historic grades and elevations (seen most prominently in reclaiming Ziegler's Ravine). The Park Service also replanted missing portions of the grove and reconstructed stonewalls along Hancock Avenue. Construction of the cyclorama center in the early 1960s necessitated landscape modifications in Ziegler's Grove, including the physical relocation of several monuments. Although each had been moved only a few feet north or west, monuments were relocated to their original positions. On September 24, 2014, work crews returned the Battery F 5th U.S. Artillery monument to its original location, and thereafter four additional Federal monuments were reset. This initiative also provided funds to reconstruct one of the commemorative features of Ziegler's Grove—the historic entrance gate to Hancock Avenue, designed and built under the direction of Superintendent Emmor B. Cope in 1923. Replete with two bronze eagles and pillars with plaques reading "Gettysburg National Military Park," this gate once led battlefield visitors into the heart of the Union army's battle line. On October 6, 2017, park and foundation staff participated in a small ceremony marking the completion of the project.[11]

Another significant improvement to the park landscape in recent years came through the efforts of what was then named the Civil War Trust, the nation's largest nonprofit battlefield preservation entity. In the summer of 2014, the Trust announced its intention to restore the site of General Lee's headquarters, located along Chambersburg Pike. At the time of the battle, the home was owned by Mary Thompson. This area, the grounds of the first day's battle, experienced considerable commercialism and modern intrusions in the decades after the battle. The Quality Inn, a forty-eight-room brick hotel complete with a swimming pool, stood adjacent to the historic headquarters. Nearby sat a popular Gettysburg restaurant, the Appalachian Brewing Company. The Trust purchased the hotel property for six million dollars and undertook an extensive renovation project to restore Lee's headquarters, a building that Civil War Trust President Jim Lighthizer described as the "most unprotected historically important building from the Civil War." On October 28, 2016, Trust officials cut the ribbon to unveil the restoration work on Lee's headquarters, marking a significant victory in Civil War preservation.[12]

Recently, the Trust has turned its attention to purchasing properties along the Baltimore Pike, a critical supply corridor for Meade's army. In late September 2017, a local miniature golf course, Mulligan MacDuffer Adventure Golf, closed its doors after twenty-nine seasons of operation. Located along the Baltimore Pike, approximately one-quarter of a mile south of the entrance to the park's visitor center, this property was secured by the Trust to further remove modern intrusions from the fields. At the time of this writing, however, the Trust has not razed this entertainment venue, and it sits abandoned with no apparent remediation plan.[13] Efforts continued with the acquisition of six acres along the Baltimore Pike, near Culp's Hill, in the spring of 2021.[14]

Such endeavors are ongoing. In November 2022, the Trust (which changed its name to the American Battlefield Trust in 2018) announced plans to purchase Pickett's Buffett, a long-standing restaurant on Steinwehr Avenue that sits prominently on the fields of Pickett's Charge, the grand Confederate offensive made on July 3, 1863. Once the restaurant property is purchased, the Trust will demolish the structure, remove the parking lot, and restore the ground to its wartime appearance. Owing to its preponderance of commercial developments, Steinwehr Avenue, as will be covered in later chapters, is a particularly attractive area for preservation efforts. Pickett's Buffett is the southern-most commercial development on this commercial strip, and its removal will only further enhance interpretive understanding of the July 3 battle action.[15]

The most stunning victories in battlefield preservation at Gettysburg in recent years, without exception, have come through the work of the American Battlefield Trust. The removal of each of these modern intrusions helps to restore the battlefield to its wartime appearance and provides a better, richer interpretive experience for Gettysburg visitors.

*****

But as dusk settled on the war's sesquicentennial, and Americans ruminated on the war's legacies and consequences, other events unfolded that forced a reckoning with the "unfinished business" of our nation's most decisive—and defining—epoch. Questions of commemoration, and in particular the appropriate place for Confederate symbolism, stood at the center of much of this discourse. While many cities and commemorative spaces became focal points for these discussions, contemporary conversations and debates over the Civil War's meaning played out prominently on the Gettysburg battlefield. That Gettysburg stood tall amidst national discourse on the tangled threads of Civil War memory should not be surprising—the battle, and indeed the battlefield itself, has always held a singular place in America's collective memory.

On the evening of June 17, 2015, a self-described white supremacist named

Dylann Storm Roof opened fire on a Bible study meeting gathered in Emanuel African Methodist Episcopal Church in Charleston, South Carolina, leaving nine dead. In the days that followed the tragedy, photos emerged on the internet of Roof posing with a Confederate flag as well as other symbols of white supremacy. These images reignited impassioned discussions over the flag as a symbol of racism, white supremacy, and oppression. To be sure, debates over the display and symbolism of the Confederate flag were hardly new. However, the shooting at Charleston's AME Church unleashed a new round of discourse on the appropriate display of Confederate symbols and, as subsequent events would reveal, ushered in a period of profound racial unrest. The Civil War's contested legacy often stood at the center of racial reckoning. Beginning in the summer of 2015, these questions played out on the streets of Richmond, Virginia, the college town of Charlottesville, Virginia, in Minneapolis, Minnesota, and on the battlefield at Gettysburg.[16]

The National Park Service reacted quickly. One week after the shooting in Charleston, the agency's director, Jonathan Jarvis, issued a statement directing National Park Service bookstores and their sales-partners to evaluate their merchandise and voluntarily pull items that only featured the Confederate battle flag. News headlines like "Gettysburg Bookstore Pulls Confederate Flag Merchandise," amplified concerns by many that history was, in their words, being erased. In reality, however, of the 2,600 items in its inventory, only eleven items were removed from the shelves of the bookstore at the Gettysburg visitor center. Merchandise that displayed both the Confederate flag and the American flag continued to be sold.[17]

Nonetheless, on March 5, 2016, a group of demonstrators met on the battlefield to honor the Confederate flag and to celebrate a Confederate heritage that they judged to be endangered. Organized by the J. W. Culp Camp of the Sons of Confederate Veterans (Gettysburg, Pennsylvania), the first-ever "Confederate Flag Day" held in Gettysburg drew approximately two hundred demonstrators. In response to the pro-Confederate flag demonstration, a group of counter-demonstrators, led by history professors at Gettysburg College, also gathered on the battlefield that afternoon. Separated into designated demonstration areas in the shadows of the Eternal Light Peace Memorial, some three hundred people sparred over deeply divided views of the Confederate flag, exchanged expletives and insults, and on a few occasions were separated by law enforcement.[18]

Tension over Confederate symbolism continued to escalate nationally and much of it centered on the appropriate place for monuments honoring Confederate generals and soldiers. When the city council of Charlottesville, Virginia, announced plans for the removal of a statue of Robert E. Lee, hundreds of white supremacists converged upon the college town in mid-August 2017, ostensibly to protest the monument's removal. White supremacists and so-called alt-right supporters, carrying both Confederate and Nazi flags, marched through the University of Virginia's campus and Lee Park. Illuminated by burning tiki torches in their hands, the marchers chanted "Jews will not replace us." The protest turned deadly the next day, as the white supremacists clashed with counter-protesters in downtown Charlottesville. A local counter-protester named Heather Heyer was killed and over thirty others injured when one white supremacist, James Alex Fields, Jr. intentionally rammed his car into a crowd gathered to peacefully protest the Unite the Right Rally.[19] Ultimately, the Charlottesville City Council removed the Lee statue, renaming the park in which the memorial had stood since 1924 Emancipation Park.[20]

To even the most casual of observers, the events at Charlottesville served as a warning about the pervasive racial fissures in American society—and how the Civil War remained both so deeply contested and relevant to that divide. The killing of a man named George Floyd on March 25, 2020, by a Minneapolis police officer, Derek Chauvin, again sparked nationwide protests over police brutality and rejuvenated the Black Lives Matter (BLM) movement. Another round of removals of Confederate symbols swept across the nation, particularly in states of the former Confederacy, and at unprecedented rates. The Southern Poverty Law Center (SPLC) reported that 168 Confederate symbols were removed or renamed in 2020, including 94 monuments. In a February 2021 statement, Lecia Brooks, the SPLC chief of staff, remarked that 2020 was "a transformative year for the Confederate symbols movement." Still, by the SPLC's account in early 2021, slightly over seven hundred Confederate monuments or statues remained on public property.[21]

Public debates over the contested nature of Civil War memory, the Confederate flag, and statues played out at Gettysburg in both subtle and alarming ways. When Republican presidential nominee Donald Trump visited Gettysburg a month before the 2016 presidential election, he harkened to Lincoln's leadership during the Civil War, declaring, "It is my hope we can look at his example to heal the divisions that we are living through right now."[22] As events would soon reveal, however, divisions only widened in America in the ensuing years, and the Civil War's legacies often amplified these fractures. Indeed, Trump added to those fissures when, as president, he seemed to defend the protestors at Charlottesville as "very fine people." Nor would he be the only individual to stand on Gettysburg's historic grounds and conjure up a particular memory of the Civil War in an effort to appeal to modern political perspectives. On more than one occasion, Ku Klux Klan rallies and protests were held on the battlefield. Such gatherings at Gettysburg were not new, but one might wonder what propels white-supremacist organizations like the Klan to rally at Gettysburg in the first place. Why do these hate groups continue to return to Gettysburg to co-opt this historic space to promote a particular version of history or a current political agenda?[23]

While Confederate memorials toppled from their pedestals in scores of communities across the nation, commemorative tributes to the Confederate soldier on the Gettysburg battlefield remained protected by federal law. There are eleven Confederate state memorials honoring southern soldiers on the battlefield, many erected in the mid-twentieth century, and several other monuments to Confederate soldiers and regiments. The official statement on the park website noted, "The NPS will continue to provide historical context and interpretation for all of our sites and monuments in order to reflect a fuller view of past events and the values under which they occurred." Park officials debated how best to respond to the reinvigorated debate over Confederate memorials. They initially considered placing contextualized wayside markers at each of the Confederate state monuments, but determined this initiative redundant. To date, there is a marker at the North Carolina Memorial that explains the monument's history, and park managers are considering placing one at the Virginia Memorial, the first of the Confederate state monuments placed on the battlefield. Important work unfolded in the digital realm, however. Park staff scanned scores of primary source documents relevant to the design and dedication of each of the Confederate monuments in the park, which are now available on the park's website.[24]

A more alarming incident that intensified racial tensions and incongruous understandings of the Civil War occurred at Gettysburg on July 4, 2020. Hundreds of armed protestors converged upon the battlefield in response to an internet-borne false threat that so-called Antifa leftists planned to burn American flags, Confederate flags, and Blue Lives Matter flags in the Gettysburg National Cemetery that afternoon. This was not the first time that false rumors of flag burnings on the Gettysburg battlefield drew a response. On July 1, 2017, for instance, the anniversary of the opening day of the battle's commemoration, hundreds of armed militiamen, members of anti-government groups, individuals from Confederate heritage groups, and Klansmen rushed to Gettysburg, responding to a similar dog whistle. Some of these would-be protectors came from as far as Michigan and Nebraska. No flags were burned on the battlefield then, nor were Confederate monuments desecrated, but crowds cheered in response to declarations that the Civil War wasn't about slavery and that Confederate memorials should remain. Fortunately, no serious disruptions occurred, although one armed protestor accidently shot himself in the leg.[25]

Three years later, the new supposed Antifa threat also proved to be an online hoax. But again it generated the desired response from individuals looking for a fight or provocation. For much of the day, individuals bearing AR-15s and AK-47s and wearing tactical gear and camouflage patrolled the grounds at Gettysburg National Military Park. Many congregated within the boundary of the Gettysburg National Cemetery, where they lounged on benches or leaned menacingly against the stonewall they adorned with "Trump 2020" flags. Others stood along West Confederate Avenue, among them Klansmen who proudly displayed their organization's flag on the back of a pickup truck near the Virginia Memorial. While some of the armed protestors were from the local Pennsylvania and Maryland region, others had traveled hours from Ohio to "protect" the battlefield and its monuments. Many carried or unfurled Confederate battle flags, while others wore Donald Trump t-shirts and hats. Some brought lawn chairs and coolers into the national cemetery, violating long-standing rules. To accompany the Trump flags, the so-called militiamen added a Confederate battle flag and a Blue Lives Matter flag over the stonewall of the national cemetery, the very ground where over 3,500 Federal soldiers killed during the battle lay in their final resting place. Doug Mastriano, then-Pennsylvania state senator and a defeated candidate for the state's governorship in 2022, participated in the event and spent hours mingling with the protestors.[26]

The culminating incident occurred in the Gettysburg National Cemetery, when an individual wearing a Black Lives Matter t-shirt got into a verbal altercation with a segment of armed protestors. A minister from Hanover, Pennsylvania, stated that he was visiting the grave of an ancestor when fifty-some people surrounded him and began verbally harassing him. Law-enforcement officials escorted the pastor from the cemetery but did nothing to his harassers. Gettysburg spokesmen reported that the minister was escorted out of the cemetery "for his own safety."[27] One observer noted that "it was immediately apparent that law enforcement officials had lost control of the event."[28]

How could such an incident occur at one of the most cherished of the nation's historic sites? In anticipation of this event, after all, the National Park Service had increased its law-enforcement presence on the field and was joined by local, state, and federal authorities, including agents from the Department of Homeland Security. But they faced a daunting task. On February 22, 2010, laws concerning firearms in national parks changed to allow visitors to carry weapons in federal parks, provided they complied with state and local laws. Since Pennsylvania is an open-carry state, the protestors in July 2020 were legally allowed to carry their weapons. For reasons that remain unclear, however, park management ignored the violation of several regulations outlined in the Superintendent's Compendium, a guiding document that stipulates rules and regulations specific to each park as implemented by 36 Code of Federal Regulations (36 CFR). For instance, section 2.51 (a) requires that public assemblies or gatherings of more than twenty-five people apply for a permit and be relegated to one of the two free-speech areas designated within the park.[29]

The July 4, 2020, demonstration far exceeded twenty-five people. Additionally, the Superintendent's Compendium provides guidelines for acceptable behavior within the Gettysburg National Cemetery; in describing the purpose of the cemetery, these guidelines specify that only activities "compatible with maintaining the solemn commemorative and historic character of these areas" are permitted. By any reasonable measure, the July 4 fiasco violated both those guidelines and the solemnity and historic integrity of the national cemetery.

Countless individuals found the events that occurred on the Gettysburg battlefield on Independence Day 2020 distasteful, and some of them actively responded. A small group organized what they described as a "teach-in" and met on the battlefield equipped with signs noting the centrality of slavery to the Confederacy and the Army of Northern Virginia. Several of these individuals were confronted and harassed by members of alt-right groups who angrily challenged the message on their signs and the importance of the Black Lives Matter movement.[30] Then, in mid-July, several dozen gathered in a First Amendment corral for a counter-protest of the July 4 fiasco. When the group departed the sanctioned area and walked into the national cemetery, they were confronted by several of the park's law-enforcement rangers. The treatment of the counter-protest group seemed profoundly inconsistent with how the Park Service had handled the agitators on the battlefield on July 4, 2020.[31]

Undeniably, Gettysburg has a long history with white-supremacist groups. Yet the event on July 4, 2020, far eclipsed any other similar incidents on the battlefield in its existence. In managing the event that date, by its own admission, the Park Service had two objectives that day: to keep people safe and to prevent damage to the historic resources. By those limited standards, the day's objectives were met. In more meaningful and symbolic ways, however, the National Park Service failed miserably. Park management allowed for a perverse defilement of the battlefield landscape and national cemetery. Worse, it abdicated its authority in not only enforcing NPS regulations to mitigate such an event occurring on the battlefield and within the national cemetery, but also in upholding its very mission to preserve and protect the park's historic resources, established in both the National Park Service's 1916 Organic Mission and the battlefield's enabling legislation. The events at Gettysburg on Independence Day 2020 and the park's tolerance of the defilement were an insult to the Federal soldiers who died at Gettysburg. How park management might react to a similar event in the future—and if history is any indicator, there will be other such protests—remains to be seen. Until then, July 4, 2020, must stand as the darkest day in the history of Gettysburg National Military Park since its establishment in 1864.[32]

* * * * *

Interpretive programming at Gettysburg, in contrast to the events of July 4, 2020, moved in quite a different direction. In the summer of 1863, Gettysburg was home to a small community of freed African Americans. One of those individuals, Abraham Brian, owned a modest twelve-acre farm on the northern slope of Cemetery Ridge, ground that quickly became integrated into the Army of the Potomac's battle line. When news that the Confederate army was moving through Pennsylvania and rounding up African Americans, Brian and his family fled, only to return to their home after the battle. The structure itself changed considerably after 1863, undergoing various additions and renovations, before being restored to its wartime appearance in the early 1950s. In the summer of 2015, for the first time, the National Park Service opened the Brian structure to park visitors. Peering through Brian's windows allowed visitors the opportunity to contemplate the ways in which the Federal soldiers along Cemetery Ridge were, as the park's chief of interpretation put it, "all that stood between their home and the specter of slavery."[33]

Other opportunities to understand the lives of Gettysburg's free blacks followed. In early December 2019, the agency began extensive work on the Warfield house, which sits along Millerstown Road, near the West Confederate Avenue intersection. At the time of the battle, this two-room stone home was owned by James Warfield, a blacksmith, and his family. Like the Brian family, the Warfields fled as the Confederate army approached. And, like the Brian property, the Warfield house saw significant additions and alterations in the generations after the battle. Park specialists removed the non-historic addition to the house and re-established the structure's historic appearance.[34] Then, in October 2022, the National Park Service installed an interpretive wayside at the house titled "Freedom Threatened," which recounts the story of the Warfields and how they experienced the Battle of Gettysburg. When considering why so few African Americans visit Civil War sites, Gettysburg included, author and former journalist at *The Atlantic* Ta-Nehisi Coates reflected on his visits to Gettysburg and the recent advancements the Park Service has made in broadening the site's interpretation beyond the Federal and Confederate soldiers. He concluded, "Of all the Civil War battlefields I've visited, Gettysburg now seems the most honest and forward-looking."[35] Indeed, it would be impossible to imagine such a panel being erected on the battlefield in the 1960s, or even in the early 1990s. The addition of these sorts of exhibits, combined with more diverse interpretive programming, also reflects the trajectory of Civil War scholarship and conversations that have already taken place in the academic community. These are important additions to the interpretive landscape and recognize how the town's small community of freed African Americans responded to the invasion of Lee's Confederate army.

Arguably, Gettysburg's "golden age" offered the best interpretive experiences in the battlefield's history, both in quantity and quality of programs. For a brief period, this level of programming continued in the wake of the Civil War sesquicentennial. For instance, in the summer of 2015, the park's interpretive daily schedule offered no fewer than twenty different programs, each focusing on a specific part of the battle or broader topical programs for visitors interested in learning about, for instance, the life of a Civil War soldier. Visitors to Gettysburg in the summer of 2015 could join a program that focused on each day of the battle or join a park ranger for an immersive hour-long program on the battle's "key moments." Park rangers also offered evening campfires and two-hour-long battle walks that detailed any number of events or personalities related to the battle or the Civil War itself.[36]

Plagued by a shrinking interpretive staff at both the permanent and seasonal level, unfortunately, Gettysburg's summer programming has slowly dissipated. The COVID-19 pandemic certainly impacted the park's interpretive abilities in a myriad of ways during the summer of 2020 and again in 2021 (and how future trends of COVID-19 might impact the park and public programming remain, of course, uncertain and unpredictable). The Park Service's summer 2022 interpretive programs represent a mere shell of previous years. On a mostly daily basis, park rangers offered nine different topical programs. This summer schedule also suggests that the Park Service is embracing a more elastic educational experience for battlefield visitors, offering programs on World War II soldiers buried in the national cemetery, for instance. Continuing their efforts to integrate diverse perspectives in their educational opportunities, park rangers now offer a program titled "Living on Freedom's Edge" that considers how Gettysburg's African American community experienced the Gettysburg Campaign. Frequent or veteran visitors to Gettysburg nonetheless quickly observe the limited and underwhelming summer program schedule. Those visitors interested in more in-depth opportunities to better understand the three-day battle and the men who fought it will find the park's interpretive programming lacking. Indeed, many areas of the battlefield now remain interpretively neglected—the majority of the nine programs that were offered in the summer of 2022 met either in the Gettysburg National Cemetery or the visitor center.[37]

Interpretive programs were not the only service trimmed back in recent years. Whereas the park library and archives had once accommodated researchers on an open basis, at the time of this writing at least, the park library is closed to outside research requests. The park archives, which house scores of original documents associated not only with the battle but also the park's history, accommodate a mere twelve researchers per year. The 2014 edition of this book, for instance, required spending thousands of hours in the park archives, reading through original, primary sources. Such a project would not be achievable under the current restrictions. No doubt a decrease in staffing compounds problems associated with the decline in interpretive programming and research access. By Gettysburg's reporting, for example, the park employed sixty-four permanent rangers and thirty-nine seasonals in 2015; in 2018, that number had fallen to fifty-two permanents and forty seasonal rangers. Certainly the decline in staffing helps to explain some (but not all) of the restricted access and questions about the park's commitment to visitor services and access remains.[38]

On the other hand, some new and exciting developments in the interpretive agenda at Gettysburg have occurred in recent years. An annual winter lecture series allowed visitors to enjoy a variety of Gettysburg and Civil War Era topics and are well attended. In an effort to broaden its outreach on social media, park staff launched "Coffee with a Ranger" in the summer of 2017. Partnering with the Lincoln Fellowship and Taps for Veterans, every evening from Memorial Day through Labor Day, visitors could experience the "100 Nights of Taps" in the Gettysburg National Cemetery. New programming also occurred at the David Wills house, where Lincoln spent the night before dedicating the cemetery. The Park Service acquired this property in 2004 and opened it to the public in 2009. Seeking to make the house "a part of every visit to Gettysburg and to provide greater opportunities to reflect on the meaning of Gettysburg and the legacy of the American Civil War," the Park Service stopped charging admission during the summer of 2018. Consequently, the home, now staffed by park rangers, has seen an increase in attendance. The park has also undertaken an extensive plan to replace old or outdated interpretive waysides at various locations on the auto tour route, which provide more context to the locations where each is placed. Park staff has also undertaken an extensive rehabilitation project on the Ephraim Wisler house, the grounds where the first shot of the Battle of Gettysburg was fired on the morning of July 1, 1863. Preservation work included the removal of non-historic, modern additions and restoration of the structure to its 1863 appearance. Located along Route 30 (the Chambersburg Pike), this property is expected to be completed in the spring of 2023 and will include a small gravel parking lot for visitor access.[39]

In recent years, park management started to reimagine the uses of historic farmsteads themselves. In the summer of 2017, Gettysburg began leasing the historic Michael Bushman home, located on the second day's battlefield, as a "vacation rental." Park managers cited the C&O Canal, which rented the lock houses for overnight uses, and Valley Forge, as two examples of nearby national parks that lease their historic structures. The park found the program a success, noting that guests have "really enjoyed the unique interpretive experience of spending time in a battle-era home in the heart of the Gettysburg battlefield." In mid-January 2023, Gettysburg announced a plan to lease four historic homes as "short-term vacation rentals (AirBNB/VRBO style)." Three of these properties are signature farmsteads, located on the southern end of the battlefield and were witness to the fierce fighting of July 2, 1863. These farms include the Bushman home, the Slyder home, and the Rose home. The fourth property, the Althoff house, is also located on the southern end of the battlefield, just east of Devil's Den, but was built after the battle. As with many of the management decisions at Gettysburg, this announcement generated considerable discussion. While some criticized the decision to turn historic homes into vacation rentals, the park maintained that such a practice is a cost effective and pragmatic way to support the preservation of these historic structures, while also providing a "unique and immersive visitor experience."[40]

It is an ambitious task to interpret history, and in particular Civil War history, during an era of intense political polarization. These challenges are amplified at Gettysburg, a historic landscape, as this book will reveal, that millions of Americans feel intensely connected to and deeply passionate about. The Park Service at Gettysburg has made important strides in highlighting the wartime experiences of the town's freed African American community. As will be discussed, for generations, Gettysburg's interpretive emphasis centered on Pickett's Charge, often through the lens of the Confederate army. Adding other perspectives in no way diminishes the efforts of Union and Confederate soldiers, but simply adds layers to the complexity of the battle and diverse perspectives to the people who experienced it.

*****

Gettysburg's "golden age" was characterized not only by stability in the park's upper management, but also by exceptional leadership talent. The perfect collision of abilities and vision in Park Service management is, of course, not easily replicated. Unfortunately, the years following the sesquicentennial have been characterized by profound instability. While other changes in upper management occurred after the 150th, frequent changes in the superintendent's position proved most consequential to the management of the battlefield. In late May 2017, the NPS permanently reassigned Superintendent Clark to the Northeast Regional Office at Harpers Ferry Center.[41] This reassignment came as a result of an Office of Inspector General investigation, which found that Clark had violated ethics rules concerning his interactions with the Gettysburg Foundation, the park's nonprofit partner.[42]

After Clark's departure, Gettysburg saw a remarkable six acting superintendents in two years. Interim superintendents are responsible for keeping the ship afloat, not for developing and executing a vision for the park's operation.

By necessity, any accomplishments at Gettysburg during this period were of a small-scale nature. A federal government shutdown, lasting from December 22, 2018, until January 25, 2019, further hindered park operations. Finally, in November 2019, the National Park Service announced the selection of Steven Sims as the new permanent superintendent. A graduate of the United States Military Academy, Sims had previously served as superintendent of Valley Forge National Historical Park. Sims assumed his new post at Gettysburg in late January 2020, becoming the agency's thirteenth superintendent. The new superintendent arrived on the cusp of what eventually became a historic moment. Two months later COVID-19 impacted operations not only at Gettysburg but around the globe.[43]

Several landscape rehabilitation projects already in progress continued under Superintendent Sims's administration. Back in 2002, the Park Service had begun to systematically rehabilitate selected parts of the battlefield. That often involved clearing large sections of non-historic woodlots and excessive vegetation. Through these efforts, impressive and historic vistas were reclaimed, such as along the Codori-Trostle thicket, the ground near the Slyder farm, the Slaughter Pen, Munshower Field, Oak Hill, and Culp's Hill. As impressive as these cuts once were, they did not last. Many of these sections of the battlefield have returned to conditions resembling their early 2000s appearance, with overgrown brush and woodlots eliminating historic viewsheds that were once achieved. For years, the park utilized volunteer labor to help maintain particular areas of the battlefield. This program, Adopt-A-Position, allowed volunteers to organize at least once a year to provide upkeep to their adopted sites. Areas around monuments were particularly attractive for adoption, often by organizations or individuals from the community that the regiment represented. This work often involved clearing weeds and brush from the designated site. Superintendent Sims's administration has pulled back from the very popular Adopt-A-Position and is currently reconsidering how to use volunteer labor.[44]

Some new initiatives fared better. Early in 2021, the Park Service and the Gettysburg Foundation undertook a program to rehabilitate a portion of Culp's Hill, the right flank of the Army of the Potomac's battle line and the site of significant fighting on July 2 and 3. These efforts targeted eighteen acres on Culp's Hill and resulted in the removal of excessive vegetation and understory. Visitors to Culp's Hill now benefit from a more accurate visual understanding of the terrain and, with the addition of new interpretive wayside exhibits, ideally a better sense of the importance of the hill during the battle.[45]

Other landscape modifications continued into the second decade of the twenty-first century, with two significant projects occurring on the southern end of the battlefield. In mid-March 2022, park staff closed Devil's Den for six months to complete critical improvements to mitigate erosion. Devil's Den is one of the most visited sections in the park, and certainly one of the most iconic landmarks on any Civil War battlefield. Consequently, pedestrian traffic around the den—both on and off established trails—resulted in considerable erosion problems. The park reopened Devil's Den on September 30, 2022.[46]

Meanwhile, in July 2022, the Park Service closed Little Round Top for similar, but more extensive, improvements to the historic landscape. This had been a long time in the making, with the initial request for funding submitted in 2009 and environmental assessment reports completed in the subsequent years. Little Round Top was not only the scene of fierce fighting on July 2, 1863, but it is also one of the most popular spots on the battlefield. Consequently, the site suffers from the congestion of vehicular and human traffic and widespread erosion. The rehabilitation work aims to provide the visitor experience on Little Round Top by installing new interpretive exhibits and designating trails and gathering areas. More importantly, this work will better preserve and protect this historic ground. At the time of this writing, the National Park Service estimates that Little Round Top will be closed for eighteen months.[47]

Aspects of Superintendent Sims's tenure nonetheless have been punctuated by controversy. The fiasco that unfolded on the battlefield and in the cemetery on July 4, 2020, stands as an irrevocable stain on his administration. Since his arrival, Sims has reviewed policies and, at times, has taken a more strident and narrow interpretation of various park regulations. Perhaps this approach to regulations stems from controversies over recent park superintendents—two of the three previous superintendents were investigated by the inspector general and reassigned. In the spring of 2021, for example, the park announced new hours of operations—from sunrise to sunset—and reviewed (and altered) policies that previously permitted marathons to be run on the battlefield.[48]

In light of the circus-like events that occurred in the cemetery on July 4, 2020, the Park Service reviewed its regulations regarding what kind of activities should be permitted (or not) in the national cemetery. Activities that were previously permitted are now restricted. For instance, the Sgt. Mac Foundation, an organization that has been placing wreaths on soldiers' graves in the national cemetery since 2008, is now restricted from holding its ceremonies in the cemetery. While flowers can still be placed on the graves at any time, ceremonies are only permitted in the Gettysburg National Cemetery on eleven designated dates of the year, days which coincide with "dates of special historic significance to the Gettysburg National Cemetery and Annex." Other long-standing events have similarly been restricted. Rather than conducting its ceremony in the national cemetery, the First-Year Walk for Gettysburg College freshmen now processes through the cemetery and concludes at the Leister house, one of the park's designated free-speech areas. These decisions, particularly the cancelation of the Sgt. Mac wreaths, have been controversial within some segments of the local community. Yet, it is important to remember how such restrictions came into place—this is a consequence of the perverse defilement that occurred in the national cemetery on July 4, 2020—and these restrictions are in place to prevent, hopefully, a similar event from happening in the future.[49]

At the time of this writing, another particularly sensitive issue centers on the condition of Plum Run Valley. Recently, a handful of beavers migrated into the Plum Run Valley and over time constructed four dams, resulting in considerable expansion of the historic run. Most significantly, this beaver infestation caused Plum Run to encroach upon the 40th New York Monument, dedicated by the regiment's veterans in 1888. To many observers, the beavers are disrupting the region's cultural and historic resources, but park management has maintained that the integrity of the space remains unmolested. Indeed, when pressed on the status of the beavers at a Rotary Club meeting, Sims declared that the creatures would remain until they cause damage to the historic resource. What constitutes damage remains unclear. "Until then," he quipped, "they continue to be our friendly, furry friends."[50]

The park's negligence in addressing the beaver habitat in the now flooded Plum Run Valley underscores concern over the park's general management philosophy and simultaneously reinforces the potential ways in which a superintendent's background could influence his vision for how the battlefield should be managed. And, at some level, the beaver habitat issue highlights what appears to be inconsistencies in park management's wildlife and natural resources policies. For instance, the park continues to cull the white-tailed deer to support "long-term protection, preservation, and restoration of critical elements of the cultural landscape and other natural and cultural resource."[51] Such a systematic effort to remove deer from the battlefields appears inconsistent when management simultaneously allows the beavers to co-exist with the historic environment in the Plum Run Valley. Additionally, while the park has undertaken erosion mitigation efforts on Devil's Den and has begun extensive rehabilitation work on Little Round Top, the negligence of Plum Run Valley seems incongruent and brings under question park management's understanding of both the 40th New York Monument and Plum Run Valley itself as historic resources. What factors might help explain these management decisions? Perhaps these newfound realities are the consequences of the individuals in the two top management positions at Gettysburg not having substantive academic training in history or extensive experience in managing historical parks.

Kristina Heister, the current assistant superintendent, has a background in wildlife and fisheries and has held several natural resource management positions in the agency.[52]

As the following chapters will show, the educational and professional backgrounds of superintendents and their deputies have profoundly influenced the battlefield's management and visitor experience over the years. And compelling arguments can be made that the most successful superintendents, J. Walter Coleman and John Latschar, were more than park *rangers* or *managers,* they were *historians.* Events in the previous decade have forced Americans to grapple, once again, with the contested legacies of the Civil War and the various ways the memory of the Civil War permeates our shared landscapes and public spaces. Now, perhaps more than ever, Gettysburg National Military Park needs strong, visionary leaders with a thorough understanding of the Civil War Era who are prepared—and capable—of facing the challenges of interpreting the Civil War in the twenty-first century. After all, more people visit Gettysburg than any other Civil War site in the national park system. The Union and Confederate soldiers, as well as modern battlefield visitors, deserve better.

*****

In September 2021, the Brookings Institute noted that a national survey found that 46 percent of Americans believed that our country was on the brink of another civil war.[53] Even casual readers of major media outlets could not escape the frequent references to a looming civil war. On March 2, 2019, two columnists for the *Washington Post* wrote an article titled "In America, Talk Turns to Something Not Spoken of for 150 Years: Civil War" in which the contributors postulated that the nation was "on the verge of civil war." Similar predictions appeared elsewhere. On October 1, 2021, *The Atlantic* ran an article noting that conservatives were "Preparing for Civil War." Two months later, Charles Blow a contributor to the *New York Times* forecasted, "We're Edging Closer to Civil War." Drawing an analogy of a then recently issued ruling from the Texas Supreme Court that restricted abortion rights to nineteenth-century white southerners' desires to control the bodies of millions of enslaved peoples, Blow suggested, "I see too many uneasy parallels between what was happening nearly 200 years ago and what is happening now. I see this country on the verge of another civil war." Just months later, in early 2022, an article in *NPR* encouraged readers to "Imagine Another Civil War, But This Time in Every State."[54]

References to an impending civil war abound as modern Americans navigate a turbulent era of toxic partisanship, profound philosophical divisions, and seemingly irreconcilable political differences. Comparing the political divide in modern America to that of the 1860s is a tempting, but dangerous analogy. Doing so fundamentally obscures, or perversely fantasizes, the realities that white and black Americans endured between 1861 and 1865.[55] Indeed, perhaps more than ever, it is imperative to understand the Civil War and all of its complexities, from the stories of white and black soldiers on a battlefield, to the experiences of emancipated peoples, to the civilians on the northern and southern home fronts. Fortunately, through the tireless work of generations of preservationists, the Gettysburg battlefield stands as a tangible landscape to help us better understand those sacrifices and sufferings.

When Lincoln traveled to Gettysburg in November of 1863, he arrived in a town that had borne witness to the destruction of a civil war. During his tenure as president, Lincoln left Washington only a handful of times, and in accepting the invitation to travel to Gettysburg, Lincoln was presented with an opportunity not only to dedicate the Soldiers' National Cemetery but also to articulate his vision for the Union war effort. Ultimately, those gathered in the cemetery on that temperate and sunny November day unknowingly faced eighteen more months of unprecedented death and destruction.[56] By the war's end, some seven hundred thousand Americans had died in the conflict, marking our nation's bloodiest war.

Indeed, the Gettysburg Address, an articulation lasting some two minutes, became Lincoln's most profound speech. Lincoln incorrectly posited that the world would "little note" the remarks made that day, but deftly understood that the sacrifices and efforts made on those fields around Gettysburg would never be forgotten. Our responsibility, whether in November 1863 or at present, is to ensure that the stories of the soldiers of the Battle of Gettysburg, and the civilians in that community, are told accurately and unfailingly.

We might ruminate on Lincoln's speech and his soaring challenge, "It is for us the living, rather, to be dedicated here to the unfinished work which they who fought here have thus far so nobly advanced." If we rise to accept Lincoln's call, how might we dedicate ourselves to the "unfinished work" of the men who fought and died at Gettysburg? How might we be better stewards for both current and future generations who visit Gettysburg to learn of the experiences of the soldiers in the Army of the Potomac and the Army of Northern Virginia and attempt to understand the war's impact on the area's civilians? What does the future of Gettysburg National Military Park look like? And what role does the National Park Service have in facilitating a battlefield experience that more broadly reflects the American people in the twenty-first century while telling an engaging and historically accurate story about our nation's most decisive epoch? Indeed, looking beyond 2023, the National Park Service at Gettysburg faces various challenges. Some are practical. The realities imposed by a shrinking staff are felt (and seen) across the park. For instance, rather than seeing a well-maintained landscape, visitors now see a battlefield that *looks neglected*. In the absence of staff to execute a systematic mowing program, weeds and grass now overtake once-maintained areas. Some of the park's historic homes, such as the Klingel farm and the Hummelbaugh property, are visibly deteriorating. Meanwhile, in 2018, battlefield visitation dropped below the one-million mark, statistical evidence that visitation to Gettysburg has been on a gradual but steady decline. Managers of historical sites across the nation are on a perpetual quest to attract new audiences, and many, like those at Gettysburg, are hindered by a declining permanent staff. Questions about the long-term impact of the current park administration also remain—and as this book shows, park managers have had and will continue to have a profound influence on the physical and intellectual integrity of the battlefield.

Yet, perhaps the 160th anniversary of the Battle of Gettysburg offers more than another opportunity to recast familiar narratives of the fighting between the two armies. It is not hard to find the relevance of the Civil War in our daily lives, and a better, more complete understanding of that epic conflict is imperative. The July 2023 anniversary encourages us to reflect on the magnitude and consequences of the war's deadliest battle and to consider the importance of a landscape once deemed "hallowed ground."

This book, in both the writing of it and the reading of it, is one small way to help ensure that the events that occurred at Gettysburg in the summer of 1863 are remembered in perpetuity. In understanding the battlefield's 160-year history, perhaps we can also better understand our collective past and shared future.

ACKNOWLEDGMENTS

Writing the history of the Gettysburg battlefield has been a herculean topic and I have received the assistance and support of many individuals during this odyssey.

For nine summers, I had the pleasure of working as a seasonal interpretive ranger for the National Park Service at Gettysburg National Military Park. I talked with thousands of visitors about the Civil War and the battle, led scores of eager pilgrims around Devil's Den, McPherson Woods, and the Peach Orchard, watched the sunset on Little Round Top, built a campfire in Pitzer Woods, and found solace and serenity walking along East Confederate Avenue. Along the way I had the fortunate pleasure of working alongside some of the finest in the Green and Gray and befriending scores of others. Gettysburg will always hold a special, personal place in my heart.

Thus, through my tenure as a park ranger at Gettysburg and more recently as a researcher on the history on the battlefield, I owe an enormous amount of gratitude to several individuals at Gettysburg National Military Park. John Heiser patiently answered numerous research requests and questions, pulled scores of files from the park library, and offered much encouragement and humor. Greg Goodell, the park archivist, gave me open access to the park's records, pulled hundreds of boxes of research material, and allowed me to establish residency in the archives. Dr. John Latschar, former Gettysburg superintendent, read every chapter of this project as it originated as my dissertation and provided keen, substantive comments. During this process I benefited enormously from numerous conversations with Gettysburg's senior historian, Kathy Harrison, whose knowledge on the history of battlefield is unmatched. I also owe a special thanks to Katie Lawhon, who helped me navigate through much of the contemporary files and photographs. Others patiently listened while I questioned them about the development of the national military park or needed access to materials, including Winnona Peterson, Jo

Sanders, Norma Lohman, Scott Hartwig, and Eric Campbell. This is a better book because of their contributions.

This project originated as my dissertation at Auburn University. My five years at Auburn University as a doctoral student stand as one of the highlights of my life. Auburn's History Department offered me a supportive and vibrant academic community. Specifically, my advisor, Dr. Kenneth Noe, patiently and professionally guided me through the stages of obtaining the PhD. He answered seemingly endless questions about classes, comprehensive exams, publications, letters of recommendation, and jobs. Through his mentoring I am a better historian and scholar. Doctoral students carry the reputation of their advisor; I am honored to call myself a Ken Noe student.

I want to thank the staff at the University of Tennessee Press. Specifically, Scot Danforth, my editor, for taking an interest in this project and skillfully shepherding it through the publication stages. Thanks as well to the outside readers for their support of this project.

I want to thank my parents, Michael and Jacqueline, and my sister, Brittany. My parents have been beacons of support and encouragement throughout my life, and I owe much of my success to them. Brittany has packed, unpacked, assembled, and disassembled my apartments more times than she has desired to, yet maintained relatively good humor in doing so. Hopefully I am un-packed for a while.

Unfortunately, the one person to whom I owe the most gratitude toward not only in the completion of this book, but in countless other facets of my life, passed before its publication. For over a decade, Clyde R. Bell was my best friend and companion. He cheerfully accompanied me on dozens of research trips, read every chapter of this book more times than he cared to, looked up random information to verify facts, and endured hours listening to me talk about this project. He never wavered in his support, continuously offering me his "full measure of devotion." This book is because of Clyde; as it is for him. I hope I have made him proud.

* * * * *

A decade after the original publication of *On a Great Battlefield,* Gettys-burg remains the singularly most important location in my professional career, as well as in my personal life. I have studied the Battle of Gettysburg now for over twenty years; my interest in the July 1863 fighting between the Army of the Potomac and the Army of Northern Virginia has only grown, and my appreciation for the battlefield landscape and its unique and complex history has only deepened. The previous ten years, 2013–2023, witnessed considerable changes, improvements, and controversy at Gettysburg National Military Park, and I am delighted with the opportunity not only to chronicle those changes, but to reflect on how contemporary Americans understand and experience Gettysburg, the Civil War's bloodiest battle.

In writing the preface to this revised edition, I wish to acknowledge several individuals who have helped bring this project to fruition. Once again, I enjoyed the opportunity to work with Scot Danforth, now director of the University of Tennessee Press, and welcomed his enthusiastic support of this updated edition. At the time of this writing, the park has imposed severe restrictions on visitor access to the park library and archives. Research access to files and documents necessary to write about the history of the battlefield, or the battle itself, is now nearly nonexistent. Fortunately, a significant part of the research needed to tell the story of the battlefield's history over the last ten years is available through determined and clever internet research. I am grateful to both Christopher Gwinn, chief of interpretation at Gettysburg National Military Park, and Teresa Bulger, senior historian at Richard Grubb & Associates, for sharing important files and documents to assist in a better, more detailed recounting of the 2013–2023 era at Gettysburg. Additionally, thanks to Ken Noe, John Heiser, and members of the OSU Department of History Writing Group for reading drafts of this preface and providing thoughtful and helpful feedback.

In the years since this book first came out, I met my husband, Michael Waricher, perhaps not surprisingly at Gettysburg. Shortly before we met, Michael had read *On a Great Battlefield* and our common interest in the battlefield and its history offered an immediate source of connection and conversation. Indeed, Michael's passion for Gettysburg's history eclipses my own, and his knowledge of the battlefield, combined with his expertise in Gettysburg's commemorative photography, is simply unrivaled. Michael's unwavering support and encouragement have made any number of my achievements possible, including this one. Each day, I am profoundly grateful that we met . . . on a great battlefield.

INTRODUCTION

Seven score and five years after the battle of Gettysburg and President Abraham Lincoln's declaration of the battlefield as "hallowed ground," the National Park Service (NPS) unveiled its new 103 million dollar Gettysburg National Military Park Museum and Visitor Center, the culmination of years of planning, fundraising, and bitter controversy. The April 14, 2008, event coincided with a broad program of battlefield landscape rehabilitation that collectively brought the most extensive changes to the Gettysburg battlefield since the 1880s. Both of these platforms—the creation of a public-private partnership to build and operate a new museum and the ongoing landscape changes—raised a firestorm of controversy among interest groups and individuals across the nation. While Civil War scholars largely applauded the Park Service's intentions to create a historically accurate landscape, now popularly referred to as reclaiming the battlefield's "historic integrity," others decried the agency's intentions to "rape" the battlefield they knew. Additional criticism centered around the new museum's more inclusive story-line that included exhibits on secession, slavery, and Reconstruction, seemingly at the expense of beloved collections and familiar stories. Such broadened interpretation challenged an entrenched reconciliationist narrative and underscored the pervasiveness of the Lost Cause mentality lingering in the twenty-first century. Some fervent opponents demanded the resignation of Gettysburg's superintendent, John Latschar, claiming the new interpretive focus defiled southern heritage. One critic declared this contextual interpretation as a "cosmic threat to all battlefields in this country." Environmental enthusiasts decried the removal of trees and woodlots, believing such a practice incompatible with the National Park Service's conservation mission.[1]

Years before, in the final decades of the nineteenth century and as part of the "golden age of battlefield preservation," Civil War veterans had first manufactured the Gettysburg National Military Park these critics defended into an enduring, physical memorial for their comrades. At Gettysburg, as well as the war's other national military parks, veterans created a landscape that embodied sectional reconciliation. Through purposeful design, Gettysburg became less a testament to the visceral realities of civil war than an iconic landscape of peace and unity with an emphasis on soldiers' courage rather than causes and consequences. Deliberate creation of national military parks served not only to "bind the nation's wounds," but established civic spaces to champion what historian Michael Kammen terms the "heritage syndrome." In his analysis of American culture and memory, Kammen identifies an omnipresent tendency of Americans to "remember what is attractive or flattering and to ignore the rest." The National Park Service's decision to shift the long-standing interpretive focus at Gettysburg from the "High Water Mark" to "A New Birth of Freedom" thus led to an ensuing outcry that underscored the "heritage syndrome" of the Civil War.[2]

Underlying this clamor, moreover, was the fact that not only had Gettysburg offered a reconciliationist slant, but also a strong Confederate focus. In 1942 the National Park Service acquired the Gettysburg Cyclorama, the 360-degree painting depicting Pickett's Charge on July 3, 1863, and made the cyclorama the central feature of its interpretive programming. Already five decades old, the painting heralded the valor and courage of the Confederate assaulting force and helped reinforce Pickett's Charge as the climactic moment of the battle, the "High Water Mark," if not of the entire war. One NPS official declared the painting to be "the most important exhibit we shall ever have" and recommended that all future decisions "be built around it." Emphasizing the cyclorama led to the perpetuation of the "High Water Mark" thesis. Subsequent management decisions driven by the prominence of the painting included the location of the agency's first visitor center, the development of a tour route, and the introduction of various interpretive programs and mediums.[3]

Today, the National Park Service manages approximately seventy other sites associated with the Civil War era. These include a variety of properties ranging from the war's battlefields, to Ford's Theatre, to the Clara Barton National Historic Site, to the Arlington House. Among these diverse sites, however, none hold the national appeal and recognition of Gettysburg National Military Park. Whether or not Gettysburg deserves its nomenclature as the war's "High Water Mark" can be debated. What is certain, however, is that since the battle, Americans made and accepted Gettysburg as the Mecca of Civil War landscapes. An examination of the public comments written to park officials in the final years of the twentieth century in light of the interpretive and rehabilitation controversies reveals a deep and often unexplainable connection to the landscape once littered with unimaginable horrors of war. "I am writing this letter to you from my heart," a Georgia woman wrote to John Latschar, "To me, Gettysburg ranks up in the top five items that I treasure the most: God, My Husband, My Family & Friends, My Church, and Gettysburg."[4]

Little Round Top. Devil's Den. McPherson Ridge. Culp's Hill. The names of terrain features of the battlefield are instantly recognizable. Union and Confederate soldiers battled in scores of small towns and farm fields across the nation, but none of those battlefields evoke the emotional, visceral connection of Gettysburg. More than with the three days of fighting, however, Gettysburg became associated with the articulation of the Union war aims and the vision of the nation's "new birth of freedom." The distinguishing feature of the Adams County battlegrounds became President Abraham Lincoln's 272-word speech dedicating the Soldiers' National Cemetery on November 19, 1863. Quickly, the national cemetery became one of the most visited spots on the battlefield and the words of the address resonated deeply with ensuing generations of Americans. Each year, over one million visitors from across the nation and around the world come to Gettysburg. The National Park Service is thus encumbered with an enormous responsibility of preserving the war's "hallowed ground" and educating the public, not only on the battle, but also about the Civil War as the nation's defining moment. Thus, the National Park Service is a purveyor of the war's popular memory. Through the landscape itself, the battlefield and museum exhibits, and ranger programs, the National Park Service assumes a proactive role in facilitating and molding Americans' understanding of the conflict.

Not surprisingly, thousands of books and articles are devoted to the battle. Year after year, historians and enthusiasts add to the litany of Gettysburg scholarship, examining, or often reexamining, various aspects of the battle. Yet for all the battle's dissection, scholars have paid only minimal attention to the battlefield itself and the process of preserving, interpreting, and remembering the bloodiest battle of the Civil War. This book seeks to provide a critical perspective to Gettysburg historiography by examining not the battle, but the national military park, and specifically how the Gettysburg battlefield has evolved since the National Park Service acquired the site in August 1933. This eight-decade period highlights the complicated nexus between preservation, tourism, popular culture, interpretation, and memory. The Park Service's management of the battlefield occurs not in a vacuum, but within a larger realm of political, social, and academic trends. Decisions made by park officials simultaneously influence the interpretive story at Gettysburg, the narrative presented to thousands of park visitors, and shape more broadly the Gettysburg experience. The story of the battle of Gettysburg has been told; the story of the Gettysburg battlefield largely has not.

This is not surprising. Only recently have scholars begun to examine the process of preserving and interpreting America's battlefields in general, much less the grounds at Gettysburg. This small field of scholarship on the history and memory of Gettysburg includes crucial narratives by Amy Kinsel, Jim Weeks, Carol Reardon, and Thomas Desjardin. Other sites have received even less attention. Timothy Smith's pioneering work has offered a deeper understanding of the establishment of the first five federally preserved battlefields: Chickamauga & Chattanooga, Antietam, Shiloh, Gettysburg, and Vicksburg. Paul Shackel and Edward Tabor Linenthal examine issues of memory and culture at several historic sites. Scholars have devoted minimal attention, however, to examining the more contemporary and complicated relationship between preservation, interpretation, broader cultural trends, and memory.[5]

While the historiography of battlefield preservation and of the Gettysburg battlefield more specifically is relatively scant, a broader, deeper scholarship now exists on historical memory, particularly as related to the Civil War. Two of the best earlier works on the birth of the Lost Cause ideology are Gaines Foster's *Ghosts of the Confederacy: Defeat, the Lost Cause, and the Emergence of the New South, 1865–1913* and Charles Reagan Wilson's *Baptized in Blood: The Religion of the Lost Cause, 1865–1920*. Another work addressing Civil War memory is Nina Silber's *The Romance of Reunion: Northerners and the South, 1865–1900*, which examines how northerners cultivated images of reunion, often grounded in perceived notions of gender and honor. Kirk Savage's *Standing Soldiers, Kneeling Slaves: Race, War, and Monument in Nineteenth-Century America* studies efforts to depict slavery and emancipation in monuments and sculptures in the years following the Confederate defeat. The foremost work on Civil War memory is David Blight's *Race and Reunion: The Civil War in American Memory*, which highlights how the Civil War generation created three competing interpretations of the war—perspectives that emphasized the nobility of the Confederate cause, the centrality of emancipation, or the reconciliationist notion of a war in which all were brave and true. In Blight's eyes, reconciliation eventually pushed aside the cause and contributions of African Americans. Subsequent books by scholars such as William Blair, Barbara Gannon, and Kevin Levin similarly explore the interplay between race, reunion, and memory in the post–Civil War nation.[6]

Tracing Civil War memory and trends in interpretation at Gettysburg can be complicated. Since the spring of 1864, three organizations have shouldered the task of preserving the battlefield: the Gettysburg Battlefield Memorial Association (GBMA, 1864–1895), the United States War Department (1895–1933), and the current administrator, the NPS. Several themes emerged after the NPS acquired the battlefield in 1933. Most apparent, the history of the Gettysburg battlefield underscores the complexity of preserving and interpreting a historic landscape. Gettysburg offers an example of how landscapes develop, or evolve, over time. One historic preservationist summarized that "landscapes are dynamic, ever-changing phenomena."[7] This characterization undoubtedly applies to the Gettysburg battlefield. Several factors account for the dynamics of Gettysburg's changing landscape. The site's first stewards, the GBMA and the War Department, managed the battlefield as a memorial to the men who fought. The National Park Service, however, struggled to develop a consistent management philosophy. Within the agency, haphazard landscape practices, promotion of tourism to the national parks, encouragement of recreational pursuits, and ill-defined policies of preserving cultural resources regularly influenced the direction of the park's management. Compounding the lack of a national directive, inevitable management change at a local level further magnified differing preservation and interpretation theories. Between August 1933 and October 2009, ten National Park Service superintendents administered Gettysburg National Military Park. The eleventh superintendent reported for duty on March 1, 2010. The changes in direction occasioned by such turnover resulted in an ever-evolving management philosophy and battlefield. Superintendents' backgrounds, whether as landscape architects, government bureaucrats, or historians, consistently shaped their vision for the battlefield.

The complexity of the battlefield's history, however, can only truly be understood by looking at events beyond the federal boundary and outside of the National Park Service. A multitude of external factors influence the operations of the battlefield, and more importantly, mold Americans' understanding of the battle and their history. Never far removed from larger political or social issues, historic preservation trends and the evolution of the Gettysburg landscape did not develop in isolation. When the National Park Service assumed control of the battlefield, for example, the Great Depression loomed large over the nation. Through unprecedented funding allocated from New Deal projects, park management oversaw the construction of a modern tour route, visitor facilities, and road repairs. Significant to the hullabaloo generated by the landscape rehabilitation program of the twenty-first century, park officials initiated the first cutting of non-historic woodlots in 1940, a practice that subsequent superintendents periodically continued. America's involvement in World War II had an indelible influence on the battlefield and Americans' association with it. During the war, the Gettysburg Address surged in popularity as individuals sought solace in the sacrifices of Union and Confederate soldiers and comfort in Lincoln's words. Beginning in 1941 and climaxing during the early years of the Cold War, Gettysburg became a platform of patriotic expression. Orators invoked the deeds of the soldiers and readily referenced selected lines from the Gettysburg Address as a call to fight Nazism or stop communist aggression. "Government of the people, by the people, for the people" became an often-quoted line in opposition of despotism and tyranny. Such patriotic appeals paralleled the postwar popularity of civic pilgrimages, which reaffirmed Gettysburg as a tourist destination and underscored the "heritage syndrome."[8]

During the Civil War Centennial, no commemorations captivated the nation more than those held at Gettysburg in 1963. Yet while the event emphasized a theme of "A Nation United," the Civil Rights Movement underscored a different national reality. For millions of Americans, the "new birth of freedom" had not yet been delivered. Beginning in 1961, both northern and southern politicians stood on the Gettysburg battlefield and articulated pleas for racial unity in a continuance of the work begun five score ago. When speaking for social and political equality for blacks, orators referenced Lincoln's Gettysburg Address and encouraged listeners to dedicate themselves "to the proposition that all men are created equal." Others, namely Alabama governor George Wallace, enunciated a different vision. The simultaneous occurrence of the Civil War Centennial and the Civil Rights Movement afforded the nation, and the National Park Service, the opportunity to reexamine the war's predominant narrative. Yet the centennial passed without modifications to the story-line; visitors to Gettysburg continued to receive a narrative centered on the generals and soldiers, devoid of social and political complexity.

Challenges to the war's "heritage syndrome" emerged at the end of the century. Within the Park Service, superintendents initiated discussions to expand the interpretive story-line at the nation's Civil War sites. As Gettysburg's management sought to fulfill this directive, Americans articulated differing understandings of the reasons for the war, and it became increasingly clear that, in the eyes of many, a discussion of slavery at the battlefield was simply not fitting or proper. Certainly, this passionate connection to the American Civil War cannot be overstated. According to a recent study by Ancestry. com, 18 million Americans have an ancestor who fought in the Civil War and an estimated two-thirds of Americans have an ancestor who lived during the conflict. Sometimes it seemed that all of them had an opinion about how to run Gettysburg.[9]

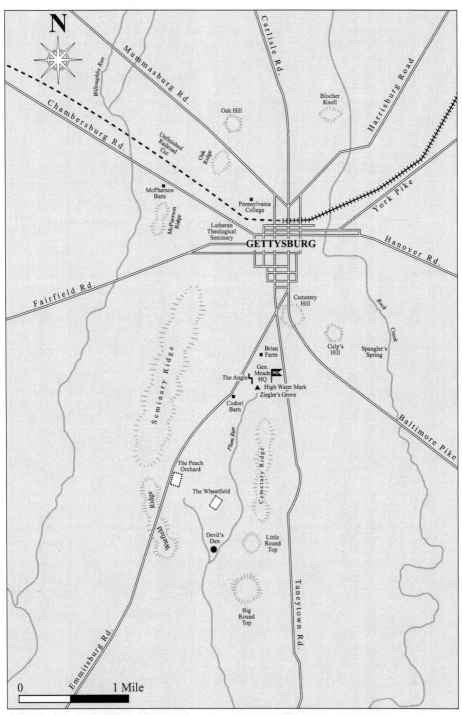

Key Terrain Features and Sites at Gettysburg, 1863. Map created by Alexander Mendoza.

CHAPTER 1

WE ARE MET ON A GREAT
BATTLEFIELD: GETTYSBURG,
1863–1933

Two weeks after the battle of Gettysburg and the climactic, disastrous, frontal assault of July 3, later to be known as Pickett's Charge, the remnants of the defeated Army of Northern Virginia rested securely on the south bank of the Potomac River. News of the three days of fighting in a small south-central Pennsylvania town headlined newspapers across the nation. Northerners rejoiced that their Army of the Potomac had finally defeated the seemingly invincible General Robert E. Lee and the Army of Northern Virginia. Upon learning of the Federal victory at Gettysburg, the *Philadelphia Inquirer* headlined, "Victory! Waterloo Eclipsed!" Yet, for the Union and Confederate soldiers who endured and survived the fighting along round tops, peach orchards, and wheat fields, their writings in the days after the battle offer a more solemn reflection. "No doubt the news of the great three days battle of Gettysburg has resounded throughout the land and fill many a heart with mourning," wrote William Calder of the 2nd North Carolina to his mother on July 18, 1863. Samuel Wilkeson, a *New York Times* correspondent who had covered the battle, offered a eulogy to the thousands slain on the battlefield. "Oh, you dead," he wrote, "who at Gettysburg have baptized with your blood the second birth of freedom in American how you are to be envied!" Among those who baptized the fields in blood was Bayard Wilkeson, a nineteen-year-old lieutenant serving in Battery G, 4th U.S. artillery. While defending Blocher's Knoll on July 1, Wilkeson fell mortally wounded. Three days later, Samuel Wilkeson identified the young lieutenant's body as his son's.[1]

The words of Private Calder and Samuel Wilkeson typified the sentiments of many of the men who fought at Gettysburg on July 1–3, 1863. By the time the 160,000 men of the two armies converged in Gettysburg, the Civil War had entered its third summer. Though the nation had become a "republic of suffering,"

Americans had yet to witness a battle as large or ultimately as deadly as the three days at Gettysburg. The number of casualties at the end of the battle was approximately 51,000, including 10,000 killed, over 30,000 wounded, and nearly 11,000 missing or prisoners of war. For the 2,400 residents living in the small crossroads and the surrounding countryside, life would never be the same.[2]

As the defeated Confederates withdrew from their battle line along Seminary Ridge on July 4, local residents struggled to regain some resemblance of their former lives. The impact of 160,000 soldiers, 50,000 mules and horses, and thousands of artillery pieces on the landscape left an indelible imprint of the "hard hand of war." Residents, many of whom hid in their basements for safety, emerged to find their fields and crops consumed or ruined, fences torn down or destroyed, and wells drained or contaminated from decomposing human and animal corpses. Wounded soldiers recovered in homes and public buildings for weeks after the battle. Over 7,000 dead men lay haphazardly buried in shallow graves on the fields where they fell.[3]

Surrounded by unimaginable tragedy and death, citizens initiated efforts to establish a cemetery for the fallen Union soldiers. David Wills, a local attorney, purchased twelve acres on behalf of the Commonwealth of Pennsylvania and seventeen other northern states, for the creation of a proper burial of their now dead sons, brothers, or husbands. Wills selected the high ground of Cemetery Hill, a key piece of terrain that had figured prominently as part of the Union battle line. This ground was adjacent to the Evergreen Cemetery, the town's civilian cemetery. Once purchased, Wills then arranged to have noted Scottish horticulturist William Saunders design the burial ground. Within weeks a reburial crew, led by Samuel Weaver, began to disinter Union bodies from makeshift battlefield graves and reinterred them in the new cemetery. In the midst of a bitter civil war, the fallen Confederates were denied burial in the newly created Soldiers' National Cemetery; they remained buried on the battlefield until the 1870s when their remains were exhumed and reburied in southern cemeteries.

Underscoring the North's collective understanding of the magnitude of the events on the Pennsylvania farm fields, approximately 20,000 spectators braved the cold autumn day to witness the dedication of the Soldiers' National Cemetery. On November 19, 1863, Boston orator Edward Everett delivered a keynote dedication speech that lasted nearly two hours. Then President Abraham Lincoln stood to say a "few appropriate remarks." In less than two minutes, Lincoln's Gettysburg Address captured the enormity of the war, while offering a "final resting place" for the Union soldiers who had sacrificed their lives so that a "nation might live." Interments in the new cemetery continued through the spring of 1864.[4]

The Soldiers' National Cemetery symbolized an effort to properly honor men who gave the "last full measure of devotion." Meanwhile, other preservation efforts were already in motion. Within weeks after the battle, local residents began to preserve key areas of the battlefield to further commemorate the Army of the Potomac's grand victory. David McConaughy, another local attorney, spearheaded the movement. This effort was unprecedented. On August 9, 1863, a little more than one month after the battle, McConaughy noted that, "there could be no more fitting and expressive memorial of the heroic valor and signal triumphs of our Army . . . than the Battle-field itself." State officials agreed and on April 30, 1864, less than one year after the battle, the Pennsylvania legislature chartered the Gettysburg Battlefield Memorial Association (GBMA). Not only was this Gettysburg's first preservation organization, it was also the nation's earliest attempt to preserve Civil War battlegrounds. The charter provided the GBMA with the authority to "hold and preserve, the battle-grounds of Gettysburg, on which were fought the actions of the first, second, and third days of July . . . with the natural and artificial defenses, as they were at the time of said battle."[5]

The GBMA, an association that consisted mainly of local residents, guided the formation of the battlefield in its early years. Essentially this organization focused its efforts on three issues. First, since the fighting occurred on dozens of farmsteads and across twenty-five square miles, the commissioners sought to purchase lands connected with the battle. Within one year of its establishment, the GBMA had acquired seventy-five acres. In 1866, an additional twenty-nine acres at the round tops and four acres where Major General John Reynolds fell on the morning of July 1 were purchased. Second, the commissioners supervised the placement of the battlefield's earliest monuments and markers. In the years after Appomattox, Union veterans eagerly sought to erect markers and monuments as visible symbols of their comrades' sacrifice. The GBMA oversaw the placement of 320 markers. Finally, the commissioners proceeded to build the battlefield's first avenues. By 1895, nearly twenty miles of rudimentary avenues along the Union battle line had been constructed.[6]

The GBMA's preservation efforts were commendable and unprecedented. Within two months after the armies retreated, and as the darkness of civil war continued to pervade the country, Gettysburg residents had the foresight to establish an organization to preserve these hallowed grounds. Hindered by a lack of money and a strict enabling legislation, however, the association was only able to purchase land on the Army of the Potomac's battle line. The Confederate battle line remained in private hands, which became a vital issue as the battlefield evolved into a landscape of reconciliation between North and South. Grander visions of the local preservation association ushered in the second phase of battlefield preservation. This phase occurred in the final two decades of the nineteenth century, in what Timothy Smith defines as the "golden age of battlefield preservation." Reflective of heightened sectional reconciliationist sentiments, Union and Confederate veterans strove to mark and commemorate the grounds recognized to be among the war's defining battles. The timing was opportune in Washington; in 1890, half of the congressmen were Civil War veterans. With their support in the final decade of the nineteenth century, Congress authorized the establishment of five national military parks under the administration of the War Department: Chickamauga & Chattanooga (1890), Antietam (1890), Shiloh (1894), Gettysburg (1895), and Vicksburg (1899).[7]

The War Department's principal purpose in providing federal protection for these battlefields was to protect the grounds and to preserve them as a memorial to the men who fought and those who had died. To prepare the transfer of the GBMA holdings to the War Department, in May 1893 Secretary of War Daniel Lamont appointed three men to a newly created park commission, organized to administer the daily operations of the battlefield. With a nod toward binding the nation's wounds, Lamont reserved one of the commissioners' seats for a southerner. The first commissioners were Colonel John P. Nicholson, a Union veteran from Pennsylvania; Brigadier General William H. Forney, an Alabamian and battle veteran; and John Bachelder, who had not fought in the battle, but served in the capacity as a civilian reporter, and acted as the battlefield's first historian. Two months later, Lamont appointed Colonel Emmor B. Cope to serve as the commission's chief engineer.[8]

After appointing the commissioners, Lamont and the War Department moved to officially acquire property held by the Gettysburg Battlefield Memorial Association. On December 6, 1894, New York Representative and former Union general Daniel E. Sickles, already a controversial figure in Gettysburg lore, introduced H.R. 8096. With little debate, on February 11, 1895, Congress approved "An Act to Establish a National Military Park at Gettysburg, Pennsylvania." Popularly called "the Sickles Bill," this legislation established the federal park boundary at 3,331.5 acres. The GBMA deeded its 522 acres to the federal government, which then formally established Gettysburg National Military Park as the fourth Civil War battlefield administered by the War Department.[9]

The enabling legislation specified three interrelated objectives: first to preserve lands affiliated with the three day battle; second to mark the lines of battle of the two armies; and third to provide access to these grounds. The legislation also granted the acquisition of additional land to preserve and mark the lines of battle. As a result, Gettysburg's park commissioners initiated an aggressive management approach to establish a landscape that would serve as a memorial to the soldiers of both the Army of the Potomac and the Army of Northern Virginia. Reconciliationist sentiment provided the much-needed impetus for the establishment of Gettysburg National Military Park, as well as the other military parks. In *Race and Reunion*, David Blight defines reconciliation as the "dominant mode" of Civil War memory. This willful construction of a palatable account of the Civil War emphasized the courage and sacrifice of both Union and Confederate soldiers. Choosing to deliberately ignore or evade the war's causes and consequences, white Americans forged a story-line devoid of conflict or controversy. Consequently, the war's defining issue, slavery, remained purposefully absent. As Blight illustrates, the emancipationist account, rooted in African Americans' remembrance of the war, was minimized or purposefully ignored by those perpetuating the prevailing white, reconciliationist version.[10]

In the spirit of reconciliation, veterans of both sides visited Gettysburg to help the commissioners accurately mark the positions of their units on the field. For example, on May 29, 1894, Edward Porter Alexander, a Confederate artillery colonel in the Army of Northern Virginia at the time of the battle, toured the battlefield with E. B. Cope to point out positions held by the Confederate artillery. By 1895, with Alexander's assistance and other veterans of Lee's army, sixty-five Confederate artillery and infantry positions were marked. By 1904, commissioners had marked and placed 324 guns with carriages, as well as 462 unit tablets on the field. For ornamental and educational purposes, ten-inch artillery shells, mounted in the form of a pyramid, were placed alongside the gun carriages.[11]

Gettysburg's enabling legislation mandated that access to the battlegrounds be provided. When the War Department took control of the battlefield, poorly developed, often dirt roads, provided the only means to access the grounds. Visitors who wished to see specific areas, such as the Confederate line on Seminary Ridge, had to traverse through thick briar patches, high grass, or dense woodlots. Other sites remained completely inaccessible. Park commissioners wanted to make the entire battlefield accessible, and they soon began a vigorous project to build an extensive road network. In 1895, just months after the transfer, contracted local laborers built telford avenues along the main battle lines that permitted visitors easier means to follow the Confederate line along Seminary Ridge, as well as the Union line down Cemetery Ridge toward the Wheatfield, the Valley of Death, and the western slopes of the round tops. By the turn of the century, much of the park's infrastructure had been built, which provided easier access to many of the battle's key sites.[12]

Additionally, the federal government authorized land acquisition for preservation efforts and the purpose of marking the lines of battle. Though the battlefield's enabling legislation defined the federal government's boundary at over 3,000 acres, commercial establishments and private homes dotted the battlefield and the surrounding landscape. The Gettysburg Electric Railway stood as one of the most blatant intrusions on the historic terrain. Shortly after acquiring the battlefield, commissioners learned that the Gettysburg Electric Railway Company had plans to expand its trolley line. Already operating lines through town, as well as along parts of Cemetery Ridge and the southern end of the field, the company planned to run tracks through Devil's Den and the Valley of Death.

In January 1896, the United States Supreme Court handed down a landmark ruling, not only for the Gettysburg battlefield, but also critical to the preservation of all historic sites. Justice Rufus Peckham delivered the majority opinion in *United States vs. Gettysburg Electric Railway Co.*, which gave legal authority to the federal government to acquire land through the power of eminent domain. Peckham declared that the federal government had a responsibility to preserve and safeguard nationally historic sites and buildings. His words rang strong: "Can it be that the government is without power to preserve the land, properly mark out the various sites upon which this struggle took place . . . for the benefit of all the citizens of the country, for the present and for the future?"[13] The court's ruling set precedence for early historic preservation law and invested the Gettysburg administrators the authority to seize lands deemed historic for inclusion into the military park.

Empowered by the court's ruling, the War Department quickly acquired several key properties. In 1899, the government acquired 194.89 acres and an additional 102 acres the following year. By 1901 the War Department's acreage totaled 1,274.57 acres. Still, park commissioners struggled to acquire lands along the Confederate line of battle. They attempted to negotiate with local residents, but found owners were only willing to sell their property for "exorbitant prices," which the secretary of war refused to pay. In 1900, the War Department condemned five tracts of land totaling 105.79 acres along Seminary Ridge.[14] For the first time in the park's history, the Confederate battle line along Seminary Ridge became available to visitors.

Union and Confederate veterans quite literally made Gettysburg National Military Park. Their efforts resulted in the preservation of key parcels of the battlefield, the marking of unit positions, and the construction of avenues to access the fields. As important, these men also created a memory of the battle of Gettysburg and the Civil War that ensuing generations of Americans faithfully accepted. The war's battlefields became physical symbols to a reconciled nation. Initially, southerners expressed little interest in commemorating their efforts at Gettysburg. It was, after all, a Federal victory that resulted in a loss of approximately 28,000 of their comrades and was located in a northern state.

In 1897, after a series of visits from Confederate veterans, the commissioners enthusiastically reported on southerners' increased interest in the battlefield and desire to erect monuments to their comrades. Applauding southerners' interest, Cope declared, "There is a growing interest developing in the South in this, The Battlefield of the War, now that we are a Band of Brothers." As Union and Confederate fraternity emerged at Gettysburg, no other site in the nation would exemplify sectional reconciliation as the Pennsylvania battlefield.[15]

As important, Cope's proclamation underscored a second emerging theme. Veterans of both sides had come to believe that Gettysburg was, to use Cope's words, "The Battlefield of the War." In *The Confederate War*, Gary Gallagher suggests that in the summer of 1863 most southerners did not view Gettysburg as an irreversible loss. Instead, he maintains, that southern civilians had constructed a nationalistic sentiment around Robert E. Lee and the Army of Northern Virginia and continued to hold an unwavering faith in their cause and independence through war's end. After the war, however, Gettysburg began to hold claim as the war's "High Water Mark," the lynchpin on which the direction of the war turned. In their postwar writings and particularly in monument dedication speeches, veterans attached a singular importance to Gettysburg,

The iconic scene of a nation reconciled; veterans from the Philadelphia Brigade Association and the Pickett's Division Association clasp hands at the stonewall of the Angle during the battle's fiftieth anniversary, July 3, 1913.

elevating the battle as the war's defining moment. Lieutenant Frank Haskell, a Union staff officer in the 2nd Corps, offered a representative statement when he declared, "The battle of Gettysburg is distinguished in this war . . . as by far the greatest and severest conflict that has occurred."[16]

Defining Gettysburg as the war's "High Water Mark" brought greater meaning and symbolism to reconciliation events on the Pennsylvania battlefield. In July 1913 the "Peace Jubilee" commemorating the battle's fiftieth anniversary exemplified the heightened sense of reconciliation that gripped the nation. By July 1, 42,000 veterans of the Blue and Gray were encamped on the battlefield. On July 3, members of the Pickett's Division Association and the Philadelphia Brigade Association clasped hands across the stone wall at the Angle, the stone wall feature that come to symbolize the disastrous failure of Pickett's Charge. Photographers captured the event, which further embedded Gettysburg as the war's "High Water Mark" and a site of fraternal reunion. The next day, America's independence day, President Woodrow Wilson, the first southern-born president since the Civil War, delivered an address befitting traditional reconciliation rhetoric. He proclaimed the fifty years following the battle had brought "peace and union and vigor." Wilson continued, "We have found one another as brothers and comrades, in arms, enemies no longer, generous friends rather, our battles long past, the quarrel forgotten—except that we shall not forget the splendid valor, manly devotion of the men then arrayed against one another, now grasping hands and smiling into each other's eyes."[17] This reconciliationist account, created by the veterans themselves to selectively remember the war's events, devoid of divisiveness, now pervaded the American consciousness.

America's entrance into World War I forced the War Department to devote its energies to conducting military affairs in Europe, and offered less time to manage Civil War sites. As a result, the secretary of war restructured the nation's battlefield management, including Gettysburg. Mostly significantly, a federal act specified that any vacancy on the park commission, either by death or resignation, would not be filled. When all seats became vacant, the secretary of war would then appoint a superintendent to manage daily operations and administration of each battlefield. Gettysburg's park commission officially ceased to exist when John Nicholson died on March 8, 1922, and shortly thereafter, former park engineer Cope became the first superintendent of Gettysburg National Military Park. Cope continued to manage the park's daily operations until his death, at age ninety-three, on May 27, 1927. The passing of Cope, one of the park's most influential commissioners and the last of the war's veterans to manage it, marked a milestone in the administration of the Gettysburg battlefield. Future management of Gettysburg, as well as the other Civil War parks, passed to sons of Civil War veterans, or in time, government officials.[18]

While Union and Confederate veterans carefully toiled to preserve the blood-stained fields of battle, another preservation effort was gaining momentum in the western United States. During the Gilded Age, a group of Americans became increasingly concerned about the decimation of the nation's significant cultural and natural resources and the federal government's relative lack of power to protect these resources. On March 1, 1872, President Ulysses S. Grant signed legislation to create the country's first national park when he authorized the preservation of two million acres at Yellowstone in Wyoming. Through the late nineteenth century, the federal government authorized the establishment of additional national parks, including Yosemite and Sequoia in California, and Mount Rainier in Washington. A monumental effort in the nation's preservation movement occurred when Congress signed the Antiquities Act on June 8, 1906. This act gave the president the authority to "declare by public proclamation historic landmarks, historic and prehistoric structures, and other objects of historic or scientific interest that are situated upon the lands owned or controlled by the Government of the United States to be national monuments." Later that year, President Theodore Roosevelt approved Devils Tower, in Wyoming, as the first national monument.[19]

America's first national monuments and national parks paralleled contemporary cultural trends of recreational tourism and heritage tourism. In *See America First*, Marguerite Shaffer explores the tourist culture from 1880 until 1940. Journeying to sites promoted as quintessentially American, such as Yellowstone or the Grand Canyon, white, middle- or upper-class families forged a link between themselves, their perception of American identity, and their national heritage. Tourism became a "ritual of American citizenship." By visiting the nation's cultural and natural parks, Shaffer argues, tourists believed they would "become better Americans." Aside from serving as an indicator to citizenship, John Sears demonstrates how nineteenth-century tourism emerged as part of the country's diverse culture. Not only did sites like Niagara Falls or Yosemite interest both men and women, they also appealed to a multitude of religious sects. These sites became "sacred places" for all Americans.[20]

Frederick Jackson Turner defined the American West as distinct to American character, identity, and development. Advancements in the nation's infrastructure, climaxed by completion of the Transcontinental Railroad, propelled Americans westward in their ideals of Manifest Destiny, settlement, and eventually tourism. On the eve of America's intervention into World War I, states west of the Mississippi River boasted thirty-five national parks and monuments, sites integral to the "See America First" campaign promoted by western politicians and boosters. Administration and management of these sites, however, remained haphazard. On August 25, 1916, President Woodrow Wilson signed legislation creating the National Park Service, within the

Department of Interior, to bring the needed uniformity. The National Park Service's guiding legislation, the Organic Act of 1916, outlined its mission: "to conserve the scenery and the natural and historic objects, and the wildlife and to provide for the enjoyment of the same in such a manner and by such means as will leave them unimpaired for the enjoyment of future generations."[21]

Stephen Mather became the National Park Service's first director, and would serve as such until January 1929. Mather recognized that the national parks could not survive merely as a preserved entity, as land unknown to the eyes and feet of the people. He encouraged Americans to tour and use the parks. As the parks became popular and relevant with the public, Mather hoped to secure congressional funding. Timing was opportune. Railroads initially served as the primary means of transportation to the parks, but soon the automobile would revolutionize American society and tourism. Park Service officials quickly encouraged automobiles and tourism within the parks. Similarly, Mather, also as a means to encourage tourism, promoted concession operations.[22]

Still, the National Park Service remained principally a western system consisting of natural and cultural sites. Opportunity to develop parks in the east lay not in natural, but in historic sites. A new director provided the stimulus for expansion. Horace Albright, who had served as the agency's first assistant director under Mather and superintendent of Yellowstone, succeeded Mather in 1929. On the eve of the Great Depression, the National Park Service administered fifty-four national parks and monuments. A history enthusiast, Albright had long pushed the National Park Service to acquire the War Department's battlefields. Albright and other service personnel argued that the department failed to effectively administer and interpret these sites. For their part, some War Department officials expressed reluctance to relinquish control of the battlefields, because they feared the National Park Service would turn the memorial grounds into recreational sites or "playgrounds." The Department of Interior and the National Park Service officials assured the War Department that they were well prepared to manage the battlefields, and to pledged to retain their military nature.[23]

These efforts were realized when President Franklin D. Roosevelt signed Executive Order No. 6166 on June 10, 1933, which transferred the War Department sites to the National Park Service. Two months later, on August 10, the Park Service added twelve natural sites and fifty-seven historical sites, among them Gettysburg National Military Park. At Gettysburg, the National Park Service acquired 2,530 acres, 1,728 monuments and markers, and nearly 24 miles of park roads. James R. McConaghie became Gettysburg's first NPS superintendent. The transition of the battlefield to the National Park Service and McConaghie's tenure would prove to be a watershed in the history of the battlefield.[24]

CHAPTER 2

WE CANNOT HALLOW THIS GROUND: THE NATIONAL PARK SERVICE'S BEGINNINGS AT GETTYSBURG, 1933–1940

When Franklin D. Roosevelt signed Executive Order No. 6166, transferring the administration of sixty-nine parks, including Gettysburg National Military Park and the Soldiers' National Cemetery, from the War Department to the National Park Service, the agency became a true national entity, the protector of America's significant natural and historic landscapes. To be sure, contemporary social and economic events undeniably defined the operations of all national parks. By the summer of 1933, the worst economic crisis in American history gripped the nation. After the stock market crash on October 29, 1929, economic investments contracted, banks collapsed, and businesses closed. Eventually 25 percent of the country's population was unemployed. Breadlines and "Hoovervilles" were common in cities throughout America, while farmers in the countryside struggled to cope with plummeting crop prices. Promising Americans a "New Deal," Roosevelt introduced a myriad of unprecedented legislation intended to provide relief, recovery, and reform to the people and nation.[1]

As the Great Depression strangled the nation's economy and Americans found themselves unemployed, the federal government pumped enormous amounts of money into creating what Roosevelt's critics called "make-work projects." Ironically, the national park system, as well as state parks, benefited enormously from the pervasive economic plight and the abundance of available labor. Roosevelt's proactive approach to the Great Depression not only employed thousands of men and women in various jobs across the nation, but also improved America's public lands, in both recreational and historic sites. New Deal monies provided significant improvements at the Gettysburg battlefield, as well as scores of other national and state parks. Between 1933 and 1940, for instance, the National Park Service received approximately 220 million dollars to fund New Deal projects. The Public Works Administration (PWA), for example, made available 40 million dollars to improve roads and trails in the national park system between 1933 and 1937. Indeed, without the infusion of federal funds and the abundance of available workmen, changes in the Gettysburg battlefield, both to the landscape and educational focus, would not have occurred on such a grand scale.[2]

The transfer of the War Department's sixty-nine parks to the National Park Service also paralleled rising, interrelated trends in American culture. This included an increase in outdoor recreation, growing popularity of a tourist culture, the proliferation of automobile ownership, and the expansion of the nation's road system. Certainly the widespread popularization of the automobile redefined Americans' leisure time and the growth of tourism, which ultimately made places like Gettysburg more accessible. For instance, in 1910 personal automobile ownership stood at one automobile for every 265 Americans; by the eve of the Great Depression, one in every five Americans owned an automobile. Consequently, sizable monetary investments went to improving road systems within the national parks.[3]

Until 1933 the majority of the parks in the National Park Service were principally in the western states. Administering mostly natural and cultural sites, the agency relied on landscape architects as supervisors, a practice that continued during the Great Depression. Trained in the fundamentals of managing and protecting natural features, these landscape architects also worked to fashion recreational and environmental opportunities within the parks. While landscape architects proved aptly suited to manage natural and cultural resources, managing historic sites was another matter.[4]

On par with wider trends within the agency, James R. McConaghie, the first National Park Service superintendent at Gettysburg, was a trained landscape architect. McConaghie received his Bachelor of Science degree from Grinnell College, in Iowa, in 1916. After being honorably discharged from service in World War I, McConaghie spent a year at the University of Minnesota studying architecture before graduating with a Master of Landscape degree from Harvard University's School of Landscape Architecture in February 1924. After graduation, McConaghie spent the next five years working for Pennsylvania's Department of Interior Affairs as a landscape architect, planning and designing parks, playgrounds, and school grounds. McConaghie also worked for the Wheeling Park Commission in Wheeling, West Virginia, where he directed the planning and construction of Oglebay Park. He then spent two years working for Pennsylvania's Department of Forests and Waters, preparing special reports and studies for the development of Penn-Roosevelt State Park, near Lewistown, and Bushey Run Battlefield State Park, in western Pennsylvania. Meanwhile, to manage the transition between the War Department and the National Park Service, the federal government administered a series of Civil Service examinations for new management positions. On February 7, 1933, McConaghie was appointed as Gettysburg's superintendent.[5]

At Gettysburg, McConaghie assumed responsibility for 2,530 acres, 1,728 monuments and markers, and nearly 24 miles of roads. His architectural background and management philosophy would define the development of the battlefield during the 1930s. He applauded the battlefield's growth under the management of the War Department, but noted it could no longer remain "stationary." Instead, the battlefield had to move "to a degree with the times." His task, as he saw it, was to improve the "imperfections." To accomplish this goal, McConaghie defined the Park Service's four primary and interrelated objectives for its new site: restoration, preservation, accessibility, and usability. Through the nexus of these four objectives, the Gettysburg battlefield evolved during the 1930s.[6]

One of the most popular of the New Deal programs, and certainly one of tremendous impact on the modernization of the national parks, was the Civilian Conservation Corps (CCC). Created by an act of Congress on March 30, 1933, and signed into law by Roosevelt the following day, the CCC put young men ages eighteen to twenty-five to work in America's outdoors. The CCC acted as a natural extension to the growing popularity of outdoor recreation. A variety of work projects included soil conservation, restructuring of natural and historic parks, and building parks, trails, and bridges. Four federal departments, including the Department of the Interior, oversaw the Civilian Conservation Corps. By the time the program was terminated in 1942, the CCC employed over two million men. These enrollees performed work in ninety-four national parks. CCC workers' contributions in the nation's state park system were staggering. Their labor resulted in the creation of 711 state parks and the development or improvement of over 3 million acres in the state park system.[7]

Eager to capitalize on the availability of labor for improvements to the park infrastructure, McConaghie requested a 200-man camp for the battlefield. His request was met; Gettysburg housed two CCC camps where workers toiled for nine years, until March 1942, creating a more accessible and usable landscape. The park's first CCC camp, located in Pitzer Woods, was established on June 17, 1933, two months before the National Park Service acquired the site, and initially enrolled 180 workers. Officials located the camp along the Confederate battle line on Seminary Ridge to showcase the camp and enrollees to tourists. One Gettysburg staffer recalled that the camp was "conveniently located" on Seminary Ridge so "that thousands of people who might never visit a CCC Camp are enabled to visit this one, and see the Camp in action." The second camp, MP-2, established on November 1, 1933, was located further north along Seminary Ridge, behind McMillan Woods.[8]

The Civilian Conservation Corps camp in McMillian Woods was established in November 1933.

Though many national parks, as well as state and local parks, sponsored CCC camps, most employed white laborers. Robert Fechner, the director of the CCC, stipulated that black enrollment would be in accordance to their population. African American enrollees, therefore, would constitute no more than 10 percent of the total enrollment. Thus, of the 2 million CCC laborers, African Americans made up approximately 250,000. As a result of the heightened racial tensions and opposition to black camps in predominately white areas, the federal government selected several national parks to host black camps, believing these areas to be in more tolerant environments. Gettysburg National Military Park housed two African American CCC camps. Other federally managed sites to use black enrollees included Colonial National Historical Park, Shenandoah National Park, and the Civil War battlefields of Shiloh, Vicksburg, and Chickamauga & Chattanooga. At each of these camps, black laborers performed tasks, namely internal improvements, comparable to those performed by workers at Gettysburg. Black camps also existed throughout the Commonwealth of Pennsylvania. The state's first black CCC camp was established in the Alleghany National Forest on April 24, 1933. Black workers also engaged in forestry improvements at Black Moshannon, Pymatuning, and Trexler-Lehigh State Parks. While black laborers on Civil War battlefields and across Pennsylvania were not uncommon, they did not represent the normal CCC experience.[9]

Gettysburg's black CCC camps differed from others, however, in their supervisory organization. When initially established, the camps were segregated. White enrollees performed clerical duties, while the black enrollees performed manual labor. Ironically, the hierarchy of black CCC camps mirrored the structure of the Civil War's United States Colored Troops (USCT); blacks could enlist, but officer positions belonged to whites. Black activists, however, pressured the federal government to place blacks in supervisory positions, and in 1935 President Roosevelt complied with their demands. By July 1935, all white CCC workers at Gettysburg had been transferred, and the park housed only black enrollees. Perhaps then it was only "fitting and proper" that the CCC camps at Gettysburg served as a model, or the nation's test case, that used both black laborers and supervisors. On August 10, 1936, Captain Frederick Lyman Slade became the first black officer commanding a black CCC camp. When the camp in Pitzer Woods closed in April 1937, black officers were assigned to the park's second camp, MP-2, which evolved into a camp exclusively staffed and supervised by blacks. While the camp at Gettysburg was exceptional for employing black supervisors, white officers always oversaw the activities of the CCC camps on other battlefields. In fact, in *At Work in Penn's Woods*, Joseph Speakman notes that only one other CCC camp used black officers. This camp, near Elmira, New York, and part of New York state parks program, was established in 1937, after Captain Slade assumed the officer position in Gettysburg.[10]

New Deal laborers constructing Meade Avenue. Note General George G. Meade's headquarters, the Lydia Leister farm, on the left of the image.

While segregation defined the "Jim Crow" South, and discrimination pervaded other areas in America, the employment of African American CCC labor blended reasonably well with Gettysburg's management and local residents. One explanation why black enrollees were tolerated, if not accepted, by local residents was that camp labor was not confined to the battlefield, but used in area projects as well. In times of need, according to a CCC historian, "the camp was always ready to lend a helping hand." Enrollees frequently removed snow from the borough streets, for instance. Yet, black enrollees confronted daily reminders that they held a secondary place in American society, even in the Pennsylvania camps. Housing was segregated by race. Conditions in the southern camps were not as harmonious. In his study of black CCC laborers at Shiloh National Military Park, Timothy Smith finds pervasive hostility to black enrollees. Tennessee's U.S. Senator, Kenneth McKellar, declared, "colored camps are problems." Local residents expressed similar opposition. "Ours is not a negro community," one resident commented, "and we do not know how to handle them." The prevailing racial climate of Tennessee explains the blatant hostility toward black CCC laborers that was generally absent in the Gettysburg camps.[11]

While Gettysburg's CCC camp stood as a vanguard to the introduction of black officers, interestingly little attention was paid to the relatively radical camp structure in the reports of the park superintendent and historians. McConaghie diligently recorded the accomplishments and labor investment, but rarely referenced the racial component of the camps, only occasionally noting the number of "colored enrollees." In his 1936–1937 annual report, he noted the transfer to black supervisors with "particular interest," and understood this to be the only camp with black officers in the country. Dr. Louis King, CCC historian and supervisor, who arrived at Gettysburg in the winter of 1934, received minimal discussion in the park correspondence. King, who earned a doctorate degree in anthropology from Columbia University, worked at the battlefield until the closure of the camp in March 1942, and produced a variety of historical reports for the park administration. McConaghie mentioned King's race on one occasion, in a memorandum to the regional director commenting on the housing for black officers. Though certainly atypical in his educational attainment for the era as a black, or even white, man, little is known about King's time at Gettysburg and the racial climate he endured while in Pennsylvania. Similarly, the sentiment and emotions of the black CCC workers are lost to the historical record. For the young African American men working at Gettysburg, the irony must have stood clear: they were laboring on a battlefield where thousands of southern men had fought just seven decades earlier to sustain a social hierarchy undeniably built on race. The black men toiled along the lines of Seminary Ridge and improved roads to allow visitors to safely drive along West Confederate Avenue to see the dominating monument honoring Robert E. Lee and the Virginians. They also manicured a landscape where President Abraham Lincoln envisioned a nation "dedicated to the proposition that all men are created equal." In the 1930s, as it had in the 1860s, race remained tightly bound to the Gettysburg narrative.[12]

In a clear break from the War Department's practices, educational initiatives and visitor services became of primary importance to McConaghie's administration and central to his philosophy of visitor usability. In fact, the new superintendent noted that educational services were the "most important work facing the service." McConaghie's determination to lay the foundation for educational services paralleled the larger trend promoting education within the National Park Service. As noted, until the expansion of the agency's holdings in 1933, the National Park Service consisted only of a few historical parks and devoted minimal attention to interpretive programs. Cultural or natural sites, such as the Grand Canyon or Yellowstone, needed little interpretation. Managing a complex historical site, such as Gettysburg, required the Park Service to explore different methods to educate visitors about the battle and use the landscape itself as a tool to achieve these objectives. The acquisition of scores of historic sites forced the agency to reinvent itself. Horace Albright, the agency's director between 1929 and 1933, and Verne Chatelain, the agency's first historian, promoted education within the parks, often as a means to foster patriotism. Chatelain saw educational programs as a means to "breathe life into American history" and in doing so create for visitors the "color, the pageantry, and the dignity of our national past."[13]

Here, too, the Great Depression provided the agency with the necessary manpower. New Deal allocations allowed the parks to hire historians, often termed "historical technicians," to conduct research on the site or to develop formative educational programming. New Deal funding provided for the employment of Dr. Louis King, hired in January 1934, and William Allison, hired in June 1933, as historical technicians. McConaghie understood that as the century moved forward visitors became further removed from the Civil War generation, and therefore lacked personal knowledge of the battle. By the battle's 75th anniversary, only an estimated 15,000 veterans were still alive, and many of them were not participants in the battle. Geared toward presenting the battlefield to an audience who had a first-hand connection to the war, the War Department believed the itinerary tablets, monuments, and markers, as well as the battlefield, served as sufficient educational tools. McConaghie and park officials sought to replace the cold, lifeless markers with a fresh and modern educational initiative. Managers lamented how visitors in the 1930s lacked that "direct touch" to or "personal interest" in the battlefield. Officials were increasingly aware of the changing demographics and recognized the necessity of an improved educational program to "replace the personal knowledge of yesterday" and in doing so provide the tools to help visitors "read" this historic landscape. McConaghie proudly declared that the park offered "conveniences" to tourists, but also expressed frustration at the apparent speed with which visitors toured the battlefield. "They do not want to spend the time here to fully understand the field," the superintendent bemoaned.[14]

With its headquarters located on the second floor of the Post Office building on Baltimore Street, and limited by space, the Park Service offered little more than the War Department in museum education. Possessing few artifacts, the park principally relied on a topographic map created by the War Department, popularly called the Cope Map, as well as historic troop movement maps and photographs to tell the story of the battle. Within six months of acquiring the battlefield, however, discussion of a new museum began. Plans recommended a display of artifacts, weaponry, uniforms, and personal effects that would supply visitors with the "best means of vitalizing and visualizing the Gettysburg Battlefield."[15]

Within a few months, however, it became apparent that the admirable ideal of a museum would not easily be realized. Several constraints prohibited its development, including the agency's inability to acquire objects, inadequate display and storage space, and the competition from privately owned museums in town. Because these museums appeared superior to anything the Park Service could develop in the foreseeable future, historical technician R. L. Jones recommended to the NPS chief historian that the government purchase and operate one of these collections.[16] His recommendation fell on deaf ears as the government grappled with higher budget priorities during the Great Depression. The economic capital necessary to purchase or develop a museum simply was not available. Instead, park employees continued to cope within a limited and antiquated facility, while they strove to develop alternative methods to inform visitors, and left museum education to the private museums.

The most extensive museum in Gettysburg was the Rosensteel's Gettysburg National Museum on Taneytown Road, located directly across from the Soldiers' National Cemetery. Visitors to this museum wandered through a cavernous structure filled with thousands of battlefield artifacts, typical of a nineteenth century "curiosity room." In April 1939, George Rosensteel unveiled a 6,000 foot addition to his museum. The added displays, now totaling sixty-seven cases, made the Rosensteel collection the most elaborate in Gettysburg. Admittedly, the Gettysburg National Museum offered little in the way of interpreting the Civil War, instead showcasing thousands of objects in glass cases. The following spring, Joseph Rosensteel, George's nephew, conceived the idea of an Electric Map, a large-scale relief map surrounded by auditorium-style seating. The thirty-minute presentation summarized the campaign and three-day battle using colored lights on a topographic map to illustrate the position of the Union and Confederate armies. The museum provided visitors what the early Park Service administration could not. Asserting his prominent role in the commodification of the battle, Rosensteel commented he observed more cars parked at his museum than any other point of interest on the battlefield.[17]

Although the Park Service did not immediately realize its plans to develop a museum, recently hired NPS historians and New Deal laborers did accomplish smaller scale educational projects. In 1937 the NPS hired Frederick Tilberg as an assistant historian to oversee the battlefield's history program. Civil Works Administration (CWA) employees established a system of walking trails, totaling nineteen miles, which allowed visitors to traverse terrain not easily accessible from the park avenues. In February 1938, in preparation for the battle's seventy-fifth anniversary, the Park Service developed one of its earliest tour maps of the battlefield. It marked points of special interest, including Little Round Top, Devil's Den, the Wheatfield, the Peach Orchard, Culp's Hill, Cemetery Hill, the High Water Mark, and the Soldiers' National Cemetery. In the summer of 1939, with CCC funds, the park published a 4,000-word orientation booklet that included fifteen pictures and two maps. Undoubtedly, without the efforts of the New Deal employees, little of significant value could have been accomplished during these years.[18]

This fence originally stood at Lafayette Square, Washington D.C. The fence was relocated to Gettysburg in the late 19th century and placed on East Cemetery Hill. As part of larger modifications to the Soldiers' National Cemetery in 1933, the National Park Service relocated the fence to separate the Soldiers' National Cemetery and the Evergreen Cemetery. Note the equestrian statue to General Winfield Scott Hancock to the right of the photo.

The Gettysburg National Museum (the Rosensteel Museum), Taneytown Road. This commercial facility opened in 1921.

In addition to advancement in educational opportunities, McConaghie recognized the need to create a park to "meet modern demands," thereby upgrading the battlefield to provide convenient, accessible amenities to visitors. Financed with New Deal money, significant time went into improving the battlefield avenues that had been built by the War Department. These roadways, constructed for nineteenth century horse-drawn carriages and not modern automobiles, were quickly deteriorating by the early 1930s. The Works Progress Administration provided Gettysburg with over $15,000 to improve avenues, gutters, and culverts. These improvements accomplished two of McConaghie's objectives: accessibility and usability. The superintendent noted that the improvements in the roads not only removed driving hazards, but offered a "vast improvement in appearance" and increased visitor safety.[19]

To complement the improved road system, laborers constructed four buildings to enhance visitor services. To replace antiquated, small wooden toilet pits, the park opened comfort stations at Devil's Den and Spangler's Spring in 1936. To further increase visitor service and contact, two additional buildings opened as entrance stations in May 1937, one along the Chambersburg Pike and another along the Emmitsburg Road. The Park Service also opened the historic George Weikert farmhouse along United States Avenue as an information station. These buildings established a NPS presence throughout the battlefield. Recognizing that a "certain amount of modernity" was necessary, these additions furthered the agency's mission of accessibility and usability.[20]

In addition to supervising the New Deal laborers and Park Service staff, McConaghie's duties included managing the Licensed Battlefield Guides, a group that had been formally recognized by the War Department in 1915. In this capacity, McConaghie intended to establish uniformity in the interpretation of the battlefield and the men who told its story. Immediately upon assuming management duties of the battlefield, the Park Service enacted numerous rules and regulations pertaining to the licensed guides. In May 1934, McConaghie put the guide service on "trial," expecting them to comply with Park Service regulations and prove themselves "worthy" of being retained. Two years later, McConaghie felt compelled to remind the guides that they were "still on trial."[21]

More telling of McConaghie's relationship with the guides, however, was his expectation that they would identify with the National Park Service. Disappointed by their unwillingness to embrace the NPS, McConaghie informed them that "there has been somewhat of a failure in recognizing the distinct value that comes from being associated with this Service." Association with the National Park Service, according to McConaghie, meant being part of a greater organization, and as the superintendent asserted, "promotion of the Service means promotion of self." In a memo to the guides, McConaghie

Civilian Conservation Corps workers landscape the area around the comfort station at the Pennsylvania Monument.

clearly defined his understanding of the Gettysburg battlefield and the National Park Service, "You are no longer concerned merely with this famous battlefield, but rather you are concerned with all of the other national parks in the country." Whereas the War Department diligently worked to preserve and commemorate Gettysburg as a singular, distinct battlefield, the park's new management firmly believed "this park is a National Park, and the public is generally being educated to the point where this Park is associated with the many well-known and famous National Parks." In McConaghie's view, visitors touring Little Round Top or the Peach Orchard needed to recognize they were touring only "one of a chain of parks."[22]

The preservation and presentation of historic landscapes develop and change over time. Battlefields, as historic landscapes, are not static entities, but experience change through various factors. One modern historic preservationist notes that "landscapes are dynamic, ever-changing phenomena." The Gettysburg battlefield has been, and continues to remain, a "dynamic, ever-changing" landscape that evolved through the efforts of the Gettysburg Battlefield Memorial Association, the War Department, and finally the National Park Service. The transition of the battlefield from the War Department to the National Park Service illustrates the dynamic progression of managing a landscape. This transition, made during the Great Depression, only enhanced the Gettysburg battlefield as a "dynamic, ever-changing" phenomenon.[23]

McConaghie placed preservation and restoration as two key elements of his philosophy. When the National Park Service acquired the battlefield, however, the agency had little understanding of how to manage a historic landscape. Prior to 1933, the Park Service consisted mostly of cultural and natural sites in the western states. Therefore, because the agency lacked a uniform landscape management policy, local park officials had the freedom to utilize the landscape at its discretion, with little oversight or direction from the national office. It is in this realm that McConaghie made his most permanent impact on the battlefield.

To be sure, McConaghie often seemed conflicted, or contradictory, in his attempts to establish and implement a landscape preservation philosophy. On one hand, he applauded the War Department's preservation efforts and stated the Park Service's mission to "preserve the intent of what they have done and to complete what they left unfinished." He viewed the battlefield as an evolving landscape, one that moved "to a degree with the times." McConaghie believed that the development, or evolution, of the battlefield could "be done without disturbing in any way the values or purposes for which the thing exists." His perception of the battlefield landscape thus mirrored modern preservation philosophies that "landscapes are dynamic, ever-changing phenomena," not static resources.[24] Yet on several occasions park staff did, in fact, alter or disturb the battlefield features, or the cultural resources for which the site was established.

Moreover, McConaghie's writings and subsequent actions suggest a preference for a multiuse landscape. In word and deed he favored a duality of the battlefield: some visitors could explore the historic landscape and learn about the battle, while others could tour the grounds and enjoy the scenic beauty. For instance, in an era of high unemployment and entrenched economic despair, park management strove to augment tourism by emphasizing the battlefield's scenic beauty. In an October 1937 letter to the agency's director, McConaghie lauded the battlefield's autumn foliage and advocated increased attention to its natural beauty. Thereafter, the park issued a press release offering a simplistic narrative of the "sanguine struggle" of July 1, 2, 3, 1863, but encouraged readers to appreciate "another side to the notable Battlefield." Visitors were encouraged to enjoy the redbuds and dogwoods that rejuvenated the springtime landscape. From McConaghie's perspective, Gettysburg offered visitors layered landscapes of different uses. The other "side to the notable Battlefield" was its scenic landscape. In encouraging visitors to travel to the park to see the budding dogwoods and redbuds, park officials purposefully transitioned the battlefield from a historic landscape to a tourist or leisure ground.[25]

Correspondingly, McConaghie's tenure emphasized promoting, creating, and cultivating an aesthetic landscape. Creating a manicured landscape, however, stood at odds with the agency's mission of preserving the cultural resources associated with the battle and its memorialization. In his 1936–1937 annual report, the superintendent bemoaned the sheer number of monuments on the battlefield. Noting they had "particular meaning" to the men who erected them, he believed that to current visitors the monuments "merely exist." Thus, to reconcile the proliferation of granite memorials with a more attractive landscape, McConaghie advocated planting trees and shrubs to obscure their view. Specifically, he offered, "The task before the field is to carefully plant so that the numerous monuments will appear to fit and be screened so as not to unduly affect the landscape." From McConaghie's perspective as a landscape architect, the Park Service should create a landscape that would minimize or deliberately hide the monuments—monuments erected by the veterans themselves to forever honor the deeds of their comrades—in order to promote a site that did not "unduly affect the landscape." To enhance the visual aesthetics of the grounds, park maintenance embarked on efforts to beautify the park. This included "tree surgery" along park avenues and around monuments in order to give the battlefield and its historic structures a "dressed up appearance."[26]

Not all park staff favored developing and presenting the battlefield as a scenic, leisure ground. Voicing opposition to McConaghie's promotion of the rosebuds, dogwoods, and autumn foliage, historical technician R. L. Jones lamented, "Gradually the area is ceasing to be a Military Park and becoming a mere spot of scenic beauty." Advocating the battlefield as a site of "scenic beauty" minimized the landscape's historical significance and simultaneously engendered a management philosophy more similar to the agency's western parks. Moreover, the National Park Service considered building amenities befitting a national park, notably picnic accommodations. Early proposals to place picnic tables on the battlefield generated extensive debate among park employees. Some among the historical staff chided the absurdity of placing picnic tables on the battlefield and voiced their opposition in letters to the superintendent. "The Nation, as a whole," Jones wrote, "is not and never can be interested in the Park as a scenic or recreational spot . . . This is a hallowed spot. We should not desecrate it by encouraging picnics, even with a few rustic tables." As important, Jones's sentiment underscored a belief in the sanctity of Gettysburg; promotion of recreational and leisure activities threatened the battlefield's sanctification. Consideration of designated picnic areas also underscored a tendency to view the battlefield less as a memorial, historical landscape and more as a national park.[27]

Some of the changes did "unduly affect the landscape," however. Physical alterations made to the Soldiers' National Cemetery between June 1933 and August 1935 compromised the site's sanctification and proved to be one of the most damaging initiatives implemented during the Park Service's era. Without doubt, the Soldiers' National Cemetery had become the most renowned cemetery in America, a "final resting place" where over 3,500 Union soldiers were eventually interred from the battle. On November 19, 1863, President Abraham Lincoln's Gettysburg Address had consecrated the landscape with an eloquence unparalleled in American history. William Saunders, an acclaimed landscape architect, had designed the cemetery. Saunders created a landscape of "simple grandeur" where the interment of the Union dead, the layout of the circular walkways, and the chosen shrubbery had been purposefully designed. McConaghie alleged that the War Department had neglected the cemetery, and proposed a plan to better preserve it. Some of the changes altered visitors' experiences, while other decisions, made primarily to facilitate accessibility and scenic purity, changed the landscape perception, but did not significantly modify the original intent.[28]

The most significant change was the resetting of the soldiers' headstones. The original stones, positioned in 1863 and 1864, were elevated approximately twelve inches above ground level, but lacked proper foundation support. After decades of harsh winter weather and frost heaves, the stones had shifted and were now no longer aligned, which, according to park officials, created an "unsightly vista" and "produced in one a feeling of a lack of care." To correct this problem, the CCC temporarily removed the headstones, dug trenches to create a concrete foundation and reset them. The workers then added new grading to the gravesites, which created a continuous and level landscape. These changes drastically affected the cemetery's original design.[29] As a result, the headstones now flush with the ground were no longer easily visible from the drives.

Other modifications were less consequential to visitors' perception of the burial spaces, but similarly compromised the original design. Saunders had included a pipe fence and an adjoining hedge to separate the Soldiers' National Cemetery from the Evergreen Cemetery, the adjacent public cemetery. In 1933 the NPS removed the pipe fence for "aesthetic reasons" and in its place relocated a much higher fence from East Cemetery Hill to separate the two cemeteries. When the CCC workers removed the pipe fencing, they also removed the arboretum of evergreens that lined the pipe fence. The Soldiers' National Monument, dedicated in 1869, stands as the only monument in the cemetery included in Saunders' design. An iron fence and shrubbery surrounded the monument until 1933, when the Park Service removed both. Workers also eliminated the gravel circular walkway between the graves, which, combined with the grading of the landscape, hindered visitors from easily seeing the headstones and forced them to the periphery of the graves.[30]

As noted, accessibility and usability dominated McConaghie's philosophy. Clearly the desire to beautify the cemetery and to provide convenient access to the grounds drove these alterations. In terms of beautification, the NPS removed many of the landscape trees, most notably the Norway spruces along the cemetery's western boundary and maples along the upper drive of its eastern boundary. In their stead, workers planted ornamental trees— rhododendrons, holly, and hemlocks—that required less maintenance. In just one month, employees planted over two hundred holly trees and rhododendrons. Decades earlier Saunders had cautioned against such additions, favoring a design of "simple grandeur." In addition, in order to provide convenient vehicular access, and to accommodate tour buses carrying veterans for the July 1938 reunion festivities, CCC workers widened the entrance gates along the Baltimore Pike.[31]

In fairness, the Soldiers' National Cemetery had undoubtedly changed since its dedication in November 1863. Saunders designed the cemetery exclusively for Union dead. Future wars, beginning with the Spanish-American War, necessitated cemetery tracts for the burial of these veterans. To offset their locations from the Civil War burials, these post–Civil War burials were placed outside the interior drive. Changes implemented during the 1930s further altered the cemetery's original design, considerably more than modifications made during the War Department administration. The resetting of the headstones was necessary to correct the alignment from frost heaves, but their resetting at ground-level was done simply for the ease for maintenance, principally mowing. Local veterans' camps adamantly spoke out against these changes. One critic observed that the Park Service treated the grounds as "public parks rather than as sacred Memorials." He further noted, "such was not the case when the Cemetery and Battlefield were in charge of the War Department."[32]

Meanwhile, other changes occurred to Gettysburg's historic structures. In planning for the construction of the Eternal Peace Light Monument, the Park Service approved the demolition of one of the historic properties along the first day's fields. Located northwest of the town on Oak Ridge, the John Forney farm was the scene of heavy fighting between General Robert Rodes's Confederate infantry and General John Robinson's Union forces. The Forney buildings stood as obstacles to Confederate movements, but also provided shelter from Union fire. The property suffered minor structural damage, mainly bullet holes. Later the house and barn became field hospitals, and the surrounding fields served as burial sites for Confederate soldiers. Excepting the addition of a postwar metal roof, the property largely remained in its Civil War configuration. By the mid-1930s, however, the Forney property had fallen into a noticeable state of neglect. In the fall of 1937, the Pennsylvania Commission for the 75th Anniversary of the Battle of Gettysburg, in consultation with the National Park Service, purchased land on the north and south sides of the Mummasburg Road, which included the Forney farm.[33]

Superintendent James McConaghie with veterans at the battle's seventy-fifth anniversary, July 1938.

According to McConaghie, the Forney buildings were in a "dilapidated condition" and their condition "indicated little in the way of salvage." In addition to the decaying buildings and the cost to salvage them, McConaghie concluded that "as far as the park knew," the buildings held "no special historical significance." He noted that the War Department had marked by tablet other historic properties, but there was no tablet for the Forney farm buildings, and he therefore concluded they were of "questionable historic value." In the end, McConaghie argued that any restoration projects were cost prohibitive and subject to "considerable guesswork." If such funding became available, the park held higher priorities. In his estimation, priority was not to restore or salvage historic buildings, but to demolish them in order to "provide a proper setting for the new monument." Shortly, thereafter, the commission signed an agreement with a third party to demolish the Forney property by January 1, 1938. Notably, not until the demolition began and subsequent concern over the importance of the Forney buildings surfaced did park historian Frederick Tilberg prepare a report on their historical significance.[34]

Finally, after the landscape alterations to Oak Ridge, the "High Water Mark" of the 75th anniversary occurred with the dedication of the Eternal Peace Light Memorial on July 3, 1938. Towering over Oak Ridge stands a forty-foot shaft adorned with a gas flame. On the shaft of the monument are two women, symbolizing unity between North and South. "Peace Eternal In

Superintendent James McConaghie speaking with a Union veteran at the battle's seventy-fifth anniversary, July 1938.

Franklin Delano Roosevelt speaking on the battle's seventy-fifth anniversary, July 3, 1938.

A Nation United" is inscribed at the base of the monument. Standing before an assembly of 1,800 aging Civil War veterans and thousands of spectators, President Franklin D. Roosevelt delivered the monument's dedication speech. "Immortal deeds and immortal words," Roosevelt declared, "have created here at Gettysburg a shrine of American patriotism."[35] At the close of the president's dedication, two veterans, one Union and one Confederate, unveiled the monument and ignited the eternal flame.

In addition to reconfiguring the Soldiers' National Cemetery and removing the Forney property, the Park Service made other alterations to the battlefield's appearance. At the time of the battle, there was minimal undergrowth in the woodlots because livestock frequently grazed among the trees and farmers actively maintained the woods for firewood and fence railings. Though the War Department commissioners attempted to maintain a historically accurate landscape, excessive undergrowth, particularly on properties not owned by the government, grew in the decades after the battle. In order to establish a more accurate vista and to return the woodlots to their historic appearance, the War Department annually burned excess tree foliage and shrubbery. War Department officials at Shiloh National Military Park followed a similar practice of clearing undergrowth and burning excess shrubbery to create a landscape that mirrored the 1862 condition. As early as 1934, however, the Park Service had stopped the practice at Gettysburg. Instead of controlling undergrowth through annual burns, the agency adopted a policy to encourage undergrowth, believing that controlled burns reduced the "fertility of the soil." Consequently, in places such as Oak Hill, the Codori-Trostle Thicket, McMillian Woods, and the slopes of Big Round Top, trees and underbrush quickly grew where no such vegetative growth existed at the time of the battle. This landscape management practice was not exclusive to Gettysburg, however. At Shiloh, Park Service officials also discontinued the burning of undergrowth and shrubbery.[36]

Aspects of the Park Service's landscape management philosophies, however, remained inconsistent. In fact, while allowing for underbrush to grow, park officials simultaneously initiated small-scale efforts to rehabilitate specific parts of the battlefield to their historic condition. At Shiloh, for example, the Park Service rehabilitated the Sunken Road, key terrain held by Union troops and later reflective of the intense fighting termed the Hornet's Nest. They also rehabilitated the area around the Bloody Pond and restored the Peach Orchard, a key battleground on April 6, 1862. Similar landscape rehabilitative efforts occurred at Gettysburg. Park historians researched historic appearances of the terrain and recommended small-scale rehabilitation projects of cutting post-battle vegetation growth in order to open historic views. Historian Tilberg suggested cutting non-historic tree growth along four vistas at the battlefield's southern end, where General James Longstreet's 1st Corps assailed the Union line on July 2. These four areas included: Little Round Top north toward the Wheatfield; Little Round Top west toward Plum Run and the Trostle buildings; Little Round Top to Devil's Den; and Sedgwick Avenue south toward Little Round Top.[37]

McMillian Woods before a landscape clearing.

Upholding McConaghie's philosophy of creating a historic viewshed, the agency approved its first vista cutting project on August 8, 1940, and CCC laborers immediately started work. By October, McConaghie reported the area around Devil's Den clear of trees and shrubbery. The following month the east side of the Wheatfield was clear-cut, opening a view from Little Round Top to the Wheatfield.[38] Each of these cuts occurred without controversy from the local community. The cutting projects marked significant and progressive advancement in the park's landscape management philosophy. In cutting and removing the non-historic trees along Devil's Den and the Wheatfield, park management advanced the agency's mission from merely preserving the landscape to creating a historically accurate appearance. In this instance, modifications to the battlefield's appearance helped to improve visitor understanding of the fighting on the battle's second day by opening viewsheds comparable to those in July 1863.

Further visual improvements helped to create a more historically accurate landscape. During the War Department's administration, park commissioners erected post and pipe fencing (concrete posts with metal piping) to delineate boundaries and to keep unwanted farm animals off the battlefield grounds. When the National Park Service acquired additional land and it became unnecessary to partition off private land from federal land, these fences became visually intrusive. Over five miles of these decrepit fencing patterns littered the fields and intruded upon key battle grounds. Much of the post and pipe fencing ran parallel with the battlefield avenues. Looking north from the Pennsylvania Monument, for example, visitors would have seen post and pipe fencing along Pleasanton Avenue, Hancock Avenue, and also parallel to the railroad line that ran across the fields of Pickett's Charge.[39]

McConaghie put New Deal laborers to work in removing them. By the summer of 1937, the deteriorating fence posts and rails had been removed, opening an accurate vista of Cemetery Ridge. At the same time, workers removed the post and fence piping along West Confederate Avenue and replaced it with more historical wooden post and rail fences. This task accomplished three interrelated objectives. First, the removal of the post and pipe fencing eliminated physical intrusions from the battlefield, and second, by doing so, improved scenic vistas. And finally, removing the fencing eliminated detailed landscape maintenance. In addition to the removal of the post and pipe fencing, laborers made other landscape alterations that improved the visual and historic conditions of the battlefield. Between 1936 and 1937, New Deal workers removed the modern intrusions of telephone poles and wires along the Chambersburg Pike and placed the wires in an underground conduit.[40]

As park officials created a battlefield that more closely mirrored historic conditions, they also had to contend with the inevitability of modern intrusions. Though the National Park Service owned 2,530 acres, the battle raged over 25 square miles, north, west, and south of the borough with various tourist and residential establishments encroaching on all fronts. One area of particular concern was Warfield Ridge, located along the battlefield's southern end. In 1863 Warfield Ridge anchored the Confederate right flank and was part of the key terrain the Confederates advanced over on the second day's fighting. By the mid-1930s, Warfield Ridge housed a refreshment stand, a dancing pavilion, and a series of tourist cabins. The refreshment stand and dancing pavilion were located at the northeast corner of West Confederate Avenue and the Wheatfield Road. The tourist cabins were scattered along West Confederate Avenue. Recognizing the inconsistencies of modern, commercial venues on historic terrain, park managers identified this area as a high acquisition priority.[41]

An increasing number of modern houses also stood along the Emmitsburg Road. This road served as a key north/south artery for the movement of troops and supplies, and it separated the Confederate battle line along Seminary Ridge from the Union battle line on Cemetery Ridge. Only a few properties stood along the road at the time of the battle, including the farmsteads of Henry Spangler and Joseph Sherfy. By 1940, however, modern homes surrounded these historic farms. After the construction of another house along the Emmitsburg Road, McConaghie took action to acquire the Spangler and Sherfy properties and to "forestall any further residential development."[42]

Eight years after becoming the first National Park Service superintendent at Gettysburg, in November 1940 McConaghie announced his transfer to Vicksburg National Military Park. Reportedly the purpose of the transfer was to use his management skills to enhance the Mississippi battlefield as he had Gettysburg. The end of McConaghie's administration offers a fitting closure to the first years of the National Park Service at Gettysburg. He established four objectives: restoration, preservation, accessibility, and usability. Too, he sought to develop a battlefield that moved "to a degree with the times."[43] To that end, he was successful. New Deal funding and workers laid the foundations for an accessible and usable battlefield, complete with a modern avenue system and visitor amenities, including comfort stations and information centers. McConaghie's record on restoration and preservation, however, remains mixed. Certainly he deserves credit for initiating the Park Service's first rehabilitation project that fashioned sectors of the landscape to its historic appearance. Removal of the archaic post and pipe fencing, undergrounding the telephone wires along the Chambersburg Pike, and eliminating garbage dumps and junk yards accomplished two objectives: it eliminated a modern intrusion from the battlefield, while simultaneously creating a visually pleasing view. Here, too, McConaghie demonstrated a relatively progressive, modern approach. On the other hand, changes to the Soldiers' National Cemetery and the removal of the John Forney farm seemingly reinforced McConaghie's background as a landscape architect, for neither modification advanced the agency's preservation or interpretation mission. Promotion of the battlefield's scenic features, landscape beautification efforts, and consideration of designated picnic areas suggest a tendency to view Gettysburg not exclusively as a memorial battlefield, but as a *park,* a philosophy certainly congruent with the practices of the National Park Service. At the end of McConaghie's tenure, events beyond the boundaries of Gettysburg would soon redefine how Americans viewed and used the Pennsylvania battlefield.

CHAPTER 3

FROM THESE HONORED DEAD WE TAKE INCREASED DEVOTION: GETTYSBURG DOES ITS PART FOR VICTORY, 1941–1945

The 1930s proved to be the definitive watershed in the history of the National Park Service, both in the expansion of the agency's holdings and the use of New Deal funds for internal improvements. During the Great Depression, the agency established parks primarily for scenic and outdoor recreation, including the Blue Ridge Parkway, Shenandoah National Park, the Great Smoky Mountains, and the Natchez Trace Parkway. On the eve of America's intervention into the Second World War, the National Park Service managed 159 sites, totaling approximately 21 million acres. By 1941, however, federal funds for improvements were becoming increasingly scarce and subsequent events soon redirected the nation's priorities. On the morning of December 7, 1941, the Japanese attack at Pearl Harbor jolted the nation out of its isolation, and forced Americans to turn their attention to world affairs. Declaring the bombing at Pearl Harbor "a date which will live in infamy," President Franklin D. Roosevelt led the nation into war.[1]

Quickly the nation mobilized into an "arsenal of democracy" and Americans fought in Africa, landed on the beaches of Normandy, and "island hopped" through the Pacific. These events on far-distant shores further defined the Gettysburg battlefield. The war years influenced the battlefield's landscape, its resources, and Americans' connection to the battle and President Abraham Lincoln's Gettysburg Address in several, and sometimes contradictory, ways. The demands of World War II would come to dictate nearly every aspect of the park's daily operations. Yet the 1863 battle continued to echo deeply in American memory. From Gettysburg's hallowed grounds, orators called on Americans to support the war effort and, if necessary, once again offer the "last full measure of devotion" for freedom. A new generation of Americans reengaged the words of Lincoln's Gettysburg Address and interpreted it to fit the uncertainty and peril of their era.

Since acquiring Gettysburg National Military Park in 1933, the National Park Service had gradually transformed the battlefield from a memorial landscape, designed to commemorate the deeds of the men who fought there, into a fledging national park. The nexus of Superintendent James McConaghie's vision and the infusion of New Deal funds had drastically altered the battlefield and, in doing so, established the foundation for a modern, accessible tourist landscape. The impact of local management, mostly superintendents, cannot be overstated. Local administrators held considerable influence over operation and management of sites within the national park system. Their educational and employment backgrounds shaped the decisions they would make on landscape alterations, preservation, and interpretation. When McConaghie transferred to Vicksburg National Military Park, James Walter Coleman arrived to become the Gettysburg's second superintendent on February 1, 1941. At this time, landscape architects comprised the majority of the agency's professional cadre; James McConaghie, an experienced landscape architect, paralleled larger professional trends within the agency. Coleman, however, was a trained historian. A Pennsylvania native, he received his bachelor's and master's degrees from Pennsylvania State College in 1929 and 1931, respectively. He worked as a Civilian Conservation Corps (CCC) historian at Vicksburg National Military Park and later as a historian at the Library of Congress. In 1936 Coleman earned a doctorate degree in history from Catholic University. Thereafter, Coleman served as superintendent of Petersburg National Military Park, a position he held until March 1938, when he returned to Vicksburg as superintendent until he was transferred to Gettysburg.[2]

Since its establishment, the National Park Service had dedicated itself to the preservation of the nation's cultural and natural resources. Stephen Mather, the agency's first director, and Horace Albright, his successor, realized that merely preserving these sites was inadequate for the agency's survival. Instead of standing as isolated and secluded lands unknown to the eyes and feet of people, Mather and Albright believed parks had to be made accessible and accommodating. Public support, they reasoned, would lead to sustained congressional funding, thereby ensuring their permanence. Through the improvements to the existing parks brought by the New Deal, combined with the establishment of recreational sites, Americans could renew their enthusiasm for outdoor leisure and tourism. And they did. During the 1940 fiscal year, approximately 19 million people visited America's national parks.[3]

The National Park Service placed itself in the tourist business, and Gettysburg would be as well. Eager to greet the new superintendent and to establish cordial relations between the park and the community, local businessmen sponsored a "Welcome to Gettysburg" dinner for Coleman. The new super-intendent stressed that amicable relations between the Park Service and the community were critical to the successful operation of the Gettysburg battle-field, and to a thriving tourist economy. Continuing an agenda established by McConaghie for visitor accessibility, he aimed to create a visitor-friendly park. "We are in the tourist business," Coleman declared, "and we are interested in attracting as great a number of visitors here as possible." Promotion of the battlefield's scenic landscape served as one method of attracting tourists. Con-tinuing a trend initiated by his predecessor, Coleman's administration encour-aged travel to Gettysburg to enjoy the picturesque vistas of blooming redbuds and dogwoods. Certainly this philosophy stood in stark contrast to the War Department's, but also reflected the battlefield's gradual evolution from a me-morial landscape into a park with multiple uses, namely historical education and recreation.[4]

New Deal improvements notwithstanding, one significant landscape practice of the McConaghie administration was the rehabilitation of small-scale features on the battlefield to create a landscape that remained relatively consistent to its historic features. To be sure, part of the problem of the ex-cessive undergrowth stemmed from the Park Service discontinuing the War Department's practice of annual burns to destroy this underbrush. As noted, the agency's first clear-cutting project began in the spring of 1940 when CCC workers removed non-historic tree growth at Devil's Den, Little Round Top, and the Wheatfield. Upon his arrival, Superintendent Coleman listed vista-cutting projects as a top priority, further shaping the landscape to a more his-torically accurate vista. During the war years, CCC workers continued to re-habilitate Little Round Top by clear-cutting underbrush along its slopes and removing brush and small tree growth along West Confederate Avenue.[5]

In addition to removing non-historic tree growth, the Park Service be-gan to restore missing historic features. In December 1941, the regional office approved the planting of 270 peach trees in the Sherfy Peach Orchard. On the afternoon of July 2, 1863, Mississippi and South Carolina troops broke the Union line at the Peach Orchard, situated along the Emmitsburg Road and approximately one-half mile from the Union position on Cemetery Ridge, and held the orchard through the remainder of the battle. Officials also proposed the "restoration for historical reasons" of the apple orchard north of General George G. Meade's headquarters to the "wartime scene in that vicinity." They also recommended planting apple orchards on the Hummelbaugh and Bliss farms. Recognizing the problem of maintaining multiple orchards, Coleman favored leasing them to a local farmer. With an eye toward economic revenue, the superintendent also suggested canned peaches or apples as an "attractive sales article."[6]

Major efforts to improve the battlefield's appearance focused on those areas that received the majority of visitation, namely Little Round Top and Cemetery Ridge, near the Angle. Simultaneous to these projects, park staff researched the wartime appearances of its historic structures and subsequently completed restoration improvements to several properties. Among the first to be restored was the Lydia Leister farm, site of General Meade's headquarters. The farm house, located slightly east of Ziegler's Grove, underwent extensive restoration to both its interior and exterior. Here, too, a consideration for historical authenticity guided policy. One park official noted that the work assisted in "recreating and perpetuating the historical scene in key areas of the Gettysburg battlefield." In the summer of 1943, improvements to its foundation were completed and an adjacent flagstone walkway was added, which now displayed an American flag.[7]

Owing to its central location on the battlefield, Gettysburg's staff also restored the Abraham Brian property. Owned by a family of free blacks in 1863, the Brian farmstead sat along Cemetery Ridge slightly north of Ziegler's Grove. In the decades after the war, the home underwent several additions, including the construction of a second story and an adjoining wing to the southern side. By the 1940s, however, the farmstead had fallen into a state of disrepair. Given its prominent location near the Angle and the area's popularity with visitors, the park initiated plans to restore the farmhouse to its historic configuration. Wartime fiscal constraints, however, prevented any improvements until April 1951, when additions on the south and east wings were removed. Yet in their efforts to restore the farmhouse, park staff subsequently did little to improve its interpretation. The story of a free black family's experience as an invading Confederate army approached their doorstep for the time being remained silent. This did not represent a purposeful omission in the agency's interpretation, but reflected a prevalent emphasis on soldiers and tactics, typical of the nationally accepted reconciliationist narrative.[8]

As noted, when the National Park Service acquired Gettysburg in 1933, the agency had minimal experience in managing historic sites. As opposed to exclusively natural sites, such as Yellowstone or Grand Teton, administering historic sites presented officials with a different set of challenges. To bring uniformity in managing historic sites, in the fall of 1943, one decade after acquiring Gettysburg and other military parks, the acting director of the National Park Service issued an administrative directive for the national battlefields. He declared, "The guiding principles of battlefield park administration and development should be to present to the public the original battlefield scene as nearly as possible." This committed the agency to a policy of creating a historically accurate landscape, a practice that Superintendents McConaghie and Coleman's staff had already been implementing in a limited manner at

The National Park Service perpetuated the "High Water Mark"
thesis by focusing on landscape and interpretive improvements
at the Angle and Cemetery Ridge. The Brian Farm, owned at
the time of the battle by a family of free blacks, was restored to
its historic configuration in the early 1950s.

Gettysburg. Wherever practical, the NPS encouraged a program of "permanent preservation" that allowed for an area to be "faithfully preserved or accurately restored." Citing landscapes as "historic documents," the NPS made
the accurate maintenance and presentation of a battlefield a primary objective.
For the first time since acquiring the chain of military parks, the Park Service
articulated a uniform policy to manage and preserve historic landscapes.[9]

Meanwhile, the National Park Service continued to view tourism as a
key component. Encouraging tourism manifested itself in different ways. Im-
itating comparable visitor amenities in the western parks, in mid-April 1941
Coleman's staff opened coin-operated scenic viewers on Little Round Top and
the Eternal Light Peace Memorial on Oak Hill. Later, one was placed at the

Angle to overlook the fields of Pickett's Charge. The scenic viewers existed solely as a pleasure amenity. These viewers facilitated a better view of the landscape, but did little to interpret the area's battle action. Moreover, the selected locations of the scenic viewers reflected the battlefield's most popular sites. Coleman reported the viewer on Little Round Top to be "far more popular" than the other two. The scenic viewer phenomenon at Civil War battlefields was not unique to Gettysburg, however. In January 1941, the Park Service installed one scenic viewer on the Chickamauga & Chattanooga battlefield.[10]

In addition to cultivating a landscape that more clearly resembled its historical appearance and simultaneously offered a pleasant view, the National Park Service also actively shaped visitors' battlefield experiences in the realm of educational development. During the War Department's stewardship, the itinerary tablets and monuments stood as the principal interpretive tools to educate visitors on the battle's events. During the summer of 1941, Gettysburg's staff premiered a series of evening campfire programs. On July 13, park staff hosted the first campfire program, "Our National Parks in Color," on East Cemetery Hill, along Wainwright Avenue. To advertise for the program, the Park Service ran press releases in the local newspapers and local radio stations announced the event. The popularity of the opening program was encouraging; over 250 people attended. Later in the summer, various rangers presented slideshow programs on Crater Lake National Park and Hopewell Village to an audience of nearly 600. Campfire programs continued to be offered the following summer, but wartime constraints and declining visitation forced the park to cancel them in 1943. They were resumed in the summer of 1944.[11]

At this time, the campfire programs were the only ranger programs presented on the battlefield. It would appear by the abundance of local advertisement that area residents were the target audience. More significant from an educational perspective, however, were the program topics. Certainly the campfires did little to explain the battle, or even broader Civil War topics. Instead they focused on other national parks, reflective of McConaghie's philosophy that Gettysburg was only one link in a chain of national parks. Many of the films explored natural, not historical sites. A park ranger did provide a ten-minute summary of the Gettysburg campaign and battle before the featured program began.[12] Park officials wanted to introduce Gettysburg visitors to other national parks rather than educating them about the Gettysburg campaign and battle. Although hundreds of visitors gathered weekly on East Cemetery Hill, a key piece of the Union army's battle line, they received little meaningful interpretation of the battle.

It is not unreasonable, however, to assume that fostering a sense of nationalism and American patriotism was an underlying purpose. During the war the government mastered the art of propaganda with productions such as Frank Capra's *Why We Fight.* Films illustrating the majestic beauty of the Grand Canyon, Yellowstone, or Olympic National Parks showcased America's natural resources, while presentations about Saratoga and Revolutionary War encampments celebrated its historical resources and reminded viewers of America's triumphant struggle for independence and democracy. In an era defined by democracy versus Nazism and good versus evil, visitors were encouraged to feel proud of their heritage, their national parks, and the United States. Fittingly, in March 1861 Lincoln urged a similar remembrance of a common history in his first inaugural address. The newly elected president spoke of "mystic chords of memory" that reached from "every battlefield and patriot grave to every living heart and hearthstone all over this broad land" in an effort to compel northern and southerners to embrace a common heritage.[13]

The decrease in battlefield visitation served as one daily reminder of the influence of World War II. Ordinary travel declined precipitously when President Roosevelt declared gas rationing in seventeen eastern states on May 15, 1942. By the end of the year, gas rationing was in effect across the entire country. Coleman estimated that gas rationing curtailed Gettysburg's visitation ninety percent. Restrictions and mass mobilization resulted in a severe decline in visitation across the national park system. For fiscal year 1940, national parks recorded 19.3 million visitors; in fiscal year 1943 a mere 7.3 million traveled to the parks. During the winter, visitation at Gettysburg, like other sites, was virtually nonexistent; in January 1943, only 84 people visited the battlefield. Coleman reported, "Park travel has virtually ceased except for men in uniform."[14]

No other event defined the site's interpretive focus and the visitor's experience as much as viewing the Gettysburg Cyclorama. The cyclorama, a 360-degree panoramic painting, depicts the climactic scene of Pickett's Charge on July 3, 1863. Painted by French artist Paul Philippoteaux in 1883–1884, the painting premiered in Boston in 1884 before being showcased in several other American cities. In 1913, local interests brought the painting to Gettysburg in time for the fiftieth anniversary and displayed it in a specially constructed rotunda on East Cemetery Hill along Baltimore Street. After much negotiation, the Park Service acquired the painting on April 1, 1942, and continued to house it in the same building.[15]

The cyclorama now became the center for the Park Service's educational efforts. Ironically, at the site of a key Union victory and the war's only notable battle in a northern state, visitors experienced a decidedly Confederate interpretation of the battle. Certainly this narrative predated the Park Service's administration, originating with the veterans themselves during the era of reconciliation. The famed "hands across the wall" gathering on July 3, 1913, gave emphasis to Pickett's Charge as the climactic moment of the battle, if not

This building, located on East Cemetery Hill, along the Baltimore Pike originally, housed Paul Philippoteaux's painting of Pickett's Charge. The Gettysburg Cyclorama premiered in Gettysburg in 1913.

the entire Civil War. The acquisition of the Gettysburg Cyclorama and the subsequent centrality of the painting in the park's interpretive experience underscored the "High Water Mark" theme. The cyclorama heralded the cause of the Confederate soldiers on July 3 and provided scant attention to the men of the Army of the Potomac defending Cemetery Ridge. Indeed, not only did the painting become central to the park's educational program, but the primacy of the cyclorama also defined many subsequent management decisions. One Park Service official declared the painting as the agency's "most important exhibit" and recommended subsequent management decisions to be based around the cyclorama. In making the Gettysburg Cyclorama the focal point, the National Park Service became an active participant in shaping the battle narrative, and more importantly, the public's understanding and memory of Gettysburg.[16]

Indeed, subsequent management decisions were centered on the Gettysburg Cyclorama and the continued cultivation of the "High Water Mark" narrative. Though the painting became the agency's "most important exhibit," park officials soon discovered the inadequacies of the building that housed it on East Cemetery Hill. A leaking roof, uncontrolled humidity, and fluctuating room temperatures had caused irreversible damage to the painting. Keenly aware of the deficiencies of their own facilities, the deplorable conditions of the cyclorama building, and the popularity of local private museums, Park Service officials opened discussions to build a museum facility. While both local and regional officials agreed that a modern building was necessary for better preservation of the cyclorama and enhanced visitor services, the Park Service could not reach a consensus about where the new museum should be built. Debate involved whether the site should be privately or federally owned, its proximity to the popular Rosensteel museum, visitor access to the tour route, and convenience from well-traveled highways. Park officials advocated sites that were conveniently located near two popular stops: Ziegler's Grove, near the Angle and the Soldiers' National Cemetery.[17]

As debate on site selection continued, no one questioned the wisdom of constructing a modern facility on historic battlegrounds. Such a decision paralleled the agency's prevailing philosophy that visitor accessibility was paramount to the integrity of the battlefield. In fact, park officials lauded the proximity to the fields of Pickett's Charge as the principle factor for any site selection. The primacy of the newly acquired cyclorama also dictated potential sites. In deliberating where to locate the new facility, management believed that visitors' battlefield experiences would be enhanced if they viewed the cyclorama painting at the end of the tour, after they had the opportunity to walk the ground of Pickett's Charge. Roy Appleman, the agency's regional historian, asserted the new facility should be "on commanding ground and in the heart of the historic area." Locating modern visitor centers on "commanding ground" of historical significance had become customary for the National Park Service. Appleman approvingly cited the newly constructed visitor center on Henry House Hill at Manassas as justification for building Gettysburg's facility on Cemetery Ridge.[18]

If some park officials were hesitant to approve construction on historic grounds, the site's interpretive potential and accessibility offset those concerns. For example, Frederick Tilberg voiced his support for a location "as accessible as possible." He downplayed the historical significance of Ziegler's Grove, stating that "only the left flank of Pickett's Charge" moved over the ground. Superintendent Coleman recognized that development on Cemetery Ridge would constitute an intrusion, but he too lauded the site's accessibility and panoramic view. Perhaps Appleman revealed the Park Service's primary justification to construct the museum on historic battleground. "Just as a monument or memorial has been placed there for a purpose," Appleman declared, "so with an interpretive center it should be placed where it will do the most good on behalf of the visitors who come to the scene." Here too a philosophy of doing the "most good" for visitors paralleled wider trends within the National Park Service. When balancing developments and visitor use, Stephen Mather, the Park Service's first director, once declared the most ideal policies were ones that offered "the greatest good for the greatest number." In terms of highway accessibility and convenience to the popular sites, a visitor center constructed near Ziegler's Grove would offer "the most good" for the "greatest number."[19]

Increase in automobile ownership forced park officials across the country to deal with their impact on parks' cultural and natural resources. At Gettysburg, Coleman's staff initiated discussions to develop a new tour route. These discussions corresponded with the acquisition of the cyclorama and the subsequent discussion of a new visitor center. Improvements to the battlefield's infrastructure during the New Deal created a modern, accessible road system. In 1938 the Park Service had designed a standard touring brochure in preparation for the battle's 75th anniversary. Yet, many visitors continued to meander throughout the grounds. Moreover, the existing tour route further complicated an understanding of the battle, since it failed to follow any logical, chronological order. The route began at the contact station along the Chambersburg Pike (U.S. Route 30 West), where park rangers greeted visitors and provided some orientation. Rangers then directed visitors to the fighting of Day 1 along Oak Ridge, which included a stop at the Eternal Light Peace Memorial. Leaving Oak Ridge, visitors drove to East Confederate Avenue to cover the fighting of July 3 at Spangler's Spring and the July 2 and 3 action on Culp's Hill. From Culp's Hill, the Union right flank, visitors proceeded to the Soldiers' National Cemetery. The tour then continued southward along Cemetery Ridge, highlighting Pickett's Charge of the afternoon of the third day's fighting. Next the tour returned to the July 2 action with stops at Little Round Top, Devil's Den, the Wheatfield, and the Peach Orchard. The tour route then continued northward along West Confederate Avenue, the position occupied by the Army of Northern Virginia on July 2 and 3. Finally, the tour concluded at the point of origin at the Chambersburg Pike.[20] Clearly the tour route was not only out of time sequence, but also difficult to navigate.

The newly planned route included eight stops that would direct visitors through the battlefield chronologically. Starting at the contact station along U.S. Route 30, the tour proceeded north along Reynolds Avenue to the second stop at the Eternal Light Peace Memorial. Next, visitors traveled south along Doubleday Avenue to stop at the observation tower on Oak Ridge, which overlooked the Federal position on the afternoon and evening of July 1. The tour continued on West Confederate Avenue to the Virginia Memorial, the fourth stop. Visitors then drove through town to reach the Union's right flank at Spangler's Spring and Culp's Hill, before proceeding to the grounds of the fighting on July 2: the Wheatfield, Peach Orchard, and the sixth stop at Devil's Den. The tour included a stop at Little Round Top. Leaving the Union left flank, visitors traveled north on Hancock Avenue to the High Water Mark, the final stop. Concluding the tour, visitors could walk to the new building, view the cyclorama, and then, if interested, take a short stroll to the Soldiers' National Cemetery. This new route accomplished three objectives. First, it provided visitors with a chronological understanding of how the battle unfolded. Second, the new route included stops at the "principle features of the park," as designated by the Park Service. And third, by designing a tour route that included eight stops, visitors could see these "principle features" in the "shortest possible time."[21]

Planning for this structured and chronological tour route further underscored the transitional nature of the battlefield. Since its establishment in 1916, the National Park Service supported automobiles in the parks as a means to promote tourism. The War Department had done little to develop a bona fide tour route; instead, visitors meandered across the battlefield avenues without any standardized method. The National Park Service, however, embarked on a proactive role to systematize visitors' experiences. Coleman sought to establish a tour route suitable for a generation of visitors who were unfamiliar with the battle. According to Coleman, the new tour route should "aim to put forth a clear, uninterrupted chronological narrative of events, readily understandable to visitors who are entirely unacquainted with the battlefield and the story." Moreover, the proposed educational facilities and the structured tour route accomplished former Superintendent McConaghie's objective of developing the battlefield into an accessible landscape, which further fashioned Gettysburg as a national park. Management continued to explore options to build a new visitor center and develop a chronological tour route, and economic and social factors of the postwar era would eventually offer the agency the timely opportunity to fulfill these objectives.[22]

Similarly, the proposed tour route paralleled Americans' changing interest in specific areas of the battlefield. In the decades after the battle, Culp's Hill and Cemetery Hill were the most visited sites, owing in part to their convenient location to the town and proximity to the Soldiers' National Cemetery. By the 1940s, however, fewer tourists traveled to these locations. While Culp's Hill and Cemetery Hill remained on the auto tour, it was not unreasonable to assume that many visitors did not drive the entire battlefield and avoided sites they may have considered to be too far or less popular. Furthermore, Culp's Hill had become heavily wooded, and, though the agency initiated small-scale vista cuttings, none had been conducted along the eastern side of the battlefield. Thus, the excessive undergrowth made understanding the fighting along the Federal right flank complicated. Consequently, the tactical and strategic importance of Cemetery Hill and Culp's Hill faded into distant memory, and the third day's action solidified its place as the "High Water Mark" of the battle.

The increasing popularity of the "High Water Mark" can be explained by several factors. Foremost, the National Park Service became an active agent in promoting Pickett's Charge as the climactic assault of the battle, if not the entire Civil War. Management made deliberate decisions that established the Angle as the central point on the landscape, thereby defining visitors' touring experiences and understanding of the battle. First, the Park Service's improve-ments along Cemetery Ridge resulted in a more historically accurate vista. During McConaghie's tenure, the post-and-pipe fencing scattered throughout Cemetery Ridge were removed. And when the NPS acquired the Round Top Railroad in 1944, the rail bed, wire fencing, and non-historic hedgerows that cut across the fields of Pickett's Charge and Cemetery Ridge were removed. These preservation efforts allowed the agency to "erase a scar" and restored historical authenticity to the fields of Pickett's Charge. To further promote the "High Water Mark" narrative, and to blend an element of entertainment with education, the park erected a scenic viewer near Battery A, 4th U.S. Artil-lery, commanded by Lieutenant Alonzo Cushing. Similarly, the restoration of General Meade's headquarters brought additional attention to the Cemetery Ridge landscape. And the recent acquisition of the Gettysburg Cyclorama firmly embedded the interpretive focus to the third day's action. Fascination with the third day's fighting at Gettysburg found support in popular literature as well. In the mid-1930s, Virginia historian Douglas Southall Freeman au-thored his multivolume biography on Robert E. Lee, which offered a distinctly positive interpretation of the Confederate general. Less than a decade later, he published his three-volume *Lee's Lieutenants: A Study in Command.*[23]

While the Park Service took an active role in emphasizing the "High Water Mark" narrative, the Soldiers' National Cemetery remained one of the most visited sites. As part of the agency's philosophy of creating an acces-sible battlefield, the cemetery entrance gates were widened to accommodate two-way automobile traffic. Following the Lower Drive, visitors drove by the graves of the Civil War soldiers, then proceeded to the Upper Drive to view the Soldiers' National Monument. President Lincoln's rising popularity in American culture in the 1940s, reflective of the patriotic mood and the tran-scendency of the Gettysburg Address, brought more visitors to the cemetery. Memorial Day speakers, as will be discussed, frequently invoked the Gettys-burg Address and crowds swarmed to the Lincoln Speech Memorial. Capi-talizing on this surging interest in the rhetoric of the Gettysburg Address, the Park Service sought to expand its interpretive presence in the cemetery. In the spring of 1942, the park erected a marker at the Soldiers' National Monument, near where Lincoln stood on November 19, 1863, and a second at the Lincoln Speech Monument. At this time, these were the only interpretive signs on the battlefield.[24]

Since their establishment in 1915, the Licensed Battlefield Guides had demonstrated varying degrees of antagonism toward the War Department and early NPS management. Shortly after arriving at Gettysburg, Superin-tendent McConaghie placed the guides on "trial" while encouraging them to foster a stronger and dedicated connection to the new National Park Service administration. By the 1940s, problems with their behavior had increased considerably. When Coleman attempted to exert more control over the often-unmanageable guides, relations between the two groups worsened. Coleman predicted a "show down" with the guides, whom he believed were intent on "pulling political strings and running this Park."[25]

Much of the antagonism centered on the guides' professional behavior, or lack thereof, with visitors. Some guides deliberately avoided giving visitors any information pertaining to park facilities or activities. Others refused to take visitors to the agency's headquarters or the newly acquired cyclorama, in the belief it would "spoil" their story. Coleman wrote the NPS director to explain the increasingly hostile relations between the park staff and the guides, claiming "no visitors are being brought to the Park Museum and it is obvious that the guides will proceed to take over the area if they are permitted to do so." The increasing number of visitors touring in automobiles only perpetuated guides' hustling. Visitors frequently encountered uniformed guides soliciting tours by "running out to the roadside upon the approach of a car, waving arms and shouting to attract attention." Unsuspecting visitors thought that they were being hailed by a police officer and stopped, only to be harassed into hiring a guide to tour the battlefield. On the town square, park management charged that guides could be frequently seen stopping cars or jumping on the running boards of moving vehicles. Even when approached for directions on how to reach a particular site on the battlefield, guides offered to take them to the requested site, but for a fee.[26]

Coleman argued that their aggressive and unprofessional behavior reflected poorly on the National Park Service at Gettysburg. Unwilling to have the park's image tarnished by some disreputable guides, he believed that the only solution to improve the guide system was to place them on civil service status, which would then make the guides directly responsible to the Park Service. The guides immediately opposed the proposal and local congressmen refused to introduce legislation.[27] Licensed guides retained their independent, self-employed status, and park management, wary of how their behavior reflected on the Park Service, kept a watchful eye.

Issues of civil service status aside, Licensed Battlefield Guides exerted a direct influence over management decisions and acted as a powerful interest group in the battlefield's development. For instance, when park officials considered developing a chronological tour route, the guides opposed the initiative. In October 1942, the acting regional director suggested that the park use interpretive waysides accompanied with short descriptive text and orientation maps to facilitate an understanding of the battle. As outlined, a purpose of the interpretive markers would allow visitors to "learn the story of the battle without the necessity of hiring a guide." After considering the proposal, Coleman postponed the installation of the exhibits, due in large part to guide opposition. Increasing tensions between the National Park Service and the Licensed Battlefield Guides over interpretive markers underscored a pervasive narrative of factions competing for ownership of the battlefield and its story. Their opposition to the wayside markers was simply a matter of self-interest; the more accessible the battlefield came to self-guiding, the less imperative guided tours would become. Clearly the Park Service could only go so far in cultivating an accessible landscape that provided visitors with the tools to explore the battlefield themselves. Licensed Battlefield Guides also claimed ownership of the battlefield and sought to determine its accessibility.[28]

Victory in World War II depended on full mobilization of the American people and resources. During the war, Americans made personal sacrifices, whether by the loss of a loved one overseas, rationing food stocks, purchasing victory bonds, or adhering to nightly curfews. Millions of people "did their part" by contributing to the war's scrap drives. Here, too, the war defined the management of the battlefield. Citizens donated spare tires and salvaged tin cans, rubber and other valuable war materials. National parks across the nation accommodated wartime requests in a variety of ways, Gettysburg included. While Civil War battlefields contributed large amounts of metals toward salvage, the federal government targeted western parks for their natural resources. The secretary of the interior authorized the mining of salt in Death Valley and the cutting of Sitka spruce trees in Olympic National Park. Several western parks, including Grand Canyon, Carlsbad, Sequoia, Acadia, Olympic, and Glacier Bay housed military rest camps, hospitalization facilities, and defense installations. Military training exercises occurred in Yellowstone, Yosemite, Shenandoah, Death Valley, and on the Gettysburg battlefield.[29]

The demands of the Second World War influenced Gettysburg's landscape in several ways. In the decades following the Civil War, the War Department had stockpiled a large supply of surplus cannon and artillery pieces, many of which were not displayed, but instead stored in maintenance sheds. During the Second World War, Gettysburg distributed excess artillery to other Civil War sites. For example, at least eighteen guns were transferred to Antietam National Battlefield. Yet millions of tons of scrap metal were needed to build and arm the nation's aircraft, battleships, and fighter planes. By September 1942 Gettysburg had contributed nearly eighteen tons of scrap metal. The salvaged items included iron fence panels and posts, various metal signs, as well as eighty-six guns from the surplus stockpile. In addition, more than eight hundred spherical shells were removed, which had been placed by the War Department as commemorative features to represent the ordnance supply.[30]

The demands of the war, however, required more. On October 13, 1942, Coleman wrote to the NPS director that a survey of available metals on the battlefield revealed that more pyramidal piles of artillery shells could be "removed without serious interference with the visitor's understanding of the battle." This included 194 pyramidal castings, totaling near 80,000 pounds. He also reported that there were nineteen Union and Confederate bronze itinerary tablets available, which had been installed in the 1880s. In their place, Coleman proposed the creation of several exhibits, including a campaign map and a short narration detailing the Union and Confederate approach to Gettysburg. Believing that the itinerary plaques added "little or nothing" to the existing interpretive program, Director Newton Drury approved their removal and disposal. Fortunately, they were never salvaged.[31]

While the nation prepared for further sacrifices, so, too, did the battlefield. In December 1942 park officials produced a report that grouped the battlefield's markers and monuments in order of priority for the scrap drives. This report divided the markers into nine groupings, essentially presenting a plan for the dismantling and melting down of many of the memorials and monuments designed and dedicated by the veterans themselves. First priority for removal were the nineteen bronze itinerary tablets. Group two consisted of 197 Civil War cannons and artillery tubes, which marked the headquarters of the generals. Group three included 256 brigade, division, and corps explanatory tablets. Group four consisted of various decorative objects on 250 monuments. The report listed nineteen symbolic statues as the fifth priority for removal. Priority group six comprised 317 bronze inscriptive tablets of regimental or state markers. Reliefs depicting battle scenes or individuals were listed as the seventh priority for removal. The forty-three statues honoring individuals appeared further down on the priority list. This group included the Union corps commanders' equestrian monuments, as well as the bust of President Lincoln on top of the speech memorial in the Soldiers' National Cemetery. The final group prioritized for scrap consisted of three monuments, listed last for their "highly artistic merit." Ironically, those monuments commemorated Confederate soldiers and included the Virginia Memorial, the North Carolina Memorial, and the Alabama Memorial.[32]

To compensate for their loss, the Park Service proposed photographing the monuments and their inscriptions for archival history. In February 1943, Director Drury added that the agency would consider the donation of the monuments only with the assurance that they would be recast after the war. In attempting to balance the preservation of the nation's historical treasures and the necessity of wartime sacrifice he wrote, "Each war memorial in the parks represents the last possible debt payment of the Nation to some soldier or group of soldiers in our national past. It would be little comfort to the soldiers of the present day if such evidence of the Nation's gratitude should come to be lightly regarded."[33] Fortunately, the hardships of the war did not become desperate enough to warrant the removal and scrapping of the tablets or monuments itemized on the inventory.

In addition to metal salvage, the federal government took advantage of the sizable acres of Civil War battlefields and procured these lands for military training and camps. In December 1942, for instance, the War Department established the Third Women's Army Auxiliary Corps Training Center (WAAC) at Chickamauga & Chattanooga National Military Park. When the camp closed on April 1, 1945, approximately 46,000 women had been trained in the WAAC camp. The superintendent proclaimed the camp to be a "real asset" to the park and noted that many of the women expressed interest in learning about the battle's history and planned to visit in the postwar era. Meanwhile, at Shiloh National Military Park in Tennessee, the War Department requisitioned land for field artillery maneuvers. During July 1942, Shiloh's superintendent reported 2,810 troops were simulating wartime conditions and noted that the maneuvers gained "much publicity" for the park.[34]

In Mississippi, the National Park Service surveyed the iron markers and tablets at Vicksburg National Military Park for the scrap drive. These markers had also been installed during the veterans' era of the late nineteenth century. Some of these interpretive tablets and markers were considered "obsolete" by park staff and were prioritized for removal. By the fall of 1942, Vicksburg's staff had condemned and removed twenty-five tons of iron interpretive markers and tablets for the scrap drive.[35] Chickamauga & Chattanooga National Military Park also donated a sizable amount of surplus metals. In his November 1942 monthly report, Superintendent C. S. Dunn reported the park had scrapped 205.8 tons of metal to date. This included surplus cast iron artillery shells, "many" historical tablets, and "various other items of loose and useless metal found over the park." The Army's Corps of Engineers also salvaged thousands of linear feet of pipe that had been laid by the War Department during World War I, when the grounds were used as a training camp for American Doughboys.[36] Undeniably, the national parks, including the Civil War battlefields, "did their part" to contribute to the Allied victory during the Second World War.

Gettysburg, as with Shiloh and Chickamauga & Chattanooga, also served a utilitarian purpose during the war. During the fall of 1942, the War Department agreed to house prisoners of war in the United States. By war's end, more than 400,000 Germans were imprisoned in approximately 500 POW camps scattered throughout the country, many in abandoned Civilian Conservation Corps facilities. One such camp was located at Gettysburg National Military Park; its relatively remote location in south-central Pennsylvania made the site ideal for a prisoner of war camp.[37]

Located south of the borough lines along the Emmitsburg Road, the POW camp occupied fifteen acres on the fields of Pickett's Charge. The first

German prisoners arrived in June 1944. They were temporarily detained in the Pennsylvania National Guard Armory, located on West Confederate Avenue, while the permanent stockades were being built. On June 22, 1944, the prisoners were transferred to this camp and by month's end the camp held over 250 prisoners. Surrounded by barbed wire fencing, the camp was four hundred feet by six hundred feet, and protected by guard towers at each corner of the stockade.[38]

By the war's midpoint most men in Pennsylvania of working age were serving in the military, leaving Adams and surrounding counties with a severe labor shortage to harvest the area's lucrative crops. Consequently, local fruit producers in desperate need of labor requested manpower assistance from the U.S. Army, which sent several hundred prisoners to work in fruit production and packaging. Prisoners also helped to harvest the pea crop and cut pulpwood. In return, they received prevailing wages, approximately one dollar per day, with a portion being credited to their account for use in the camp PX, and the remainder given to the federal government. The prisoners performed a much needed and appreciated service for the local community by processing thousands of dollars worth of food that otherwise would have spoiled.[39]

Beginning in the 1880s and reaching climactic high points in the 1913 and 1938 reunions, Gettysburg stood as a symbol of reconciliation and embodied fraternity among the veterans of the Civil War. When a new generation of Americans responded to their nation's call of duty, only a few thousand Civil War veterans were still alive, and the war faded slowly into a distant memory. Entrance into World War II and subsequent hardships endured by millions revitalized Americans' connection with the battlefield and brought forth a new generation to interpret the Gettysburg Address to the contemporary crises abroad and the sacrifices at home. As the country's men marched off to war in distant lands, Americans sought to reconnect with the heroism and sacrifices of their ancestors, to find strength and conviction to triumph in a war against evil. Reviewing orations delivered at Gettysburg during the war years, often at Memorial Day commemorations, two themes emerge. First, speakers continued to promote Gettysburg as a "shrine" to sectional reconciliation. This pervasive narrative underscored national unity in a time of unprecedented foreign crisis. "Gettysburg echoes the call to the service of a united and determined nation," noted one orator. Second, in the face of the stark realities of expanding Nazism, Fascism, and despotic rulers, Americans interpreted the Gettysburg Address as a call for democracy and freedom. For the permanence of freedom, Americans committed to giving, if necessary, "the last full measure of devotion."[40]

Heightened patriotism, continued designation of Gettysburg as a site of reconciliation, and contemporary interpretations of the Gettysburg Address as an appeal to democracy manifested themselves in Memorial Day commemorations. Memorial Day had long been an integral part of the commemorative and reconciliation process at Gettysburg. The events of the 1940s, however, made honoring those who sacrificed their lives for freedom more relevant. Memorial Day regularly included a recitation of the Gettysburg Address as prelude to the keynote speech. In May 1941, William C. Storrick, a Gettysburg resident present at the dedication of the Soldiers' National Cemetery nearly eight decades earlier, recited the address to open the occasion.[41] Two years later, in 1943, more than 2,200 gathered for the Memorial Day ceremonies. Pennsylvania governor Edward Martin delivered the keynote. His opening statement made clear the contemporary interpretations of the Gettysburg Address. "Four score years ago, on this hallowed field, the Great Emancipator declared that 'government of the people, by the people, for the people shall not perish from the earth.'" The Second World War tested the strength of the American people to uphold Lincoln's vision of "government of the people." The governor proceeded to describe the dark realities of the totality of the war in Europe and the fight to uphold a peoples' right of self-government. He noted the governments of Europe had been "blotted out," their people living in "slavery or exile." Global "Armageddon" waited if the war for freedom and independence was lost. The war's outcome, according to Martin, would "determine whether Lincoln's great words remain true."[42]

Orations the following year, 1944, underscored this belief. Befitting to a landscape that epitomized regional unity, the 1944 Memorial Day ceremonies included keynotes speeches from a "representative" of the "Old South" and one from "the Old North." North Carolina governor J. Melville Broughton opened with a declaration of national unity, forged at Gettysburg eight decades ago. "We are assembled before a shrine sacred to North and South alike," Broughton stated. Borrowing phrases from the Gettysburg Address, Broughton echoed the declarations of the veterans themselves during the era of reconciliation. "It is all together fitting that these great sections of our nation," he declared "once divided but now united, should in this momentous hour of world history join in solemn pledge of unity and loyalty." Gettysburg stood, noted Broughton, as a memorial to "two of the greatest Americans of all time"—Abraham Lincoln and Robert E. Lee. As important, for contemporary Americans, the Gettysburg Address was not only a tribute to the Union dead, but also a vision for a united nation and the permanence of democracy. Lincoln's "immortal address," as interpreted by Broughton, was a "prayer" for "the preservation of the government created by democracy." In 1944, Americans and freedom-loving citizens around the globe fought valiantly against "evil forces" intent on exterminating democracy.[43]

Representing the Old North, Massachusetts governor Leverett Saltonstall's address echoed themes of reconciliation and the relevance of the

Gettysburg Address as the ultimate test of the survival of democracy against conquering rulers abroad. Eight decades removed from the divisiveness of the Civil War, descendants of Union and Confederate veterans now fought "side by side" around the globe against aggression and injustice, in a testament to the "united spirit" of America. Appealing to those on the home front, Saltonstall urged domestic unity and commitment to safeguard the values of freedom and opportunity, ideals that Lincoln "so clearly advanced."[44]

In *Lincoln at Gettysburg: The Words That Remade America,* Garry Wills claims Lincoln's speech to be an "authoritative expression of the American spirit." His words, according to Wills, cast a "spell" over Americans that has yet to be broken. Uses and interpretations of the Gettysburg Address during the Second World War suggest that Wills's assertion of the speech casting a "spell" is correct. The power of Lincoln's address, however, comes not from its static interpretation, but from its malleability and the ways successive generations have applied his words to interpret contemporary crises. At a time when totalitarian and dictatorial governments eliminated personal liberties and freedom for millions of people, the passage declaring that "government of the people, by the people, for the people shall not perish from the earth" became ever more pertinent. In the 1940s, the Gettysburg Address remained an "authoritative expression of the American spirit" because it embodied the spirit of democracy, freedom, and, if necessary, militancy to preserve these freedoms.[45]

To evoke Lincoln's memory was not a phenomenon exclusive to Gettysburg, however. In his article on Lincoln and the Second World War, Barry Schwartz finds that the federal government often made reference to Lincoln's wartime actions and speeches. Lincoln became a means to explain increased federal powers in wartime, to inspire individuals to vanquish tyranny, or to console those who lost loved ones in the current battles for freedom. As the Roosevelt administration painted the Second World War as part of the nation's grand historical narrative, the Civil War stood at the center. And Lincoln emerged as the foremost figure representing freedom and equality. In a government advertisement used to encourage the purchase of war bonds, an image of the Lincoln Memorial and a silhouette of a mortally wounded G.I. soldier dominated the poster. The headline, "That We Here Highly Resolve That These Dead Shall Not Have Died in Vain," drew a clear connection between the sacrifices of generations past and a nation rising to assume the new burdens of sustaining freedom.

World War II forced Americans to reconnect to their past and to reshape the meaning of the battle of Gettysburg to make it relevant to their lives and struggles. During this national crisis, Americans continued to look toward Gettysburg to find meaning as well as a sense of national identity. True, other national parks contributed to the war effort through salvage drives, natural resource extractions, and hosting military training camps. But no other landscape inspired the same degree of sentiment as Gettysburg. Orators used Gettysburg to inspire Americans to become better citizens, and interpreted the Gettysburg Address as a call to uphold the virtues of freedom and the nation's heritage. While standing on the battlefield and reflecting upon the heroism of the Americans who fought and died on these fields, modern Americans found the resolve and commitment to fight the enemies of peace and freedom. No other landscape brought the stark clarity to the war for freedom and sovereignty more than Gettysburg. Through these "mystic chords of memory," Gettysburg helped to renew Americans' commitment to preserve a nation.[46]

CHAPTER 4

THE WORLD WILL LITTLE NOTE NOR LONG REMEMBER: POSTWAR TOURISM, PATRIOTISM, AND THE NEW BIRTH OF COMMERCIALIZATION, 1946–1955

Victory in Europe on May 8, 1945, and the surrender of Japan four months later on September 2, ended mankind's deadliest and costliest war. As the military demobilized, American GIs returned home and took their place in a bourgeoning, vibrant domestic economy. The emerging national highway system, pent-up buying power, and shorter work weeks increased leisure time. Free of the economic hardships of the Great Depression, in the years immediately after the war, millions of people took to the road to reacquaint themselves with America and its national treasures in what Susan Sessions Rugh has termed "the golden age of family vacations." As Rugh notes, the proliferation of the automobile "democratized" the family vacation. Slightly over half of American families owned automobiles in 1948; by 1960 automobile ownership extended to 77 percent.[1]

Taking advantage of postwar prosperity, increased leisure, and the advantages afforded by the automobile, Americans traveled in large numbers to the country's national parks because it solidified "their status as citizens in the American nation." Heritage tourism in itself was not a new phenomenon. In *See America First,* Marguerite Shaffer explores the interplay between tourism and national identity in the six decades before the Second World War. Beginning in the late nineteenth century, the bourgeoning tourist industry "actively promoted tourism as a ritual of American citizenship." By visiting sites that personified America, such as the Grand Canyon, Yellowstone, or traveling through the west, Shaffer argues that "tourists would become better Americans." This practice of promoting heritage tourism as a critical component of citizenship accelerated in the years following World War II. Individuals and families journeyed, or pilgrimaged, to historic sites in unprecedented numbers as a means to reinforce their association to America and its culture. At the height of the Cold War, Americans searched for ways to strengthen their connection and loyalty to the nation, its history, and its patriots. Visits to historic, civic sites demonstrated this association and reinforced a celebratory national narrative of American exceptionalism. Certainly postwar travels for African Americans reflected a different experience, one determined by the confines of racial discrimination. The practices of racial discrimination, Rugh notes, "complicated the claims of African Americans to American identity," claims which white Americans in the postwar era so readily sought to reaffirm.[2]

Beginning in 1945, as Michael Kammen suggests, an "anxious mood" pervaded American society that ushered in a "pronounced sense of discontinuity between past and present." Kammen argues that Americans forged a feeling of continuity by visiting historic sites and museums, as well as participating in a variety of historic endeavors in their local communities. The result of the impulse to associate with the nation's history and an increasing popularization of the past manifested itself in what Kammen terms the "heritage syndrome." He defines the "heritage syndrome" as an "impulse to remember what is attractive or flattering and to ignore all the rest."[3]

To connect with this dominant, triumphant national narrative, Americans journeyed to historic places. Across the nation, historic sites recorded approximately 48 million visitors in 1954. Colonial Williamsburg, a popular site since its opening in 1933, recorded over 166,000 visitors in 1946, an approximate increase of 76 percent from the previous year. A decade later Colonial Williamsburg received 341,000 visitors. The "heritage syndrome" also drove visitation to the nation's natural vistas. The Grand Canyon enjoyed a dramatic spike in visitation in the years immediately following the Second World War. By the end of the 1946 fiscal year in September, park officials recorded nearly 489,000 visitors, representing an increase of 325 percent from the 1945 fiscal year. The National Park Service felt the impact of this surge in visitation and the popularity of the "heritage syndrome." In 1945 visitation to all national parks reached 11.7 million; within two years visitation had doubled to 25.5 million. In 1956, the national parks reported 61.6 million.[4]

Unsurprisingly, Gettysburg National Military Park stood as a beneficiary of this surge in tourism. During August 1945 approximately 45,000 people toured the battlefield, and the following month park staff reported over 57,000 visitors. In 1946, the first full year after the war, visitation to the park totaled 508,641. The following year, in 1947, the park recorded 630,805, or a 25 percent increase from the previous year. Gettysburg's visitation for the 1948 to 1949 fiscal year reached 659,222, the third busiest year in the battlefield's history at this time. Visitation continued to increase annually, and by 1955 the park recorded 724,037 visitors.[5]

Other Civil War battlefields enjoyed an increase in visitation as well. In Mississippi, visitation trends at Vicksburg National Military Park reinforced an evident rise in nationwide tourism. For the 1945–1946 fiscal year, James McConaghie, new superintendent at Vicksburg, reported approximately 82,000 visitors. Two years later, he recorded an annual visitation of 122,184. Increase in visitation aside, more revealing of the nature of postwar tourism is that McConaghie reported that visitors traveled from across the nation, specifically representing no less than forty states. The nation's first federally preserved Civil War battlefield, Chickamauga & Chattanooga, reported 218,527 visitors between June 30, 1947, and April 30, 1948. Thus, as illustrated by the postwar visitation statistics of Vicksburg and Chickamauga, Gettysburg's visitation surpassed all battlefields. While Americans visited historic and cultural sites to reaffirm their heritage and patriotism, the shared reverence for the Pennsylvania battlefield compelled more Americans to visit Gettysburg than any other Civil War battlefield.[6]

Immediately at war's end, park officials sought to promote Gettysburg as a site of patriotic reckoning. Superintendent Coleman identified patriotic expressions among the agency's most important activities. Events associated with the battle's anniversary not only displayed "sound patriotic motives," but also allowed "the community to profit in a material way." Blending patriotic occasions with capitalistic gain benefited Americans seeking a means to reconnect with their history, the Park Service, and the economic interests of the town. Coleman recognized the battlefield as a desirable destination in postwar tourism. "People want to come to Gettysburg at such times," he commented, "and they look to our community to provide them with patriotic programs."[7]

Interpretative programs at Gettysburg took two forms in the postwar years. First, the park resumed its campfire programs, which had been curtailed during the war years. The park historian reported an average attendance of two hundred at each program. Like those held previously, many of these programs explored America's national parks, offering minimal discussion of the battle of Gettysburg. In the summers following the war, for instance, visitors enjoyed films on Yellowstone, Zion, Bryce, Mount McKinley, Carlsbad, and Grand Canyon National Parks, as well as programs on Skyline Drive, the Shenandoah Valley, the assassination of Abraham Lincoln, the Statue of Liberty, Historic Pennsylvania, Colonial Williamsburg, and Saratoga National Historical Park.[8]

More significantly, Memorial Day ceremonies revealed the increased association between the postwar political environment, the pervasive reverence for the battlefield, and accepted uses of the landscape. Now civic ceremonies offered the traditional reverence for the sacrifices of the Civil War soldiers, an interpretation of Lincoln's Gettysburg Address as a call to an enduring democracy, and highly partisan Cold War rhetoric. In May 1945, as American soldiers continued to wage deadly campaigns in the Pacific, Republican senator Robert Taft of Ohio delivered the keynote speech. Taft opened his remarks with an acknowledgement of "reverence" to the soldiers who fought at Gettysburg, a site he defined as the "greatest battlefield of the Civil War." Drawing parallels to those Civil War soldiers who fought for freedom eight decades ago, Taft addressed the current global struggle for freedom and Americans' commitment to preserving freedom and liberties. Then, before a crowd of nearly 3,500, Senator Taft launched into a narrative of the inherent dangers of peacetime conscription and, foreshadowing popular Cold War discourse, warned listeners of the dangers of a growing government bureaucracy. The following year, for the first peace time Memorial Day event, fellow conservative and Ohio Republican John Bricker imparted a comparable oration proclaiming "confusion" in the nation's domestic and foreign policy. Interpreting President Lincoln's Gettysburg Address as a testament to "liberty and free representative government," Bricker urged listeners to recall Lincoln's conviction that government served to "provide a fair chance for all the race of life," not to "direct the lives of people." Over 4,000 people gathered in the Soldiers' National Cemetery to hear Bricker's speech, while thousands more listened through a radio broadcast.[9]

The decidedly political overtones left some listeners unhappy and calling for more traditional commemorations. Local residents voiced their opposition to speakers "who deliver orations on party politics." Regional officials also found the practice of using the battlefield to promote a political agenda unsavory. The month following Senator Bricker's address, the acting regional director informed Coleman that future Memorial Day events "ought to be free of expressions of party politics." As the memo from the acting regional director and the opposition from the local community suggests, using Gettysburg to further a partisan message violated the battlefield as a place of reconciliation and consecration. Future Memorial Day events offered more traditional tributes to the Civil War soldiers and less overt attention to Cold War politics. In May 1947, Pennsylvania governor James Duff delivered the keynote speech. Speaking to the meaning of Gettysburg, Duff summarized, "Gettysburg has become a symbol of sacrifice of those who have given their lives for their country—not only here, but in every field of battle and in whatever faraway place." Too, Lincoln's words offered an enduring call-to-arms for the preservation of American ideals. At the dawn of the Cold War, Duff warned of the shadow of totalitarianism spreading through Europe, a shadow that undermined the very soul of freedom once espoused by Lincoln. Offering the much-quoted passage, Duff decried this communist menace that threatened Lincoln's ideal of "government of the people, by the people."[10]

Subsequent Memorial Day speakers continued the tradition of honoring the courage and sacrifice of the Civil War soldier. As had become common during the Second World War, speakers harnessed the appeal of Gettysburg and Lincoln's speech and applied it to contemporary political struggles. In May 1948, Massachusetts Republican congressman Joseph Martin spoke of the landscape's consecration noting, "On this field of sacrifice, the most beautiful evaluation of the service rendered our Nation by those who have fought in her defense was uttered by the immortal Abraham Lincoln." Breathing relevance from events in 1863 to listeners, Martin linked the sacrifice of those who fought for the Union and words of the "immortal" Lincoln to the present threats to free government. The Union preserved by the soldiers of the 1860s "has become the nation which is the last bulwark of liberty in this world." Interpreting the Civil War as a clear testament to the viability of "government of, by and for the people," Martin summoned listeners to the current global war for peace and freedom. The duty of contemporary Americans, he challenged, was to see that "freedom does not perish from the earth." Other speeches similarly found inspiration and relevance in the deeds of the Civil War soldiers. In May 1951, Maryland governor Theodore McKeldin summarized the hardships endured by the Civil War populace. As had become common, McKeldin interpreted the Gettysburg Address as a lasting call for democracy. Using an often-quoted passage, the governor declared that America "must set the good example and foster once more the good life so that 'government of the people, by the people and for the people shall not perish from the earth.'"[11]

Poet Carl Sandburg noted that Abraham Lincoln became the "mirror" in which Americans could "see themselves." Americans saw the meaning of their nation and fate of democracy in the words the president spoke on a bloodstained field in Pennsylvania. The Second World War served to revitalize Abraham Lincoln and the Gettysburg Address. Faced with unprecedented hardships caused by global war and an ever-looming threat to the American way of life, Americans interpreted the Gettysburg Address as an enduring testament to democracy, patriotism, and sacrifice. The power of Lincoln's speech, then, lay in its malleability and in its transcendent ideals. Orators brought relevance into the two-minute speech, thereby democratizing it for contemporary crises. Reflective of this popularization of the Gettysburg Address, in the fall of 1946 Congress declared November 19, the date of the dedication of the Soldiers' National Cemetery, "Dedication Day." The joint resolution stated that the president's words would continue to "touch the hearts of men and inspire them with faith in our matchless democracy as long as time endures." Lincoln's speech on November 19, 1863, as understood by writers of the resolution, was a call for his countrymen to "dedicate themselves to the principles of democracy." Unsurprisingly, congressmen inserted the often-quoted line of "government of the people, by the people, for the people" as a testament to their understanding of the Gettysburg Address as a commitment to democracy. Dedication Day, then, became less an occasion to honor the Union dead at Gettysburg and more an event to celebrate the cause of democracy and freedom. President Harry S. Truman proposed that the Gettysburg Address be read in public settings wherever "the American flag flies."[12]

On November 19, 1946, Gettysburg celebrated its first Dedication Day. Congressman Jennings Randolph from West Virginia delivered the keynote address. Sponsored jointly by the Lincoln Fellowship of Pennsylvania and the Sons of Union Veterans (SUV), the Dedication Day events soon became as popular as Memorial Day, attracting several thousand spectators, as well as notable politicians and distinguished guests. For example, on November 19, 1951, on the 88th anniversary of the dedication of the Soldiers' National Cemetery, Illinois governor Adlai E. Stevenson served as the keynote. Befitting to contemporary interpretations of the Gettysburg Address as an oration on democracy, Stevenson declared, "When we realize that Lincoln saw the dissolution of the Union as a threat to democratic aspirations throughout the world, his words at Gettysburg become more meaningful." For the occasion, the Library of Congress donated an original copy of the Gettysburg Address, which was displayed at the Gettysburg National Bank.[13]

Dedication Day paralleled an increasing popularization of Abraham Lincoln. Boy scouts and local chapters of the Sons of Union Veterans began to hold annual celebrations of the president's birthday in Gettysburg. In 1949 the Harrisburg Council of the Boy Scouts of America initiated an annual pilgrimage for Pennsylvania Boy Scouts to Gettysburg. On February 12, nearly 2,000 scouts gathered to commemorate Lincoln's birthday and to participate in a nationwide program to "Strengthen the Arm of Liberty." The following year, nearly 3,000 scouts attended the ceremonies and paraded through town to the Soldiers' National Cemetery. Actress Colleen Townsend recited the Gettysburg Address, reportedly the first time a woman read the speech at the Gettysburg ceremonies. Each of these events were broadcast by radio, which permitted thousands more to join in the commemoration and further increased Lincoln's popularity, as well as increasing the nation's interest in Gettysburg. The 100th anniversary of the opening of the Western Maryland Railroad line provided another occasion for townspeople to commemorate Lincoln. Screen actor Ray Middleton, aboard a Civil War–era train, portrayed President Lincoln's arrival at the rail station on Carlisle Street. Upon disembarking, "Lincoln" and his accompanying party proceeded to the town square and stopped at the David Wills House, where the president stayed the night of

November 18, 1863. After a brief stop, the party continued to the Soldiers' National Cemetery for the Dedication Day ceremonies. Over 50,000 reportedly attended, and NBC later broadcast the event.[14]

When the National Park Service acquired the battlefield in 1933, then-Superintendent James McConaghie recognized the need to modernize the park's educational opportunities. The War Department's commissioners installed hundreds of explanatory itinerary tablets that described the movements of brigades, divisions, and corps of the two armies. The itinerary tablets, complemented by scores of monuments, told the battle in great detail. From corps to brigade to regimental level, these markers and monuments presented a complete narrative of the battle. For example, the 2nd Corps marker of the Army of the Potomac, located along Hancock Avenue, detailed the unit's arrival to the field, its part on the second day's fighting along Cemetery Ridge, and its role in repulsing Pickett's Charge. The tablet also included a list of casualties. Suitable though they were for an audience with first-hand knowledge of the battle, these plaques failed to stimulate the mind of the modern-day visitor.

During the Second World War, Superintendent Coleman proposed the installation of interpretive markers, but vocal opposition, especially from the Licensed Battlefield Guides, forestalled the project. After the war, however, the Park Service did successfully design and install interpretive tablets, or "field exhibits." Unlike the War Department's itinerary markers, the Park Service tablets provided a simplified explanation of the battle's critical moments. In doing so, the agency helped to shape the way visitors understood the battle. The first interpretive field exhibits were installed at Spangler's Spring, the Angle, Devil's Den, Little Round Top, and General Meade's headquarters in 1947. The following year exhibits were placed on Culp's Hill, East Cemetery Hill, McPherson Ridge, Oak Ridge, and Seminary Ridge near the North Carolina State Memorial. The park historian observed that these exhibits "attracted considerable attention."[15]

These exhibits are noteworthy because they represented the National Park Service's first attempt to interpret the battle to visitors using the landscape and a bona fide educational medium. As noted, the campfire programs did little to offer a substantive account of the battle, and they failed to make effective use of the terrain to interpret the fighting. Gradually the National Park Service became an active agent in facilitating visitor understanding of the battle. These new field exhibits accomplished two key objectives: they interpreted the terrain and explained the battle action that occurred on that particular site. Mounted as glass-enclosed standing displays, the exhibits included several photos of the commanding officers and a short narrative explaining the events of the area. They also displayed an aerial map, indicating the battle line of the two opposing armies, and placed the visitors' position on the map with

In the years following World War II, the National Park Service installed interpretive "field exhibits" on the battlefield. These exhibits broadened visitors' understanding of the battle by connecting the terrain to the specific battle action. These waysides, installed at the Angle, explain the fighting on July 3, Pickett's Charge.

the "you are here" arrow. This helped to orient visitors to the position held by the two armies and showed their location relative to other key points. For example, the exhibit installed at Seminary Ridge included a panoramic picture of the terrain related to Pickett's Charge, including Cemetery Hill, Ziegler's Grove, the Angle, the Copse of Trees, and Little Round Top. Standing at the exhibit, visitors could now look eastward toward the Union line and interpret the landscape that defined the fighting on July 3.[16] These interpretive exhibits allowed visitors as they drove through the battlefield to stop at one, receive a basic explanation of tactical complexities, and "read" the terrain to learn more about the fighting that occurred there.

Installation of waysides marked a key advancement in the interpretation of the battle and the landscape. Still the agency continued to explore other means to assist the increasing number of visitors to better understand the battle. In the summer of 1947, park rangers were posted on the battlefield to contact visitors and offer informal interpretation. In August, a ranger at Little Round Top reportedly contacted over 2,000 visitors. Superintendent Coleman reported that the rangers "rendered a real public service." Other than the summer campfire programs and the rangers on the battlefield, the National Park Service still did not offer regular, structured interpretive programs. On special occasions, however, rangers presented detailed tours to military, student, or organized groups. For a thorough discussion of the battle, the Park Service recommended visitors hire a Licensed Battlefield Guide.[17]

As historian Jim Weeks demonstrates in *Gettysburg: Memory, Market, and an American Shrine,* mass culture and the automobile redefined the battlefield landscape and the means by which visitors experienced Gettysburg. Proliferation of individual automobile ownership and a modernized highway system brought Americans to Gettysburg in increasing numbers. While the majority of visitors preferred to see the battlefield from the comfort of their automobile, taking advantage of the newly installed interpretive exhibits and self-guided tour route, the Park Service added another way to see the battlefield when it approved bus tours. In 1949, Charles Pitzer, manager of the Pitzer Bus Company, approached Superintendent Coleman with the suggestion of providing tours of the battlefield during the summer. He proposed charging a fee of one dollar and employing a licensed guide to describe the battle action. Coleman enthusiastically supported the proposal, as did the regional and national offices. Bus tours, while commercializing the battlefield, received approval from the park offices as they provided a "desirable service to the public." Director Drury, however, cautioned park management to consider the reaction from the Licensed Battlefield Guides, whose influence was recognized not only in Gettysburg, but also among the NPS leadership in Washington. Opposition from the guides notwithstanding, the Park Service approved Pitzer's proposal for bus tours of the battlefield.[18]

While the National Park Service operated its headquarters in the downtown post office building on Baltimore Street, the cyclorama building on East Cemetery Hill served as the primary visitor contact station. The interpretation of the cyclorama consisted of a seventeen-minute audio presentation that explained the Gettysburg campaign, the three-day battle, and concluded with a brief history of the painting. Owing to the painting's significance, Congress designated the Gettysburg Cyclorama a National Historic Object on October 5, 1944. This designation notwithstanding, visitors still found an unattractive exterior and a rapidly deteriorating painting. In 1947 Congress appropriated

$10,000 for its restoration.[19] This restoration work, however, was only a temporary solution to a long-term problem.

The country's only exhibited cyclorama of the Battle of Gettysburg remained a popular tourist attraction. For instance, in 1951, over 20,000 viewed the painting. Public relations further increased interest in the painting. The July 5, 1954, issue of *Time* magazine presented a feature article on the cyclorama. Later *Time* donated five thousand color prints of the cyclorama to the park with permission to sell the prints for profit at twenty-five cents apiece. Other promotional flyers encouraged visitors to see "The World's Largest War Painting" and declared that the "cyclorama is the key to the battlefield. The Battlefield Park can only be intelligently understood by seeing the cyclorama." Such deliberate emphasis on the Gettysburg Cyclorama furthered the primacy of the "High Water Mark" thesis.[20]

The acquisition of the cyclorama defined not only the battle's interpretation, but also park planning, namely the construction of a new visitor center and continued discussion of redesigning the tour route. After considerable debate, on January 28, 1946, Director Drury wrote the regional director approving the site of Ziegler's Grove, located between Taneytown Road and Emmitsburg Road, for the new museum. Park Service officials cited the proximity to the fields of Pickett's Charge as one key reason for the site's selection. Roy Appleman, the NPS Regional Historian, asserted that the new facility should be "on commanding ground and in the heart of the historic area." One of the Park Service's fundamental tenets since its establishment had been accessibility. Stephen Mather, the agency's first director, once declared that the most ideal policies were ones that offered "the greatest good for the greatest number." Constructing a visitor center in "the heart of the historic area" would provide convenient access for "the greatest number."[21]

Sensitive to the impact that the increasing number of automobiles had on visitation and the visitor experience, park staff continued to consider other means to improve touring the battlefield. For example, park officials considered a proposal to paint directional arrows at avenue intersections and crossings, which would guide visitors to the next direction of the tour route. Superintendent Coleman approved, but again warned the regional office that the licensed guides would likely voice opposition because such markings would facilitate greater access to the battlefield. As with the opposition to the installation of wayside exhibits, the guides' stance was purely self-serving. Greater access to the grounds threatened the guides' perceived monopoly on battlefield tours. Ultimately the agency approved the plan to paint directional signs, but the park failed to gain approval from the state highway department and abandoned the plan. Regional officials then suggested that the battlefield tour route be marked with mileage signs to allow visitors to gauge their progress as they drove along the tour road. In November 1950, the Park Service contracted with a local sign company to install fifty-five directional signs along the tour route. Placed along the battlefield avenues, the metal disc signs, containing the words "Battlefield Tour" in white on a background of blue and gray, directed visitors from stop to stop on the auto tour. This decision made the battlefield more accessible to self-guiding, upholding former Superintendent McConaghie's objectives to make the field more user friendly.[22]

Not surprisingly, the implementation of the chronological tour route and bus tours raised red flags with the Licensed Battlefield Guides. Relations between the guides and the Park Service, always contentious, continued to rapidly deteriorate. As the battlefield became more accessible for self-guided tours, the guides worried that NPS initiatives would detract from their popularity and services. Meanwhile, Coleman and the regional director continued to receive complaint letters regarding improper guide conduct. Such complaints reinforced the superintendent's belief that the Park Service needed to exercise greater control over the guides. The disagreements over accessibility and the tensions among the park staff, the guides, and eventually local merchants illustrate the tendency of various groups to claim ownership of the battlefield and use it to promote an often self-serving agenda.

Matters came to a head in 1951 when the Gettysburg Chamber of Commerce called upon the district congressman to investigate Coleman's conduct with the guide association. Henry Garvin, president of the Gettysburg Chamber of Commerce and a Licensed Battlefield Guide himself, spearheaded the allegation. He accused Coleman of threatening to eliminate the guides if they refused civil service status, a proposal put forth during the Second World War. Garvin asserted that "the guide service has made Gettysburg," not the War Department or the National Park Service. As evidence of the guides "making" Gettysburg, Garvin offered a comparison to Antietam: "no one goes there because there are no guides," he stated. Coleman issued a "blanket denial" of the allegations and noted that when he learned that a majority of the guides opposed civil service status, he withdrew the proposal. Congressman James Lind mediated between the two sparring parties and quelled the issue of converting the guides to civil service status.[23]

Coleman continued to strive toward an accessible battlefield, which, of course, placed him at odds with the guides. The situation worsened when the Park Service produced a self-guided fifty-page booklet, complete with tour maps, pictures, and accompanying historical text. The publication and sale of the brochure created a firestorm of controversy among the guides, as well as local businessmen. Garvin insisted that the booklet would minimize the role of the guides. Giving visitors a self-guiding booklet as an option to tour the battlefield presumably meant fewer would be interested in hiring the services of the guides. Proving themselves an emerging interest group, local business-men opposed the brochure because it competed with several other brochures locally produced.[24]

Coleman maintained a hard line in dealing with criticism of the self-guided auto tour and booklet. In doing so, he furthered the agency's goal to create a more accessible battlefield. In fact, the majority of visitors opted to tour the grounds themselves. Coleman found that 87 percent of visitors did not employ battlefield guides, which, in turn, necessitated the explanatory brochure and directional signs. In response to the guides' and Chamber of Commerce's complaints, Coleman replied, "It appears preposterous to me that we should limit visitor aids to such an extent that our tourists must employ a guide or get lost." When accused of trying to establish a monopoly on battlefield tours, the superintendent reminded his critics of the Park Service's favorable treatment of the guides. Coleman noted that the Park Service provided the guides with two contact stations (one along the Chambersburg Pike and another along Business 15) and also recommended their service to visitors. He then appealed to his detractors' higher sense of purpose, urging them to place the sanctity of the battlefield over personal and profiteering interests. "Certainly Gettysburg is too important and sacred a shrine," he declared, "for us to deny this assistance to visitors for purely commercial reasons."[25]

Yet many guides remained sensitive to any perceived threat to their business. Not only did their relations with the Park Service prove antagonistic, but their relations with local interests also deteriorated. In December 1951, the Retail Merchants Association (RMA) began operating an information booth on the Lincoln Square. Coleman agreed to supply the association with park brochures to distribute to interested visitors. This decision created a new controversy between the Licensed Battlefield Guides, the RMA, and the National Park Service. When guides learned of the distribution of this brochure, they lashed out at the association just as they had against Coleman earlier in the year. Guides blamed the association for simply distributing self-guided brochures, not endorsing the guided tour. Representatives from the RMA responded that they had, in fact, recommended the guide service, but if a guide was unavailable suggested the visitors tour the field themselves. The association, meanwhile, maintained that the guides had grown "abusive" toward them. One guide allegedly threatened a volunteer staffer, "If the merchants association doesn't take you out of the booth, I'll burn it down." The merchant association, like Coleman, reminded the guides that they did not have a monopoly to guide on the battlefield.[26]

Coleman remained concerned over the behavior, or more appropriately misbehavior, of the guides. This concern was perhaps not unfounded, as shown both by RMA reports and in correspondence from visitors. Visitors complained that guides were unprofessional and, at times, deceitful. Winnie Langley, in a letter to the NPS director, recounted the story of a guide who refused to give directions to her family on how to get around the battlefield, and instead emphatically stated that they should hire him because only he knew how to negotiate the tour roads. When Mrs. Langley reported that they merely wanted directions, and not a guide, the guide abruptly retorted, "Go to the crossroads and turn any way you want to." A visitor from McVeytown, Pennsylvania, reported his unpleasant experience with a guide in a letter to the editor published in the *Gettysburg Times* on July 21, 1953. He wrote, "It has been such a long time since I have had such an unpleasant, uninteresting, sonorous-toned and rushed conducted tour than I had."[27]

The ongoing conflict with the Licensed Battlefield Guides and the emerging tension with local businesses illustrated the perpetual discord among interest groups over ownership of the battlefield. It also reinforced the eternal effort to extract capitalistic gains from the fields of battle. In this instance, three defined interest groups emerged, each with its own vision and agenda to advance. The National Park Service wanted to promote a self-guided tour route in order to make the field more accessible. On the other hand, the guides and the local merchants aligned more closely and were clearly acting more on economic interests. Licensed guides opposed any efforts by the Park Service to promote an accessible battlefield, on the assumption that fewer visitors would employ their services. Local merchants similarly began to oppose the Park Service's intentions to create an easier-to-use battlefield when the latter produced their self-guiding tour booklet. Businessmen opposed this initiative because it competed with locally produced brochures, which forced local businesses to compete with the National Park Service. Coleman reminded the guides that Gettysburg was "national in scope and not the property of the local community." One merchant aptly noted the emerging conflict over battlefield ownership and stated, "People who cannot afford or do not want guides cannot be forced to take one. The battlefield belongs to the public, not the guides."[28] Differing perspectives on possession of the battlefield would continue to emerge as a dominant theme.

To better understand the guides' concern over declining tours, it is valuable to examine battlefield visitation and the number who hired the services of the guides. In 1955 the Park Service reported 724,037 battlefield visitors. Of these, 71,910 toured with a guide in an automobile and 47,796 toured with a guide on a bus. Thus, approximately 119,000 visitors toured the battlefield with a guide, either by personal automobile or by bus, representing 16 percent of yearly visitors. The following year, 1956, 756,320 visited the battlefield. Of this total, 135,549, or just 18 percent, used the services of a licensed guide either in an auto tour or bus tour. For all the power that the Licensed Battlefield Guides exerted over the management of the battlefield, the majority of visitors chose not to hire their services. Based on visitation statistics and individuals who hired the services of the guides, Garvin's assertion that the "guide service has made Gettysburg" was simply erroneous.[29]

Since July 1863, the Gettysburg battlefield has been an ever-evolving landscape. The inevitable growth of the town paralleled the evolution of the battlefield topography and in some instances directly altered it. The struggle to control modern development certainly was not a new problem, and in fact had plagued battlefield administrators since 1864. As chronicled in Jim Weeks's *Gettysburg*, local businessmen had been selling Gettysburg to consumer tourists since the armies departed the battlefield. "By the 1950s," Weeks argues, "a post–World War II wave of automobiling families had transformed battlefield, lodgings, restaurants, and commercial attractions." America's postwar economic and population boom exacerbated the underlying conflicts among battlefield preservation, landscape utilization, and commercialization. The Park Service owned over 2,500 acres, yet hundreds of acres of battle ground remained privately owned or in the hands of developers. Modern intrusions encroached on the historic terrain from all directions, and the National Park Service remained helpless to stop such development. If the battlefield was not a popular enough attraction in its own right, Gettysburg received increased attention when, in 1950, Dwight Eisenhower purchased a 189-acre farm adjacent to the southern end of the battlefield. During his presidency, Eisenhower hosted prominent dignitaries, which in turn made Gettysburg even more popular to contemporary Americans.[30]

Landscape philosophy during Coleman's administration centered on two objectives. First, in order to generate a historically accurate landscape, Coleman continued the practices of rehabilitating sectors of the battlefield to its 1863 appearance. Workers devoted considerable efforts to improve the fields of Pickett's Charge and Cemetery Ridge. In the winter of 1949, workers cleared grounds between Cemetery and Seminary Ridges, including the removal of trees that had grown to full height and had blocked the view from one ridge to the other. In the same area, park maintenance completed the rehabilitation of the Round Top Railroad bed, and by the summer of 1950 most of the railroad bed had been leveled and the terrain restored to its 1863 appearance. In the spring of 1950, a series of postwar trees around the famed Copse of Trees southward to the Pennsylvania Monument were removed to recreate the open, clear vista of Cemetery Ridge as seen in 1863. The park's campaign to create a historically accurate landscape remained a primary effort. In regards to vistas along Cemetery Ridge, Tilberg summarized, "It is our aim to establish a wartime pattern of tree growth on the ridge and to maintain this pattern." Other cuts occurred along the southern end of the battlefield at Plum

Aerial view of the Peach Orchard at the intersection of the Emmitsburg Road, Millerstown Road, and Wheatfield Road (ca. 1941). Note the commercial and residential developments. The Pennsylvania Memorial can be seen in the top right.

Run and along the northeastern side of Little Round Top. Tilberg reported that "clearing in this area now ties in closely with the appearance of the valley in a war-time Brady photograph." Coleman also expanded the vista cutting to the first day's fields. He approved a cut at Oak Ridge, opening a historic vista eastward that overlooked the position of the Union army's 11th Corps. Two years later, in the spring of 1952, the park completed a clear-cutting project on McPherson's Ridge.[31]

Second, Coleman advocated the acquisition of land threatened with commercial development, which further increased the preservation efforts. For example, in 1952 the Park Service owned 2,564.12 acres and, by 1956, had acquired 2,707 acres. The landscape philosophy of acquiring additional grounds stemmed from the wave of postwar commercialism that engulfed the surrounding area. Hotels, inns, restaurants, and other attractions inevitably developed in order to accommodate battlefield visitors. A small victory in preservation occurred in the spring of 1949 when the three-story Battlefield Hotel, located at the intersection of Baltimore Pike and Steinwehr Avenue, was demolished. Yet, while the razing of the Battlefield Hotel opened a viewshed from the Soldiers' National Cemetery, in its place soon stood a single story automobile station.[32]

Because of their location along the main route into Gettysburg, the Emmitsburg Road tracts were the most desirable for hotels, restaurants, gas stations,

The Lee-Meade Inn underscored the prevalent struggle to remove commercial intrusions from the battlefield landscape. The NPS acquired this property in 1953. View from the Longstreet Tower, along West Confederate Avenue. Big Round Top can be seen to the far right of the image and Little Round Top to its left.

and other commercial developments. For that reason, the National Park Service listed areas along the Emmitsburg Road as "high priority" for acquisition. One of the most popular, and certainly one of the most intrusive on the historic landscape was the Lee-Meade Inn. Built in 1930 and situated on thirty acres of land along the Emmitsburg Road, near the Peach Orchard, the Lee-Meade Inn consisted of eighteen cabins and a lodge. In September 1952, Superintendent Coleman reported that the park received approval to acquire an option on the Lee-Meade Inn, after learning that the owner wanted to add a drive-in theater. In October 1953, the federal government accepted the deed to the property. Like the Lee-Meade purchase suggests, the acquisition of private properties remained a piecemeal effort.[33] Commercial developments, nonetheless, continued to squeeze the battlefield from every direction.

When trying to protect threatened land, National Park Service officials faced difficult decisions on which tract(s) should be acquired, and in what order of priority. In 1947 Coleman developed a land acquisition program for Gettysburg National Military Park, wherein he prioritized high-risk tracts and their acquisition. One such high-risk area included a forty-acre tract below East Cemetery Hill, key terrain where General Jubal Early's brigades attacked the Union position on the night of July 2. A year earlier, park officials learned that Luther Sachs, a local contractor, had purchased a tract along Wainwright Avenue with the intention of building a housing development. Park historian

Frederick Tilberg, among others, urged the NPS to acquire the property before it was developed. Meanwhile, simultaneous to this development, the Gettysburg Area School District sought land near Culp's Hill, along East Confederate Avenue and Wainwright Avenue, to construct new school facilities in close proximity to town.[34]

Beginning in the fall of 1952, negotiations opened among Gettysburg National Military Park, the Gettysburg Area School District, Luther Sachs, and Pennsylvania congressmen on the feasibility of a land exchange. In a letter to the chairman of the Adams County Republican Committee, U.S. senator Edward Martin observed that the land in question was primarily used for farming and stated that the development of school facilities "would not harm the National Park in any way." Martin also wrote NPS director Conrad Wirth, inquiring into the possibility of the school district procuring the twenty-acre parcel of government land.[35]

Congress needed to approve the transfer because the school district's desired tract fell within the established federal boundary. In October 1952, Director Wirth wrote Senator Martin to explain the agency's position. Wirth reminded the senator that it was "not customary" to permit the use of federal lands for school purposes. The director believed, however, that this case was "worthy of special consideration." Wirth recommended that the government sell the Culp tract to the school district and use the received monies to purchase privately owned land to include into the federal boundary. Negotiations continued through the following year. Congress authorized the land exchange in July 1953. Shortly afterwards, President Eisenhower signed the legislation relinquishing twenty-three acres of government-owned land along East Confederate Avenue to the school district. The Gettysburg School District then purchased the Luther Sachs tract for $15,000, and upon obtaining title to the twenty-nine acre tract, conveyed the deed to the National Park Service. Once the Park Service acquired the Sachs property, the process began to restore the terrain to its historic appearance and convert it to farmland.[36]

The land exchange with the school district demonstrated the challenges to historic preservation, in particular in prioritizing sites to preserve. Though the exchanged land was clearly historically significant, management chose to downplay the value of the site of the new school. On January 27, 1953, the *Gettysburg Times* reported Coleman as saying, "The Park Service has felt that sale of this particular section of battlefield land would not seriously affect the battlefield." When faced with unfavorable choices, Park Service management had opted to exchange preserved government land for the construction of school facilities in return for the acquisition of private property that could have easily been developed in the future. Over the next three decades the school district constructed an elementary school, a high school, and athletic playing fields on the grounds where Confederates attacked East Cemetery Hill on the evening of July 2, 1863. The new high school football stadium rose on the grounds where Confederate colonel Isaac Avery fell mortally wounded and hastily scrawled his legendary note, "Major: Tell my father I died with my face to the enemy."[37]

In the decade following World War II, Gettysburg National Military Park implemented several significant reforms. Superintendent Coleman oversaw the agency's first attempts to interpret the battle to visitors using the site's most valuable asset, the landscape. The installation of wayside exhibits and the stationing of park rangers on the battlegrounds moved the agency toward implementing former Superintendent James McConaghie's vision for a proactive educational program. Simultaneously the NPS established the cyclorama as the keystone to its interpretive features; the centrality of the Gettysburg Cyclorama perpetuated the "High Water Mark" narrative. Equally important, Coleman continued the practice established by McConaghie to rehabilitate small sectors of the battlefield to their 1863 appearance. The popularity of Abraham Lincoln and the Gettysburg Address continued to manifest itself in the years following the Second World War. Contemporary Americans interpreted Lincoln's address as an enduring testament to freedom and democracy. In the shadow of the Cold War and communist expansion, the words "government of the people, by the people, for the people" held special relevance. Congressional establishment of November 19 as Dedication Day further underscored Gettysburg's place as a special, unique landscape. Though scores of fields had been consecrated by the blood of men in blue and gray, no others had been sanctified with such elegant oration. Yet larger improvements loomed on the horizon. In January 1956, the federal government initiated MISSION 66, a ten-year program to improve the national parks. MISSION 66 coincided with the Civil War centennial and the fiftieth anniversary of the establishment of the National Park Service. In the upcoming years, Gettysburg would experience tremendous changes that further redefined the battlefield experience.

CHAPTER 5

THE GREAT TASK REMAINING BEFORE US: MISSION 66 AND COLD WAR PATRIOTISM, 1956–1960

Characterized by Susan Rugh as the "golden age of family vacations," Americans took to the roads on weekend journeys and extended vacations as never before. As the shadow of the Cold War loomed ever larger, Americans traveled to the nation's natural and cultural treasures. Looking to the past served as a way to alleviate an unsettling present and uncertain future. The National Park Service recognized its role in promoting education as a component of civic virtue. "It is very important to the welfare of our nation," wrote Gettysburg's historian Frederick Tilberg, "that the youth of our country learn to understand and appreciate their great American heritage of history."[1]

For decades the proliferation of the automobile had been linked intrinsically to the operation and promotion of the national parks. Automobiles brought the first visitors to Mount Rainer in 1908, and since its establishment in 1916, the National Park Service had promoted automobiles as a means to increase visitation. On the eve of the Civil War centennial, more than 61 million Americans owned automobiles, with one automobile in circulation for every 2.3 Americans. In 1956, Congress passed the Federal Highway Act, which would eventually fund the construction of 41,000 miles of federal highways. Taking to the highways for extended vacations reinforced "family togetherness" and at the same time bolstered American heritage.[2]

Reconnecting to their heritage brought many Americans to national parks. By 1940 the agency's 161 parks recorded nearly 17 million visitors. The agency's operating budget in 1940 was approximately $34 million. During World War II, however, it quickly became a victim of fiscal constraints. In 1945, for example, the entire Park Service budget was a meager $4.7 million. While the postwar years brought a dramatic increase of visitors, park facilities and infrastructure continued to steadily decline; many sites were simply ill-equipped to handle the increasing number of visitors. More significantly, the Park Service's budget actually decreased during this period. By 1955, there were 181 parks with over 56 million visitors, yet the agency received $32 million in appropriations. Despite visitation tripling since 1940, parks were forced to operate with less fiscal allocations than they received prior to the war.[3]

In the mid-1950s, the rapid deteriorating conditions of the national parks became a common subject for columnists and editors. Historian Bernard DeVoto's column, "Let's Close the National Parks" published in *Harper's,* lamented the condition of the national parks. DeVoto estimated that in order to effectively maintain them, the NPS would need an annual operating budget of at least $250 million. Without such money forthcoming, DeVoto believed the only way to continue to preserve the country's historic and cultural resources was simply to close the national parks. In January 1955, Charles Stevenson wrote a scathing critique, "The Shocking Truth About Our National Parks," in *Reader's Digest.* Stevenson cautioned Americans planning a trip to a national park, "I must pass along a warning: Your trip is likely to be fraught with discomfort, disappointment, and even danger."[4]

The Park Service did not deny that deplorable conditions existed at many of its sites. As far back as June 1949, National Park Service director Newton Drury outlined the gloomy status in "The Dilemma of Our Parks."[5] The agency's situation was complex. Faced with increased visitation, the agency was expected to offer quality services, while at the same time following its mission to protect the historic, cultural, and natural resources. Continual budget woes only compounded this tension between visitor access and historic preservation.

In December 1951, Conrad Wirth became the director of the National Park Service. A trained landscape architect, who had earned a Bachelor of Science degree in Landscape Gardening from Massachusetts Agricultural College, Wirth began his career with the agency in 1931 as an assistant director for land planning. During the New Deal, Wirth managed the Department of the Interior's Civilian Conservation Corps. After the war, he returned to his duties in land planning and served briefly as the agency's associate director. On December 7, the secretary of interior appointed Wirth as director of the National Park Service.[6] To secure long-range funding for the agency, improve infrastructure, and promote recreational tourism, Wirth conceived the MISSION 66 initiative. A decade-long project intended to improve the condition of the national parks, MISSION 66 evolved as a manifestation of the agency's long-standing tradition to promote recreational tourism.

Wirth's program gained momentum through a favorable change in the presidency. Whereas Franklin Roosevelt had been an avid proponent of the national parks, his successor, Harry S. Truman, did not share the same enthusiasm. Wirth now found a sympathetic ally in newly-elected President Dwight D. Eisenhower. Having purchased a farm on the southwestern boundary of Gettysburg National Military Park in 1950, Eisenhower became a frequent visitor to the Pennsylvania battlefield. Wirth's MISSION 66 proposal received a public relations boost when Eisenhower mentioned the current status of the national parks in his inaugural address, declaring, "The visits of our people to the parks have increased much more rapidly than have the facilities to care for them." On January 27, 1956, Wirth and his team met with the president and his cabinet to discuss the proposal. Two weeks later, on February 8, Wirth announced the MISSION 66 initiative at a banquet in Washington, D.C., sponsored by the Department of the Interior, the National Park Service, and fittingly, the American Automobile Association. Over the next decade, Congress allocated $1,035,225,000 for operation and improvements within the national park system.[7]

The improvements made during MISSION 66 were impressive, to say the least. Many parks received significant funding to improve facilities, roads, and trails. Program funding included resources for the development and improvement of 2,767 miles of roadways and over 900 miles of new or reconstructed trails. During MISSION 66, the National Park Service constructed 82 campfire amphitheaters, added 471 buildings, built 584 comfort stations, and improved 17 others. In addition, over 1,100 wayside exhibits were improved throughout the parks. A major component of MISSION 66 was the construction of modern visitor centers. Over the decade of the initiative, the Park Service constructed 114 new visitor centers, which provided information, interpretive displays, museums, as well as food services and souvenir concessions. These visitor centers included such diverse parks as Dinosaur, Rocky Mountain, Death Valley, Cape Cod, Yellowstone, and, of course, Gettysburg.[8]

Yet MISSION 66 was not uniformly embraced. Its principal purpose to modernize the parks underscored inherent tensions over the function of the national parks. For a half century, the agency had encouraged recreational tourism. On the eve of the nation's environmental awareness movement, conservationists and environmentalists charged the agency with overdeveloping heretofore pristine environments. These critics, including the Sierra Club, cited a literal interpretation of the agency's mandate to maintain the park's "unimpaired," charging that the MISSION 66 initiatives irrevocably damaged ecological and natural environments. Modern developments now littered previously undisturbed areas of the Everglades, Grand Teton, Yosemite, and Yellowstone. Modern, obtrusive visitor centers, like the ones at Antietam and Gettysburg, were built on historic terrain. In a 1961 article in *National Parks Magazine*, Weldon Heald charged the agency with urbanizing the parks and summarized, "engineering has become more important than preservation."[9]

While Director Wirth championed MISSION 66 in Washington, he instructed park officials to prepare plans to guide their sites through the next decade. Civil War sites across the nation developed proposals to modernize their visitor services and interpretive opportunities. MISSION 66 had a considerable impact on all the federally managed Civil War battlefields, not just Gettysburg. The situation at Antietam National Battlefield remained the most critical. The government owned a mere 200 acres of the historic battlefield; MISSION 66 brought land acquisition to the forefront of the park's management priorities and recommended the purchase of 1,300 acres. In addition, Antietam received funding to build a new visitor center. Two sites dominated discussions for potential location: near the New York and Maryland State Memorials or adjacent to the Antietam National Cemetery. As with Ziegler's Grove at Gettysburg, proximity to key battle action and visitor accessibility drove the selection. Roy Appleman, a proponent of Ziegler's Grove for Gettysburg's facility, argued that Antietam's visitor center should be located close to the state monuments, since it would be "near the center of the most important field of action" and conveniently located to the Hagerstown Road. Director Wirth made the decision and chose the New York Monument location.[10]

Western Theater battlefields faced similar dilemmas with encroaching development and seemingly inadequate resources. Established in 1890, Chickamauga & Chattanooga was not only the first national military park but, at 8,190 acres, was also the largest. Yet that park only received approximately $460,000 through the decade-long initiative, roughly half of Gettysburg's funding. MISSION 66 projects included road improvement, additional parking areas at Chickamauga and at Point Park at Lookout Mountain, and improved visitor access to Snodgrass Hill. Vicksburg National Military Park, meanwhile, received slightly over 1.7 million dollars from MISSION 66, which would help to fund the construction of a closed-circuit tour route, interpretive displays, informational literature, and exhibits. Shiloh National Military Park received approximately $1,550,000. Timing was opportune; visitation reached an all-time high in 1956, with a recorded 644,387 visitors. Conscious of the objections to overdevelopment, Shiloh's MISSION 66 plan noted goals to "preserve the battlefield in its wartime condition to the fullest extent possible." To detractors, planners noted that the program did not mean "radical or unwarranted change" for the battlefield, but instead brought "logical and carefully planned development and operation of the park to preserve the scene and tell the story of an epic chapter of the Nation's past for the benefit, enjoyment, and inspiration of all the people."[11]

Back in Pennsylvania, after seventeen years as superintendent, James Walter Coleman transferred to the Washington office as a staff historian in July 1958. On July 1, 1958, James Myers, a career NPS employee, became Gettysburg's third superintendent. Myers began immediately to explore ways to capitalize on the infusion of federal funding, totaling $1,014,750, to improve the Gettysburg experience. In preparing their MISSION 66 reports, park staff articulated key management goals, for both the interpretive and physical presentation of the battlefield.[12] Superintendents McConaghie and Coleman had taken steps to improve the park's educational program. Each championed a modernized agenda that moved beyond the static narration of the tablets and markers. Key advancements in education resulted with the installation of several wayside exhibits. This marked the agency's first attempt to connect the landscape with the battle's events. Whereas the War Department's bronze tablets narrated the battle by listing a unit's role in the fighting, the Park Service's waysides incorporated historic photographs, images of selected commanders or soldiers, panoramic pictures of the landscape, battlefield maps, and textual summations to explain the battle. With the funding from MISSION 66, park staff looked at additional ways not merely to *inform* visitors, but to *interpret* the battle action and landscape.

Gettysburg's advancement in interpretation corresponded with larger trends in the National Park Service. Beginning in 1953, the Park Service conducted new training programs to instruct park rangers to develop methods of interpretation in order to connect the site's natural or cultural resources with the visitor. The Park Service did not detail the methods of interpretation, however. Instead, acclaimed newspaper reporter, novelist, and playwright Freeman Tilden produced the agency's guiding interpretive philosophy. Tilden began writing about the national parks in the 1940s and authored *The National Parks: What They Mean to You and Me* in 1951. Six years later, Tilden produced what would become the agency's principal guide to interpretation, *Interpreting Our Heritage*. In this book, Tilden outlined six fundamental tenets of interpretation. Most central, he declared, "Information, as such, is not interpretation. Interpretation is revelation based on information. But they are entirely different things. However, all interpretation includes information." As important, Tilden maintained, "The chief aim of interpretation is not instruction, but provocation."[13]

Tilden's interpretive philosophy guided the National Park Service's educational programs, including those at Gettysburg. Seeking not merely to instruct, but to provoke, park officials strove to "assist the visitor to convert the Park's resources, the battlefield and its monuments and the National Cemetery, into meaningful concepts." In this sense, the park utilized the battlefield, through its own power, to elicit an emotional connection from visitors. In the planning of new educational initiatives, park staff demonstrated progressive thinking. Sensitive to the changing visitor demographics and the evolution of the landscape, Gettysburg advocated additional interpretive methods with the understanding they would be periodically updated to "conform with the needs of the time." Such practices represented a stark contrast to the War Department's methods to present only factual information on the itinerary tablets.[14]

National parks became places not only to understand a particular battle or a cultural landscape, but they also became classrooms to reaffirm a sense of patriotism. Gettysburg served, according to Tilberg, as a place for the nation's youth to "learn to understand and appreciate their great American heritage of history." This sentiment underscored a familiar theme. While sensitivity to patriotism increased during the Cold War, Gettysburg had often served as a special place, hallowed ground, for Americans to connect to their heritage. Since the dedication of the Soldiers' National Cemetery and a shared recognition of Gettysburg's exceptionality, scores of Americans pilgrimaged to the battlefield. Without a doubt, the "heritage of history" experienced at Gettysburg told of the honor and valor of the Union and Confederate soldiers. The veterans themselves had promoted this narrative as they molded Gettysburg into a landscape of reconciliation. The "heritage of history" continued to remain triumphant and reconciliatory, and devoid of any discussions of the causes of the Civil War or the unfilled aspirations of Lincoln's "new birth of freedom."[15]

The National Park Service's mission statement reflects the agency's inherently contradictory objectives of preservation and visitor enjoyment. As stated, the agency is to "conserve the scenery and the natural and historic objects," while leaving the resources "unimpaired for the enjoyment of future generations." Gettysburg sought to enact MISSION 66 objectives that would maintain a careful balance between preservation and use. Detractors to this program, including some of Gettysburg's staff who voiced concerns for the battlefield, lamented the modernization of the parks. They cautioned that modern accommodations "must be made with care, over-development avoided, and unnecessary service facilities eliminated."[16]

Gettysburg's "Master Plan" had identified a new visitor center as a key objective to facilitate visitor use and education, which was made possible with MISSION 66 funding. As noted, the Park Service had talked about a new visitor center as early as the 1930s and in January 1946, then-Director Newton Drury approved Ziegler's Grove as the site for the facility. Drury's decision to locate a non-historic building in the center of the battlefield reflected contemporary philosophies that placed visitor convenience and accessibility as paramount. The National Park Service selected renowned architects Richard J. Neutra and Robert Alexander to design the visitor center and museum. Known for his modern architecture style, Neutra stood as one of the leading architects in the mid-twentieth century. Born in Vienna in 1892, he immigrated to the United States in 1923, first settling in New York City before moving to Chicago. While in Chicago, Neutra joined the architecture firm of Holabird and Roche, where he met noted architects Louis Sullivan and Frank Lloyd Wright. Greatly influenced by their architectural styles, Neutra eventually moved to Los Angeles to establish his own design firm. There, his vision came to dominate California landscapes.[17]

The site and design for the new visitor center demonstrated the Park Service's efforts to modernize the battlefield and provide visitor access. The Ziegler's Grove location placed convenience over preservation. Though the Rosensteel Museum had already intruded on the northern spur of Cemetery Ridge, the location of the Park Service's visitor center irrevocably altered the historic landscape of Ziegler's Grove. Neutra's building, located just north of the Angle, stood as a visible symbol of the contradiction between preservation and visitor use. The design for the building included a large rotunda to hang the cyclorama painting and an observation platform, allowing visitors to overlook the fields of Pickett's Charge, which gave them the similar vantage point as Paul Philippoteaux, the artist who painted the cyclorama. Some of the building's aesthetic features included a reflecting pool along the eastern side and an outside assembly space. Trees and shrubbery were planted in the attempt to minimize the visual impact of the building.[18]

The new visitor center situated at the center of the Union line on Cemetery Ridge necessitated extensive changes to the historic landscape. In preparation for construction, for example, contractors excavated and landscaped portions of Ziegler's Grove, moved monuments, and realigned historic avenues. The War Department's observation tower in Ziegler's Grove was deemed an intrusion that served no useful purpose, and it was removed in July 1961. Other changes were also necessary. The new visitor center rested on key battle ground, where, in the 1880s, veterans erected monuments to honor their units and comrades. Prior to construction, five monuments had to be moved and relocated. To facilitate automobile access from the Taneytown Road and Steinwehr Avenue, contractors realigned Hancock Avenue. This roadway had originally run northward along the spine of Cemetery Ridge, and then continued past Ziegler's Grove and the Brian farm, before angling northeast to intersect with the Taneytown Road, several hundred yards south of the Rosensteel Museum. A section of the avenue that ran northeast from Ziegler's Grove toward the Taneytown Road was removed for a parking lot. Hancock Avenue now terminated at the new visitor center. At the same time workers removed the historic entrance gates to Hancock Avenue. Contract work began on November 20, 1959; the new visitor center was to be completed by December 12, 1961.[19]

While efforts to modernize the battlefield and the visitors' experiences centered on the construction of the new visitor center, other projects included

Construction of the Gettysburg Visitor and Cyclorama Center. Placement of this building required the alteration of several commemorative features, including the removal of the observation tower seen in the left-center of the image. Situated prominently in Ziegler's Grove, this building opened on March 18, 1962.

the restoration of the cyclorama painting, which had begun in the fall of 1959. By July 1960, restoration crews had completed over half of the painting's second restoration. As these projects progressed, park officials continued to pursue several minor interpretive initiatives that had marked the first half of the decade. For example, workers installed new field exhibits on Barlow's Knoll and Oak Hill, areas of relative neglect, as well as West Confederate Avenue and the Wheatfield Road. Like those previously installed, these exhibits included a panoramic picture to interpret the landscape, an aerial photo to orient visitors, and a narrative to describe the battle action.[20]

In August 1962, the park debuted a High Water Mark Walking Tour consisting of ten exhibits and stops. As designed, the walking tour encouraged visitors to get out of their automobiles and walk the fields of the July 3 fighting. Not only did this walking tour complement the new visitor center's location and the interpretive centrality of the Gettysburg Cyclorama, but it also reinforced the "High Water Mark" as the principal interpretive narrative. Initially, regional officials proposed an elaborate walking tour complete with benches and a flagstone terrace at the Angle. Local staff, however, opposed such developments, arguing that the benches and terrace would be a "serious intrusion" on Cemetery Ridge. To access the High Water Mark Walking Tour from the facility, visitors had to cross Hancock Avenue. For visitor safety, the regional office recommended Hancock Avenue be removed, but Superintendent Myers noted the infeasibility of such a measure, because it was a main avenue on the tour route.[21]

Jim Weeks recounts in *Gettysburg: Memory, Market, and an American Shrine* that commercialization had stood as an integral part of Gettysburg's history since the days following the battle. Developments around the battlefield and the marketing of Gettysburg was not a new phenomenon. The national outcry against such defilement on a sanctified ground, however, represented a new public debate on acceptable uses of Gettysburg. In the years leading up to the Civil War centennial, park rangers, historians, politicians, civilians, and newspaper editors engaged in vociferous debates over commercialization in and near the battlefield. As housing developments and commercial establishments continued to expand, preservationists opened a "Second Battle of Gettysburg." Some of the developments, without a doubt, stood as a by-product of the National Park Service promoting the battlefield as a tourist destination. Surging numbers of family vacationers produced the inevitable developments of hotels, restaurants, shops, and other tourist amenities.[22]

In the spring of 1959, a series of newspaper articles reported on the increasing development of the town and Gettysburg National Military Park. "Commercialism Launches 2nd Battle of Gettysburg" headlined the April 5 issue of the Harrisburg (Penn.) *Patriot News*. "Unless America cares enough to prevent subsequent development," writer Hans Knight warned, "commercialization would eventually overrun the battlefield." While only one sign marked the entrance to the battlefield, he added, state roads proliferated with commercial signs advertising museums, souvenir shops, and visitor accommodations. Three days later, Jean White of the *Washington Post* authored a comparable article entitled, "The 2nd Battle of Gettysburg." White offered that, "If they restage the battle of Gettysburg on the centennial four years from now, some of Pickett's men may be making their charge through a custard stand or souvenir shop." Picking up on the theme of custard stands dominating the fields of Pickett's Charge, an editorial titled "Custard's Last Stand" appeared in the April 12 issue of the *Reading Eagle* of Reading, Pennsylvania. Once again, patriotism and preservation came in conflict with commercialization as the author asked, "Why do Americans insist on blighting even a historic site like the battlefield with blinding neon signs, garish souvenir shops and junky frozen custard stands?"[23]

These editorials and articles deliberately forged a connection between preservation and patriotism. Each contended that development and commercialization of Gettysburg was un-American. "Patriotism," Adlai Stevenson had extolled in 1952, "is the love of something." To be American and patriotic meant opposing commercialization on the historic battlefield, and only unpatriotic Americans, those who disregarded the nation's heritage, favored neon lights and tourist trappings. Others focused on profiting from the sacrifice of American soldiers. "On each field where the trumpets sounded, the cash register now jingles," summarized Ashley Hasley of the *Saturday Evening Post*. The outcry against souvenir shops, accommodations, and neon signs underscored an accepted belief that these establishments defiled a sacred landscape. Commercialization seemingly dishonored, or trivialized, the sacrifices of the men who fought and died on these fields.[24]

Increasing patriotism during the Cold War and the desire to thwart the perceived defilement of the nation's historic treasures offered the proper timing for the National Park Service to ask Congress to increase funding for land acquisition. Informing Congress that it was "now or never" to acquire additional land at Gettysburg, Director Wirth requested over $2 million to purchase approximately 600 historic acres. Some members of Congress did not share Wirth's sense of urgency; his proposal met opposition in Washington and the House immediately cut the national park budget. Several congressmen argued that the federal government already owned a sufficient amount of land at Gettysburg. Ohio representative Michael Kirwan, for example, opposed any further land acquisition, remarking, "We have enough land at Gettysburg. There is no use in taking any more . . . They have the land where the important part of the battle was fought."[25]

Other congressmen and Civil War preservationists disagreed and fought to restore the National Park Service appropriations into the bill. On April 20, 1959, Pennsylvania representative James Quigley appealed to his fellow congressmen to increase appropriations for land acquisition. Quigley acknowledged the necessity of limited development and commercialization. Tourism, after all, had become the town's most profitable business, and visitors had to be fed, housed, and entertained. Quigley's emotional plea rested on the historical significance and collective memory of the Pennsylvania battlefield. "Gettysburg just isn't any battlefield of any war," he stated. "It isn't even just any battlefield of the Civil War. Gettysburg is Gettysburg: the site of one of the truly decisive battles in the whole of history." More important than merely urging that funding for land acquisition be restored, Quigley's reasoning rested on a popular belief in Gettysburg's exceptionality. In the minds of Americans, Gettysburg was far from "just any battlefield" of the war.[26]

The backlash against commercialization and congressional budget cuts was immediate. Newspapers throughout the country printed letters from concerned citizens speaking out against development on America's battlefields. Jess Gorkin, editor of *Parade*, led the national appeal. In an open letter to

Congress, he challenged representatives to restore the appropriations, declaring, "And for each day lost, a part of our heritage is lost. Next year or the year after may be too late to save Gettysburg." Gorkin concluded that Gettysburg's historic grounds "must be worth more to America than the $750,000 needed to stop the advance of commercialism."[27] As the Congressional debates and the articles in the *Saturday Evening Post, Washington Post,* and *Parade* further demonstrated, events on the Adams County battlefield garnered national attention. The battlefield would no longer be exclusively operated by local management, but influenced by national interests.

In mid-May, the Senate appropriations committee held hearings to fund the National Park Service. Major General Ulysses S. Grant III, the grandson of the Civil War general and recently appointed chairman of the Civil War Centennial Commission, voiced his support for the purchase of threatened areas before the upcoming centennial celebrations. The media coverage and public pressure proved successful, but resulted in a hollow victory. Congress approved $650,000 for land acquisition at Gettysburg National Military Park. Congress made their authorization, however, dependant on the enactment and ratification of community zoning laws. In June 1959, Cumberland Township formed a planning commission to consider zoning laws, but despite the Park Service's encouragement, the township failed to enact the necessary laws. Consequently, while commercialism pressed the battlefield from multiple directions, Gettysburg received no federal funding for land acquisition.[28]

Though federal funding for the preservation of the battlefield remained virtually nonexistent, local, grassroots efforts emerged to protect threatened parts of the battlefield. The surge of Americanism during the Cold War combined with timely media releases concerning the "Second Battle of Gettysburg" and the excitement of the approaching Civil War centennial, helped to raise public awareness for the need to protect the historic grounds. Patriotic fervor and concern for historic preservation led local citizens to form the Gettysburg Battlefield Preservation Association (GBPA) in September 1959. Formation of the GBPA demonstrated a collective interest in the battlefield's future. The association focused its efforts on acquiring threatened land. They solicited donations to purchase areas and then donated the land to the National Park Service. Ulysses Grant III and Robert E. Lee IV, the great-grandson of the Confederate general, served on the GBPA Advisory Board. Local interests responded; within three months of its establishment, the association had reportedly received $6,000 in donations. By March 1960, six months after its formation, the GBPA raised over $25,000 for land acquisition.[29]

Local historically-minded residents had cause for concern. At the height of the "golden age of family vacations," entrepreneurs capitalized on the battlefield's popularity. Businessmen sought to blend battlefield education with family entertainment, which resulted in the establishment of several entertainment-driven businesses. While the National Park Service provided visitors a self-guided automobile tour route, a local company offered bus tours, and beginning in 1959 visitors could tour the battlefield in a helicopter. Carroll Voss established his helicopter business directly across from General Meade's headquarters, along the Taneytown Road. During the summer, helicopters ran continuous flights, giving customers a birds-eye view of the battlefield. Taking off near Meade's headquarters, pilots directed their aircraft south along Hancock Avenue, then towards Little Round Top and Devil's Den, before returning. When pilots approached Little Round Top, they dropped their altitude to one hundred feet, which forced visitors to scurry when they saw them approaching so low. After receiving many complaints regarding this disruption, Myers informed Voss that the helicopter tours interfered with visitors' enjoyment of the battlefield. Though unwilling to abandon his profitable enterprise, Voss did agree to stop "buzzing" Little Round Top.[30]

Taneytown Road, meanwhile, remained a popular strip for commercialization. In addition to the helicopter service, just a few hundred yards further south, a local resident opened an amusement park for children. On July 18, 1959, Fantasyland, described as a "child's paradise," opened to the public. Designed and operated by Kenneth Dick, a Biglerville native and World War II veteran, the forty-acre park offered a "wonderful world of make believe." Fantasyland consisted of a number of children's attractions, including a twenty-foot Mother Goose, The Old Lady Who Lived in a Shoe, Santa's Village, and Rapunzel's Castle. It also offered a sugar plum snack bar that overlooked a miniature lake with ducks, nursery rhyme time, a playground, and a caboose. Assailed immediately by preservationists as being unconcerned for the importance of the battlefield, Dick maintained his operation did not interfere with the historical setting. Not only was Fantasyland built in a wooded area relatively concealed from the battlefield tour route, but the amusement park stood on ground that saw little fighting during the battle.[31]

Fantasyland's construction on the periphery of historic battle ground reinforced the changing nature of tourists by the mid-twentieth century. During the Cold War, mass consumption and marketing of Gettysburg centered on families touring in personal automobiles. As Jim Weeks argues, the postwar wave of family tourists necessitated the development of family-oriented lodging, as well as attractions that would appeal to families with young children. Fantasyland met this need. As families made "civic pilgrimages" to Gettysburg, in other words, commercial businesses such as Fantasyland capitalized. They attracted and provided families with the opportunity to spend a few hours on the battlefield and then relax with Mother Goose and other storybook characters.[32]

Influenced by the heightened sensitivities of the Cold War, patriotism and the desire to connect with historical events became widespread. Several historians have examined the relationship between the nation's anticommunist attitudes and the surge of Americanism. John Fried offers a compelling examination of how the Cold War shaped the country's commemorative events. The Cold War, he writes, "encouraged efforts to patriotize the American calendar." Such events included Flag Day, Armed Forces Day, and Constitution Day. In 1954 Congress added the phrase "under God" to the Pledge of Allegiance. Anniversaries of historic events or people were popularized during the Cold War, as well. One of the most spectacular displays of patriotism occurred at Jamestown's 350th anniversary in 1957. England's Queen Elizabeth attended the ceremony. Like Fried, Stephen Whitfield forges a connection between patriotic displays and the Cold War. "The search to define and affirm a way of life, the need to express and celebrate the meaning of 'Americanism,' was the flip side of stigmatizing Communism," concludes Whitfield. In each instance, these celebratory occasions demonstrated the widespread acceptance of what Michael Kammen terms the "heritage syndrome." Americans readily remembered, celebrated, and advocated the attractive, positive aspects of the national history, ignoring eras and events of strife and conflict.[33]

Meanwhile, events such as the battle anniversary and the commemoration of Dedication Day continued to draw sizable crowds and also reflected the popularity of the battle and the centrality of the Gettysburg Address. In July 1959, the Gettysburg Fire Company hosted a series of celebrations on the 96th anniversary that foreshadowed future battle festivities. This provided the occasion not only for Gettysburg's first battle reenactment, but also the first reenactment on any Civil War battlefield. Not surprisingly, they recast Pickett's Charge, the event commonly accepted as the "High Water Mark" of the Confederacy. On July 5, several hundred members of the newly formed North-South Skirmish Association reenacted the last moments of Pickett's Charge near the Angle. Superintendent Myers reported that over 8,000 spectators attended this "pageant" display. Events of the following July presented a fitting preamble to the planned festivities for the Civil War Centennial. To celebrate the battle's 97th anniversary, the North-South Skirmish Association again reenacted Pickett's Charge before a crowd of 14,000. Events at the Angle commenced at 2:45 pm with a short narration of the Confederate assault. Promptly at 3:00 pm, a signal gun fired from the Virginia Memorial symbolized the beginning of the artillery barrage. Thirty minutes later the reenactors advanced toward Cemetery Ridge. As the Confederate infantry approached the Union center, the American Legion and the V.F.W. unfurled the American flag.[34]

While reenactment events offered spectators an element of entertainment, Dedication Day offered a more "fitting and proper" occasion to commemorate the Gettysburg Address and the establishment of the Soldiers' National Cemetery. As noted, in the midst of the Cold War and global threats to democracy, Americans interpreted Lincoln's address as an enduring call to self-government. The importance of his rhetoric rang worldwide, for in November 1959, Voice of America offered a global broadcast of a special program "In Search of Lincoln." During the broadcast, several of the world's leading statesman paid tribute to America's sixteenth president, including President Eisenhower, British Prime Minister Harold Macmillan, India's Prime Minister Jawaharlal Nehru, and President General Ngo Dinh Diem of the Republic of Vietnam.[35]

CHAPTER 6

DEDICATED TO THE PROPOSITION THAT ALL MEN ARE CREATED EQUAL: THE CIVIL WAR CENTENNIAL AT GETTYSBURG, 1961–1965

As the 100th anniversary of the Civil War approached, the nation and the world remained mired in national and international turmoil. The Cold War loomed large and dictated foreign and domestic politics. National celebrations of the Civil War Centennial offered occasions to celebrate America's past and to bolster national unity in the face of an increasingly volatile world. The dawn of the centennial paralleled aggressive communist expansion around the globe. On April 12, 1961, the centennial of the firing on Fort Sumter, Russian cosmonaut Yuri Gagarin became the first human in space, recording a 108-minute orbit of the earth. That summer, construction began on the Berlin Wall, a physical testament to the divide between communism and democracy, and President John Kennedy sent the first American military personnel to South Vietnam. The next few years saw the nation at the brink of nuclear war with the Soviet Union, continual communist expansion, and deteriorating conditions in Southeast Asia.

The situation at home was no better. Racial discord highlighted domestic tensions. The simultaneous occasion of the Civil War Centennial and the emerging Civil Rights Movement brought the unrealized proposition that "all men are created equal" to the forefront of national discussion. The American South became a battleground for racial equality and the true fruition of President Abraham Lincoln's vision of a "new birth of freedom." The early 1960s witnessed an increase of civic activism and resistance to long-standing segregation laws and customs. In February 1960, four African American college students challenged long-held segregation practices by sitting at a lunch counter at Woolworth's in Greensboro, North Carolina. By the end of the year, approximately 70,000 had participated in the "sit-ins" in 100 cities across the country. The following year a band of "Freedom Riders" challenged segregation laws in southern transportation facilities. Widespread protests against entrenched segregationist practices forced Americans to grapple with racial equality and, in the process, forced the country to reexamine the Civil War and its implications. Not since the 1860s did Lincoln's call for a "new birth of freedom" ring more true.[1]

Asserting the role of race in the Civil War narrative, however, proved a difficult task and one that defied conventional interpretations. In the hundred years since the surrender of General Robert E. Lee to General U. S. Grant at Appomattox Courthouse, the causes, meanings, and sacrifices of the Civil War had been willfully constructed and distorted by generations of Americans. Quick to selectively forget the causes of the war or the sufferings on the battlefield, scores of Americans readily embraced a romanticized account that trumpeted the courage and valor of Civil War soldiers. As David Blight demonstrates in *Race and Reunion,* the national acceptance of the reconciliationist narrative overshadowed alternative memories of the war, namely those of African Americans in what Blight terms the emancipationist narrative. Even within this mode of memory, interpretations of the war remained complex. For African Americans, remembering the Civil War meant revisiting the realities of slavery. For white Americans, it was easier to ignore the role of race in the war than to confront it as an undeniable cause of the war. As a result, African Americans became divorced from the culture of reunion and reconciliation. "A segregated society," notes Blight, "demanded a segregated historical memory." The emerging racial discord of the 1960s, however, offered an opportunity to incorporate the emancipationist narrative into the Civil War story.[2]

Gettysburg stood as the iconic site for reconciliationist sentiment. The battle's fiftieth anniversary, in 1913, typified fraternal reunion. Purposefully absent from the occasion was any discussion of slavery or emancipation. Orators heralded the courage of the soldiers. "We are not here to discuss the Genesis of the war, but men who have tried each other in the storm and smoke of battle are here to discuss this great fight," Virginia Governor William Hodges Mann declared. "We came here, I say, not to discuss what caused the war of 1861–1865," he continued, "but to talk over the events of the battle here as man to man." Twenty-five years later, at the 75th anniversary, aging Union and Confederate veterans gathered once again in a display of sectional reconciliation. The dedication of the Eternal Light Peace Memorial, with its inscription "Peace Eternal in a Nation United," stands as a physical reminder of the dominance of reconciliation.[3]

When the National Park Service acquired Gettysburg in 1933, the agency continued to promote the battlefield as hallowed grounds to pay honor to the deeds of the soldiers. The focus on the "High Water Mark" underscored this approach. Racial issues, whether overt or inconspicuous, however, remained interwoven to Gettysburg's history. Seemingly, the centennial observance and the ongoing Civil Rights Movement presented the nation, as well as the National Park Service, with an ideal opportunity to integrate the racial issues into the Civil War narrative. Yet the centennial and the social unrest brought no such broadened interpretation. Though orators used the occasion of the centennial as a platform for racial unity, the Civil Rights Movement did little to influence the predominant interpretation at the nation's Civil War battlefields. At the twilight of the centennial in 1965, and after scores of sit-ins, freedom rides, freedom summers, and a stand in a schoolhouse door, visitors to Gettysburg still found a romantic, reconciliatory narrative devoid of the bitter conflicts of the war itself and its implications.

Meanwhile, the National Park Service continued to implement MISSION 66 and the initiative to improve the infrastructure of the nation's parks. The decade-long program infused one billion dollars for operation and improvements. MISSION 66 provided Gettysburg National Military Park with over $1 million. Throughout the national park system, the most visible achievement of MISSION 66 was the construction of new visitor centers. The National Park Service had long desired to build a modern visitor center and museum at Gettysburg; MISSION 66 provided the revenue to do so. After a series of construction fiascos and reoccurring completion extensions, on March 18, 1962, the Park Service opened the Gettysburg Visitor and Cyclorama Center. Appropriately, former president Dwight D. Eisenhower, signer of the MISSION 66 initiative, spent more than an hour touring the visitor center later that spring. The new visitor center marked a significant departure from the park's existing facilities. Confined to small office spaces on the second floor of the federal building along Baltimore Street, the Park Service had offered little in the way of museum exhibits or displays. As a result, few visitors, estimated at less than five percent of total park visitors, bothered to stop at the headquarters. Certainly the cyclorama building on East Cemetery Hill received more visitors. Now with the opening of this new visitor center and museum, visitors increasingly stopped at the building as part of their Gettysburg experience. For example, in July 1962, almost 80,000 toured the new museum, a number that represented nearly 20 percent of the battlefield's visitors.[4]

The visitor center offered several modern interpretive experiences. A sixteen-minute introductory slide program was shown in the auditorium. This program emphasized the battle as the turning point of the Civil War and asserted Gettysburg as the "supreme battle of the Civil War." The museum featured thirty exhibits that narrated the battle and the Civil War, as well as four dioramas that depicted scenes from the battle. The main attraction, however, remained the Gettysburg Cyclorama. After years of inadequate display in a poorly ventilated and heated building, the restoration crew hung the painting in the new facility in May 1962. Too, a new, modernized program now accompanied the restored painting. Previously, visitors to the cyclorama on East Cemetery Hill viewed the painting while listening to a guide who summarized the fighting on July 3. In the new facility, visitors listened to an audio tape and viewed an accompanying light and sound program. As they entered the cyclorama rotunda, and stood on the center of the platform with the painting surrounding them, a dim purple light slowly came up with a voice telling them they were about to "witness a vision of the past." Suddenly, full lights came on to the painting, while the narration of the third day's action proceeded accompanied by audio effects of artillery shots, rifle firing, and soldiers' yelling. The audio program pointed out key features on the painting relevant to the third day's battle action, including Little Round Top, Seminary Ridge, Cemetery Ridge, and the Copse of Trees. As the program concluded, the lights faded and a voice recited the Gettysburg Address.[5]

This new presentation sought to immerse visitors in the experience of Pickett's Charge. After watching the introductory slide program and viewing the painting, visitors were encouraged to complete their experience with a walk to the observation deck to overlook the fields of the third day's fighting. Interested visitors could then walk along the newly constructed High Water Mark Walking Tour, which park officials described as a "walk into history" and "a more intense experience." Soon after the painting was moved into the new visitor center, the old cyclorama building was demolished and the landscape restored to its condition prior to erection of the building in 1913. The Gettysburg Travel Council would eventually develop this land into a parking lot for one of their visitor centers.[6]

Though the dedication of the Soldiers' National Cemetery had always stood as an integral part of the Gettysburg story, beginning in the 1940s and continuing through the Cold War, Lincoln's Gettysburg Address assumed increased meaning to a nation in a global struggle against communism. After President Harry Truman proclaimed November 19 Dedication Day, this served as an occasion not only to commemorate the Union dead, but also to pay tribute to the transcendent ideals of freedom and democracy. Fittingly then, on November 19, 1962, the 99th anniversary of the Gettysburg Address, the agency formally dedicated the new visitor center.

Richard Neutra, the building's designer, had intended to construct a facility that would draw attention to Lincoln and his "inspiring two-minute address." He wanted to give emphasis to the "wondrous words" of the Gettysburg Address and regularly referred to the facility as the "Lincoln Memorial Museum." Superintendent Myers gave the welcoming remarks and Regional Director Ronald Lee served as the master of ceremonies. Director Conrad Wirth, the architect of MISSION 66, presented the keynote speech before 350 invited guests and a crowd estimated at 30,000. Wirth proclaimed November 19, 1962 a "great day" in the history of Gettysburg National Military Park.[7]

MISSION 66 had also made funds available to install interpretive field exhibits. Presentation of the battle to visitors progressed with each generation. As noted, the War Department relied exclusively on monuments and tablets to narrate the battle to visitors, many of whom were Civil War veterans. When the National Park Service acquired Gettysburg in 1933, it recognized the need to modernize the park's educational programming to appeal to visitors now several generations removed from the war. Wayside exhibits interpreted the battlefield and used historic photographs, maps, and narrative text to explain the fighting. Now, with MISSION 66 funds, the Park Service continued to modernize its interpretive field exhibits by installing several audio-visual exhibits. The first audio station was installed near General George Meade's headquarters on May 12, 1964. A year later, audio-visual stations were mounted on Little Round Top, alongside the Virginia Memorial, and on Oak Ridge, at the observation tower. These exhibits consisted of a traditional wayside marker with a historic map, photographs, and a textual summary, but now included a push-button account that gave an oral summation of the fighting that had occurred in the immediate vicinity. The audio-visual station at the Virginia Memorial, for example, gave a brief account of the Confederate infantry assault on July 3. These four audio stations further demonstrated the park's ongoing efforts to upgrade its interpretive media. Not only did the audio stations complement the cyclorama's new light and sound show and the dioramas in the new visitor center, but they also allowed visitors to engage the battle with differing sensory experiences, instead of reading scores of monuments and itinerary tablets. Instead of passively driving through the field, the audio-visual stations offered an interactive medium. The battlefield slowly evolved into an interactive experience.[8]

Observing the pageantry of the Civil War Centennial in April 1962, distinguished historian John Hope Franklin declared, "One searches in vain for an event in our history that has been commemorated with the same intense and elaborate preparation that characterizes the Civil War Centennial." Centennial celebrations occurred across the nation, but none compared to the glamorous and exciting festivities planned for Gettysburg in 1963. In preparation since April 1956, the nation's centennial celebrations would culminate on the Pennsylvania battlefield.[9]

Roots of the centennial were found in the popularization of the Civil War during the mid-twentieth century, in what Edward Tabor Linenthal terms

"Civil War subculture." This subculture popularized and democratized the study of the Civil War; outside the halls of academia, scores of Americans sought to learn more about the conflict. Chicago founded the first Civil War round table in 1940. The establishment of the North-South Skirmish Association followed in 1950. On the literary front, historian and the preeminent author on the Civil War, Bruce Catton, probably did more than any other contemporary individual to highlight the "Civil War subculture." A Michigan native and founder and editor of *American Heritage,* Catton's prolific prose and readable narratives entertained and educated millions. In 1954, Catton received the Pulitzer Prize for *A Stillness at Appomattox,* the final installment of his "Army of the Potomac" trilogy.[10]

The popularity of the "Civil War subculture" created an amicable atmosphere for the centennial celebrations that blended education with entertainment. Civil War enthusiasts and historians became the driving forces behind the creation of a centennial commission. Just as President Eisenhower warmly received Director Wirth's MISSION 66 proposal, he was equally receptive to celebrating the Civil War Centennial. In the summer of 1957, Congress passed bipartisan legislation to establish the Civil War Centennial Commission (CWCC) and Eisenhower signed the bill in September. Officially the CWCC fell within the authority of the National Park Service, and its purpose was to plan and coordinate events with the NPS, interested organizations, and state commissions. Wirth facilitated CWCC's first meeting. The commission unanimously approved as its chairman Major General U.S. Grant III, grandson of the Union commander.[11]

Preparation for the centennial celebrations in Pennsylvania, however, had actually predated the establishment of the CWCC. On April 20, 1956, the Pennsylvania General Assembly formed "The One Hundredth Anniversary of the Battle of Gettysburg and Lincoln's Gettysburg Address Commission." The legislation set up a nine-member commission and charged it with the "proper and fitting recognition and observance" of the events. Acting independently from the national CWCC, Pennsylvania's commission, in cooperation with the National Park Service and other local agencies, assumed responsibility for the events at Gettysburg. On April 22, 1961, Gettysburg and Adams County kicked off the centennial by reenacting the "Departure of the Independent Blues." Over four hundred men participated in the event to commemorate the first men from Adams County to volunteer.[12]

In anticipation of Gettysburg's centennial, national media attention increased. During the winter of 1961, CBS television and the *New York Times* visited Gettysburg to film for a special television show, "Carl Sandburg at Gettysburg." Not to be outdone, on April 1, 1961, NBC aired "The Gettysburg Address Story." In addition to special television programming, *National Geo-*

graphic, Life, Trailways, and *Ford Times* ran articles on touring the battlefield complete with color photographs. Just months before Gettysburg's centennial, on March 31, 1963, President John Kennedy, accompanied by his wife Jackie and daughter Caroline, spent nearly two hours touring the battlefield in their Mercury convertible.[13]

While the news media continued to draw attention to Gettysburg in anticipation of the July 1963 commemorations, the first major centennial reenactment occurred at Manassas National Battlefield Park in Virginia. Over the weekend of July 21, approximately 2,000 reenactors participated in the event held on the battlefield, executing artillery barrages, infantry assaults, and simulating hand-to-hand combat. Confederate reenactors, many clad in gray clothes from Sears and Roebuck, portrayed Virginia soldiers holding their position on Henry Hill, as General Thomas Jackson's brigade had successfully done one hundred years earlier. The mostly southern crowd stood and applauded as Union troops retreated. Nearly 100,000 visitors attended the event.[14]

Manassas, for better or worse, set the standard for subsequent commemorations, or perhaps more accurately, celebrations. While the reenactment offered spectators a chance to visualize and imagine a Civil War engagement, some newspaper reporters decried the spectacle. Several declared it a "sham" or "farce." Others criticized the commercialization, noting a "Coney Island" atmosphere. In Gettysburg, the local newspaper declared the Manassas reenactment a "strange spectacle" that mocked the sacrifices of the soldiers in an arena befitting a "Roman circus." The writer appealed to the CWCC to abandon future plans for similar events. Looking toward the events of July 1963, the *Gettysburg Times* declared, "There can be no such excuse for desecration of Gettysburg and other Civil War battlefields. Future commemorative events should be conducted with dignity and in a spirit befitting to the occasion." The National Park Service expressed similar concerns. The sheer volume of people, grandstand bleachers, cannon, and horses caused considerable damage to the historic terrain. Moreover, as a preservationist agency, the Park Service's role in the reenactment seemed misguided. Out of concern for historic preservation, Director Wirth banned future reenactments on Park Service property.[15]

Yet the ban was not ironclad. The Park Service permitted the 1962 Antietam reenactment to go on as scheduled since its planning was already underway. More importantly, however, for one of the war's defining battles, the nearly three weeks of observances at Antietam passed with relatively little fanfare and public attention. The climactic event took place on September 17 and 18, when nearly 2,000 reenactors staged the fighting at Bloody Lane. An estimated 18,000 watched the event. Low attendance paralleled minimal national media coverage; the reenactment of the nation's bloodiest day received only a few snippets on the eighty-sixth page of the *New York Times*. During its centennial year, a mere 175,000 visitors journeyed to Antietam. During the remainder of the centennial, visitation to Antietam dropped to an annual average of 100,000. In terms of domestic and international implications, the September 1962 battle at Antietam, arguably, held more significance than Gettysburg. Few, however, challenged Gettysburg as the war's "High Water Mark." Quite simply, none of the war's other battlefields held the same appeal, attraction, or symbolism as Gettysburg.[16]

Meanwhile, on March 11, 1963, three months before its own centennial observances Gettysburg National Military Park received a new superintendent. Secretary of the Interior Stewart Udall announced the appointment of Kittridge A. Wing to succeed Superintendent Myers, who transferred to Cape Hatteras National Seashore in North Carolina. A World War II veteran, and now Gettysburg's fourth NPS superintendent, Wing brought considerable management experience. Before his arrival he had served as the assistant superintendent at Shenandoah National Park in Virginia; the assistant superintendent, then superintendent at San Juan National Historic Site in Washington state; and superintendent at Fort Union National Monument in New Mexico.[17]

The centennial theme of "A Nation United" could not have brought deeper irony. More than any time since the 1860s, the country was fiercely and violently divided. The vision of a nation where "all men are created equal" remained unrealized and a deep-seated implication of the 1860s conflict. The timely observance of the Civil War Centennial and the Civil Rights Movement offered Americans the opportunity to reflect on slavery and freedom, equality and segregation, secession and sit-ins, and Manassas and Birmingham. By the time the Union and Confederate soldiers arrived at Gettysburg, the Lincoln administration had clearly articulated the war's dual objectives: restoration of the Union and emancipation of four million enslaved people. In his dedication speech of the Soldiers' National Cemetery, to consecrate the grounds where over 3,500 Federal troops lay buried, Lincoln shared his vision for a new Union. Inevitably then, perhaps it was only "fitting and proper" that in 1963 the battlefield served as a landscape to once again champion ideals of freedom, democracy, and a nation's "new birth of freedom."

Tensions mounted in the Deep South over integration of public schools and facilities. Governor George C. Wallace vowed to defy a court order to integrate the University of Alabama. Meanwhile, in Pennsylvania, Vice President Lyndon B. Johnson traveled to Gettysburg to deliver the keynote speech during the Memorial Day commemorations. Speaking to a crowd of 3,000, Johnson paid tribute to the battle's soldiers and Lincoln's dedication. Johnson used the occasion to appeal to a realization of Lincoln's vision of a "new birth of freedom" in the contemporary battle for civil rights. "Our nation found its soul in honor on these fields of Gettysburg one hundred years ago," Johnson asserted, "We must not lose that soul in dishonor now on the fields of hate." Echoing words of Martin Luther King, Jr., who declared that desegregation of public schools across the South was moving at a "snail-like pace," Johnson declared that white Americans could no longer ask for patience from their black brethren. In his concluding words, Johnson offered, "Until justice is blind to color, until education is unaware of race, until opportunity is unconcerned with the color of men's skins, emancipation will be a proclamation but not a fact. To the extent that the proclamation of emancipation is not fulfilled in fact, to that extent we shall have fallen short of assuring freedom to the free."[18]

Johnson's remarks set the tone for subsequent speeches given during the battle's centennial. "A Nation United" observances commenced on June 21 with a ceremony at the Pennsylvania State Memorial. On June 30, former president Dwight D. Eisenhower, now a Gettysburg resident, stood before an audience at the Gettysburg High School and addressed the significance and legacy of the battle within the contemporary context of the Cold War. Whereas Vice President Johnson's remarks offered a decidedly civil rights message, Eisenhower's comments focused not on domestic strife, but on national unity in the face of communist expansion. "It remained for one man," Eisenhower told a crowd estimated at 6,000, "not a soldier or a historian, but the President of the United States, Abraham Lincoln, to tell us in a few immortal words the true meaning of the battle fought here." Linking the words of the Gettysburg Address to current events, as so many speakers had done before, Eisenhower continued, "Lincoln's words should be read, pondered and pondered still again, by every American, for they apply today as profoundly as they did on that November day when they were first spoken." The former president warned of the threats imposed from the communist world, which the free world could not ignore. In the Cold War environment that pitted democracy against communism, Eisenhower extolled, "We, in our time, shall win the battle for freedom!"[19]

On July 1, activities commenced with an "Our Heritage" ceremony at the Eternal Light Peace Memorial. Narrated by NBC's Ben Grauer, the ceremony paid tribute to the sacrifices of the men on both sides. The program included speeches from several governors from states that had contributed troops to the battle and a welcome address from Pennsylvania governor William Scranton. In addition, the Gettysburg Battlefield Preservation Association and the Military Order of the Loyal Legion presented the National Park Service with titles to tracts of land they had purchased for inclusion into the federal holdings. At the conclusion of the program, attendees moved throughout the battlefield to witness rededication ceremonies of various monuments. In addition to the expected orations, beginning on July 1 and continuing through the three-day event, visitors traveled through the battlefield to witness "vignettes of history." Over one hundred Adams County residents participated in recreating historical scenes, including the "Barlow-Gordon Incident," "John Burns, Venerable Citizen-Warrior," "A Sharpshooter's Roost" at Devil's Den and a vignette on General Lee titled "A Valliant General, a Noble Man." The Park Service designed these vignettes to immerse visitors into the battle and to humanize and personalize the experience of combat. As advertised, the vignettes gave visitors a chance to experience the "daily behavior of men under the stress of battle." Here too the park used the occasion to create an interactive experience that allowed spectators to visualize elements of Civil War combat.[20]

A "Strength Through Unity" parade highlighted July 2. Over 6,500 people marched in the parade, including reenactors, women dressed as Civil War era belles, several thousand active military personnel, Armed Forces bands, and nearly 1,500 Sons of Union Veterans. Newspapers reported that over 35,000 turned out for the parade. The two men who portrayed President Lincoln and John Burns, the aged local resident who defended his home and town, received favorable applause from the crowd. But the loudest applause was for Robert E. Lee IV, the great-grandson of the Army of Northern Virginia's leader, who rode through the town streets in an Army Jeep.[21]

The cheers for Lee were not surprising. Gettysburg's centennial coincided with a reemergence of the Lost Cause phenomenon. Taking their cues from Lee's farewell address at Appomattox, Lost Cause advocates persevered in the belief that the Confederate Army surrendered not because they were inferior soldiers, but because they were forced to yield to "overwhelming numbers and resources." At Gettysburg, this quixotic, nostalgic version of the Civil War manifested itself in the unveiling and dedication of several Confederate state memorials. Lacking economic resources and reluctant to commemorate a Confederate defeat, only three southern states (Virginia, North Carolina, and Alabama) had placed memorials during the first half of the twentieth century. The nation's renewed interest in the war, combined with a reemergence of white southern heritage in the midst of a civil rights struggle, provided the catalyst for the remaining former Confederate states to erect monuments to honor their soldiers.[22]

Georgia led the second wave of monumentation across the nation's Civil War battlefields. On September 21, 1961, Georgians dedicated a monument to her fallen sons at the Antietam battlefield. This was the first Georgia monument erected on any Civil War battlefield and Antietam's first monument honoring former Confederate states. The day following the dedication at Antietam, a similar monument was unveiled at Gettysburg. The dedication blended a mild Lost Cause rhetoric with a strong call for unity in the face of international aggressions. The ceremony began with the playing of the Star Spangled Banner, followed by the invocation and the recitation of the Pledge of Allegiance. Mrs. Max Flynt, Co-Chairman of the Georgia Centennial Hall of Fame Committee, then led a salute to the Confederate Battle Flag, "I salute the Confederate Flag with affection, reverence, and undying remembrance." In a modern display of reconciliation, if not irony, the U.S. Second Army Band played "Dixie."[23]

Regional Director of the National Park Service Ronald F. Lee accepted the Georgia State Memorial. Lee's speech narrated the deeds of the Georgia soldiers on the afternoon of July 2; he recalled their "desperate" fight for the Wheatfield and their triumphant victory in Devil's Den. In Lee's rendition, Georgians nearly captured Little Round Top, and "had they gained it, they could then have rolled up and smashed the entire Union line . . . it was Georgia's greatest moment at Gettysburg." James Myers, then Gettysburg's superintendent, also praised efforts of the men from Georgia. "The Georgia men who fought at Gettysburg were typical of the Southern soldier," declared Myers. "They were dedicated men—men of courage, of endurances and of faith in a burning cause." Each speaker shaped the deeds of the Georgia soldiers as those committed by men who fought for principles, "for what they believed was right."[24]

Moving beyond an expected overture of Lost Cause gallantry, the speakers appealed to those in attendance to "consecrate the past" and "pay tribute to the dead." Lee, Myers, and Georgia Governor Ernest Vandiver encouraged a remembrance of the sacrifices of all Civil War soldiers and from these reflections bring meaning, or inspiration, to future generations. In a testament to the pervasiveness of the "heritage syndrome," Governor Vandiver declared that Americans "can look back at the Civil War as a matter of pride, not with shame and regret." In their efforts to consecrate an acceptable version of the past, Vandiver challenged listeners to "learn the lessons" taught by the sacrifice of the soldiers and to "find a way to let the dead serve the living."[25]

The recounting of the gallant efforts of the Georgians was to be expected. More significantly, Vandiver directly confronted contemporary issues of racial violence and injustice. Vandiver did not rattle the sabers of white southerners, but instead offered a plea for unity in brotherhood. His timing was opportune. At the dawn of the Civil War Centennial, state and local officials in southern states grappled with ways to implement, or more often defy, the federal court ruling in *Brown v. Board of Education* (1954), which legalized the integration of public schools. While some southern officials refused to comply with the court order, in January 1961, Governor Vandiver accepted the enrollment of two African American students at the University of Georgia. The governor's progressive stance spared the University of Georgia the racial hostility seen in the integration at other southern universities, such as the University of Alabama and the University of Mississippi. Shortly thereafter, Vandiver encouraged the Georgia state legislature to repeal a law that barred integrated schools from receiving state funding.

The lesson learned by the sacrifice of hundreds of thousands of men on Civil War battlefields, according to Vandiver, was unity. The bond of brotherhood, he declared, permitted disagreements but also granted the "common welfare of the national family." This fraternalism led the way toward domestic tranquility, yet enhanced the nation's prestige on the world's stage. Hinting at the current divisive racial issues as a threat to the nation's security, Vandiver urged, "Never in our history has there been such a need for this nation to present to the world a united front so impregnable that no Communist, no American-Nazi, no agitator group, no lunatic fringe, can even pin-prick our armor of solidarity."[26]

Governor Vandiver was not the only southern representative to use the centennial as an occasion to plea for racial justice. On July 3, 1963, after the dedication of the Georgia monument, Floridians gathered on West Confederate Avenue to dedicate their state monument. Congressman Sam M. Gibbons, of the 10th Congressional District of Tampa, delivered the dedication address. His words mirrored those of Vandiver. Reminding listeners of the bloodshed on the fields of Gettysburg, Gibbons linked the sacrifices made by the men in 1863 to the struggle for freedom a century later. He declared that the "burden for the right for freedom now" lay with those present. Gibbons made direct reference to the violence and disorder experienced in the Deep South and urged that racial conflicts be removed from the streets and resolved in courts, legislative bodies, and the ballot box. "As responsible Americans working for better human relations we abhor the use on our citizens of the snarling police dog, the fire hose, the electrically-charged cattle prodding stick," he declared.[27]

Like Georgia's governor, Gibbons placed the country's racial divisiveness in the larger context of the Cold War and the need for a unified front in foreign affairs. "America's racial conflicts have immediate world-wide significance," he declared. "We cannot hope to win men's minds in the battle with communism if America becomes a land in which freedom, equality and opportunity are reserved only for the white men." In sum, Gibbons maintained that if racial conflicts could not be settled peacefully and equitability and if America failed in its fight against communism, then those who fell and died at Gettysburg and on other battlefields would "then have died in vain."[28]

Not all southern orators pleaded for racial justice, however. Just weeks after his stand on the doorsteps at the University of Alabama, George Wallace, Alabama's segregationist governor, attended Gettysburg's centennial celebrations. On July 2, he placed a wreath at the Alabama State Memorial and later that day gave the dedication speech for the South Carolina State Memorial. Wallace's speech echoed familiar rhetoric. "This is a solemn occasion," the governor said, "We stand among the descendents of brave men who fought for North and South and we still stand for defense of the Constitution of the United States."[29]

With the exception of Governor Wallace, centennial speeches delivered on Seminary Ridge mirrored those by orators along Cemetery Ridge. Northern liberals used the centennial and their understanding of the sacrifices made by the Union soldiers to emphasize the ideal that America, as Lincoln stated, was "dedicated to the proposition that all men were created equal." At a mass held at the Eternal Light Peace Memorial on the morning of June 30, Father Theodore Hesburgh, President of Notre Dame, spoke of African American equality. Appointed as Notre Dame's fifteenth president at the age of thirty-five in June 1952, Father Hesburgh boasted a strong civil rights record. Before an estimated crowd of 4,000, Hesburgh declared that Union soldiers had fought for black freedom, but because of continued racial oppression, the Civil War remained "unfinished business." Hesburgh echoed Lincoln's call to the dedication of a great task. "It is freedom denied from one American to another American," Hesburgh postulated, "and until every white American decides to act morally towards every Negro American, there is no end to the unfinished business." The following day, New Jersey Governor Richard Hughes made a similar appeal. Hughes extolled, "The Civil War was not fought to preserve the Union 'lily white' or 'Jim Crow,' it was fought for liberty and justice for all." He declared it a "shame" that the "full benefits of freedom are not the possession of all Americans a full century after the war which was fought to save America's soul."[30]

Beyond the fanfare, theatrics, and flag-waving, Gettysburg's centennial offered the nation's political leaders an opportunity and platform to address prevailing political and social issues. Speeches given by northern and southern speakers alike did more than commemorate the battle's centennial by recounting the brave deeds preformed and heroic sacrifices made. These orators capitalized on the battle's symbolism and the power of its landscape to urge Americans to find peaceful reconciliation to racial strife. By standing on the battlefield, by being at Gettysburg, their words resonated more deeply and profoundly than if given in Tampa, Florida, or on the campus of Notre Dame. Also recognizing the symbolic power of place, one month after Gettysburg's centennial, Martin Luther King, Jr., stood before the white marble statue of Abraham Lincoln and made a plea for Americans to move beyond the "manacles of segregation" and break the "chains of discrimination."[31]

The association between the Civil War Centennial and the Civil Rights Movement manifested itself most clearly at Gettysburg. No other battle-

The centennial reenactment of Pickett's Charge, July 3, 1963. The National Park Service recorded over 404,000 visitors to the battlefield that month.

field witnessed the apparent connection between race and freedom. It was at Gettysburg that Lincoln offered the nation a "new birth of freedom," and it would be at Gettysburg that speakers urged the realization of this promise a century later. Moreover, these calls for freedom exemplified how the nation defined itself in the midst of racial and social conflict. Similarly, the attention given to current discord, namely civil rights, illustrated how Americans used the battlefield and its symbolism in contemporary times. Americans went to Gettysburg, a place of unimaginable suffering, to appeal for racial justice. Much as Lincoln did in his second inaugural, speakers hoped to "bind the nation's wounds." A battlefield consecrated by those who "gave the last full measure of devotion" certainly served as a fitting platform.

As expected, the climax of the centennial celebrations was the July 3rd "Reunion at the High Water Mark." To honor the one hundredth anniversary of Pickett's Charge, with the Stars and Bars unfurled, five hundred Confederate reenactors advanced from Seminary Ridge toward Cemetery Ridge. As they advanced, sound systems reproduced the effect of cannon and rifle fire, while a smoke screen simulated the smoke of black powder. Across the battlefield, five hundred reenactors representing the Union Army's 2nd Corps

Stuckey's Pecan Shop, Emmitsburg Road, view looking west from the Peach Orchard. Commercial venues, like Stuckey's, underscored Gettysburg's postwar tourist boom.

waited to greet the "Confederates" with handshakes when they reached the Angle. When those in gray and those wearing blue grasped hands, all sang the Star Spangled Banner and then recited the Pledge of Allegiance.[32]

Two years earlier, the centennial events at Manassas brought immediate backlash. While those at Gettysburg were, for the most part, carried out in a more dignified and solemn manner, some observers remained critical. On July 14, Don Robertson of Cleveland's *Plain Dealer* reported on the "Vulgar Show at Gettysburg" and reminded readers of the sacrifices made at Gettysburg by poignantly listing the casualty statistics. Robertson found the commercialization of the centennial deplorable, writing, "Observances should be kept out of the reach of commercial elements. The anniversary of a battle should be no occasion for a hot-dog proprietor to triple his business." The editorial included a famous Matthew Brady photograph of the Confederate dead at the Rose Farm. Its caption declared, "Some dead at Gettysburg. This picture is no reenactment."[33]

Indeed, local businesses did capitalize on the battle's bloodshed, just as Robertson observed. By 1963, the main roads surrounding the battlefield—Steinwehr Avenue, Baltimore Pike, Emmitsburg Road, and Taneytown

Road—had become littered with commercial businesses. Jim Weeks has explored how mass culture defined Gettysburg, and climaxed during the centennial. Strategically positioned across from the park's visitor center, the National Civil War Wax Museum opened in time for the centennial events. This museum offered life-size soldier replicas, displays of weapons and relics, and a dramatization of the Gettysburg Address. On Baltimore Street, actor Cliff Arquette, more famous as Charley Weaver, had opened the Soldiers' Museum in 1959. But it was LeRoy Smith, a Midwesterner by birth, who served as a primary force behind the marketing. He opened the Lincoln Train Museum, directly west of Ziegler's Grove, and also the Hall of Presidents Wax Museum on Baltimore Street. Several years later Smith opened the Old Gettysburg Village, a period shopping mall. Since Adams County lacked zoning ordinances, the Park Service remained powerless to stop such development on the battlefield periphery. By the battle's centennial, Weeks concludes, "Gettysburg resembled Niagara Falls or Gatlinburg."[34]

In addition to the anniversary activities, the Park Service used the centennial as an opportunity to expand its interpretive programming and inaugurated a series of campfires at its newly constructed amphitheater. Though summer campfires had been presented since 1941 on East Cemetery Hill, the park staff envisioned a more "suitable place" to hold these evening programs. Upon examining several sites, Pitzer Woods, the former site of the Civilian Conservation Corps camp along West Confederate Avenue, was selected as the most suitable location.[35] The outdoor programs at the amphitheater differed from the campfires held in previous years. The park now planned to hold campfire programs at the new venue six days a week, beginning on July 1 and continuing through Labor Day. Each program was standardized: a ranger read from a script that summarized the historical significance of Pitzer Woods and included an overview of the life of Civil War soldiers. The ranger then demonstrated the nine-step process of loading and firing a rifle, gave a brief discussion on the battlefield's memorialization, and then led a group sing-along. After the scripted narration, the program concluded with a viewing of the MGM film "Gettysburg." The campfire program premiered on the opening day of the battle's anniversary, July 1, 1963. George Wallace attended the inaugural program. Approximately 3,000 people enjoyed the campfire programs held during the three-day battle anniversary, and by the end of the month the park estimated nearly 7,600 had attended these programs.[36]

As expected, visitation reached an all time high during July, with 404,017 visitors. Four months later, Gettysburg's centennial observances concluded with the commemoration of the dedication of the Soldiers' National Cemetery. In the years after July 1863, the defining aspect of the battle of Gettysburg had become Abraham Lincoln and the Gettysburg Address. Other battles across the country exacted high casualties; places like Spotsylvania, Antietam, Allatoona, or Cold Harbor offer ready comparisons to each day of fighting at Gettysburg. High casualty rates or heroic fighting at Little Round Top or the Peach Orchard, then, did not define Gettysburg; Lincoln and the Gettysburg Address had. A century after the two-minute oration, Lincoln's Gettysburg Address evolved into more than a speech to consecrate battle grounds and to pay tribute to the Union dead. Instead, in the words of one speaker at the centennial event, Lincoln and the Gettysburg Address became "worldwide" symbols of freedom and democracy. Fundamental values of liberty, equality, and self-government, articulated by Lincoln, became aspirations to people all around the world.[37]

Fittingly, then, the centennial of the Gettysburg Address included not just noted American politicians, but a contingent of international dignitaries. Gettysburg College held the opening ceremony on November 17 and hosted John Chadwick, minister of the British Embassy; Italian ambassador Sergio Fenoaltea; and Herve Alphand, ambassador of the French Republic. Ambassador Alphand summarized the sentiment of millions when he stated, "Lincoln's words belong not only to one country but to mankind as a whole." Secretary of State Dean Rusk spoke on the "International Aspects of Lincoln's Address." Acknowledging the global relevance of Lincoln's speech, Rusk declared, "And the words of Gettysburg assume new depth, new meaning—not only for Americans, but for all who, under God, love freedom!" Later the attendees proceeded to the Soldiers' National Cemetery. Here, former president Dwight D. Eisenhower delivered a rededication speech and Pennsylvania Supreme Court justice Michael Musmanno recited the Gettysburg Address.[38]

Forced to decline the invitation to speak at the November ceremonies because of an impending trip to Texas to quell tensions within the Democratic Party, President John Kennedy telegrammed a statement to the centennial commission. Unlike his vice-president, who months earlier had spoke in support for racial equality, Kennedy's statement described the significance and lasting symbolism of Lincoln's address. He telegrammed, "Lincoln and others did indeed give us 'a new birth of freedom,' but the goals of liberty and freedom, the obligations of keeping ours a government of and by the people are never-ending." Three days later, in Dallas, an assassin's bullet claimed the president's life. The media attention and the centennial celebrations seemed to reinforce Americans' interest in Gettysburg. By the end of the year, the battlefield set a record for visitation with over two million visitors.[39]

The nation's centennial observances reached their "High Water Mark" at Gettysburg in July 1963. As noted, Antietam's centennial events passed with little fanfare or national attention. The western Civil War battlefields mirrored more the small observances of Antietam. At Vicksburg National Military Park, 200,000 visitors were recorded, or half of Gettysburg's total, during its centennial month, also in July 1963. Here too, events passed with minimal attention when compared to Gettysburg's. The *New York Times* reported commemorations in Vicksburg with a mere paragraph, simply noting that the grandsons of General U.S. Grant and General John C. Pemberton met each other on the battlefield. Meanwhile, to commemorate the battle of Chickamauga, which occurred on September 19 and 20, 1863, scheduled events included two days of parades, contests, and ceremonies. The park reported 2,115 visitors attending.[40]

Americans' interest in Gettysburg continued to increase in the wake of the centennial. By comparison, visitation to Antietam peaked in 1962 with 175,000 and then decreased to an average annual visitation of 100,000 the following two years. Visitation to Gettysburg during the balance of the centennial remained high. In 1964, over 2.2 million people toured the battlefield. Visitors continued to see changes to the park's interpretation and the battlefield landscape. In the summer of 1964, the National Park Service produced and distributed a self-guiding, descriptive brochure complete with fourteen stops. Maintaining a practice established by Superintendent James McConaghie during the Great Depression, park officials continued to create historic vistas. Workers removed brush on the slopes of Little Round Top, but consistent with the goal of simultaneously managing a recreational landscape, made a "special effort to preserve the healthy redbud and dogwood trees which color the hill's slope in the springtime." Over 130 acres at Devil's Den, along Crawford Avenue, and the Rose farm were also cleared.[41]

The surge of patriotism engendered by the Cold War and the Civil War Centennial reinforced the nation's attachment to the battle of Gettysburg and continued engagement with President Lincoln and the Gettysburg Address. Unparalleled commemorative events in July and November 1963 underscored this association, as did the record-setting attendance of two million visitors. The simultaneous occasion of the Civil War Centennial and the Civil Rights Movement presented the nation with an opportunity to reengage the entrenched reconciliationist narrative. While some spoke for full equality for African Americans, the centennial's theme of "A Nation United" proved to be more idealized than realized. To many African Americans, the Civil War Centennial continued to remind them of the war's "unfinished business." While societal discord brought racial equality to the forefront of the nation's domestic issues, the interpretation of the war remained a romanticized, reconciliationist account. Across the nation, race remained disassociated with the centennial celebrations and the emancipationist narrative muted from the dominant mode of memory. America's "heritage syndrome" relating to the Civil War remained deeply entrenched. Those with the ability to redefine the war's national narrative, including the National Park Service, continued to perpetuate long-standing interpretations. The National Park Service at Gettysburg, as well as at Civil War sites across the nation, remained wedded to a story of heroic soldiers and commanders. "National temper and mythology," notes David Blight, "still preferred a story of the mutual valor of the Blue and Gray to the troublesome, disruptive problem of black and white."[42]

CHAPTER 7

OUR FATHERS BROUGHT FORTH ON THIS CONTINENT A NEW NATION: THE NEW GETTYSBURG EXPERIENCE, 1966–1975

MISSION 66 marked a major milestone in the history of the National Park Service. At a time when the nation's "heritage syndrome" drove thousands of Americans to historic and cultural sites, the decade long initiative provided the desperately needed improvements to modernize the parks' infrastructure. MISSION 66, in part, reaffirmed the National Park Service's tradition of promoting recreational tourism. Improvements in roads, trails, camping facilities, amphitheaters, and visitor amenities encouraged a recreational aspect to many of the national parks. When MISSION 66 began in 1956, the agency recorded 61.6 million visitors. At the close of the program in 1966, approximately 133.1 million visitors had visited the national parks. In 1964, George Hartzog became the agency's new director. Where Conrad Wirth focused on improving infrastructure, Hartzog advocated the acquisition of important, threatened lands. The new director promoted a program known as "Parkscape U.S.A." This initiative continued to champion multiple uses of the landscapes, and simultaneously sought to create recreational tourism opportunities in urban environments. During Hartzog's nine-year tenure, from 1964 to 1972, the agency added sixty-nine units, which included the first urban recreational parks at Gateway, New York City, and Golden Gate in San Francisco.[1]

Meanwhile, the end of MISSION 66 paralleled the conclusion of the Civil War Centennial. The observances of the Civil War Centennial aptly demonstrate the dominance of the "heritage syndrome" and a tendency to remember and glorify the soldiers, commanders, and battles without engaging in a meaningful discussion of the war's causes or consequences. Inability to come to terms with historical truths, in this instance the social and cultural implications of the war, produced what Michael Kammen terms a "false consciousness" of history, or historical amnesia.[2] While the rising social conflict over racial equality occurred simultaneously with the centennial observances, the Civil Rights Movement did not generate any significant change in the prevalent narrative of the 1861–1865 conflict. At Gettysburg, the National Park Service continued to promote a reconciliationist account, focusing on the glorification of the Union and Confederate soldiers.

In the years following the end of MISSION 66 and the conclusion of the Civil War Centennial, Gettysburg continued to remain a popular destination. The national "Civil War subculture" and the pervasive acceptance of the "heritage syndrome" produced record high visitation. During 1963, and for the first time in the history of Gettysburg National Military Park, over two million people visited the battlefield. Centennial activities only piqued interest in the battle; the following year, over 2.2 million people visited the park. Most significantly, the National Park Service placed itself squarely in the "tourist business" and, as a result, redefined the concept of a national military park.[3] For the men of the Gettysburg Battlefield Memorial Association and the War Department, the preservation of the landscape served to honor those who fought and died on the fields. This transformation of a national military park began when the National Park Service acquired the battlefield in 1933, but rapidly evolved in the years immediately following the Civil War Centennial. Paralleling larger trends within the agency, Gettysburg was promoted as a multiuse landscape and tourist destination, which helped to redefine the Gettysburg experience.

From a practical perspective, the increase in visitation in the years after the centennial combined with the increase in commercial development surrounding the battlefield compelled the National Park Service to reexamine its management philosophy and operational strategy. Higher visitation underscored inevitable tensions in the agency's mission to preserve the battlefield while at the same time providing visitor access. Administrative structure within the agency itself compounded these circumstances. When the National Park Service acquired Gettysburg National Military Park, it had little understanding of how to manage or preserve a historic battlefield. Superintendents' educational or professional backgrounds often guided daily operational policies. Between 1933 and 1965, Gettysburg had only four superintendents: James McConaghie, J. Walter Coleman, James Myers, and Kittridge Wing. In the decade immediately after the Civil War Centennial, the park had three: George Emery (January 1966–November 1970), Jerry Schober (December 1970–August 1974), and John Earnst, who arrived in August 1974.

This leadership change cannot be understated; neither the agency's national office in Washington, D.C. nor the regional office in Philadelphia directed preservation and operation decisions at Gettysburg, or other sites within its regions. Instead, local management enjoyed broad authority and discretion to shape the individual park as each superintendent deemed appropriate. Consequently, preservation and interpretive decisions at Gettysburg were not implemented based on uniform, academic principles, but were often dictated by the superintendent's background and personal vision. This frequent change in leadership made it difficult to establish continuity in management. The inevitable transition in authority and individuals' perceptions of the military park reinforced the evolutionary nature of the battlefield.[4]

The National Park Service continued to advocate a multiuse philosophy that encouraged differing forms of use. The "Parkscape U.S.A." movement supported the diversity of activities, including hiking, camping, horseback riding, fishing, and skiing. Adapting a historic battlefield for popular uses of recreational activities ran counter to the park's enabling legislation. Yet Gettysburg management allowed, if not encouraged, a broad variety of recreational activities.[5] In the process, park officials actively participated in the transformation of Gettysburg from a hallowed battlefield, a memorial to those who fought, into a national park.

The Park Service at Gettysburg had often promoted the duality of preservation and recreation. During the Great Depression, for example, park officials encouraged visitation to the battlefield for its scenic vistas, especially the spring and fall foliage. Now park staff moved beyond promoting the scenic vistas, which allowed for a passive use of the battlefield, and began to promote active recreational uses. Management recommended building picnic and camping facilities at a non-intrusive area of the battlefield, as befitting to a national park.[6] Certainly the construction of picnic areas had little adverse impact on the historic integrity of the battlefield, but subsequent proposals did undermine the park's primary purpose. In early 1962, for instance, park staff began to promote recreational pursuits. Harry Pfanz, park historian, noted that few visitors found the battlefield to be a "pleasant place for hiking and nature study," noting "this activity will be encouraged" by construction of hiking and nature trails. Subsequent proposals included using areas of the battlefield for off-season recreational activities that included sleigh riding, ice skating, Easter egg hunts, and kite flying. Horse trails were built and visitors were encouraged to explore the battlefield on horseback. Park staff noted these activities fell within the "proper uses" of the park and simultaneously served as a means to further community relations. As explained, these recreational uses were to "complement" existing historical programs.[7]

Across the nation, the Park Service established Environmental Study Areas. As intended by Director Hartzog, the purpose of these areas was to allow students the opportunity to explore environmental issues in an outdoor classroom. In January 1970, the agency reported sixty-seven operating study areas, reaching 50,000 students.[8] Gettysburg National Military Park hosted an Environmental Study Area in the southern part of the battlefield, where students studied the battle's historical narrative, man-made features, and the site's natural characteristics. Using the theme of "Man and the Land at Gettysburg," the area provided students with an "understanding of the total environment and the individual's relationship to it." For example, the natural features of Devil's Den, Big Round Top, Plum Run, and the historic Slyder Farm, were used to interpret "man's impact on and relationship to his environment." The Park Service conducted environmental education programs for the local schools and used the recently acquired Little Round Top Museum for the new Environmental Center. Park historians contacted school superintendents to promote visitation to the battlefield to learn about deer, pheasants, Native Americans, and geological and ecological features. Park officials noted that Gettysburg was not "just a battlefield," but offered a diversity of educational opportunities.[9]

In the years following the Civil War Centennial, Park Service management broadened the uses of the battlefield and in doing so redefined both the agency's understanding and the public's expectations of a national military park. To be sure, Gettysburg's enabling legislation clearly defined the battlefield's purpose: to preserve the lands affiliated with the three-day battle. Now, Gettysburg's administrators promoted a multi-use landscape that included exploring its environmental features and encouraging recreational activities. Certainly none of these activities were compatible with the primary reason for the battlefield's establishment as a national military park. Neither the Gettysburg Battlefield Memorial Association nor the War Department championed the environmental or ecological facets of places where Union and Confederate soldiers once battled. Now Park Service superintendents sought to create an impression that blended historical authenticity with entertainment. One Park Service official declared, "Let's really have concern for the visitor and let's really give him the 'time of his life.'"[10]

One method of providing the visitor with the "time of his life" included the advancement of the interpretive programming. For decades, the self-guided auto tour had been the park's primary educational tool. Simply driving through the battlefield, reading the occasional tablet or marker, and perhaps intermittent walks on the fields, instilled a passive learning experience. The park ranger's role to stimulate the educational experience remained minimal, if not nonexistent. Beginning in the 1970s, however, rangers started to take a more proactive role in shaping the visitors' experiences and premiered a series of interpretive programs. Rangers now became a vehicle to educate the visitor on the battle, sparking a deeper appreciation for the site, while also creating a participatory experience.

Meanwhile, academic and professional historians worked to broaden the dominant historical narrative to include the roles of women and minorities. Popularly termed "social history," this approach sought to challenge the consensus history, often the white-man's history, and write history "from below." This new trend produced a historical narrative far more dynamic, diverse, complicated, and, of course, accurate. The impact of social history could be seen at the nation's Civil War sites. Gettysburg likewise developed interpretive programs that explored not only the battle, but also the impact on the civilians and its aftermath. Other parks across the country also broadened their programming, which slowly breeched the entrenched reconciliationist narrative. At Petersburg, for example, park rangers offered programs on the role of the United States Colored Troops at the battle.[11]

By the early 1970s, the new interpretive programs at Gettysburg fell under three principal themes: "The Man Lincoln," "The Men Who Fought," and "The Folks Who Stayed Home." A twenty-minute guided walk in the Soldiers' National Cemetery discussed the impact of Lincoln's Gettysburg Address. Park rangers recounted soldiers' experiences in both first-person and third-person programs in "The Men Who Fought." Rangers conducted tours that explored Pickett's Charge, Little Round Top, Devil's Den, the Valley of Death, and the first day's fighting. The frequency of the programs reflected the popularity of particular aspects of the battle and the promotion of the "High Water Mark" narrative: the Pickett's Charge tour was presented seven times daily. Other programs were offered less frequently. The account of the fighting on July 1, the opening day of the battle, remained poorly interpreted. One reason, according to park officials, was because the terrain was "not as scenic as Little Round Top" and the narrative "not particularly exciting."[12]

First-person narration represented a new trend in the National Park Service. During Hartzog's administration, the agency broadened its interpretive programs to include "living-history" presentations. Delivered in first-person, interpreters dressed in period costume and assumed a personality to convey the message. By the mid-1970s, over 100 parks offered living-history programs. At Gettysburg, first-person was used to educate visitors about Civil War soldiers. During the summer, after visitors viewed the cyclorama, a ranger would escort them to the nearby Brian farm for the "Civil War Soldier" program. This program not only offered a demonstration on weapons and uniforms, but also explored the life of 1860s Americans. To authenticate the image of a soldier, male interpreters were instructed to chew tobacco, go barefoot, and not shave. The men wore Union uniforms equipped with a "distinctive aroma" that complemented their "authentic" appearance. Crowds of up to 200 gathered around the fence at the Brian farm to listen to the living historian explain the life of "Billy Yank." During the summer of 1969, for example, nearly 108,000 visitors attended the "Civil War Soldier" demonstration. Its popularity encouraged the development of two additional living-history programs, "Civil War Cavalryman" and "Women in the Crises," which debuted during the summer of 1972.[13]

"The Folks Who Stayed Home" offered an interpretive story beyond the soldiers and fighting. The "Women in the War" living-history program (originally titled "Women in the Crises"), explored how women coped with the "heat, stench, pain, and sorrow" caused by the battle. Beginning in the summer of 1973, the historic Slyder farmstead was used as a living-history farm. Dressed in period costume, rangers demonstrated the daily workings of an 1863 Adams County farm in the program "Man and the Land at Gettysburg." This interpretation blended the battle narrative with the landscape and historic structures, presenting visitors with a tangible connection to the past and an immersive experience. Park brochures noted that the recreated farmstead offered an opportunity to "visualize the farms and farmers whose lives changed irrevocably during the battle of Gettysburg." Over 11,000 people visited the living-history farm in 1976.[14]

More than ever before, park rangers directly engaged visitors in the Gettysburg story. Moving beyond the previous methods of interpretation, namely the wayside exhibits and the audio stations, rangers were now helping visitors to better understand the battle. Arguably the most effective way of instilling this connection was living-history presentations. These programs gave visitors an impression, both visually and educationally, of the life of soldiers or civilians. Park staff submitted a critical evaluation of its interpretive programs at the end of the 1973 summer season. They concluded the programs were informative but lacked *interpretation* and provocation, the principal goals of NPS educational programs. The third-person programs failed to "provoke" the visitors or "change their lives or thought patterns." Moreover, the programs failed to take advantage of the battlefield's terrain, and instead mirrored classroom lectures. Officials championed the success of its living-history programs, and felt they most effectively *interpreted* the battle and the Civil War. One park official noted that these living-history programs "engaged visitors' thoughts and emotions; they provoked instead of just informing."[15]

Contemporary social issues correspondingly influenced the educational programming. Following the publication of Rachel Carson's *Silent Spring* in 1962, heightened concern for the environment became a social and political issue. Beginning in the 1970s, the federal government became proactive in regulating environmental policies. Through a bipartisan effort, Congress established April 22 as Earth Day. Reflective of an emerging environmental consciousness, approximately 20 million people participated in the nation's first Earth Day in 1970. In the same year, President Richard Nixon signed legislation to create the Clean Air Act and authorized the Environmental Protection Agency.[16]

In a natural alignment, the National Park Service, the protector of the nation's historic and cultural treasures, promoted environmental consciousness at its sites. Director Hartzog's administration championed environmental awareness, as seen in the establishment of Environmental Study Areas. In the summer of 1969, park historian Thomas Harrison supervised an "experiment in awareness" by inaugurating a series of new environmental programs at the park amphitheater. This evening program featured an environmental film, followed by a discussion on the natural environment. At the conclusion of the program, rangers were given the opportunity to "stump speak" on a myriad of environmental issues. A total of thirty-six programs were presented to 6,905 visitors. Here, too, larger societal concerns influenced the management of the Gettysburg battlefield and stood at odds with the primary reason for establishing the battlefield.[17]

The emergence of recreational uses of the battlefield and promotion of ecological and environmental features of the landscape helped to redefine the Gettysburg experience. Acceptance of the multi-functionality of the landscape underscored the transformation of Gettysburg from a *military park* into a *national park*. In the years following the Civil War Centennial, the Park Service struggled to adopt a stable, consistent philosophy for visitor use, land acquisition, and cultural and historic resource management. Short-term and long-range planning required the agency to adapt to changing circumstances within the community and evolving interpretive trends. Equally significant, for the first time in its history, the National Park Service at Gettysburg presented its management plans to the general public for a period of review. As a consequence, the agency opened a line of communication that allowed interested individuals to comment on the proposed changes to the battlefield. In this sense, the Park Service recognized a shared ownership with the American people; the agency acted as the steward for Gettysburg to hold the site in perpetuity for the American people.[18]

By the mid-1960s, two primary issues dominated long-term planning. First, the rapid increase in visitation led park officials to reevaluate how best to preserve the battlefield and its historic structures. The second issue, ironically, was the construction of a new visitor center. Discussions of a new visitor center represented clear inconsistencies in the Park Service's management philosophy. Plans for a new visitor center, a mere five years after the Neutra building opened, demonstrated the relative lack of national oversight and the significant amount of leeway local park officials had to dictate policy. Although local and regional National Park Service personnel had carefully selected Ziegler's Grove as the site for the visitor center, by the mid-1960s, management concluded that the building was not conveniently located.

In the wake of the centennial, the Park Service examined the inherent tensions between visitor access and protection of the resource. With the opening of the new visitor center in 1962 and the centrality of the Gettysburg Cyclorama, the "High Water Mark" remained the dominant interpretive theme. As a result, Cemetery Ridge, Ziegler's Grove, and the Angle endured a steady increase of automobile and foot traffic. In an effort to better preserve the historic landscape along Cemetery Ridge, minimizing motorized traffic became increasingly important. To accomplish this goal, park staff proposed to remove Hancock Avenue from the Pennsylvania Memorial north to the visitor center. They also proposed prohibiting automobile traffic from the battlefield during the summer season. Instead, visitors wanting to see the battlegrounds would board a concession-operated tour bus for an eleven-mile ride that included stops at ten key locations. "It is cars, not people," management indicated, "which congest roads and parking areas, such a system would increase the number of visitors who could visit the park without crowding or damaging the resource." Yet, in a final decision to allow easy visitor access to the battlefield, Hancock Avenue was not removed and automobiles remained on the park roads.[19]

Consideration of a new visitor center dominated management decisions. As noted, a principal reason why the Park Service selected Ziegler's Grove was because of its proximity to U.S. Route 15 and Steinwehr Avenue. Over 60 percent of traffic to Gettysburg now traveled along the east-west corridor of U.S. Route 30, which ran directly through the borough, taking visitors through the town's narrow streets and around the Lincoln Square. Such traffic congestion led Pennsylvania's Department of Transportation (Penn DOT) to propose a seven-mile U.S. Route 30 bypass north of Gettysburg. To capitalize on the traffic along Route 30, the Park Service recommend the construction of a visitor center on the northern edge of the battlefield. The plan for the new facility, predicated upon the building of the bypass, called for the purchase of approximately fifty acres near Barlow's Knoll, ground temporarily held by the Union Army's 11th Corps on July 1. In a May 1972 meeting, Penn DOT officials informed local political representatives and Park Service officials that the Route 30 bypass, estimated to cost $21 million, remained a low priority project. Undeterred, the following year, park officials selected the historic Cobean farm directly north of town and within proximity of the proposed location of the bypass as the most suitable site for the new visitor center. In May, A. W. Butterfield, the owner of the Cobean farm, announced his intention to sell his ninety-six acre farm.[20]

Meanwhile, the Park Service explored several short-term alternatives. One such improvement came with the acquisition of the Gettysburg National Museum along Taneytown Road. The Park Service had wanted to acquire the privately owned museum as early as the 1930s. Finally on August 18, 1971, the federal government secured the museum for a sum of $2,350,000. The purchase included 6.76 acres along Taneytown Road and Steinwehr Avenue, the museum building, and the popular Electric Map. The Rosensteel family donated its extensive artifact collection. On October 31, 1973, the National Park Service assumed daily operations.[21] Ultimately, the National Park Service made the Rosensteel museum, equipped with the artifact collection and Electric Map, its primary visitor center.

The Neutra building, now referred to as the cyclorama building, continued to house the Gettysburg Cyclorama, several dioramas, and orientation films. Here visitors could watch the MGM film "The Battle of Gettysburg," and beginning in 1969, they could also view the eleven-minute feature film "From These Honored Dead." Upon review, the agency's interpretive planner found this film to be "just-right," evoking the appropriate "mood and theme." No improvements to the existing interpretative displays were recommended. "No attempt will be made," Alan Kent, an interpretive planner noted, "to tell the story of that conflict from beginning to end." Instead, the facility presented several thematic displays on infantry, artillery, and cavalry. Still, in the wake of the Civil Rights Movement and the emergence of social history, the park continued to present a reconciliatory version of the war that ignored its complexities and consequences.[22]

The main interpretative tool remained the Gettysburg Cyclorama. Yet, by the mid-twentieth century, the 1880s painting stood as an anachronism to the modern mass cultural attractions that surrounded the battlefield. The acquisition of the Rosensteel facility led to an evaluation of the existing interpretive offerings. Upon review of the Cyclorama, an interpretive planner characterized the presentation as "anticlimactic" and "not very exciting or dramatic." The cyclorama painting itself no longer seemed an adequate interpretive or educational tool; park officials sought to "bring the painting to life" and to enhance the cyclorama experience by adding additional sensory features. Instead of the taped narration, a "live performer" told the story of Pickett's Charge, as had been done when the painting was privately owned. This enhanced presentation, as planned, would "leave visitors literally limp and has no ands, buts or thereafters." Park officials proposed to modernize the Electric Map in a similar fashion, providing for a "shorter, more punchy and more dramatic" presentation. Though the dramatic overhaul of the cyclorama and Electric Map did not come to fruition, the planning underscores an evolving debate on how best to educate the battlefield's visitors, and of more contemporary concern, how to engage them in the narrative and landscape.[23]

Plans for a new visitor center north of town progressed and unleashed a firestorm of controversy within the local community, often centering on economic investments and business interests. Commercial establishments had proliferated along roads adjacent to the current visitor center, particularly along Steinwehr Avenue. Quite simply, businessmen were concerned about the adverse impact on their business if the existing visitor center closed and traffic concentrated at the new museum north of town. This debate illustrated intrinsic tensions between the Park Service's management plans and the desires of the local community. Paul Armstead, Vice President of the Fudge Kitchen, located on Baltimore Street, voiced his objections in a letter to the National Park Service's director. "With the building of a new Visitor Center," Armstead contended, "visitors have virtually no access to the town and its merchants who depend so heavily on their traffic." Businessmen who stood to profit from the proximity of the existing visitor center were not the only ones who remained skeptical of the park's ambitious proposal. Other local residents expressed similar concerns as years of resentment toward the National Park Service came to the forefront. One lifelong Gettysburg resident informed the superintendent, "I have seen a lot of poor management and bad decisions by park officials. Each time a new superintendent and new historians come in we get more poor management and more bad decisions." Based on a survey conducted by the Gettysburg Area Chamber of Commerce, 80 percent opposed the proposal for a new facility.[24]

Adams County commissioners led the way in taking steps to oppose the plan; they filed a suit in the U.S. Middle District Court on December 24, 1974, to prevent the federal government from acquiring the Cobean tract. Commissioner Harry Biesecker reminded residents that the Park Service had only recently built a million dollar facility, and argued the current economic crisis did not justify such an unnecessary expense. Reinforcing the commissioners' arguments, however, was a simple concern for economic reality: federal property was not taxable and would not contribute to the local tax base. Judge William J. Nealon ruled against the commissioners' claim on January 30, 1975, stating that since the Cobean farm was within the fixed boundary of Gettysburg National Military Park, the National Park Service could purchase the property. And the NPS did, within an hour of the ruling.[25]

In the midst of debate to relocate the visitor center and the increased tensions with the local business community, the nation's attention turned to the ongoing "Second Battle of Gettysburg." Hindered by economic constraints, inadequate or non-existent zoning regulations in Adams County, and a profit-oriented business community, historic lands fell victim to the construction of hotels, gas stations, fast food restaurants, and an assortment of tourist venues. Certainly this mass-marketing was not new; local residents and entrepreneurs had promoted Gettysburg as a tourist destination immediately after the armies retreated from the fields in July 1863. And, as Jim Weeks has argued, such purposeful commercialization of Gettysburg contributed to its central place in American history and culture.[26]

The war against commercialization and profiteering crystallized in September 1970 when Thomas Ottenstein, a Maryland attorney and developer, proposed to build a 307-foot observation tower near the battlefield. This "classroom in the sky" was to offer visitors a bird's eye view of the battlefield while interpreters presented an audio-visual presentation on the battle. Ottenstein estimated that his million-dollar investment would attract 700,000 visitors annually. Of primary concern was the tower's commanding size. Compared to the War Department's observation towers at a mere 75 feet high, the 307-foot tower would dominate the landscape. Indeed, the "space needle" would stand taller than any other building in Gettysburg, taller than the Statue of Liberty or the U.S Capitol in Washington.[27]

The debate over the National Tower polarized the two sides: those favoring scenic integrity and historic preservation against those championing economic interests. The National Park Service, the Gettysburg Battlefield Preservation Association, Gettysburg's Civil War Round Table, the Pennsylvania Historical Association, and the Lincoln Fellowship all voiced their opposition. The secretary of the interior and the director of the National Park Service declared that the tower would destroy the "integrity" of the battlefield. Secretary Rogers Morton postulated that, "The tower will wholly dominate this historic scene and may well constitute one of the most damaging single intrusions ever visited upon a comparable site of American history." Local residents, meanwhile, formed the "Concerned Citizens of Adams County for a Quality Environment" and opposed the tower on the grounds that it constituted "visual pollution."[28]

Ottenstein easily sold his idea to the local government by arguing on economic grounds. He emphasized the National Tower would support the borough's economic base with revenue from the annual 10 percent admissions tax; in contrast, when the federal government acquired properties, the land was removed from the local tax rolls. This approach worked. Mayor William Weaver and the Gettysburg borough enthusiastically supported the tower, eager to receive the estimated tax return of $500,000 within ten years. Evidently poorly informed of the significance of the events of July 1863, Commissioner Biesecker stated, "we're a small county with not much to boast about but this thing is beautiful. It's like someone came in here and built a new Eiffel Tower, right here in Adams County."[29]

Yet without zoning regulations in Adams County, even the federal government was powerless to stop the construction of the "new Eiffel Tower." Ottenstein initially wanted to build the tower in Colt Park, a residential community located on a sector of the field of Pickett's Charge. Realizing it could not prevent the tower's construction, the Park Service decided to at least minimize its impact by quietly proposing a less historically significant location.

NPS officials and representatives recommended a site bordering the Soldiers' National Cemetery along the Baltimore Pike. On July 2, 1971, both parties agreed to a land exchange. This agreement specified that Ottenstein would cease construction in Colt Park and within five years donate that tract of land to the National Park Service. Ottenstein further agreed to donate 5 percent of the tower's taxable income to a nonprofit preservation organization. In exchange, the federal government granted Ottenstein a twenty-two foot unrestricted right-of-way across its property. After months of firm opposition, the agency's acquiescence to the tower seemed surprising to most, including local park staff, who had played a minimal role in the details of the land exchange. All in all, the National Park Service failed to provide a consistent stance on the tower's construction between the national and local offices. Voicing displeasure with the seeming hypocrisy, Superintendent Schober declared it "unethical to do an about-face and come out supporting the tower after publicly denouncing it for more than a year."[30]

The National Tower opened on July 29, 1974, immediately becoming part of the market culture of Gettysburg. In its opening week, Ottenstein reported approximately 30,000 visitors. Still, critics bitterly complained that Ottenstein, with his 307-foot steel monstrosity, was financially benefitting from the battle's casualties. Detractors characterized him as a crass profiteer and labeled the tower the "cash register in the sky." With a nod toward the Gettysburg Address, the *New York Times* offered: "One score and eighteen months ago, Thomas R. Ottenstein, a wealthy Washington news dealer and real estate developer, brought forth on this hallowed ground the massive concrete footings of a new tourist observation tower, dedicated to the proposition that all men among the millions of persons who visit this historic Civil War battlefield every year should see it better from the air—at $1.35 a ticket."[31]

Commercialization persisted and intruded on the battlefield from many directions. In an effort to restrain this increasing commercial blight, the Park Service concentrated much of its land acquisition efforts to purchase tracts along the roads leading into town. On April 5, 1974, the federal government purchased the 43.04-acre Fantasyland amusement park, once a vital component of the family touring experience at Gettysburg. Under the provisions of the agreement, A. Kenneth Dick, Fantasyland's owner, would continue to operate the site while leasing it from the government for ten years. This allowed Dick to continue to pay county, township, and school taxes. One year later, the Park Service purchased the 22-acre Peace Light Inn, located on Mummasburg Road, along the battlefield's northern boundary.[32]

Certainly the acquisition of non-historic tracts remained a principal goal, yet economic constraints and practicality forced the Park Service to explore more economically feasible means to protect the battlefield from commercial establishments. By the 1970s, Steinwehr Avenue and Baltimore Pike had become a hodgepodge of tourist attractions, complete with souvenir shops, hotels, restaurants, and private museums. Located directly across from the visitor center and cyclorama center, Steinwehr Avenue, which bisects the fields of Pickett's Charge, in particular drew a tremendous amount of criticism for its overdeveloped and zealous commercialization. Unable to contain the perpetual growth of profiteering businesses, the National Park Service adopted a landscape management program, termed "tree screening." Workers planted seedlings or mature trees to conceal these intrusions. In theory, this practice seemed incongruous with the agency's landscape philosophy to generate historically accurate viewsheds. The tree screenings, however, created a visual partition between the battlefield purity and the market sprawl, which ensured that visitors recognized the boundary of the sanctified and commercial landscape.[33]

Much of the commercial development was the result of haphazard, if not nonexistent, historic preservation policies. In the late 1960s and early 1970s, changes in historic preservation legislation and philosophy, both at the federal and state levels, influenced future preservation efforts on the battlefield. First, in 1966, Gettysburg National Military Park was placed on the National Register of Historic Places with the passage of the National Historic Preservation Act. While the battlefield had received federal recognition and protection since its enabling legislation in 1895, the borough of Gettysburg did not have status as a historic site. As a result, residents and business owners made structural changes to buildings in historically significant areas with little or no state or federal oversight. In 1972, the Commonwealth of Pennsylvania recognized the borough as a historic district. One year after the National Tower opened and after years of development around the battlefield boundary, Adams County finally implemented zoning restrictions. More significantly, although the battlefield had been listed on the National Register in 1966, no documentation defined its significant features or stipulated preservation practices. Finally, on March 18, 1975, the Gettysburg Battlefield Historic District (GBHD), which incorporated approximately 11,000 acres of the battle action area, including much of the surrounding townships, was added to the National Register of Historic Places.[34]

The National Tower crystallized the debates over historic preservation at Gettysburg and stood as a physical symbol of commercialization. The establishment of the Gettysburg Battlefield Historic District delineated more clearly the boundaries between the battlefield's hallowed ground and land acceptable for development. Elsewhere, the perpetual battle against modern intrusions remained ominous. Park Service officials and preservationists at Manassas National Battlefield Park fought continual urban sprawl in northern

Virginia. In *Battling for Manassas,* Joan Zenzen recounts the ongoing struggle to preserve Manassas since its inclusion as a national park in 1940. While
tensions escalated in Gettysburg over the National Tower, the Marriot Corpo-
ration proposed the construction of a theme park alongside the Manassas battlefield. As with Gettysburg, the National Park Service had minimal influence
on development outside the federal boundary. Officially, the agency assumed a
neutral stance on the Marriot proposal. After a congressional inquiry into the
possible impact on the battlefield and subsequent concerns over the projected
environmental impact, Marriott abandoned the proposal.[35]

Certainly, controversies over preservation and land use at Manassas
stemmed from the battlefield's close proximity to Washington, D.C., and
prime location in the burgeoning area of northern Virginia. Though the Marriott theme park proposal did not come to fruition, future plans forced the
Park Service to reexamine its stance on preservation of the battlefield and the
surrounding area. In the years following World War II, an ever-increasing dis-
approval with overt commercialization of the nation's historic sites emerged.
As more Americans accepted a shared interest in the protection and future
of these battlefields, plans for incompatible uses for the sanctified landscapes
drew more scrutiny. In a *Detroit Free Press* article, "The Hucksters Close in
on Gettysburg's Grandeur," preeminent Civil War historian Bruce Catton
summed up critics' feelings on the tower, writing, "The tower is a damned outrage . . . I only hope that someday people will come to their senses and remove
the tower." Less than three decades later, efforts to recover the battlefield's
historic integrity would see Catton's desire realized.[36]

CHAPTER 8

So Conceived and So Dedicated: Balancing Preservation and Visitor Access, 1976–1988

The discord over the opening of the Gettysburg National Tower in July 1974 illustrated a growing concern for unacceptable development on or near hallowed battle grounds. Comparable objections against the proposal for a theme park adjacent to Manassas National Battlefield Park further demonstrated a widespread opposition to defilement of the nation's battlefields. Americans began to assume a more proactive role in the fate and protection of the grounds where so many men had fought and died. The preservationist canon that emerged guided future decisions on battlefield preservation, development, and compatible uses of the grounds. At Gettysburg, the Park Service continued to struggle to reconcile the inevitable tension between protecting the historic resource, the battlefield and its structures, and allowing for visitor use. This debate manifested itself in a proposal to modify visitor access to Devil's Den, one of the most popular sites on the battlefield.

The fading enthusiasm for the Civil War Centennial helped to redefine Gettysburg's place in contemporary culture and American memory. Tourists, at the time of the Cold War, visited the nation's historic sites, such as Gettysburg, as an expression of civic faith. The heightened patriotic fervor produced a culture of heritage pilgrims who sought to reaffirm American loyalty and explore the nation's history. By the early 1970s, however, these civic pilgrimages had declined. For years Gettysburg had been used by a myriad of orators, offering emotional appeals for a variety of causes—intervention into World War II, enduring commitment to destroy Nazism, cautionary tales of a growing military industrial complex, or pleas for racial equality and social unity. In the years following the centennial, however, Americans no longer came to Gettysburg as a testament to patriotic faith. "Once the celebratory national

The Gettysburg National Tower, which opened in July 1974,
crystallized the debate over historic preservation and commercialization. Statue to General George G. Meade in the foreground.

narrative ended," Jim Weeks declares, "Gettysburg ceased its role as a shrine
offering inspiration and symbolic importance for national progress." Visitation statistics reflect the larger trend in the decrease of civic pilgrimages at
the time of the nation's bicentennial. In 1978, Gettysburg received 1.56 million
visitors and the following year recorded slightly over 1 million, representing
an approximate 32 percent reduction. In part by the National Park Service's
management, Gettysburg now became a site to be experienced. Yet Americans retained a fervent and emotional connection to this hallowed ground,
and regularly articulated opinions on how the battlefield should be preserved,
used, and managed.[1]

The summer of 1976 witnessed one of the last great patriotic expressions
at Gettysburg. Timing was opportune. In the wake of widespread disillusion-

ment with the Vietnam War and Watergate, these patriotic celebrations bolstered Americans' sense of national identity and a purposeful historical narrative. Here, too, the National Park Service, both at a national and regional level, actively promoted this patriotic sentiment. Bicentennial events occurred across the country in 1975 and 1976. The national parks, Gettysburg included, hosted a variety of commemorative and celebratory activities. Chester Brooks, a regional director of the NPS, impressed upon superintendents that the Park Service needed to "enhance the heritage of each citizen we contact." Similarly, the Commonwealth of Pennsylvania capitalized on the state's role in two critical events in American history: the signing of the Declaration of Independence in Philadelphia in July 1776 and the battle at Gettysburg in July 1863. The state promoted tourism in 1976 for the 200th anniversary of "Our Glorious Nation" and the 113th anniversary of the "Battle That Saved Our Nation."[2]

The bicentennial events underscored the often-unwavering acceptance of the "heritage syndrome." Michael Kammen identifies this sentiment as "an impulse to remember what is attractive or flattering and to ignore all the rest." Patriotic zeal pervaded Gettysburg during the summer of 1976. In fact, bicentennial celebrations were nearly as elaborate as the Civil War Centennial held thirteen years earlier. John Earnst, who arrived as the battlefield's new superintendent in August 1974, reported, "our participation in Bicentennial activities was surprisingly extensive for a 'non-Bicentennial' park." Activities kicked off in the summer of 1975 with the raising of America's bicentennial flag and a display of traveling exhibits. The following summer, Gettysburg hosted several special bicentennial performances. In May, Gettysburg sponsored a film festival featuring films on revolutionary sites within the national park system. Two national traveling plays, "We've Come Back for a Little Look Around" and "People of '76," depicting historical figures of the American Revolution, were performed at Gettysburg. In addition to the traveling shows, the park produced a series of bicentennial vignettes. Described as "light-hearted playlets," these vignettes celebrated the "courage and character of America." During the summer of 1976, park staff performed "The Carol of Courage" on 464 occasions to nearly 20,000 people. Certainly the commemorations, or more appropriately celebrations, of the bicentennial represented a clear manifestation of the "heritage syndrome." In 1976, Gettysburg National Military Park recorded 1.77 million visitors.[3]

While the battlefield's role as a place for patriotic expression declined in the years following the Civil War Centennial, Americans continued to retain a strong affinity for Gettysburg and its meanings. Locally, Gettysburg National Military Park experienced what was now becoming a regular change in superintendents, which often resulted in inconsistent and sometimes conflicting management philosophies. Tensions between park management and the local community remained volatile. Commenting on the considerable leeway given to park officials and the lack of a stable, consistent management philosophy, one local resident summarized, "What one administration thinks should be done one way, another administration will probably think should be done differently." Under John Earnst the park produced a series of planning documents in order to stabilize management objectives.[4]

As the Park Service finalized its management plans, it actively engaged the public in the planning process. Many local concerns centered around plans to relocate the visitor center. Some expressed fears that any relocation would bring financial calamity to local establishments on Steinwehr Avenue and Baltimore Street, leaving only "skeletons" in the town's business district. Others believed the cost incurred from building a new facility would be an "extravagant waste of public funds," since the agency had opened a million dollar facility in 1962. These ongoing planning initiatives brought resentment of the agency's management to the forefront. One angered resident noted, "The National Park Service is a bigger threat to the town of Gettysburg than the Confederate Army ever was!"[5] Though the agency continued to advance a new visitor center as a key component to its planning documents through the late 1970s and early 1980s, once Pennsylvania's Department of Transportation nixed the Route 30 bypass proposal, the Park Service abandoned its plans to build a new visitor center.

Auto tourism had been an integral part of touring the national parks for decades. Stephen Mather, the agency's first director, actively promoted the usage of automobiles in the pristine, virgin landscapes. "Taking everything into consideration," Mather noted, "No policy of national park management has yielded more thoroughly gratifying results than that which guided the admission of motor-driven vehicles to the use of the roads of all of the parks." At Gettysburg, the policy on vehicular use in the Soldiers' National Cemetery had evolved through the decades. James McConaghie, the park's first superintendent, had actively promoted visitor access and usability, and in the late 1930s, the cemetery gates were widened to accommodate more automobiles and also buses. Establishing an accessible battlefield was an essential component of the agency's larger promotion of tourism. In 1941, Superintendent James Walter Coleman declared the Park Service to be in the tourist business.[6]

Beginning in the late 1970s, park management became more sensitive to the impact that the increasing automobile and pedestrian traffic had on the battlefield's historic landscape, and rightfully so. Visitation peaked during the Civil War Centennial with over 2 million visitors. Thereafter, visitation declined, but still the battlefield received over 1 million visitors annually. Consequently, park officials began to explore means to alleviate the pressures on the landscape posed by excessive automobile traffic. Specifically, the Park Service recommended closing the Soldiers' National Cemetery to vehicular traffic. The rationale behind the recommendation stemmed from the seemingly improper use of automobiles on hallowed ground. This proposal was not new, however. In 1942, then Superintendent Coleman recommended that the park consider eliminating vehicle traffic from the cemetery. Now, thirty years later, Earnst argued that prohibiting vehicles in the cemetery would engender a "solemn environment" befitting to the soldiers buried there. He reasoned, "How does a visitor in a car or bus driving through this 'hallowed ground' develop any sense of respect or awe for the deeds of the dead soldiers and the words of President Lincoln?" Respect for the sacrifices of the Union soldiers buried there or for the elegant power of Lincoln's dedication address could not be obtained by driving leisurely through the cemetery. Respect and awe came only by walking through the consecrated grounds.[7]

Unsurprisingly, the proposal brought immediate opposition from the community. Full vehicle access in the cemetery had allowed locals to use the cemetery as a short cut between Taneytown Road and Baltimore Pike, to avoid the often-congested Steinwehr Avenue. In response to the local reaction, Earnst compromised and decided to close only the upper drive. Visitors desiring to see the cemetery would enter at Taneytown Road and proceed along the lower drive, exiting on the Baltimore Pike. While this compromise was offered as an olive branch, the superintendent warned that if the "appropriate atmosphere does not prevail," the cemetery would be closed to all vehicular traffic. Similar to the debates about a visitor center north of town and the construction of a chronological tour, discussion of curtailing vehicle traffic in the cemetery once again demonstrated the power of local opposition to the Park Service's initiatives. Local interests persisted in their utilitarian view of the battlefield: that it served to provide both economic gain and simple convenience. Often self-interested agendas prevailed, and it became clear that any new visions for the battlefield would likely be met with strong opposition, even hostility.[8]

While auto tourism was encouraged, the agency remained unable to develop a consistent policy toward visitor access. High visitation led Earnst to explore the best methods to protect the historical resource while simultaneously providing access to the battlefield. These discussions were not new. Immediately following the Civil War Centennial, staff looked at means to protect the battlefield and its resources from "intensive visitor use." Places of particular concern included Devil's Den, Little Round Top, the Pennsylvania Memorial, and the Soldiers' National Cemetery. In 1966, the park first proposed developing a mass transit system to serve visitors and to "relieve the park from excessive automobile traffic." Years later, officials went a step farther and proposed a ban of automobiles during the peak visitation season. Through the mid-1970s, management continued to advocate a concession-operated tour at peak season as a means to control and limit traffic.[9]

Management now focused its concerns on Devil's Den, one of the battlefield's most popular sites for its historical significance, panoramic vista, and unique geological features. Consistent with its assessment of vehicular traffic in the Soldiers' National Cemetery, staff concluded that high visitor use in Devil's Den was steadily damaging the resource. To alleviate pressure and to better protect the historic scene, the park recommended removing all modernized features of visitor access to include the roads, parking lot, and the 1930s comfort station. The rationale to prohibit vehicle traffic in Devil's Den centered on efforts to restore the area's "historical integrity." Automobiles, quite simply, were incongruent with the prevailing atmosphere of a sanctified landscape. The site's historical integrity could only be retained through the elimination of modern intrusions and automobile traffic. "By eliminating the roadway, with its lumbering cars and buses," Earnst reasoned, "the massive boulders will look all the more majestic and forbidding when not dwarfed by the confusion brought into its very heart by an intrusive belt of asphalt."[10]

Reclaiming the historical integrity of Devil's Den, however, required more than eliminating automobile traffic. In order to recapture the historic scene, while at the same time permitting visitor accessibility, a new roadway, or bypass, was proposed around the western boundary of Devil's Den. Planners first recommended the bypass in 1977, and as they revised the proposal, the specifics of the bypass took different forms. As finally decided, the new road would follow the tracings of the abandoned nineteenth century electric trolley bed that ran from Brooke Avenue across Plum Run to the western slope of Big Round Top.[11]

This proposal intended to meet three key objectives: scenic purity, historic restoration, and visitor safety. The proposal to create a historic vista took its origins from the first Park Service administrations. Beginning in the 1930s, then Superintendent James McConaghie succeeded in removing non-historic features, including post and pipe fencing, as well as telephone wires along the Chambersburg Pike. The second objective, creating historic viewsheds, also dated to early Park Service practices. In 1940, the park implemented its first cutting of non-historic woodlots, which on a small-scale had continued through subsequent years. In fact, one of the first areas to be restored to its 1863 historical appearance was along the western slope of Little Round Top, facing Devil's Den. Removal of non-historic woodlots, however, resulted in an unfortunate by-product: vehicle traffic on Crawford Avenue and Devil's Den became visually intrusive. The final justification was more practical. Upon surveying the road conditions in Devil's Den, especially Sickles Avenue, engineers discovered that the extreme curves and grades did not meet minimum transportation standards for buses.[12]

As previously noted, this was not the first time the park sought to balance its preservation philosophy with its mission to provide visitor access. When the Devil's Den bypass was first introduced in 1977, the public responded unfavorably. Local opposition continued to gain momentum in the following decade. Speaking on the philosophical conflict between preservation and visitor access, one Gettysburg resident wrote the superintendent, stating, "if you wish to have visitors you must make it convenient for them. This means roads and cars that intrude on the historic scene." At the grassroots level, the Licensed Battlefield Guides and other concerned citizens formed the Devil's Den Access Committee. On September 12, 1988, standing before local press and a small gathering of witnesses in Devil's Den, the citizen's group and a state representative presented U.S. Congressman William Goodling with approximately 11,000 signatures opposing the changes to Devil's Den. Earnst, however, remained steadfast in his vision and reaffirmed that the proposed changes were necessary to preserve the historic landscape. He reminded detractors that the Park Service has "an obligation to preserve the park for infinity."[13]

Inherently, Earnst's proposal reflected inconsistencies in the agency's preservation mission. Certainly limiting vehicular access in Devil's Den would have achieved the objective of better protecting its historic landscape. Earnst effectively counteracted any preservation benefit, however, with the proposition to construct a new road on theretofore undisturbed historic terrain. A new road along the western side of Devil's Den would offset any preservation advantages of closing the den to vehicular traffic. Civil War historian William Marvel noted these inconsistencies, writing, "Must the Park Service step in and turn its own hand to destruction?" He argued, "That bypass road will do nothing but disturb another yet untouched portion of our most precious National Park." The bypass proposal failed to gain consensus from park staff as well. Park historian Kathy Georg voiced her opposition to the proposed construction, indicating such a roadway would "irretrievably alter the topography of the Gettysburg battlefield."[14]

As a result of his commitment to a flawed preservation plan, Earnst's popularity precipitously declined, both within the community and among his staff. In late August, after fourteen years of service at Gettysburg, Earnst announced his transfer to North Cascades National Park in Washington State. To succeed him, the National Park Service named Daniel R. Kuehn, a twenty-year veteran of the agency. Shortly after arriving, Kuehn, aware of the controversy surrounding the Devil's Den plan, promised to review the proposal. Even though Earnst and Regional Director James W. Coleman, Jr., son of the Gettysburg superintendent in the 1940s, had approved the plan, the Park Service had failed to secure the necessary funding. Subsequently, in early February 1989, much to the delight of many, Kuehn announced that Devil's Den would remain open to vehicle traffic. In order to protect this historic landscape and yet still provide access to the area, Kuehn decided to remove Devil's Den as a designated stop from the auto tour. Interested visitors could continue to enter the area from Warren Avenue.[15]

The proposal to eliminate vehicular traffic from Devil's Den and the subsequent decision to remove the site as a stop on the driving tour demonstrated the inevitable tensions between two conflicting goals: preserving the historic resource and providing visitor access. Yet, each time the park considered proposals to moderate visitor access—prohibiting automobiles on the battlefield in the peak summer season, regulating traffic on Cemetery Ridge, or eliminating traffic from the Soldiers' National Cemetery—the agency ultimately decided in favor of visitor convenience and accessibility. As important, this episode further demonstrated two interrelated themes of the National Park Service's stewardship. First, the agency's preservation philosophies remained inconsistent, both at a national and local level. Without the guidance of standardized philosophy, local managers remained the sole decision makers on preservation matters at their parks. This discretion by site managers underscored the second theme. Preservation decisions often did not fall within the parameters of prevailing academic practices, but were conceived and implemented by individuals. The power of one person, in this instance the park superintendent, defined preservation and accessibility issues. Consequently, historic preservation policies and academic philosophies aside, the practices at Gettysburg were often at the whim of each superintendent. Also of significance, the Devil's Den case demonstrated the contentious relationship between park management and the local community. Often the Park Service backed down from ideas and acquiesced to the demands of local interests.[16]

The disagreement between the Park Service and area residents over the management of Gettysburg illustrated the transition of the battlefield from its initial purpose as a site for reconciliation, to a landscape of patriotic commemoration, and ultimately into a memorial of shared national ownership. Twentieth-century associations to the battlefield placed a clear emphasis on patriotism and civic pilgrimages. Honoring the deeds of the soldiers who fought at Gettysburg and the timeless sentiment to Lincoln's Gettysburg Address, Americans, as well as the National Park Service, continued to champion Gettysburg as a site of sectional reconciliation. In doing so, they advanced a consensus account of the Civil War, rooted in the reconciliationist language of the late nineteenth century, devoid of the divisiveness and horrors of the 1860s. During World War II, speakers stood on the battlefield and encouraged Americans to join the fight against Germany and Japan. In the early 1960s, northern and southern representatives stood on the same fields to urge full equality for all Americans in the hope of realizing Abraham Lincoln's vision of a "new birth of freedom." The 1976 bicentennial celebration would effectively end the battlefield's usage as a site of national heritage. Americans would no longer congregate on these fields to find inspiration and encouragement in the deeds and acts of their Civil War forefathers. In the final decades of the twentieth century, Americans nationwide reengaged their association to Gettysburg and began to take a proactive interest in changes to the battlefield. As the nation moved toward the battle's 125th anniversary, Americans began to lay claim to the battlefield and regularly voiced their opinions on how it should be shaped.

As part of the planning process of the late 1970s and early 1980s, park officials reevaluated their practices in managing the site's 3,800 acres. Small-scale rehabilitation work continued. Admittedly, creating the 1863 appearance remained an ambitious task. In 1981, the park produced a Natural Resources Management Plan, which provided guidelines to landscape rehabilitation and maintenance. In the 1930s, then Superintendent McConaghie noted the ever-evolving nature of the battlefield, where he envisioned a landscape that moved "to a degree with the times." Now, five decades later, management offered a comparable vision, noting that the battlefield's natural features "are not static but are dynamic and constantly changing." Establishing a clear vision on how to manage the park's acreage, the objective became "to restore, maintain, and perpetuate as closely as possible the historic scene and character that existed on this battlefield in July of 1863." The plan also addressed the long-held propensity for a multiuse landscape. Stating that Gettysburg National Military Park was "not created for its natural significance," but "for its place in history," planners affirmed as the primary goal to "recreate and perpetuate the 1863 scene."[17]

During the Great Depression, Civilian Conservation Corps workers had removed non-historic post and pipe fencing from the battlegrounds. By the early 1980s, twenty miles of fencing, representing approximately 23 percent of the 1863 fences, had been restored. Historical fencing patterns contributed to the agency's mission of authenticity. In addition to serving as boundary markers for local farmers, fences impacted troop movements. In order to reasonably maintain farming patterns, the Park Service permitted farmers to use selected fields to plant corn, wheat, hay, or barley. As a result, this Special Use Permit (SUP) allowed the cultivation of approximately 1,400 acres of crop fields, which represented nearly 95 percent of the land in production at the time of the battle. The park also issued Agricultural Special Use Permits to provide for the pasturing of sheep, horses, and cattle. This, too, facilitated the objective of creating a "historic scene" and served as a cost effective method to maintain such large acreage.[18]

Yet the attempts to create and maintain a historical viewshed remained an elusive goal. Since the summer of 1940, several vista cuts to remove non-historic tree and shrub growth had been completed. Without a long-term management plan, however, the woodlots easily regenerated. This uncontrolled growth "obscures the historic scene," hindered interpretation of the battle, and impeded creation of the "character that existed in 1863." Now, planners recommended the removal of an additional 150 acres of non-historic vegetation. They also specified any future cuts must have a long-term maintenance program to assure these cleared areas retained their historic appearance. While taking proactive steps toward accurate vistas, management recognized limitations in achieving this objective. Modern development had already encroached upon the battle grounds from all directions. In order to provide visitors with a clear delineation between the modern, non-historic grounds and the historic battlefield, park officials continued to approve vegetative screening. This entailed planting tree screens of sixty to seventy-five feet wide.[19]

Widespread concern for the environment that emerged in the early 1970s impacted the administration and operation of the national parks, Gettysburg included. While he served as the director of the National Park Service, George Hartzog advocated that more recreational sites be included in the system and that parks initiate environmental programs. In 1979, Director William H. Whalen called for superintendents to "substantially" increase attention to environmental education. He indicated the primary objective of these environmental programs would be to encourage visitors to "appreciate more fully the natural, historic, and cultural values of the park system." In addition to the Environmental Study Area on Big Round Top and the environmentally focused campfire presentations, Gettysburg's staff also constructed a trail on Big Round Top, which included twenty-six stops to explore the area's natural resources.[20] In championing Gettysburg's natural features, however, Park Service actively redefined the meaning of a national military park. Certainly environmental awareness and the natural resources of Big Round Top were not in accordance with the battlefield's enabling statement or the earlier mission of the Gettysburg Battlefield Memorial Association and the War Department.

Meanwhile, park staff continued to offer engaging interpretive experiences. Using MISSION 66 funds, the first audio stations were installed at several locations on the battlefield. By 1980, a total of ten audio stations had been selectively placed to describe key actions of both the Union and Confederate armies. The living-history demonstrations continued to garner popular appeal and immersed spectators in the Civil War. Interested visitors could travel to the Granite Farm for a "rare opportunity for one to come face-to-face with the past."[21]

Still, one of the greatest shortcomings of the National Park Service was its incomplete relationship with its visitors. Simply stated, the agency had little understanding of the demographics of its visitors, or their expectations, satisfactions, or displeasures. Annually, park superintendents reported visitation totals and attendance on various interpretative programs, but these statistics failed to reveal any deeper analysis or understanding of park visitors. In the early 1980s, the National Park Service carried out a concerted effort to learn more about the millions of people who visited the nation's natural and cultural sites. In 1982, in order to accomplish this effort, the agency partnered with the University of Idaho to form the Cooperative Park Studies Unit.[22]

In July 1986, researchers from the Cooperative Park Studies Unit surveyed Gettysburg's visitors and their experiences while in the park. Researchers spent one week on the battlefield distributing questionnaires to visitors at eleven different sites. Following trends established during World War II, their findings revealed that the majority of visitors were families. Moreover, many were first-time visitors. The average visitor arrived in the early afternoon and spent three to six hours touring the park. Of those surveyed, over 80 percent had spent time in the visitor center, but only 60 percent went to the cyclorama center. When touring the battlefield, visitors generally stopped at the battle's significant sites, such as the Virginia Memorial, the Soldiers' National Cemetery, Little Round Top, Culp's Hill, and the Eternal Light Peace Memorial.[23]

Visitors found much to like about the battlefield and its presentation. Many responded favorably to the efforts to create an immersive experience and to present a landscape that mirrored the 1863 appearance. One visitor noted an appreciation for this touch of authenticity: "The stone and rail fences, stake and rider fences, lend a tremendous sense of historical flavor to the battlefield, as do the present historic buildings." Others expressed a scorn for the gaudy nearby commercial establishments. "The adjacent commercial strip distracts from the park," noted one visitor. Some lamented the visual intrusion created by the National Tower.[24]

Those surveyed also revealed a change in America's connection to the battle and the battlefield landscape. Americans traveled to Gettysburg for two purposes: education and enjoyment. Some visitors even offered suggestions on how the enjoyment, or pleasure, experience could be improved through the means of comfort amenities such as additional water fountains. One responder complained that their family "could not locate enough places on the tour to buy refreshments." The surveys revealed that fewer visitors now traveled to Gettysburg as an expression of patriotic faith. Instead, the new generation of visitors sought an immersive educational experience, or in some cases just an enjoyable time. This changing sentiment, however, was not unique only to Gettysburg. Visitor surveys in other national parks revealed a preference for recreation, entertainment, and, certainly, plentiful amenities. One visitor expressed displeasure at Everglades National Park because his family had to drive out of the park to find suitable groceries. One responder lamented the lack of comfortable chairs, not benches, at Colonial National Historic Park.[25]

The 125th anniversary demonstrated Gettysburg's transformation from a site of patriotic faith to a landscape to promote tourism and interaction with

Gettysburg's 125th anniversary, July 1988, emphasized a commemorative theme of "Let Us Have Peace." Approximately 60,000 spectators gathered for the battle reenactment between the Union soldiers, shown here, and the Confederates.

visitors. Borrowing a phrase from Union General U. S. Grant's 1868 presidential campaign, the 125th anniversary commemoration "Let Us Have Peace" presented a perfect theme for a battlefield and town that had recently been embroiled in controversy. For nearly two weeks programs included reenactments, living-history encampments, lectures, monument rededications, and concerts. Organizers promised "an action-packed calendar of events both educational and fun for the public." Approximately 60,000 spectators gathered at a private farmland south of the battlefield to watch the reenactment. The occasion provided visitors not only an opportunity to be a spectator, but also a chance to be a participant. Reenactors and vendors opened encampments for spectators to stroll through and interact with "soldiers." Visitors could also witness drills and marching maneuvers, learn about Civil War medicine at the "Sanitary Fair," or purchase an array of period products and souvenirs.[26]

Correspondingly, the National Park Service offered a range of interactive experiences. The living-history demonstrations, which became popular in the early 1970s, gave visitors a firsthand interpretation of Civil War life, as well as the life of local farmers. For the 125th, the park planned a three-day living-history encampment, with over 1,000 reenactors. Located near the Pennsylvania Monument, reenactors educated and entertained thousands of visitors with tactical maneuvers and weapons demonstrations. Curious tourists strolled through the encampments, listened to Civil War music, and chatted with the reenactors. These hands-on demonstrations proved popular; approximately 1,000 attended the July 1 demonstrations.[27]

Later that year, the 125th anniversary of the dedication of the Soldiers' National Cemetery witnessed the usual parades and speeches, demonstrating Americans' continual connection to the Gettysburg Address. As in previous years, the local community celebrated by recreating Lincoln's arrival and speech. James Gettys, a local resident, portrayed Lincoln, and with his entourage arrived at the rail station on Carlisle Street aboard a 1902 steam train, greeted by "David Wills" and Gettysburg's mayor, Frank Linn. They then proceeded to the Wills House where the "president" briefly addressed a crowd of spectators from the second-story window. After his brief statement, "Lincoln" rode on horseback to the Soldiers' National Cemetery as part of a ceremonial parade that included 2,000 reenactors. Approximately 15,000 gathered in the cemetery in a steady rain to listen to "Lincoln" recite the address. United States Supreme Court Chief Justice William H. Rehnquist delivered the keynote speech.[28]

CHAPTER 9

NOW WE ARE ENGAGED IN A GREAT CIVIL WAR: FINDING A VISION AMIDST A SEA OF TURMOIL, 1989–1997

Between 1989 and 1991 events around the globe rapidly changed the face of world affairs. The collapse of the Berlin Wall, the reunification of East Germany with West Germany, the beginning of free elections in former communist regimes in Eastern Europe, resignation of Mikhail Gorbachev, and the collapse of the Soviet Union lifted the "Iron Curtain" and ended the Cold War. For Americans who had lived under the looming threat of nuclear war, communist global expansion, and internal subversion at home, the end of the Cold War brought tranquility not enjoyed for decades. Domestically, however, Americans found themselves mired in controversy, the "civil war" of the era. Emerging in the late 1980s and reaching their crescendo in the mid-1990s, intense cultural, intellectual, moral, and philosophical divisions fractured the nation. Polarizing issues such as homosexuality, abortion, separation of church and state, censorship, and pornography engulfed the nation and divided Americans into factious groups. At the core of the debate over the nation's "culture wars" lay a fundamental understanding of national identity and history.[1]

Dissention over the national narrative took several forms. The National History Standards, developed over a two-year period at the National Center for History in the Schools at University of California at Los Angeles, immediately came into question. In a 1994 op-ed published in the *Wall Street Journal,* Lynne Cheney, former head of the National Endowment for the Humanities, criticized the standards for politicizing history. Titling the piece "The End of History," Cheney assailed the standards for seemingly undue attention on divisive issues like McCarthyism or the Ku Klux Klan and minimal consideration to national figures such as George Washington or Robert E. Lee. Writers of the standards, she asserted, reserved "their unqualified admiration for people, places, and events that are politically correct." Accusations of politicizing history climaxed in the early 1990s over the Smithsonian Institute's Air and Space Museum's proposal for the *Enola Gay* exhibition. As planned, the exhibit would explore the dropping of the two atomic bombs on Japan in August 1945. The Air Force Association and various veterans' groups led the opposition to the exhibit, arguing that the display overtly sympathized with the Japanese. Under intense political and social pressure, the Smithsonian cancelled the exhibit in January 1995. In each instance Americans manifested discomfort with challenges to traditional, consensus historical interpretations. A preference to selectively remember historical events—the valor of American GIs in World War II and not the implications of the dropping of the atomic weapons, for instance—demonstrated the pervasiveness of the "heritage syndrome."[2]

Elsewhere, managers charged with preserving the nation's historic sites battled against encroaching development and reoccurring capitalistic ventures. In an effort to capitalize on the popularization of education, in the fall of 1993 the Walt Disney Company announced plans for "Disney's America," a historic theme park to be built in Haymarket, Virginia. The proximity to the Manassas battlefield—less than five miles—unleashed a firestorm of nationwide criticism from historians, the Civil War community, and historic preservationists, the latter led by the National Trust for Historic Preservation. Nearly a year later, in the face of immense opposition, the Walt Disney Company abandoned the plan. National attention to the Disney proposal revitalized discussions concerning the purpose and preservation of national battlefields and what constituted acceptable developments near these hallowed grounds.[3]

As the nation moved through a period of cultural volatility, so, too, did Gettysburg National Military Park. Admittedly much of the turmoil in Adams County resulted from the Park Service's inability to provide consistency to its management of the Gettysburg battlefield. Increased sensitivities to perceived assaults on the traditional historical narrative brought closer scrutiny to those charged with managing and preserving the nation's historic sites. Meanwhile, popular culture, led by Hollywood movies and television productions, rejuvenated the "Civil War subculture." While these films and documentaries often portrayed a romanticized interpretation of combat, they nonetheless heightened popular interest in the war. *Glory*, featuring Denzel Washington and Matthew Broderick, premiered in 1989. This film captured the story of the 54th Massachusetts Infantry, an all-black regiment, and their heroic, but failed, effort to capture Battery Wagner in South Carolina. The following year, scores of Americans tuned in to PBS to watch Ken Burns' miniseries *The Civil War*. Narrated by David McCullough, and featuring Barbara Fields, Shelby Foote, Ed Bearss, and Stephen B. Oates, *The Civil War* became one of television's most watched programs. While historians proclaimed the series a "major contribution to how Americans perceive this central event of their history," some were equally as quick to take Burns to task for historical inaccuracies, questionable interpretations, and improper use of sources. Notwithstanding the nit-picking of some academics, Burns reached and captivated a far larger audience than the works of professional historians; nearly 14 million Americans watched the series.[4]

Gettysburg's popularity in American history and culture reached new heights with the release of the movie *Gettysburg* in 1993. Based on Michael Shaara's 1974 Pulitzer Prize–winning novel, *The Killer Angels*, Ron Maxwell's film introduced a new generation to the heroics of the Union and Confederate soldiers on the Pennsylvania farm fields. The success of *Gettysburg* contributed greatly to increased tourism. In 1993, for example, the battlefield recorded 1,485,853 visitors. In 1994, the year following the release of the film, 1,748,932 visitors were recorded. In the wake of the film's release, the park saw a 19 percent increase in visitation and 1994 marked the highest visitation since the centennial years.[5] While Gettysburg, James Longstreet, Joshua Chamberlain, and Lewis Armistead readily became household names, the Park Service now managed a landscape that drew even more national attention and acclaim. Management decisions no longer played out only within the boundaries of Adams County, but across the nation.

Undeniably the relationship between the American public and the battlefield stewards had changed considerably since its establishment in 1864. The battlefield's first two stewards, the Gettysburg Battlefield Memorial Association and later the War Department, managed the site with relatively minimal influence from outside. As a result, park commissioners held near exclusive power to administer the battlefield as they deemed appropriate. By the mid-twentieth century, however, management suffered increasingly from external factors, including fiscal considerations, the prevalent political climate, and expanded national media attention, holding sway over the future of the battlefield. Internal forces, namely the park superintendent and his staff, continued to define the Gettysburg experience. Between 1989 and 1994, three superintendents served at Gettysburg National Military Park. This frequency in management change further contributed an inability to establish, but more importantly implement, a consistent management philosophy. While popular with park staff and the community, principally for his resolution of the Devil's Den bypass controversy, Daniel Kuehn retired in November 1989, after serving only eleven months. On March 26, 1990, Jose Cisneros reported as the new superintendent. In the midst of deteriorating credibility of Park Service's management at Gettysburg, John Latschar arrived in August 1994, inaugurating a new era in the battlefield's history.[6]

The management of the battlefield's 3,800 acres remained a vexing problem. When established as a national military park in 1895, the battlefield's enabling legislation clearly defined the preservation of the fields and features associated with the battle as the primary purpose. When the National Park Service acquired the site, it inherited a landscape that had been maintained and preserved by Civil War veterans who managed the grounds as a memorial to honor those men who gave their "last full measure of devotion." In the years after the battle, scores of veterans dedicated monuments in tribute to the deeds of valor and heroism displayed by their comrades. By preserving both the key terrain features of the battle, such as Little Round Top, and erecting monuments on the battlefield, the veterans created two interrelated landscapes: the 1863 terrain and the post-battle commemorative features.

James McConaghie became the first National Park Service superintendent to assume responsibility to manage and preserve the historic landscape and the commemorative features. McConaghie articulated a management philosophy that rested on four principles: restoration, preservation, accessibility, and usability. During his tenure, the Park Service implemented its first cutting of non-historic woodlots, a practice that his successors continued in an attempt to provide some resemblance to the 1863 landscape. On the other hand, McConaghie lamented the numerous monuments, noting that while they had "particular meaning" to the men who erected them, to current visitors the monuments "merely exist." He viewed the commemorative features as secondary, or relegated to minimal importance, and recommended that trees and shrubs be planted to obscure their view. "The task before the field," the superintendent wrote, "is to carefully plant so that the numerous monuments will appear to fit and be screened so as not to unduly affect the landscape."[7]

Local administrators, more than any external variable, defined the management of the battlefield. Though the park had recently produced a guiding management document, the 1982 General Management Plan, Gettysburg's newest superintendent Jose Cisneros declared the plan "outdated" and recommended new management objectives be explored.[8] Reed Engle, the cultural resources manager, spearheaded the new landscape philosophy. Convinced that the battlefield could never be recreated to its 1863 condition, Engle proposed to rehabilitate the grounds to the time of the veterans' commemorative, or memorial, period. Engle and staff outlined this concept, termed the Memorial Landscape, in May 1991. Cisneros explained the new philosophy: "To manage the park as a memorial landscape which not only reflects the pre-battle 1863 agricultural environment, but includes those superimposed post-battle elements (monuments, avenues, interpretive devices, facilities, etc.) which are necessary for commemoration and visitor understanding of the battle." In essence, this new philosophy would acknowledge two distinct, but interrelated, landscapes: the pre-battle 1863 agricultural landscape and the commemorative memorial landscape. The most obvious features of the latter were the approximately 1,300 monuments and markers dedicated to and by the veterans. Other features of the memorial landscape included park avenues, identification plaques and tablets, and ornamental fencing. Park planners now described this memorial landscape as "superimposed" on the 1863 pre-battle terrain.[9]

The basis for the Memorial Landscape philosophy rested on four fundamental assumptions. First, the Park Service believed that the battlefield could never be rehabilitated to its 1863 appearance simply because it "no longer exists." Moreover, complete, exact rehabilitation to 1863 would require the removal of the features placed on the battlefield by the veterans, including the monuments and markers. Second, whereas earlier superintendents wanted to minimize the commemorative landscape, now planners believed them to be as important as the battle terrain. Third, any attempt to create an 1863 appearance could not be accomplished due to lack of "sufficient evidence." While "sufficient evidence" did not exist to rehabilitate the battlefield to 1863, adequate documentation, according to park staff, was available to create a commemorative appearance. Consequently, the Park Service maintained that the earliest the battlefield could be rehabilitated "with any consistency," "accuracy," or "respect for those who fought in July 1863," was to its 1895 appearance, when Gettysburg National Military Park received congressional recognition. Finally, Engle argued that emphasizing the commemorative landscape would enhance the visitor experience because it was the most accurate landscape.[10]

Demonstrating the emergence of a widespread sense of ownership of the battlefield, both at the local and national level, concerned individuals expressed their opposition in letters to park staff, regional Park Service administrators, and congressional representatives. Most often critics interpreted this new philosophy as an effort to deemphasize the 1863 terrain in favor of the commemorative period. "Visitors, knowledgeable historians and novices alike, come to Gettysburg to learn about the battle that took place there," one Pennsylvania resident stated. "Visitors do not come because of the memorials," he continued, "The memorials are there because of the battle." Concern about the Memorial Landscape concept came from across the nation. In a letter to National Park Service director Roger Kennedy, Ohio's Congressional Representative James Traficant, Jr., wrote that "thousands" of his constituents had contacted him expressing displeasure with the Memorial Landscape philosophy. He alluded to the popularity of an immersive experience, and noted that his constituents "tour the battlefield to get a feel for what it was like those three fateful days in 1863. They don't care or are not particularly interested in what visitors saw at Gettysburg in the 1890s."[11]

Yet in the face of criticism of the Memorial Landscape philosophy, the Park Service remained steadfast. Park historian Kathy Harrison summarized the park's intentions, writing, "While we can't let you see what it looked like the first time, in the battle, we can still make it the way it was the second time, when the veterans came back. We can still look at it with the veterans' eyes." Director Roger Kennedy reminded detractors that the National Park Service had the dual responsibility of preserving not only the terrain associated with the battle, but also the monuments and memorials created by the veterans. The most revealing comment concerning this landscape philosophy came from Reed Engle. Preservation of the battlefield, he stated, "is like a mattress, and we're putting a different sheet on top of it. It's all restorable—we can always put it back." Certainly Engle's views paralleled contemporary geographers claims of landscapes as a "dynamic, ever-changing phenomena." In this instance, Gettysburg management viewed the battlefield as a landscape that could be manufactured or disassembled.[12]

Park officials, however, proved unable to consistently define the commemorative era. Some documents defined this period from 1863 to 1900; others dated it from 1863 to 1910, while other documents fixed the period of commemoration as 1895 to 1922. While the beginning dates of 1863 or 1895 corresponded to the time of the battle or when the battlefield acquired federal recognition, respectively, park officials established relatively arbitrary dates for the conclusion of the commemorative period.[13]

Cisneros and Engle's concept, however ill-conceived, demonstrated the challenges of preserving a historic landscape. This new management philosophy also underscored the difficulties in preserving a landscape with multiple layers of history, in this instance the 1863 battle grounds and the post-battle commemorative features. While the Park Service did not intend to deemphasize the battlefield terrain, it did intend to highlight those features created by the veterans, the site's first preservationists. Thus, as Cisneros summarized, the Memorial Landscape philosophy allowed the NPS to "preserve a preservation." The desire to "preserve a preservation" reflected the conflicting ideas of the purpose and function of a national military park. Gettysburg's enabling legislation granted federal authority to preserve lands associated with the three-day battle. Consequently, the new management initiative to "preserve a preservation," which principally focused on preservation efforts from the 1895 landscape, remained incongruent with the purpose of the battlefield as a national military park. Visitors usually did not come to Gettysburg to see the commemorative landscape; they came to see the fields as the soldiers saw them in the summer of 1863.[14]

In the end, park officials never systematically implemented the Memorial Landscape program. A change, once again, in management brought about its swift termination. Reed Engle transferred to Shenandoah National Park and Jose Cisneros left Gettysburg for Big Bend National Park in Texas. This short-lived Memorial Landscape philosophy demonstrated the fluidity, if not the inconsistencies, in Gettysburg's landscape practices. Idealistic notions of preservation and interpretation philosophies aside, managers habitually made decisions that affected the presentation of the battlefield. Engle conceived the Memorial Landscape concept; it was not part of larger, uniform National Park Service practices. Unsurprisingly, when the new superintendent, John Latschar, arrived in the summer of 1994 he immediately abandoned the Memorial Landscape concept. He embarked on a vision to create a battlefield that mirrored its 1863 appearance.

Meanwhile, other dilemmas ensued. In 1974, the federal government authorized a 3,874-acreage limit for the battlefield. This limit and boundary would guide Gettysburg's land acquisition program for the next decade. In the late 1980s, at the request of Congress, Gettysburg National Military Park initiated a boundary study to explore land holdings and desired acquisitions. The National Park Service submitted its final version of the boundary study to Congress in October 1988. From a historic preservation standpoint, the existing boundary failed to include several major areas of battle, including South Cavalry Field, the Spangler Farm, and East Cavalry Field. The planning team proposed an expanded boundary that granted federal protection to most of the existing lands, as well as an addition of approximately 1,900 acres over fourteen different areas. Recognizing the fiscal impracticality of purchasing this much land, the boundary team recommended the purchase of only 250 acres, while the remainder would be preserved through scenic easements.[15]

On August 17, 1990, President George H. W. Bush signed Public Law 101–377, which added 1,900 acres to the battlefield and established a process for disposing of any nonessential lands. Gettysburg National Military Park now consisted of 5,733.05 acres. In this study, park staff also noted areas within the boundary that should be considered for removal because of minimal historical value or more practical reasons, such as maintenance difficulties. One area considered for removal was a small parcel of land located between the existing federal boundary and land owned by Gettysburg College. The small liberal arts school, founded in 1847 and located north of town, buttresses the battlefield's boundary to the east along the first day's fields. College representatives wanted to reroute a section of the Gettysburg Railroad that bisected the eastern edge of the campus because it created safety hazards to students and faculty who crossed the tracks to get to the west side of campus. They proposed the railroad track be moved off campus to the base of Seminary Ridge, near Larson's Motel on the Chambersburg Pike (U.S. Route 30 West), the section of land the boundary team had earlier recommended for removal. Removing this eight-acre parcel of land seemed reasonable— it did not witness any major action during the battle. In 1987, park planners met with representatives from the college to discuss a land exchange.[16]

In return for the eight-acre tract along Seminary Ridge, Gettysburg College offered the National Park Service a scenic easement on forty-seven acres of college land stretching from the Carlisle Road on the east to the Mummasburg Road on the west; ground where the Confederate 2nd Corps routed the Union 11th Corps on the afternoon of July 1. Eager to construct new facilities for the student body, college officials led by William VanArsdale, the college's treasurer and business manager, announced intentions to use this forty-seven acre tract for athletic fields. Herein lay the college's strong-armed proposal to the Park Service: if the agency would not relinquish title to the eight-acres near the Seminary Ridge railroad cut, which would prevent the college from rerouting the railroad line off its campus, the "only alternative" would be to continue developing the area north of town along the first day's battlefield. Prioritizing the scenic easement on forty-seven acres of key battle terrain over an eight-acre parcel of land with minimal action, the Park Service accepted the land exchange proposal. On September 26, one month after Bush signed the boundary bill, the National Park Service and Gettysburg College signed the agreement.[17]

National interest in the battlefield and its uses placed the land exchange at the center of a firestorm of public criticism that swelled across the country. In mid-December 1990, crews began bulldozing the Seminary Ridge railroad cut to reroute the rail line. During the next several months crews excavated approximately three acres of the Seminary Ridge railroad cut, destroyed nearly four acres of woods, and removed original sections of Civil War earthworks. Soon, many Americans expressed their displeasure with the demolition of the Seminary Ridge railroad cut. Critics assailed the Park Service for its failure to protect this piece of battle ground. Rudolf Jayer, from California, declared in a letter to the NPS director that the NPS had "utterly failed" in its mission to protect the battlefield. He sarcastically suggested, "Why not carry this ineptness further and use the Grand Canyon for a garbage landfill for the entire country?" Another letter from an Illinois State University professor vented a similar sardonic reaction; "Will the rest of our national parks be sold off for condominiums, landfills, or shopping malls?"[18]

Nearly four years after the destruction of the Seminary Ridge railroad cut, in the spring of 1994, Congress investigated the land exchange. Upon review of alternatives to address the damaged terrain, Director Roger Kennedy, in early May 1995, announced that the Park Service would "mitigate" the Seminary Ridge railroad cut. Paid for by the perceived culprits of the fiasco, Gettysburg College, mitigation included screening the area to minimize the appearance of the ridge and the construction of a gabion wall to prevent further erosion of the adjacent battlefield land. As expected, Americans weighed in on the decision to "mitigate" the damage. "Why should Gettysburg College," wrote

Steven Cassel of Ohio, "be treated any different than the Exxon Cooperation, after the Exxon Valdez oil spill disaster." While some criticized Gettysburg College, others placed the blame directly on the shoulders of the National Park Service. In Gettysburg, former superintendent Cisneros became a particular target. "Let's give Cisneros a pick and shovel and let him begin to clean up the mess he started," demanded one individual. Another responded, "If a travesty of this magnitude occurs again, I will personally recommend to your superior that you be sent to One Tree, Idaho, giving guided tours to foreign tourists in the mating habits of earthworms."[19] The land exchange serves as a case study in the dilemmas facing historic preservationists. Logistically and fiscally unable to protect every parcel of land associated with the battle, the National Park Service is often forced to make difficult decisions regarding preservation priorities. Although the agency did obtain a scenic easement on the forty-seven acre tract, college students regularly play sports on the fields where men once fought and died.

In *Battling for Manassas,* Joan Zenzen outlines the complexities and challenges to preserve historic battlefields. Disney withdrew its proposal for a theme park near Manassas as a result of national criticism over the seemingly ill-considered proposal. A key to success in preservation, Zenzen notes, is the cooperation of support groups and partnerships. Gettysburg National Military Park has benefited from two successful preservation-minded partners. In 1959, local residents established the Gettysburg Battlefield Preservation Association (GBPA), the battlefield's first partner association. A guiding mission of the GBPA was to acquire key parcels of battlefield grounds. Three decades later, in 1990, similarly minded residents formed the Friends of the National Parks at Gettysburg. Often called "the Friends," this association advocated the Park Service's mission of preserving the battlefield and quickly rose to become one of the most influential partners in the National Park Service. Demonstrating Gettysburg's national appeal, membership rapidly increased. Americans eagerly assisted in the preservation of the nation's most renowned battlefield by means of economic contributions or donation of labor and supplies. In its charter year, 1990, approximately 2,000 people became members, and by 1994 the Friends boasted over 12,000 members, making their organization the largest "Friends" group in the United States.[20]

The Friends wasted no time in generating projects. Foreshadowing future accomplishments, the Friends partnered with the GBPA to purchase and remove the last remaining house at the intersection of Taneytown Road and Steinwehr Avenue. In 1990, the Friends began planning for one of its most significant and visible contributions towards battlefield preservation—burying the overhead power lines along the Emmitsburg Road. This idea was not new. In the mid-1930s, then Superintendent James McConaghie's administration removed telephone poles and buried lines along the Chambersburg Pike. Sixty years later, a partner association advanced a similar project. On July 5, 1994, the group signed an agreement with the Park Service, Metropolitan Edison Company, Sprint/United Telephone Company of Pennsylvania, and the Pennsylvania Department of Transportation to underground nearly three miles of the power lines visibly obstructing the fields of Pickett's Charge. At a total project cost of $1.2 million, the lines were buried from the southern edge of town to the park's southern boundary, at the intersection of the Emmitsburg Road and South Confederate Avenue.[21]

By the 1990s, popular culture had affected Americans' understanding of the Civil War, and specifically the battle of Gettysburg, in an unprecedented fashion. As noted, the influence of the film *Gettysburg* cannot be overstated. Increased visitation between 1993 and 1994, the year of the film's release, stand as a clear indicator of its influence. The National Park Service readily responded to the film's popularity and directed its interpretation to parallel certain themes from the movie. The novel *The Killer Angels*, as well as *Gettysburg*, featured Colonel Joshua Lawrence Chamberlain and the 20th Maine and dramatized Chamberlain's efforts to "save" Little Round Top on July 2. Both the novel and the film made Chamberlain a household name. The National Park Service promoted the Chamberlain obsession and presented visitors with the interpretation they expected from the book and the movie. First, after the release of *The Killer Angels,* the Park Service improved its interpretation of Little Round Top. To signify the position of the 20th Maine, the Park Service installed a sign along Sykes Avenue, directing visitors to the regimental monument. To date, this stands as the only sign on the battlefield that directs visitors to a specific regimental marker. Workers also constructed a small parking lot near the 20th Maine monument. A wayside exhibit depicting Chamberlain's orders to hold the Union flank at "all hazards" was also added after the release of *Killer Angels.* Here, too, the Friends assisted in improving Little Round Top's interpretation. In 1995, they purchased a six-acre tract on the grounds where Company B of the 20th Maine defended its position against the attacking Alabamians. Little Round Top had always been a popular spot for veterans and park visitors alike, but the novel and film brought unintentional consequences to the landscape. To keep visitors on designated paths, and to reduce excessive foot traffic on areas prone to erosion, in 2000, park maintenance installed a post and chain fence along the established pathways on the summit.[22]

The film did restore the reputation of General James Longstreet, commander of the Army of Northern Virginia's 1st Corps. For decades, southerners had exonerated their beloved General Lee for defeat at Gettysburg and instead placed the blame squarely on the shoulders of Longstreet. After the war, southerners found Longstreet an easy scapegoat, for not only did he join the loathed Republican Party, but he openly criticized Lee's leadership at the battle. In the early 1940s, Longstreet's wife, Helen Dortch Longstreet, initiated a movement to build a monument along Warfield Ridge to honor her husband. Subsequent economic constraints of the Second World War, however, prevented her from raising the money needed. In the wake of *Gettysburg*, however, a surge of Longstreet devotees pressed for a monument to Lee's "Old War Horse." Longstreet historians joined in the nationwide appeal to solicit money for the monument. Their efforts were realized when, on July 3, 1998, the Longstreet Memorial Fund dedicated the Longstreet equestrian memorial in Pitzer Woods.[23]

This resurgence in the battle's popularity dramatically impacted the economic windfall of Adams County. In 1994, the Gettysburg-Adams County Area Chamber of Commerce initiated a series of annual studies on the economic impact of tourism to Gettysburg National Military Park and the Eisenhower National Historic Site on the town and county. The findings of the *Economic Impact Studies* underscored Americans' relationship to the battlefield and testified to the predominance of a culture of historical tourism. Of the visitors surveyed, the overwhelming majority of them, 88 percent, came to Gettysburg to learn about the battle. Education, however, balanced entertainment. A majority of visitors indicated that they also traveled to Gettysburg for recreational purposes. The intermingling of education with recreation was not a recent phenomenon. In the midst of the Great Depression, park officials promoted Gettysburg as a scenic landscape that emphasized the battlefield's springtime beauty. As established in the post–World War II era, the majority of park visitors arrived as family groups. Most traveled from Pennsylvania, Maryland, New Jersey, New York, and even a significant number came from as far away as California. Interestingly, only a few hailed from southern states.[24]

Certainly, as Jim Weeks demonstrates in *Gettysburg: Memory, Market, and an American Shrine,* the battlefield's commercial value had been realized since the late nineteenth century. In fact, soon after acquiring the site, the National Park Service cultivated a tourist culture. Commercial establishments proliferated in the years after World War II that created an inevitable conflict between preservationists and entrepreneurs. Similarly, on prior occasions when park officials considered moving the visitor center from its prominent location along Steinwehr Avenue, local businessmen bemoaned the potential relocation for fear of the adverse impact upon their establishments. The battlefield was certainly the town's primary economic producer, giving life to scores of restaurants, gift shops, hotels, and for-profit museums. This symbiotic, if not parasitic, relationship of heritage tourism and commercial establishments undeniably drove the economic engine of Adams County. In 1995, for example, visitor expenditures in the local area exceeded $106 million.[25]

By the mid-1990s, Gettysburg National Military Park desperately needed a new superintendent. Inconsistencies in management decisions combined with deteriorating relations with the local community had created a tense atmosphere. Meanwhile, the nation's increasing interest in Gettysburg further necessitated a new, mission-oriented leader. In August 1994, John Latschar became the park's tenth superintendent. His arrival brought someone with a diverse and accomplished background, not only in the National Park Service, but also in academic and military careers. After earning bachelor's and master's degrees from Kansas State University, in 1969 and 1973 respectively, Latschar received a doctoral degree in American history from Rutgers University in 1978, becoming only the second superintendent at Gettysburg to hold a Ph.D. Prior to his transfer to Gettysburg, Latschar served as the first superintendent of Steamtown National Historic Site in Scranton, Pennsylvania.[26]

Since 1933 when the Park Service acquired Gettysburg National Military Park, few superintendents conceived, much less implemented any long-term management philosophy. Latschar wasted no time in bringing the battlefield the vision it needed. Less than one year into his new post, he announced his goals for the battlefield. Appropriately, he listed protection and preservation of the park's historic resources as his top priority. Next, he sought to provide excellent interpretation. Finally, he hoped to improve relations with the local community, which had been considerably strained in the wake of the land exchange with Gettysburg College.[27]

The arrival of this vision-oriented superintendent combined with a surge in visitation, spurred by the success of *Gettysburg,* laid the foundation for a radically new battlefield experience. Continuing a trend that defined the Park Service for decades, park officials again bemoaned the inadequacies of their visitor center. Gettysburg National Military Park holds one of the largest collections of Civil War artifacts, estimated at 400,000 objects; nonetheless, the park lacked proper facilities to adequately preserve them. With no other alternative, the park stored these priceless objects in the basement of the visitor center, which exposed them to improper temperatures and humidity fluctuations. Conditions in the cyclorama building were equally deplorable. Subject to variable changes in temperature and humidity, the Gettysburg Cyclorama slowly deteriorated. Yet congressional funding for a new facility seemed unlikely. In 1996, Congress allocated the National Park Service $1.5 billion of the $1.6 trillion budget, less than one-tenth of 1 percent of the entire federal budget. Gettysburg's operating budget for 1996 totaled $3,052,000, for example.[28] If the Gettysburg Cyclorama and the park's artifacts were to be protected and preserved, funding would have to come from sources other than the federal government.

The answer seemed to have arrived in the winter of 1994. That December, Robert Monahan, Jr., a local businessman and former staffer in President Ronald Reagan's administration, approached Latschar with a proposal to construct a new visitor center at no cost to the federal government. His plan rested on the establishment of a public-private partnership, where all funds for the construction of the visitor center, estimated to cost $25 million, would be acquired from the private sector and donations. As proposed, the NPS, the Friends, and the to-be-established Monahan Group, would form the partnership. Monahan's proposal also included an element of historic rehabilitation: once the new facility was constructed, at a location slightly south of the current visitor center, the existing visitor center and cyclorama center would be removed and Ziegler's Grove fashioned to its 1863 appearance. The Park Service would operate and maintain the museum, and after a negotiated period, the NPS would assume ownership. In April 1995, the Park Service unveiled these plans. While Monahan's proposal offered a multi-million dollar facility at no cost to the federal government, the concept proved hard to sell. Two main issues drove the opposition: the noncompetitive selection of a partner and suspicion at the rate at which the negotiations had progressed. Reacting to the public's concerns over the Monahan proposal, in late August 1995, the Park Service and the Friends decided to defer further consideration of the partnership.[29]

After withdrawing from negotiations with Monahan, Latschar initiated a multi-year planning process to explore park goals, management problems, and feasible solutions. Thereafter, the planners identified four goals to guide the future management of the battlefield. The first goal underlined the protection and preservation of the artifacts, to be accomplished by the construction of a new facility. The second goal sought to preserve the Gettysburg Cyclorama. The third goal recommended that the park improve its interpretation. The fourth and final goal called for the rehabilitation of Ziegler's Grove, which aimed to reverse the prevailing Park Service philosophy of the 1960s that maintained the best location for visitor centers should be in the heart of historic terrain.[30]

After two years of planning and a nationwide request for proposals for the design and construction of a new museum, on November 6, 1997, National Park Service Director Roger Stanton announced the selection of Kinsley Equities, of York, Pennsylvania, as the contractor. Similar to the Monahan proposal in 1995, Robert Kinsley recommended the formation of a non-profit partner to administer the new facility.[31] With the selection of a partner to construct the new museum complex, Latschar and staff embarked upon a new *General Management Plan* to define a long-term management vision, which ultimately centered on the rehabilitation of the battlefield and the development of a public-private partnership for a new museum and visitor center.

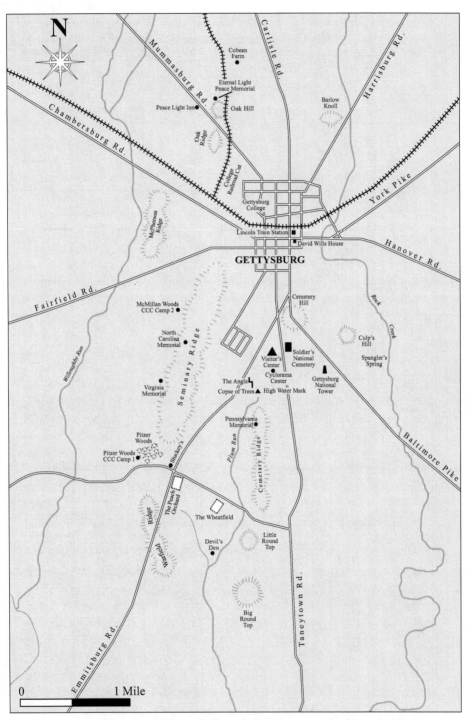

Post–1863 Features of Gettysburg National Military Park. Map created by Alexander Mendoza.

CHAPTER 10

THEY WHO FOUGHT HERE: CULTURE WARS AND A NEW DIRECTION AT GETTYSBURG, 1998–2000

In the late twentieth century, three critical factors collided to drastically alter the landscape at Gettysburg National Military Park and the battlefield's prevailing interpretation. Congress sought to redirect the interpretive focus at several of the nation's historic sites, including sites of the Civil War era, leading to a reevaluation of the popular reconciliationist narrative. Second, internally, the National Park Service instituted a treatment philosophy for cultural landscapes, to include historic sites such as Gettysburg. And finally, Gettysburg's newest superintendent, John Latschar, became the impetus to formulate and implement a clear, long-term vision to manage the historic terrain and to interpret the battle and the broader issues of the Civil War. At no time since the New Deal had Gettysburg seen such stark changes to its physical landscape. And in no time since the veterans laid the foundation for the widely accepted reconciliationist interpretation of the "High Water Mark" did visitors to Gettysburg experience such a significant change in the site's interpretation.

Certainly the clamor generated by the "culture wars" and the subsequent accusations of politicizing history would eventually have a profound effect on the events at Gettysburg. From the outside, Congress pushed the National Park Service to alter its traditional interpretation at existing sites and simultaneously authorized the establishment of new historic parks, to include places associated with social divisiveness in the country's history. Instead of letting individual military parks continue to determine their own narrative, which overwhelmingly offered a drum and trumpet presentation, Congress urged the Civil War sites to include a discussion of slavery in their interpretive exhibits. Fredericksburg and Spotsylvania National Military Park became the first of the national military parks to include a broader socio-cultural narrative as part of its interpretive mission. In 1989, as part of a boundary revision for the two parks, Congress encouraged the secretary of the interior to pursue the necessary action to interpret the battles "in the larger context of the Civil War and American History, including the causes and consequences of the Civil War and including the effects of the war on all the American people, especially on the American South." The following year, 1990, as part of Gettysburg's boundary revision, Congress inserted identical language in the park's legislation. Ensuing events underscored the nation's heightened sensitivity to the discussion of slavery at Civil War battlefields. Certainly this uproar over interpreting "the causes and consequences of the Civil War" demonstrated the relevance of what Michael Kammen terms the "heritage syndrome," the tendency to "remember what is attractive or flattering and to ignore all the rest."[1]

The Civil War parks were not the only historic sites or museums revising their long-held interpretive narrative. In 1991, Congress mandated the National Park Service provide a broader and balanced interpretation at Custer Battlefield National Monument. This legislation changed the park's storyline from the traditional narrative that praised the role of Colonel George Custer and his 7th U.S. Cavalry, to one that offered an objective portrayal of the Native Americans and their struggle to retain their ancestral land. Reflective of this balanced narrative, the site was renamed Little Bighorn National Monument. Meanwhile, Congress authorized the establishment of several historic parks associated with social and cultural divisiveness, places termed "sites of shame" by Yale professor Robert Winks. Several of these newly established parks interpreted sites or events which pertained to the Civil Rights Movement: *Brown v. Board of Education* National Historic Site (1992), Selma to Montgomery National Historic Trail (1996), and Little Rock Central High School National Historic Trail (1998). In 2000, Congress expanded the "sites of shame" and authorized the establishment of Sand Creek Massacre National Historic Site and two years later Manzanar National Historic Site. The establishment of these sites challenged the entrenched preference for selectively ignoring eras in American history rife with social and cultural discord.[2]

Guidance from the National Park Service also influenced management decisions at Gettysburg and subsequently changed the way visitors would experience the battlefield. In 1992, the National Park Service revised the standards for the preservation of historic resources and landscapes. The "Secretary of Interior's Standards for the Treatment of Historic Properties" brought uniformity to the practices of cultural landscape management and identified four treatment methods for the care of historic buildings, sites, or landscapes. These four methods were preservation, rehabilitation, restoration, and reconstruction. In brief, preservation sought to "sustain the existing form, integrity and materials of an historic property." Rehabilitation retained historic features and then aimed to "make compatible uses for properties through repair, alterations, and additions while preserving those historic features that remain and that are significant and convey historical values." Essentially, historic features that have changed or deteriorated could be improved or repaired. Restoration, on the other hand, was "the process of accurately depicting the form, features and character of a property as it appeared at a particular period of time." And finally the fourth method, reconstruction, was the process of depicting in "new construction, the form, features, and details of a non-surviving site, landscape, building, structure or object for the purpose of replicating its appearance at a specific period of time and in its historic location." An example of reconstruction would be replacing a fence in its historic location.[3]

Underscoring each of these preservation methods was an effort to recapture the "historic integrity" of a site or building. The National Park Service defined historic integrity as "the authenticity of a property's historic identity, evinced by the survival of physical characteristics that existed during the property's historic or prehistoric period." More precisely, the agency listed seven characteristics of integrity: location, setting, feeling, association, design, workmanship, and materials.[4] Though not defined in official government terminology, Americans had long recognized the need to protect Gettysburg's historic integrity. In the debates over commercialization on or near the battlefield, opponents readily decried these intrusions as a desecration to the battlefield's hallowed ground. Such defilements were now verbalized as a threat to the landscape's historic integrity.

Meanwhile, the concept of a "cultural landscape" gained popularity within the National Park Service. Charles Birnbaum, coordinator of the agency's Historic Landscape Initiative (HLI), advanced the philosophy on the protection and management of cultural landscapes. A cultural landscape was defined as "a geographic area, including both cultural and natural resources and the wildlife or domestic animals therein, associated with a historic event, activity, or person or exhibiting other cultural or aesthetic values." Birnbaum offered four categories of cultural landscapes. One classification, a historic site, was a landscape significant for its association with an important person or event. The nation's battlefields, Gettysburg included, fell into this category. Birnbaum encouraged a practice of "reading the landscape." This "landscape interpretation," served to connect the visitor to the landscape with the "tools to experience the landscape as it existed during its period of significance, or as it evolved to its present state."[5]

Amidst congressional involvement to redirect the interpretation of Civil War sites and standardization within the National Park Service in the methodology on how to manage and preserve cultural landscapes, John Latschar arrived in August 1994 as Gettysburg's new superintendent. Through Latschar's steadfast leadership, and after years of inconsistencies in administrative philosophies, the National Park Service finally established a clear, consistent management policy. After a thorough evaluation of its management objectives, in November 1997, the National Park Service selected the proposal submitted by Robert Kinsley, of York, Pennsylvania, to design and construct a new visitor center. By the end of the year, the Park Service entered into negotiations with Kinsley and the newly created non-profit partner, the Gettysburg National Battlefield Museum Foundation, now called the Foundation, to construct the Gettysburg Visitor Center and Museum.[6]

In short, once Director Robert Stanton approved the Kinsley proposal, this plan became the foundation for a new *General Management Plan* (*GMP*). Two main philosophies guided the *GMP*. Central to the plan stood the construction of a museum complex by means of the recently established public-private partnership. This new museum brought to fruition interpretive goals which had been outlined earlier: protection of the collection of objects and artifacts; preservation and conservation of the Gettysburg Cyclorama; increased interpretation and educational opportunities for visitors; and the rehabilitation of Ziegler's Grove. Second, and part of the agency's newly defined standards for managing cultural landscapes, was the effort to rehabilitate the battlefield to its 1863 condition, which in turn, helped to reestablish the battlefield's historic integrity. On August 14, 1998, the Park Service released the *Draft General Management Plan* (*Draft GMP*) and less than one year later, on June 18, 1999, the agency released its two-volume *Final General Management Plan and Environmental Impact Statement*. Collectively, the implementation of this new policy dramatically redefined the Gettysburg experience and proved to be a watershed period in the battlefield's history.[7]

On one level, it seemed that every time a new superintendent arrived to Gettysburg, a change in policies became par for the course, as each new leader tried to implement his own vision for the park. Most recently, Jose Cisneros and Reed Engle attempted to apply the poorly conceived Memorial Landscape philosophy. Not only did this proposal receive little support from the public, but it also conflicted with the battlefield's enabling legislation by emphasizing a commemorative landscape. And now, once again, a new superintendent, John Latschar, had his own vision on how to improve the landscape. As noted earlier, the Park Service had initiated small-scale cuts in non-historic woodlots as early as 1940, but failed to sustain these vistas; consequently, any opened viewshed quickly became overrun by the growth of underbrush and foliage. Visitors who now looked upon these fields, which were clear and open in 1863, saw instead dense, overgrown woodlots. Licensed Battlefield Guides and park rangers often used historic photographs when interpreting battle action so as to help visitors obtain a better sense of the 1863 landscape. Shortly after his arrival, Latschar took a tour with a licensed guide, who employed historic photographs to explain the battle's landscape. Latschar readily declared that "something had to be done" not only to enhance interpretation, but also to effectively manage the battlefield.[8] His background as a military officer enabled him to observe the battlefield as a soldier, while his training as a historian allowed him to see the battlefield as a historic source. He envisioned a philosophy that would correct the inaccuracies in the landscape.

The new *General Management Plan* provided a framework for future decisions concerning the park's three interrelated cultural landscapes: the battlefield, the Soldiers' National Cemetery, and the commemorative features. Reflective of larger trends in managing cultural landscapes, in order to accomplish this objective, Gettysburg's staff presented a program to *rehabilitate* the battlefield landscape, "making possible a compatible use for a property through repair, alterations, and additions while preserving those portions or features which convey its historical or cultural values." The fundamental tenet of this new philosophy would create a landscape that presented an accurate portrayal of the 1863 vistas. In doing so, the Park Service proactively focused on creating a visually authentic and historically accurate landscape.[9]

At Gettysburg, park planners evaluated the battlefield's 5,900 acres and formulated a plan to reclaim its historic integrity and restore significant features of the battle. Specifically, planners recommended the rehabilitation of the large-scale areas present at the time of the battle, as well as small-scale landscape features that were significant to its outcome, which included fences, woodlots, and orchards. Planners maintained that these improvements would provide visitors with a better understanding of the landscape features that influenced troop movement and the tactics of the battle. To refashion Gettysburg to its historic appearance, the plan called for the removal of 576 acres of non-historic woodlots. It also recommended the replacement of 115 acres present in 1863, but currently missing. Nearly forty miles of missing fence would be rebuilt. Originally built by local farmers, the fences were an obstacle or an impediment of approach for the soldiers. Planners further recommended the replanting of 160 acres of orchards and the trimming of 65 acres of thickets to their historic height. Nineteenth-century Civil War buildings would be restored to their historic appearance.[10]

Perhaps more than the battlefield landscape itself, the Soldiers' National Cemetery did not accurately represent its original configuration because of alterations made by the Park Service during the 1930s. New modifications to the cemetery included reinstalling the pipe-rail fencing that had initially separated the Soldiers' National Cemetery from the adjoining Evergreen Cemetery. Moreover, the plan called for the restoration of the cemetery grade and Civil War headstones to their original level. The Soldiers' National Cemetery, like the battlefield, had become a landscape that had been created and subsequently altered; now plans called for the rehabilitation of the grounds to an original appearance.[11]

The new management prescription also included the removal of the cyclorama building, which complemented the construction of a new visitor center complex. Though the facility had been plagued by constructional problems since its opening in 1962, the announcement to demolish it created a firestorm of protests. The resulting battle over its fate represented an interesting dilemma of preservation. Civil War historians viewed the building as an intrusion on historic ground and wanted it removed. Architectural historians, on the other hand, argued the building, designed by Richard Neutra, held historical significance in its own right. After much debate and argument, Civil War preservationists prevailed. On May 14, 1999, the Advisory Council on Historic Preservation approved the park's plans to demolish the building, concluding, "There are other Neutra buildings; there is only one Gettysburg Battlefield . . . the Building must yield."[12]

Latschar's intent to remove the cyclorama building from Ziegler's Grove demonstrated change in the Park Service's philosophy on the compatibility of non-historic structures on historic grounds. Only recently had the NPS brought standardization to managing and preserving competing layers of resources. At a superintendent's conference held in Nashville in 1998, site managers outlined four preservation priorities to manage Civil War cultural resources. The highest priority went to structures that existed at the time of the battle. Commemorative features placed by the veterans received second priority. Nationally significant postwar structures were the third priority. Finally, postwar facilities built by the government were the lowest priority; the 1962 Neutra building fell into the fourth category.[13]

Attempting to rehabilitate the battlefield to an 1863 appearance remained an ambitious, if not ambiguous, task. Union and Confederate soldiers fought over twenty-five square miles, and by 1998 the federal boundary included 5,989 acres. It now became necessary for park officials to determine what historic features should be restored, and which ones were impractical to replace. Relying on his background as an army officer, Latschar, along with his team, used the KOCOA method developed by the U.S. Army to determine the effect specific terrain features had on a battle. KOCOA is an acronym that analyzes: (K) key terrain; (O) observation points; (C) cover and concealment; (O) obstacles to the movement of troops; and (A) avenues of approach used by soldiers to reach their desired position. Relying upon thousands of historic documents, including officers' official reports, soldiers' accounts, photographs, newspaper accounts, and maps, park historians used KOCOA to document the entire battlefield in order to evaluate specific features that had a major impact on the battle. Park historians then mapped the battle action for each of the three-days of fighting to illustrate how KOCOA influenced where troops were positioned, moved, and engaged on the field.[14]

To some observers, the plans to remove 576 acres of trees seemed to conflict with the agency's charter to protect natural and historic sites. Unsurprisingly, some local residents rallied against the plan and presented management with a petition of approximately 1,400 signatures opposing the landscape rehabilitation program. Meanwhile, letters poured in from across the country weighing in on the new plans. The opinions and emotions expressed in these letters offer insight to the myriad of meanings and feelings that Americans had come to associate with Gettysburg. Some writers denounced the proposal to remove woodlots as a "rape" of the battlefield and voiced concern for the environment and ecosystem. Others believed that most visitors would not appreciate a landscape rehabilitation program because the average tourist does not "give a hoot about whether the trees were there in 1863." One individual declared, "Saying that visitors cannot understand and interpret the Civil War battle without removing the trees that have grown since then, is like saying that visitors to Japan cannot appreciate the devastation of Hiroshima without keeping the city like it was at the end of World War II." Sarcastically taking the rehabilitation efforts to an impracticable extreme, some decried that if the Park Service was serious in its intent to create an 1863 appearance then all the post-battle structures, including monuments and avenues should be removed.[15]

Assessing Gettysburg's meaning or explaining why Gettysburg holds such a powerful, emotional place in American history and culture remains an ambiguous and often indefinable task. The public response to the landscape alterations, however, offers a window into the meanings Americans have come to attach to the battlefield. To some, Gettysburg was not only a battlefield, but a hometown and a place of childhood experiences and personal memories. Todd Jones, a professor of philosophy at the University of Nevada, declared Gettysburg to be his "home" and more than a Civil War battlefield. In his perspective, any changes to the landscape meant that "autobiographical histories of the people of Gettysburg would be bulldozed and destroyed forever." He implored, "The forests of the battlefield are covered with private monuments from our personal histories, places where we lost teeth in snowball fights . . . a place where we experienced first kisses with our sweethearts."[16]

Other letters denounced modifications to the landscape as a desecration of the "shrine." Writers regularly used religious symbolism, terming the battlefield as "sacred" or a "shrine." Christine Riker, of California, offered a typical expression, "It is a shrine, a holy place." Illinois resident, Nathaniel Reed, described Gettysburg as "America's most hallowed ground," while Richard

Rogers of New York portrayed the battlefield as "sacred ground." A San Diego resident wrote that Gettysburg is "the most significant place in American history." In an especially emotional letter, a Georgia resident ranked Gettysburg in importance with her family, friends, and God. Describing Gettysburg as sacred and hallowed, however, was not new. Characterization of the landscape's sanctity began with Abraham Lincoln in November 1863. Now commentators used emotional, religious allusion as an appeal to keep the battlefield in its current form. Any changes to the battlefield would violate and defile this sanctity.[17]

During 1998, the NPS received over 3,700 written comments on the management proposals. While opponents generally received the most media coverage, the park received many enthusiastic letters of support. Based on the responses received, approximately 85 percent supported efforts to rehabilitate the battlefield. "I applaud the Park Service's goal of restoring this landscape closer to its 1863 appearance," wrote one Virginian. Another Virginia resident reminded critics of the Park Service's mission to preserve the battlefield: "The National Military Park is not a wildlife refuge. It was not established to protect squirrels or birds or deer or wetlands. The National Military Park is not an arboretum . . . The National Military Park is a battlefield. The battlefield is the most important artifact of the battle we have, and it is the Park Service's mission to preserve and protect this artifact."[18] While a multiuse landscape had been popular within the agency, Gettysburg included, rehabilitation plans

Breaking ground for the Gettysburg National Military Park Museum and Visitor Center, June 2, 2005. Photo courtesy of Barbara Adams.

redirected the management focus from recreational activities befitting a *park* toward historic preservation of a national battlefield.

Of the two principal components of the *General Management Plan,* the one that received the most local and national media attention was the creation of the public-private partnership for the new museum facility. By and large, the landscape proposal received only minimal consideration from the public. Objections to the museum centered on two facets: the creation of the public-private partnership with the Gettysburg Foundation and the reshaping of the site's interpretive narrative. Outrage over the revision to the battle's narrative reflected, in part, the larger cultural wars and debates over politicizing history.

Unsurprisingly, opposition to the new visitor center came from the local business establishment. Certainly these arguments were not new, but reflected long-standing trends. With over 110 businesses located less than one half-mile from the existing visitor center, the Gettysburg borough undeniably thrived on tourist spending. For decades, commercial establishments along Steinwehr Avenue and the Baltimore Pike had benefitted handsomely from their convenient location near the existing visitor center. Now the newly proposed visitor center would be moved just far enough from the commercial trappings of Steinwehr Avenue that visitors could no longer simply walk across the street to frequent local businesses. The Gettysburg Area Retail Merchants Association (GARMA), an association collectively representing the town's business establishments, unanimously passed a resolution to oppose the new visitor center. The variety of commercial venues proposed for inclusion in the new museum also drove the opposition. The Gettysburg Convention and Visitor Bureau went on record as opposing the plan because of its many commercial elements. Eric Uberman, owner of the American Civil War Wax Museum, located directly across from the existing visitor center became a vociferous critic of the new museum. He asserted that "commercialization within the Park is cannibalization of the business community by duplicating existing services."[19]

Profiteering from the battle began as soon as the armies left the field, and by the mid-twentieth century, the battlefield and commercial interests had developed a symbiotic, if not a parasitic, relationship. Yet some area residents condemned merchants for hastily opposing the plan simply to protect their self-interests. "I abhor the fact that anything new presented to the greedy businessmen of Gettysburg is immediately disfavored," one resident stated. During a public meeting, a resident of Dillsburg, Pennsylvania, expressed his frustrations with the intense local opposition. "These are *national* parks," he emphasized, "not local parks. They belong to all of us, not just the local residents." The *Harrisburg Patriot-News* came to a similar conclusion, stating, "The idea that the interests of the owners of wax museums, restaurants and other businesses catering to the tourist trade should be put ahead of preserving the historical integrity of the battlefield is both selfish and short-sighted."[20]

Certainly the agency's role in cultivating a tourist culture had changed considerably since the National Park Service first acquired the battlefield. Earlier superintendents declared the park to be in "the tourist business," and park managers often acquiesced to the demands of local interests. Debates over the elimination of automobile traffic in the Soldiers' National Cemetery in the early 1970s offer an example of an administration catering to the needs of the local community. Latschar, however, proved steadfast in implementing a vision to best preserve the historic terrain. In response to the concerns of the businessmen, Latschar declared, "There's nothing in our mission statement that says we're supposed to look out for businesses surrounding the park."[21]

Latschar's seemingly unilateral management style and apparent disregard for local business interests quickly made him unpopular with the business community. On October 1, 1998, the Park Service held a public meeting to discuss the new management plan. In front of approximately one hundred people, Robert Monahan, who had initially proposed the partnership concept in 1995, bluntly called for the removal of the superintendent, claiming Latschar acted irresponsibly in his management capacity. "I think this administration has lied, misrepresented, and misinformed the American public and the people of this community," Monahan decried, "and I think that the Superintendent for the National Military Park at Gettysburg should be removed."[22]

Still, in an effort to mollify some of the concerns of local business owners, the Park Service and Kinsley's team agreed to considerable changes in the visitor center. First, they agreed to eliminate three commercial venues and replaced the fine dining restaurant with a smaller cafeteria. In addition, while the concept of a feature film theater would be retained, the Foundation agreed to use a standard design theater instead of an IMAX production, as originally proposed. After these modifications, Northeast Regional Director Marie Rust, on July 10, 1998, signed a letter of intent with Kinsley Equities to construct the new facility.[23]

The local uproar, combined with the implications for future partnerships, drew the attention of Congress, which led to two hearings, one in February 1998 and the other the following February. On February 24, 1998, the Senate Subcommittee on National Parks requested a hearing on the merits of Gettysburg's planned partnership. Somewhat surprisingly, opposition to the new visitor center came from two battlefield preservation organizations: the Association for Preservation of Civil War Sites (APCW) and the Gettysburg Battlefield Preservation Association (GBPA). Dennis Frye, former park historian at Harper's Ferry National Historical Park and now president of the APCW, professed that the Park Service had misinterpreted its priorities by emphasizing presentation over preservation. Declaring that the battlefield, not a museum, should accomplish the goals of education, he argued, "The NPS should focus its presentation—and hence achieve its goal of education—on the *battlefield*, and not in an artificial environment of marble and glass." A year later, as the Park Service moved toward finalizing negotiations with the Foundation and releasing the *Final General Management Plan*, Congress once again investigated the partnership. On February 11, 1999, the U.S. House Subcommittee on National Parks held an oversight hearing that rehashed much of the same arguments offered during the Senate's hearing. The 1999 House hearing proved to be little more than a political exercise in grandstanding. In October 1999, Congress officially endorsed the "need" for a new facility and the partnership in the National Park Service appropriations bill.[24]

Still, the proposed partnership generated skeptics, many who expressed concern about private interests managing the nation's historic treasures. Former Gettysburg superintendent Daniel Kuehn warned that the partnership constituted "one more step down the road to privatization of the parks," which, Kuehn argued, would likely place the NPS in a secondary role in the management of the battlefield. Others expressed frustration that the federal government would not appropriate the necessary funding for a new museum. "It is ridiculous to say that the greatest country in the world can't afford to do what is needed in the most hallowed of ground," wrote Philip Stewart of Middletown, Virginia, "It is like privatizing the Arlington National Cemetery." A Columbia, South Carolina resident offered a similar sentiment, "We spend zillions to support a Bosnian peace, yet we won't put up a few lousy dollars to adequately fund this National Treasure." Overall, however, the Park Service received enthusiastic support for the partnership. During the period of open public comment, approximately 75 percent of the comments received approved the plan.[25]

While the partnership and commercial venues drove much of the public comments on the management plan, the second contentious component of the new visitor center proved to be the plan to reshape the historical narrative. As proposed, the new museum would address the war's causes and consequences. This proposal significantly diverged from the entrenched reconciliationist storyline that emphasized the "High Water Mark." The ensuing decade of planning and subsequent controversy over promoting a narrative of the Civil War to include its causes and consequences fit squarely within broader cultural wars of the late twentieth century. This debate also demonstrated the transience of the "heritage syndrome" and the pervasiveness of the Lost Cause mentality.[26]

At the core of this debate was the simple fact that Gettysburg generally presented a pro-Confederate storyline. The "High Water Mark" emphasized the Confederate perspective of the battle. This prevailing interpretation, termed the "reconciliationist memory" by David Blight, originated with the veterans themselves. Certainly by 1913, the battle's fiftieth anniversary, the landscape had been deliberately cultivated and promoted as a site of sectional reconciliation. The July 3, 1913, meeting of Union and Confederate veterans at the Angle, shaking hands in reconciled fraternity, best exemplified this spirit. Virginia Governor William Hodges Mann further reinforced the spirit of reunion and the construction of a reconciliationist narrative in a speech delivered on July 3, 1913. "We are not here to discuss the Genesis of the war, but men who have tried each other in the storm and smoke of battle are here to discuss this great fight," Mann declared. "We came here, I say, not to discuss what caused the war of 1861–1865," he continued, "but to talk over the events of the battle here as man to man."[27]

Undeniably, interpretation at Gettysburg continued to focus, not on "what caused the war of 1861–1865," but on the "events of the battle." When the National Park Service acquired Gettysburg in 1933, the agency, an active shaper of public understanding of the war, continued to promote the reconciliationist narrative. The Park Service's main interpretive presentation, the Gettysburg Cyclorama, likewise heralded the Confederate soldiers on July 3. Subsequent construction of the visitor center in Ziegler's Grove further reinforced the "High Water Mark" narrative. On the battlefield, interpretive media, which included several audio stations and wayside exhibits, further gave emphasis to Confederate valor and stressed the symbolic significance of Lee's defeat as the Confederate "High Tide."[28] The nation's Civil War Centennial brought a timely occurrence to address social and cultural implications of the war. Yet in the midst of the Civil Rights Movement, interpretation at the nation's battlefields remained static. Though orators used the battlefield to call for a "new birth of freedom," none demand the integration of slavery into the war's narrative.

Additional factors perpetuated the propensity to glorify the military events of the battle. First, the success of the book *Killer Angels* and later the film *Gettysburg,* based on the novel, reinvigorated the battle's popularity and personalized many of the battle's key figures. Thousands of visitors journeyed to Gettysburg to stand on Little Round Top, where Colonel Joshua Lawrence Chamberlain and the 20th Maine held the Union line at "all hazards" on the afternoon of July 2. *Gettysburg* climaxed with the glorified portrayal of Pickett's Charge. Brigadier General Lewis Armistead, played by Richard Jordan, personified combat, moving viewers with his emotional address to his Virginians minutes before the charge. The popularity of the film allowed a new generation to acquaint themselves with the "High Water Mark." They came to Gettysburg to explore the fields of Pickett's Charge, to walk the same terrain once covered by 13,000 Confederates in their attempt to break the Union line on Cemetery Ridge. Moreover, the battle reenactments and living-history demonstrations also actively solidified interpretation and interest toward battle action, regiments, tactics, and weaponry. Since the battle's first reenactment in July 1959, reenactments remained the climatic event of the town's summer festivities. Throngs of visitors gathered to view artillery "firing" to soften the enemy line as a prelude to scores of "soldiers" gallantly "charging" the enemy position amidst trumpeting battle cries and flag waving fanfare. Certainly the majority of visitors left the "battlefield" without engaging in a discussion of the war's causes or similar socio-cultural issues.

Meanwhile, visitors to the park museum on Taneytown Road found thousands of artifacts displayed in glass cases, once described by noted historian Eric Foner as a "hodge-podge," which provided minimal explanation of the battle and even less of the Civil War. Scant interpretive opportunities were not unique to Gettysburg, however, but demonstrated the prevailing narrative presented at other Civil War sites. This storyline permitted the Park Service to avoid confronting and presenting the war's controversial issues, such as slavery, and instead focus on cultivating and perpetuating a narrative that emphasized the valor of soldiers. Thus, in a rather active manner, the National Park Service at Gettysburg continued to perpetuate the Lost Cause. Historian Gaines Foster addresses this "heritage syndrome" of the Civil War noting, "Rather than looking at the war as a tragic failure and trying to understand it, or even condemn it, Americans, North and South, chose to view it as a glorious time to be celebrated."[29]

As a consequence of the nation's larger cultural wars and the 1990 boundary revision, Gettysburg's staff began to explore ways to broaden educational opportunities. At the park's fourth annual seminar, held in March 1995, Superintendent Latschar confronted the traditional, static interpretation. In a speech entitled, "Gettysburg: The Next 100 Years," Latschar argued that Park Service needed to make a more concerted effort to appeal to a larger and diverse American public. Admitting bluntly that Civil War enthusiasts were mostly white males, he recommended for the park to "survive," the trend of attracting primarily white men "must be reversed." The park superintendent stated that interpretation at Gettysburg had "utterly failed" to appeal to African Americans, as well as the nation's Hispanic population, a growing minority group. In the current interpretive efforts to honor Union and Confederate soldiers, Latschar declared that the Park Service had "bent over backwards to avoid any notion of fixing blame for the war."[30] This effort permitted visitors to embrace and celebrate the common narrative that glorified the valor and sacrifice of the soldiers, while deliberately ignoring the war's controversial issues.

Latschar's remarks quickly attracted a firestorm of criticism after *Civil War News* reprinted his speech in their July 1995 issue. As expected, some interpreted Latschar's comments as a direct assault on southern heritage and a misrepresentation of the Confederate cause. Certainly this perspective illustrated the heightened sensitivity to political correctness of the late twentieth century. On letterhead adorned with Confederate battle flags, Scott Williams of Missouri, for example, informed Secretary of the Interior Bruce Babbitt that slavery had relatively little to do with the "Second American Revolution." Outraged by Latschar's perceived anti-Confederate comments, Williams further advised the secretary that "it is time to find another superintendent or send Mr. Latschar to the Antarctic National Park where he can do no damage." Meanwhile, the Sons of Confederate Veterans' Heritage Committee, based in Columbia, Tennessee, embarked on a vigorous campaign to express their displeasure with the Gettysburg superintendent. SCV members sent hundreds of prepared comment cards to Babbitt, claiming that Latschar had "modified" and "altered" historical events in order to make them "more palatable to a greater number of park visitors." Each card insisted the superintendent "discontinue the policy presenting an altered version of history in attempts at stimulating greater attendance and greater revenue for the park service." G. Elliott Cummings, Commander of the Maryland Division, Sons of Confederate Veterans, demanded that Latschar "publicly repudiate" his "anti-Confederate remarks" and requested the NPS stop its "continual attacks on the history and heritage" of the Confederacy.[31]

In response to the claims that he deliberately dishonored Confederate heritage, Latschar maintained that he did not intend to offend anyone, but merely wanted to open a discussion on ways the NPS could improve its interpretation. Some remained dissatisfied; management continued to receive letters in opposition to an "altered" and "modified" version of history. The outcry against the broadened interpretive proposal underscored how the discussion of slavery and the war's causes made many Americans uncomfortable. Clearly, to some, a public discussion of slavery as a cause of the war threatened dishonor to their fundamental beliefs and heritage. Moreover, as the remark from G. Elliott Cummings underscored, the connection of slavery to secession, and the Civil War, was seen as "anti-Confederate" and disrespectful to those who claimed Confederate heritage. In this vein, an inclusion of the war's socio-cultural issues typified prevailing efforts to present a politically correct view of American history. A statement by Jerry Russell, the Director of HERITAGE PAC, a national battlefield preservation action committee, exemplifies this view. "Battlefields are not about 'blame' or any other political agendas or any socio-cultural agendas or any arguments about political correctness," he professed. Echoing words from Virginia Governor William Hodges Mann delivered eighty years earlier, Russell summarized, "Battlefields are about honor."[32]

The emotional and often personal attachment to the American Civil War cannot be overstated. According to a recent study by Ancestory.com, 18 million Americans have an ancestor who fought in the Civil War and an estimated two-thirds of Americans have an ancestor who lived during the conflict. Noting the Civil War's continual passionate appeal, Lloyd Garrison, the great-great-grandson of William Lloyd Garrison, a prominent abolitionist and editor of the *Liberator*, commented, "It's *our* war. All the blood fell on *our* soil." As important, this personal, ancestral connection helps to explain the impassioned discourse on the war's causes and consequences. Modern descendants of noted nineteenth-century Americans who took clear, defined stances on slavery, including William Lloyd Garrison, John Brown, or Harriet Tubman, are tangible connections to the Civil War, as well as reminders of its legacy.[33]

While the overwhelming majority of opposition to the park's expanded interpretation came from the general public, academic and professional historians enthusiastically supported the change. In the fall of 1998, on behalf of the Organization of American Historians (OAH), three Civil War historians—James McPherson, Eric Foner, and Nina Silber—after completing a two-day site review, announced their support for the new museum and agreed upon the necessity of a more comprehensive narrative. "Without slighting tactics, strategy, and movement of regiments or the courage of soldiers on either side," wrote Foner, "the museum ought to place the battle of Gettysburg in context—or rather in a series of contexts, military, political, and social." James McPherson, author of Pulitzer Prize–winning *Battle Cry of Freedom*, the standard history of the war, echoed the same conclusions as Latschar and championed efforts to make Gettysburg relevant to women and minorities.[34] The OAH team's recommendations embodied the current trends of academic Civil War scholarship, labeled the "new military history," which shifted the emphasis away from pure military facets toward larger socio-cultural issues and the interplay between battlefield and home front.

While external forces, namely Congress, pressed for a significant modification to the interpretive presentation at Civil War sites, internally the National Park Service began to reevaluate the story presented at its parks. The Park Service did not have a defined philosophy on how to present or interpret its Civil War sites. On August 24–27, 1998, Civil War battlefield superintendents convened a conference in Nashville to discuss the issues facing Civil War sites. This meeting, "Holding the High Ground," proved to be significant for several reasons. First, the superintendents proposed and directed the meeting; it did not originate at the national office in Washington. During this four-day conference, superintendents discussed problems mutual to their sites. Most significantly, they opened a dialogue on expanding interpretation and, in doing so, laid the foundations to ensure their parks would "remain a vital and vivid part of the American social and cultural landscape for centuries to come." They acknowledged that their interpretive focus remained similar to that of the war's veterans, which had emphasized a decidedly military account that focused on strategies, tactics, and soldiers. "In doing so we have forgotten that the audience of the veterans in 1910 knew the context of the war far better than do Americans of 1998," they concluded. Consequently, the current interpretive focus failed to recognize that the "experience of war went far beyond the ordeal of soldiers in the field."[35]

Moreover, the superintendents characterized the existing interpretation to be "biased racially and socio-economically." With this understanding, they established a guiding principle which declared, "Battlefield interpretation must establish the site's particular place in the continuum of war, illuminate the social, economic, and cultural issues that caused or were affected by the war, illustrate the breadth of human experience during the period, and establish the relevance of the war to people today." At the conference's conclusion, they agreed that any future action would include close cooperation with the Organization of American Historians to integrate the latest academic scholarship into interpretive programs and media.[36]

When the results of the meeting became public, the Sons of Confederate Veterans and HERITAGE PAC led the opposition against the proposed interpretative trajectory at national military parks. As they had responded three years earlier to Latschar's proposal to present a more inclusive narrative, the Sons of Confederate Veterans undertook a vigorous campaign against this initiative. Members sent over 2,200 cards and letters to Secretary Babbitt. The preprinted postcard noted that the agency's current proposal "does a great disservice to the military strategists and to the soldiers who sacrificed their all at these important battlefields." HERITAGE PAC likewise championed a traditional interpretation. In a July 1999 newsletter, Jerry Russell claimed that the National Park Service's new focus directly ignored the reason for which Congress originally established the military parks. This misguided management, Russell declared, was a "cosmic threat to all battlefields in this country." While acknowledging that the war's causes were "factors to be considered," he argued that they "must not supplant the interpretation of the military actions."[37]

Yet, the National Park Service would not be deterred from reshaping the storyline at its Civil War sites. Superintendents continued to lead the way toward a more inclusive narration. In May 2000, the National Park Service sponsored the "Rally on the High Ground" seminar at Ford's Theatre to facilitate a discussion on how to best expand its interpretation. Invited speakers included Illinois Congressman Jesse Jackson, Jr., who had been championing discussions of slavery at Civil War parks, as well as historians Ira Berlin, James McPherson, David Blight, Edward Linenthal, James Horton, and Drew Gilpin Faust. Robert Sutton, superintendent of Manassas National Battlefield Park, concluded, "people should expect to visit a Civil War battlefield and come away with an understanding of not only who shot whom, how, and where, but why they were shooting at one another in the first place." The "Rally on the High Ground" gained national attention from the coverage by C-SPAN and other national media outlets. The seminar also opened a discussion between Park Service managers, park interpreters, Civil War academics, and the general public. Sutton envisioned the discussions as "a new paradigm for interpreting our Civil War battlefields."[38]

Consequently, in 2000, Congress directed the secretary of interior to "encourage Civil War battle sites to recognize and include in all of their public displays and multi-media educational presentations the unique role that the institution of slavery played in causing the Civil War and its role, if any, at the individual battle sites."[39] The appropriation reinforced proposals that the agency had been considering for a decade and echoed language already inserted into the boundary proposals of Fredericksburg and Gettysburg. Though Congressman Jackson received considerable credit for redirecting interpretation, superintendents at Civil War parks had already been moving toward this narrative. As important, Congress "encouraged" each site to find ways to discuss slavery in their interpretive media. Still, Congress never mandated this goal; instead, it was left to each park to address and accomplish this objective as appropriate.

With this "new paradigm" of interpretation in play, Gettysburg initiated plans to develop its museum. Eight prominent Civil War historians agreed to help develop the storyline and to serve on the newly created Gettysburg Museum Advisory Commission. Latschar explained that the academic advisors were to help the Park Service "create the most compelling, inspirational, and accurate museum experience that is possible, and to help us avoid "Enola Gay" type situations." In their OAH review, Foner, McPherson, and Silber recommended Gettysburg change its interpretive emphasis from the "High Water Mark" to "A New Birth of Freedom." This shift in theme would present visitors a better understanding how the battle and the Civil War brought forth a "new birth of freedom" for millions of Americans, which would appeal to a wider audience. As important, this new interpretive emphasis brought forth the primacy of Abraham Lincoln's Gettysburg Address. Since November 1863, generations of Americans had returned to Lincoln's words and interpreted his speech to fit contemporary issues and crises. Each generation found new inspiration in Lincoln's rhetoric. It was Lincoln's speech that defined for the Civil War generation the purpose of the war and outlined a vision for the nation's "new birth of freedom." In many ways, these words made the Gettysburg battlefield exceptional among the war's many blood-stained fields. Thus, it was only "fitting and proper" that "a new birth of freedom" become central to the battle's interpretive focus.[40]

Demolition of the Gettysburg National Tower on July 3, 2000, represented the inaugural implementation of the National Park Service's new vision to rehabilitate the battlefield landscape to its historic condition. This structure had dominated the Gettysburg skyline since 1974.

Meanwhile, on June 18, 1999, after two years of planning, a plethora of public meetings, workshops, and open houses, thousands of public comments, two congressional hearings, construction of interim collections storage, and often contentious debates, the National Park Service released its two-volume *Final General Management Plan.* On November 23, after a required thirty-day waiting period, Regional Director Marie Rust signed a "Record of Decision," officially approving Gettysburg's plans, which included the public-private partnership and the battlefield rehabilitation. Director Stanton, on June 30, 2000, signed the necessary agreements with the Gettysburg National Battlefield Museum Foundation to proceed with the construction of the new visitor center. The Foundation board selected Robert C. Wilburn, former president of Colonial Williamsburg, as its president on October 24.[41]

The first implementation of the approved *General Management Plan*, fittingly, occurred on July 3, 2000. Thousands gathered at the battlefield to witness the demolition of the Gettysburg National Tower, an obstruction that the *USA Today* had once described as "the ugliest commercial structure ever to intrude on the sanctity of a national park." Speaking at Gettysburg on Earth Day 1999, Secretary Babbitt identified the tower as an intrusion on the historic scene and declared, "There is no better symbol for the need to preserve the Gettysburg battlefield than taking down this tower." Later that year, the

Department of Justice, acting on behalf of the National Park Service, filed a condemnation suit to acquire the tower in pursuant of the Park Service's preservation goals. On June 15, 2000, the U.S. District court granted possession of the property to the National Park Service. Ceremonies began with speeches given by Latschar; Barbara Finfrock, president of the Friends; and NPS Director Stanton. Speaking on behalf of the National Trust for Historic Preservation, Richard Moe summarized, "Sometimes we can correct the mistakes of the past." Seconds later, Controlled Demolitions fired twelve rounds of charges and within ten seconds the two million pound steel structure, which had dominated the Gettysburg skyline and landscape since 1974, crumbled to the ground.[42]

The National Tower seemed always to generate controversy with the Civil War community, and sure enough, removal created a similar uproar. The park received a barrage of comments from individuals who expressed their "disappointment" in the tower's removal. Some viewed the tower as a source of architectural beauty and believed it enhanced the visitor experience. John Vockroth of Hanover, Pennsylvania, characterized the tower as a "historic structure" and a "work of art." Another comment offered, "Please don't tear down this beautiful tower . . . there will be many fewer visitors to your plain, drab, boring park without the tower." Clearly oblivious to the significance of the Gettysburg battlefield, one individual declared, "The National Tower has made Gettysburg more famous as far as I am concerned" and alleged that the removal of the tower would ruin the local economy and "send Gettysburg underground." Notwithstanding the predictable controversy, the National Park Service saw the removal of the tower as an opportunity to reclaim the area's historic integrity. "The demolition of the Gettysburg Tower is more an act of creation and restoration than destruction," remarked Secretary Babbitt. Perhaps the most indicative comment on why the tower should be removed came from Barbara Finfrock, who declared, "We stand as this battlefield's caretakers only for a short time—a very short time. The measure of our devotion and our success as its temporary caretakers is: did we leave the battlefield better than we found it?" Finfrock envisioned visitors looking upon the field where the tower formally stood and remarked, "They will see nothing . . . and they will be able to see everything."[43]

The removal of the National Tower served as a fitting "High Water Mark" to the National Park Service's management of the battlefield during the twentieth century. Three score and seven years after the National Park Service acquired Gettysburg National Military Park, through the agency's clearly defined philosophy on managing cultural landscapes and the vision and resolution of Superintendent John Latschar, the agency had established a definitive, if not uncontroversial, plan to manage the battlefield. External and internal factors combined to redirect Gettysburg's interpretive trajectory, which removed the interpretive focus from the "High Water Mark" to "A New Birth of Freedom." The resistance to this new, broader narrative illustrated how deeply the Lost Cause mythology resonated with Americans. The turmoil surrounding the new interpretive agenda demonstrated that, 140 years after secession, segments of the nation remained uncomfortable in discussing the causes of the war, reinforcing very evidently the pervasiveness of the "heritage syndrome." A clearly articulated long-term landscape philosophy, a new interpretive focus, the creation of the public-private partnership, and the continued evolution of the Gettysburg experience ushered the battlefield into the twenty-first century.[44]

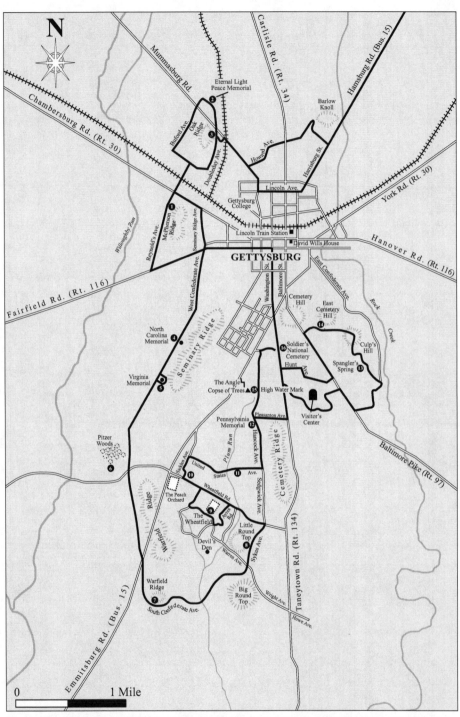

Contemporary Features of Gettysburg National Military Park, Including Tour Stops. Map created by Alexander Mendoza.

CHAPTER 11

SHALL NOT PERISH FROM THE EARTH: A NEW BEGINNING AT GETTYSBURG, 2001–2009

The demolition and removal of the Gettysburg National Tower offered a fitting closure to the twentieth century and symbolized "a new birth of freedom" for the battlefield. Appalled at the crass commercialization that the tower represented, noted Civil War historian Bruce Catton once characterized the tower as a "damned outrage" and expressed hope for its removal. By the new century, the National Park Service sought to remove modern intrusions from the historic grounds and simultaneously create a landscape more closely resembling the one seen by the men at the time of the battle. Preservationists now began to speak in terms of reclaiming the battlefield's "historic integrity." Within the Department of Interior, revisions to the Secretary of the Interior's Standards for Historic Preservation clearly defined treatment prescriptions for historic properties and cultural landscapes. These standard classifications include preservation, rehabilitation, restoration, and reconstruction. Following these new guidelines, Gettysburg's staff began an unprecedented rehabilitation project. This included creating an accurate landscape, replacing missing historic features, and removing features not associated with the battlefield.[1]

Alterations to the battlefield landscape coincided with changes to the interpretation of Gettysburg National Military Park. Beginning in the 1990s, National Park Service officials considered the need to expand and broaden the narrative of several of its parks, Civil War battlefields included. New sites preserved and interpreted "sites of shame" and gave due attention to events neglected on both the nation's physical landscape and in popular memory. These challenged the pervasiveness of the "heritage syndrome," Americans' penchant for selectively ignoring periods of conflict and divisiveness. Part of this broadening of educational emphasis included a challenge to the reconciliationist narrative at the Civil War national military parks.[2]

Responsible for the preservation of approximately seventy sites associated with the history of the Civil War, the National Park Service stands as a defining entity in how Americans have come to understand the war. When the agency acquired the war's battlefields, it continued to advocate the story of sectional reunion, which had been created and promoted by the veterans of the war. This reconciliationist storyline trumpeted soldier valor and sacrifice, intentionally ignoring many of the war's causes and implications. Consequently, as David Blight has shown, nineteenth-century Americans shaped a "segregated historical memory," one that overshadowed the role of African Americans in the conflict and the war's racial context. Even the Civil War Centennial and the Civil Rights Movement failed to challenge or dispute this ingrained narrative. In 1965, much as it had in 1895, popular study and understanding of the Civil War centered around soldiers and generals, tactics and strategies. Three decades later, at a conference in Nashville, superintendents of Civil War parks advocated interpreting battles in a "continuum of war," to illustrate the multidimensional political, social, economic, and cultural components of war. Congress endorsed these efforts, and in the Department of Interior's 2000 appropriation bill directed the secretary of the interior to support them.[3]

Never before in the history of Gettysburg National Military Park, or any other Civil War battlefield, had the Park Service attempted to implement such a broad, aggressive rehabilitation program. Two key objectives drove the project. First, using now popular terminology, Superintendent John Latschar declared that landscape improvements would recapture the "integrity" of the battlefield. To restore the "integrity" implied that post–Civil War modifications and modern-day intrusions had violated the accuracy and sanctity of the historic landscape. Second, landscape rehabilitation would improve interpretation, allowing visitors to observe the terrain as the soldiers saw it and "read" the landscape. The battlefield had stood as the primary artifact to understand the fighting and specific character-defining features, such as fencing patterns or woodlots, enhanced a better understanding of troop movements and tactics. "Historical benefits of the project are obvious," Latschar noted. These benefits would now permit visitors to explore the complexities of battle, from the decisions made by generals to the face of battle as experienced by soldiers.[4]

Since 1933, when the National Park Service acquired the battlefield, the agency had completed minor rehabilitation projects. In 1940, workers cut non-historic woodlots on the southern end of the battlefield, near Little Round Top and Devil's Den. McConaghie's second project removed and undergrounded telephone poles and lines along the Chambersburg Pike. In addition, the post-and-pipe fencing that had dotted the landscape since the late nineteenth century was removed. Certainly, McConaghie's accomplishments to remove non-historic features were commendable and represented a progressive preservation philosophy. Unfortunately, the Park Service failed to sustain the cuts, and the woodlots soon regenerated. Hence, when Latschar initiated his rehabilitation program, it was not the first time in Gettysburg's history that the Park Service attempted to establish an accurate, historic landscape. Latschar's plan differed in scope; it was the first time such extensive cutting projects involved large areas of the battlefield. And it also proved to be the first time the public had the opportunity to actively comment on the agency's landscape management initiatives.

Latschar's vision to create a historically accurate landscape indicated a clear shift in management philosophy. Charted in 1864, the Gettysburg Battlefield Memorial Association's primary purpose was to "hold and preserve, the battle-grounds of Gettysburg, on which were fought the actions of the first, second, and third days of July . . . with the natural and artificial defenses, as they were at the time of said battle." When the War Department acquired the site in February 1895, the federal government continued a similar mission, namely to preserve and mark the "lines of battle of the Union and Confederate armies at Gettysburg." In both instances, the GBMA and the War Department intended to preserve the battlefield as a means to honor the men who fought there. By all accounts, the National Park Service's philosophy of managing the battlefield had evolved since acquiring the site 1933. Latschar's philosophy directed efforts not simply to preserve the landscape, but to transform it to its historic condition. Jim Weeks notes this distinction "between preserving land to remember an event" and "transforming the land to look like it did when the event occurred."[5]

The first rehabilitation project commenced at the Codori-Trostle thicket, located toward the southern end of the battlefield and west of the Pennsylvania Monument. On July 2, 1863, the 1st Minnesota Infantry rushed toward this thicket to thwart the advance of a brigade of Alabamians. During the attack, the 1st Minnesota sustained approximately 82 percent casualties. In the years since the battle, extensive undergrowth obscured what in 1863 had been relatively open, unimpeded terrain. Rehabilitation efforts began in the spring of 2001 with the removal of three acres of non-historic trees. A second cut occurred later that fall, with the removal of an additional twenty-three acres of non-historic trees in and around the vicinity of the thicket. As part of an effort to reestablish character-defining features significant to the fighting and outcome of the battle, Friends volunteers restored historic fencing patterns in the thicket near Plum Run and along the Trostle Lane.[6]

The rehabilitation program assisted the park's objective to improve interpretation, allowing visitors to better "read the landscape." Restoring features significant to the battle's outcome afforded visitors a level of understanding theretofore absent from the historically inaccurate terrain. Interpretive benefits gained from the cutting of twenty-six acres in the Codori-Trostle thicket were immediate and stark. For example, at the time of Pickett's Charge, Union artillery, commanded by Colonel Freeman McGilvery, occupied ground just east of the thicket and poured devastating artillery fire into the advancing Confederates. As the woodlot grew in the century after the battle, it became difficult to visually comprehend the role of McGilvery's artillery in repulsing the assault. The removal of the thicket dramatically enhanced the understanding of the fighting in this part of the battlefield.[7]

Gettysburg's first rehabilitation project received enthusiastic support from the Civil War community. The removal of non-historic woodlots offered a viewshed not seen in over a century. On his first visit to the battlefield since the Codori-Trostle thicket rehabilitation, one individual remarked, "I'm impressed to say the least, the view is magnificent! Keep up the good work!" In response to the continual rumblings of opposition, one supporter reminded detractors that "The battlefield is not the Gettysburg National Arboretum, nor is it the Gettysburg National Bird Sanctuary . . . clearing trees to restore the battlefield to the vistas of 1863, as well as restoration of orchards and fence lines . . . is exactly the right thing to do." Latschar's large-scale rehabilitation

In 2004 the NPS removed eighteen acres of non-historic woodlots from the Rose Woods Gap and the vicinity of the Slyder and Bushman Farms. This rehabilitation effort opened up historic vistas to better interpret the fighting of July 2, 1863. The Rose Farm can be seen in the right rear and the 2nd Company Massachusetts Sharpshooters Monument in the foreground. Photo courtesy of Barbara Adams.

projects received attention inside the Beltway as well. During the summer of 2002, several congressional staffers visited the battlefield, met with park management, and received a tour of the newly rehabilitated thicket. The following year Congress earmarked $300,000 for the project. By 2009, the federal government's funding had reached $1.5 million.[8]

The second rehabilitation project took place near Warfield Ridge, along South Confederate Avenue, and the right flank of General Robert E. Lee's battle line. On July 2, as part of General James Longstreet's en echelon assault, General John Bell Hood's division formed along this ridge to assault the Union position at Little Round Top and Devil's Den. Here too, the growth of woodlots and shrubbery obscured what in 1863 was a relatively clear view from Warfield Ridge to the dominating position of Little Round Top. Beginning in the winter of 2003, approximately ninety acres of trees along Warfield Ridge and in the vicinity of the Slyder and Bushman farms, located between Warfield Ridge and the base of the round tops, were removed or thinned out. When the park completed this project, for the first time in over a century visitors driving along Warfield Ridge could see what the Texans and Alabamians saw before beginning their assault upon the Union left flank.[9]

Rehabilitation project completed in the Valley of Death, 2009–10. The NPS removed the 1930s era restroom and placed the utility lines underground in April 2010. Little Round Top is visable to the left of the image. Photo courtesy of Barbara Adams.

The National Park Service removed non-historic woodlots from Munshower Field, located north of Little Round Top, to more accurately reflect its 1863 appearance. The historic Jacob Weikert house is visible in the background. Photo courtesy of Barbara Adams.

Most of the interpretive and landscape maintenance had centered on grounds associated with the fighting on July 2 and 3, in particular the areas around Little Round Top and Cemetery Ridge, near the Angle. These two sites were the most visited areas on the battlefield, owing to the popularization of Little Round Top and Pickett's Charge. Now the Park Service began to rehabilitate the historic appearance along the eastern and northern sectors of the battlefield. At Culp's Hill, the right flank of the Union army, restoration crews performed a series of "health cuts" to thin out the dense underbrush. A "health cut" on the north side of Culp's Hill removed seventy-four acres of undergrowth in 2004, and another "health cut" the following year thinned an additional forty acres. Improvements were also made on the fields of the first day's fighting, north and west of town. Between 2006 and 2007, woodlots adjacent to the Eternal Light Peace Memorial on Oak Hill were removed. In July 1863, General Richard Ewell's Second Corps held this position. Now the openness of the terrain afforded visitors the opportunity to understand the dominating position of Oak Hill and how the terrain influenced the fighting on July 1 between Ewell's soldiers and the Federal army's 11th Corps.[10]

As the decade neared to a close, Gettysburg's staff had conducted the most intensive and extensive landscape rehabilitation program in its history. By 2009, large sections of the battlefield revealed a landscape similar to the one seen by the soldiers. Just six years after the inaugural cut at the Codori-Trostle thicket, 296 acres of non-historic woods had been removed. Additionally, 381.70 acres of health cuts were completed in several of the historic woodlots. While the removal of woodlots generated much debate, the park also planted trees in areas that were wooded at the time of the battle. This included planting over forty-three acres of trees at eight different locations on the battlefield. Furthermore, character-defining features significant to the battle's outcome were replaced. By 2009, workers had replanted 110 acres of historic orchards at 35 different sites. Significant to understanding troop and tactical movements of the armies on the field, 12.07 miles of historic fence patterns were rebuilt.[11]

As noted, the Park Service's current philosophy of cultural landscapes and replacement of character-defining features directed the idea and implementation of Gettysburg's landscape management program. Without a doubt, Gettysburg established a precedent for other national military park's landscape management practices. John Nau, chairman of the Advisory Council on Historic Preservation, for instance, visited Gettysburg on multiple occasions to explore the impact of the rehabilitation efforts. Smaller scale projects would be carried out at Chickamauga and Chattanooga, Vicksburg, and Antietam. Latschar spoke to the staff at Vicksburg National Military Park as they proceeded to plan and implement their own program. Like Gettysburg, by the twentieth century Vicksburg bore little resemblance to the 1863 siege landscape. Park officials, like those at Gettysburg, wanted to "enhance preservation of the landscape's historic character and integrity and improve visitor understanding and experience." For example, starting in 2005, workers removed non-historic vegetation in the Railroad Redoubt, a Confederate fortification built to protect a railroad line into Vicksburg. Certainly landscape improvements at other Civil War sites were not as expansive as those at Gettysburg, nor did they generate a similar level of controversy.[12]

Within the Park Service, however, officials remained divided on the benefits of landscape rehabilitation. Creating a historically accurate landscape is not unique to Civil War battlefields. The practice of "landscape freezing" is implemented at other historic sites. Colonial Williamsburg, where John D. Rockefeller advocated rehabilitation of the town to its 1770s condition, is a classic example of "landscape freezing." Opponents to "landscape freezing" maintain that it leads to "purposeful amnesia" because it encourages visitors to recall a romanticized version of American history. Similar to what Michael Kammen terms the "heritage syndrome," rehabilitating battlefields to their historic condition seemingly presents the landscape in isolation by focusing only on the specific days relevant to a particular battle. In her study of landscape management at Antietam, Martha Temkin, a cultural resource specialist with the NPS, argues that "landscape freezing" narrowly constrains the

In 2002 the Friends of the National Parks at Gettysburg secured title to the Home Sweet Home Motel, located along Steinwehr Avenue. This 1950s era hotel, prominently located in the fields of Pickett's Charge, characterized commercial development on the battlefield. Photo courtesy of Barbara Adams.

interpretive opportunities. Rehabilitating Antietam to its September 17, 1862, appearance prevents interpretation of the landscape on the eve of the battle or in its aftermath. She maintains "landscape freezing" can mute or minimize particular events and narratives. Returning Civil War landscapes to their historic condition, Temkin argues, also "takes us back" to the era of slavery.[13]

One method used to reclaim Gettysburg's historic integrity included the removal of post-battle structures. In 2001, the Park Service purchased Adams County Motors, a Ford dealership located along the Carlisle Road. This structure sat on the field where heavy fighting occurred on the afternoon of July 1. Ultimately the agency demolished the building and rehabilitated the ground to its historic appearance. The following year, in one of their most important acquisitions, the Friends secured title to the Home Sweet Home motel, located along Steinwehr Avenue across from the visitor center. Occupying 1.52 acres, this 1950s period motel tarnished the field where Confederates under General Isaac Trimble's command advanced toward the Union line during Pickett's Charge. As the North Carolina soldiers approached Cemetery Ridge, the 8th Ohio counterattacked and enveloped the Confederates, pouring devastating fire into their flank. On July 3, 2002, the 139th anniversary of Pickett's Charge, the Friends presented the Park Service with the deed to the property. In March 2003, contractors removed the motel. By the 140th anniversary the fields of Pickett's Charge were finally free of modern intrusions.[14]

Planning for the new museum and implementing landscape improvements dominated the NPS agenda for much of the early twenty-first century.

Still, the NPS and its partners also worked toward expanding interpretive opportunities. Seven decades after acquiring the battlefield, Gettysburg's staff developed an interpretive program considered by many to be unsurpassed by any other Civil War site. Gettysburg's summer programming now consisted of a daily rotation of approximately twenty different programs. As the result of expanded interpretive efforts, these programs not only discussed specific aspects of the battle, but also civilians, Civil War medicine, and the aftermath of the battle. During the battle anniversary, rangers presented special "real-time" programs, offered at the same time of day as the 1863 battle action. In addition, rangers offered a series of anniversary battle walks, which lasted three hours and presented visitors with a detailed account of a specific aspect of the battle, such as the fighting of General James Kemper's brigade on July 3. As a testament to their popularity and visitors' yearning for an immersive experience, hundreds of visitors endured the often-stifling July heat to follow rangers across the historic fields. Beginning in 1996, thousands more enjoyed

By the battle's 140th anniversary, the fields of Pickett's Charge were free of commercial intrusions.

these programs from the comfort of their own homes when Pennsylvania Cable Network (PCN) began coverage of the anniversary battle walks.[15]

Meanwhile, the Park Service continued to create an experience that allowed visitors the opportunity to immerse themselves in the Civil War culture. Popularized in the 1970s, the Park Service continued to promote the living-history experiences. Portraying various infantry, artillery, cavalry, medical, signal, or musical units, volunteer reenactors set up camps on the battlefield and conducted demonstrations. This form of interpretive educational programming proved popular with visitors, who enjoyed strolling through the camps and witnessing live-firing demonstrations. Such experiences were generated to give visitors what David Glassberg terms, a "sense of history." This connection often instilled feelings of patriotism, identity, and a sense of belonging. Surveys of visitors underscored their desire to obtain a "sense of history" when visiting the battlefield; they noted their wish to "get a feel for" or "connect with" or "imagine" the historic event. Rehabilitation of the battlefield now helped to create a landscape that permitted visitors the opportunity to imagine, within reason, the battle action on July 1, 2, and 3. These interpretive programs also reinforced the powerful emotional feeling of being on the battlefield. Rangers' battle walks, for instance, allowed visitors to "follow the footsteps" of a particular unit. On these occasions, walking the battlefield, feeling the terrain, hearing the rangers read quotes from soldiers who were engaged in the fighting, and viewing photographs of the soldiers significantly reinforced the personal connection for many visitors. For many, even 150 years after the battle, the emotional, some would even say spiritual, connection to the battle and the Civil War has not lessened.[16]

Abraham Lincoln's dedication of the Soldiers' National Cemetery defined the battle grounds of Adams County. On one hand, Gettysburg was a field of battle like so many others; grounds where thousands gave their "last full measure." Casualties mounted from horrific fighting in places like Sharpsburg, the Wilderness, Cold Harbor, Nashville, and Franklin. The dedication of the Soldiers' National Cemetery and particularly President Lincoln's Gettysburg Address, which defined the nation's war aims and put forth a vision for America's "new birth of freedom," set Gettysburg apart from other battle grounds. Since November 1863, Americans have turned to Lincoln and his address as a continual source of inspiration and guidance. Beginning in the twenty-first century, the National Park Service actively interpreted Lincoln as part of the Gettysburg story. To demonstrate the significance of Lincoln's visit, the National Park Service acquired the David Wills House, located on the town square. The president stayed with the Wills family the night of November 18, prior to the dedication of the Soldiers' National Cemetery. In March 2004, the Park Service, after acquiring the home from the borough, began efforts to

Construction of the Gettysburg Visitor Center and Museum began in 2006. Photo courtesy of Barbara Adams.

restore the Wills House to its historic appearance. On February 12, 2009, the 200th anniversary of Lincoln's birthday, and after a $7 million fiscal investment, the Wills House and its museum opened to the public. By the end of the year, the Wills House recorded over 35,000 visitors.[17]

On April 13, 2008, the Park Service closed the doors to its old visitor center, which had been operating as the park's main museum since October 1973. The following day, April 14, after fourteen years of planning, six years of fundraising, and three years of construction, at a price tag of $103 million, the new Gettysburg National Military Park Museum and Visitor Center opened to the public. As with the battlefield's history, the opening of the new visitor center and subsequent decisions involving its operations and management were not without controversy.[18]

As previously noted, in consultation with the Organization of American Historians (OAH), the National Park Service agreed to shift its interpretive emphasis from the "High Water Mark" to "A New Birth of Freedom." This new interpretive focus offered a broader, contextual understanding of the Civil War and redirected the story from the reconciliationist, consensus narrative, initially manufactured by the veterans after the war. Abraham Lincoln and his two-minute address made the Gettysburg battlefield exceptional. Since November 1863, thousands of Americans had referred to the Gettysburg Address in a multitude of ways and interpreted it to fit contemporary issues. Now "A New Birth of Freedom" placed the address where generations of Americans had already—central to the Gettysburg story. Specifically, the museum consists of eleven galleries to guide visitors from secession to the battle of Gettysburg and through Reconstruction. Still, and rightfully so, the battle receives considerable attention in the museum. One gallery explores the campaign to Pennsylvania. The largest gallery discusses the battle. This gallery is divided into five smaller ones, with the first one focusing on the battle's opening, followed then by a gallery for each of the three days of fighting, and concluding with the battle's outcome.[19]

Criticism of the museum and its galleries were immediate. Whereas the old visitor center continued a curiosity style display that exhibited hundreds of rifles, shell fragments, bullets, and accoutrements, park curators selectively picked artifacts that would complement and enhance the "A New Birth of Freedom" storyline. Objects were now used to interpret, not simply to be displayed. Repeat visitors and Civil War buffs found the new museum disappointing. Peter Jorgensen of the *Civil War News* declared that the new facility was "not a museum at all" and "has little on display regarding the battles of July 1, 2 and 3 in 1863." Jorgensen addressed a frequent complaint when he noted that the Park Service praised the partnership as an opportunity to build a museum that would better preserve the artifacts, but the new museum now displayed fewer objects. In the attempt to address the critics and reaffirm the new mission, Latschar explained, "What we're creating is a storyline museum, where you use artifacts to illustrate the storyline. So we have no need for 40 varieties of rifle muskets." To placate weapon enthusiasts, however, curators designed a traditional weapons display in the museum rotunda, complete with rifles, shell fragments, belt buckles, and bullets.[20]

Dissatisfaction over the display of artifacts aside, the other contentious issue centered on the famed Electric Map. As originally planned, both the Electric Map and the Gettysburg Cyclorama were to be included in the new museum. Initially, the Park Service planned to upgrade the Electric Map, but ultimately because of costs, interpretive benefits, and an outdated system, decided not to display the twelve-ton map in the new museum. This decision was met by virulent criticism. For over six decades, the Electric Map stood as an integral part of the Gettysburg experience. Returning visitors often reflected on seeing the map on previous visits. Shortly after the announcement that the Electric Map would not be used, concerned locals and battlefield visitors formed the "Save the Electric Map" group, led in part by Christine Rosensteel, Joseph's daughter, to oppose its exclusion from the new visitor center.[21]

In the place of the Electric Map, *A New Birth of Freedom*, narrated by well-known actor Morgan Freeman, serves as the museum's principal orientation program. To accomplish the secretary of interior's recommendation to discuss slavery as a primary cause of the Civil War, the twenty-two minute film places the battle into the larger social and political issues of war and its aftermath. In addition to summarizing the three-day battle, the film discusses secession, slavery, and emancipation and connects the Civil War to the Civil Rights Movement. After viewing the film, some lamented it as a poor replacement for the Electric Map. Others found the film's discussion on slavery and freedom to be too politicized and inappropriate for a battlefield orientation. One writer noted that the film overemphasized slavery as the "only cause for the Civil War" and found the connection between the battle and Martin Luther King, Jr., and the Civil Rights Movement as artificial. Alluding to the heightened sensitivities of political correctness and the cultural wars, the commenter continued, "Not to be too sarcastic, but in this political season, I half expect Barack Obama to come out at the end and say, 'I am Barack Obama and I endorse this message."[22]

Other disappointments soon loomed. Visitation to the Gettysburg Museum and Visitor Center in its first year of operation reached over 750,000. Despite high expectations, revenues for the building fell short of projections. Most importantly, the film earnings were substantially below estimates. Many visitors, satisfied with the interpretive opportunities in the free museum, opted not to see the film, while others believed the film to be priced too high. Park officials soon concluded that "the free museum was outdrawing the fee venues" which resulted in a "negative impact on the fee revenues." During the first four months of operation, between April 14 and August 28, the percentage of visitors who paid the admission fee to the film ranged from 18 to 24 percent. The Foundation's pro forma revenue projections were based on 33 percent of visitors purchasing the ticket.[23]

The solution to this shortfall seemed simple: charge an admission to the museum. Consequently, even before the museum's grand opening and the premier of the restored Gettysburg Cyclorama, the NPS and Foundation decided upon an "all-in-one fee" that included admission to the film, cyclorama, and now the museum. According to Superintendent Latschar, "the proposal spreads the burden of supporting the new facility across a wider percentage of park visitors." He stressed, however, that the "majority of the visitor experience," meaning the battlefield, would remain free. As for historical precedent, since acquiring the battlefield in 1933, the National Park Service at Gettysburg had never charged an admission fee to the museum. More importantly, the fee proposal represented a reversal of the pledge made to the American public and Congress in the *General Management Plan*. The *GMP* states, "The museum, like the visitor center, would be free to all visitors to encourage them to visit and learn from its exhibits." A deciding factor in the National Park Service selection of the Kinsley proposal was that it did not require an admission fee to the museum.[24]

Visitors and congressional members who had supported the plans for the new facility and the partnership based on the belief that the museum would be free remained far from pleased with the fee proposal. Tom Vossler, a Licensed Battlefield Guide and former board member of the Friends, commented, "How sad it is now that the museum exhibits are proving to be the most popular part of the new complex, you are going to tax the visitor in order to increase revenue!" Others felt deceived that the NPS and Foundation made an "irrevocable pledge" that the museum and its artifacts would be free. One Virginian offered a common sentiment, "The museum was promised to be free to the public. This was a key selling point from the start." More significantly to the purpose of the partnership, park historian Kathy Harrison stated "the public-private partnership was instigated and implemented in order to relieve the taxpayer of the additional burden of paying off a new interpretive complex. But the proposal seems to contradict that notion." Notwithstanding the outrage over the fee proposal, on October 1, the Park Service and Foundation announced the approval of a new fee structure. The $7.50 admission to the museum, film, and cyclorama went into effect the next day.[25]

In the midst of the fee proposal controversy, the Park Service and Foundation celebrated the Gettysburg National Military Park Museum and Visitor Center grand opening. On September 26, 2008, Superintendent John Latschar; Robert Wilburn, president of the Gettysburg Foundation; Robert Kinsley, constructor of the facility and Gettysburg Foundation board member;

Grand opening of the Gettysburg National Military Park Museum and Visitor Center, September 26, 2008. Pictured left to right: Robert Wilburn, President of the Gettysburg Foundation; Secretary of the Interior Dirk Kempthorne; Superintendent John Latschar; Robert Kinsley, President of Kinsley Construction Company.

After a decade of planning, a series of controversies, and a $103 million investment, the Gettysburg National Military Park Museum and Visitor Center opened to the public on April 14, 2008.

Secretary of the Interior Dirk Kempthorne; and Pennsylvania Governor Ed Rendell cut the ceremonial ribbon. "For the first time ever at Gettysburg," remarked Wilburn, "we have a museum that does justice to what happened here." Ceremonial events included Civil War music, a reading of the Gettysburg Address, special ranger programs, living-history demonstrations, guest lectures, and book signings.[26]

The highlight of the weekend, however, was the premier of the restored Gettysburg Cyclorama. Closed to the public since November 2005, conservation crews completed full-scale conservation on the painting. Years of improper display and poor preservation practices had caused severe damage to large portions of the painting. With the addition of the fourteen feet section of heretofore missing sky and the vibrant display of colors and detail, the painting bore little resemblance to its former self. Moreover, the three dimensional objects in the foreground, features which were part of Philppoteaux's original work, blended seamlessly onto the canvas. When properly restored and hung in a hyperbolic shape, and with the addition of the three-dimensional objects, including carriages, mannequins, and accouterments, the Gettysburg Cyclorama was now displayed in a way not seen in over a century. By the time the restored painting premiered, Congress had allocated a total of $15 million for the project.[27]

The interpretive theme of "A New Birth of Freedom" contextualizes the three-day battle of Gettysburg into the larger social, political, and military context of the Civil War.

A year after the opening of the Gettysburg National Military Park Museum and Visitor Center, and after obscuring the landscape since the early 1920s, on March 23, 2009, the park's old visitor center was demolished. A wrecking ball smashed into the Rosensteel brick building and one by one the white porch pillars toppled to the ground. The cyclorama building, however, still remained. Built in 1962 and purposefully situated in the heart of Ziegler's Grove as part of the National Park Service philosophy at that time, its fate was contested. In December 2006 the Recent Past Preservation Network (RPPN) sued the NPS for its alleged failure to comply with the National Environmental Policy Act and the National Historic Preservation Act. The National Park Service initiated an Environmental Assessment plan to explore various alternatives for the building, and continued to champion demolition and rehabilitation of Ziegler's Grove to its historic appearance.[28]

Meanwhile, controversy continues to surround the National Park Service and its partnership with the Gettysburg Foundation. Since its inception and the opening of the visitor center in 2008, the Foundation has been plagued with revenue shortfalls. After implementing the $7.50 museum fee in October 2008, eight months later the Foundation increased the admission fee to $10.50. This fee increase caught the attention of the Park Service's national office. Displeased with the apparent fiscal instability of the Foundation and increasing fees, the NPS sent a budget team to examine the Foundation's 2010 operating

Demolition of the Park Service's Visitor Center, March 2009. Photo courtesy of Barbara Adams.

budget. More significantly, approval of the Foundation's budget, especially any increase in venue fees, would no longer fall within the jurisdiction of Gettysburg's superintendent, but would now have to be approved by the Park Service regional director. Each of these measures should provide some degree of additional fiscal oversight of the Foundation.[29]

After fifteen years of service at Gettysburg National Military Park and unparalleled accomplishments, John Latschar's tenure came to an abrupt end. On October 22, 2009, Latschar learned that he had been involuntarily reassigned to serve as the associate director of cultural resources, stationed in Frederick, Maryland.[30] John Latschar indisputably stands as the most influential manager in the Park Service's history. His fifteen-year tenure, August 1994 to October 2009, witnessed the most dramatic, far-reaching changes to both the battlefield's physical landscape and its interpretive trajectory. The battlefield's earlier managers, the Gettysburg Battlefield Memorial Association and the War Department, created a landscape as a means to remember the battle of Gettysburg, as well as the men who fought and died on these grounds. Latschar's philosophy shifted the site's preservation and interpretation mission. Changes in attitudes toward preserving and presenting cultural landscapes within the National Park Service provided the guiding philosophy of landscape rehabilitation. Small-scale rehabilitation projects were accomplished at other Civil War battlefields, but none as extensive and pronounced as those at Gettysburg. These unprecedented accomplishments are owed to the management, persistence, and commitment of Latschar. Through a hailstorm of controversy over alterations to the battlefield, the Park Service created a landscape that more closely authenticates the 1863 appearance. In addition, more than ever before, the National Park Service maintains a proactive influence in shaping visitors' experiences. When Gettysburg ceased to be a landscape to extol patriotic virtues, the agency began to mold the battlefield into an immersive experience. The creation of a historically accurate landscape, the myriad of living-history demonstrations, and ranger programs that allow visitors to "follow in the footsteps" of the soldiers collectively form a "sense of history." Gettysburg stands firmly entrenched in American culture and memory; the battlefield remains a place that will not "perish from the earth."[31]

Conclusion

It Is for Us the Living: Gettysburg's Old and New Challenges

Undeniably, the final years of the twentieth century and the first decade of the new century stand as a watershed in the history of the Gettysburg battlefield. Excepting James McConaghie's administration (1933–1940), which owed its improvements to New Deal funding, no other period in the National Park Service's administration brought such expansive modifications to the battlefield. Multiple factors collided during this era to lay the foundation for these changes, which redefined the Gettysburg experience. Since 1933 when the National Park Service began managing the battlefield, the agency had only loosely defined a policy of how to preserve and present its historic landscape. McConaghie inaugurated the practice of removing non-historic woodlots for both historical accuracy and scenic improvements. Though landscape modifications in the final years of the twentieth century resulted in a vitriolic outcry, the Park Service had been cutting non-historic woodlots for six decades. Not until the final decade of the twentieth century, however, did the NPS clearly define standards on how to manage a cultural landscape. The ongoing removal of over 500 acres of non-historic woodlots, the replanting of over 100 acres of historic orchards, and the replacement of over 12 miles of historic fencing patterns create for today's visitors a visual impression similar to how Union and Confederate soldiers viewed the terrain in 1863. After contentious debate, in March 2013 the cyclorama building was demolished. The removal of the cyclorama building, which had dominated Ziegler's grove since 1962, represents on-going efforts to eliminate non-historic structures from the battlefield.[1]

Broadening the battlefield's interpretive narrative similarly improved the Gettysburg experience. Through the centrality of the Gettysburg Cyclorama, interpretive medium, and ranger programs, the Park Service served an active role in reaffirming Americans' romantic, nostalgic understanding of the Civil War. The newly installed exhibit galleries and film in the Gettysburg Visitor

Removal of the cyclorama building, March 2013. This structure had dominated Ziegler's Grove since its opening in 1962. Photo courtesy of Barbara Adams.

Center and Museum challenge the traditionally accepted reconciliationist narrative and defy the "heritage syndrome." For decades the Park Service had promoted the story of reconciliation, initially established by the Civil War veterans during the late nineteenth century. The ensuing clamor over the congressional directive of 2000 and Gettysburg's announcement of plans to address the "unique role that the institution of slavery played in causing the Civil War and its role, if any, at the individual battle sites" demonstrates the intransience of the Lost Cause narrative. Yet for all the saber-rattling over the broadened narrative, Civil War interpretive Armageddon did not occur; the "cosmic threat" to the battlefields did not emerge.[2]

In fact, the shift in the interpretive focus from the "High Water Mark" to "A New Birth of Freedom" brought to the fore the battlefield's defining event. Whether or not Gettysburg was the war's turning point is debatable, but the battlefield stands indisputably as the Mecca of this nation's hallowed grounds. President Abraham Lincoln's dedication of the Soldiers' National Cemetery and his articulation of the Union war aims made the Adams County battle grounds unlike any other. In the following decades, the Gettysburg Address has resonated deeply in American culture and memory. On multiple occasions, orators cited passages from the address to fit contemporary issues. In the 1940s, for example, speakers used the address as a call to arms and endurance of hardships in a global war. After the Second World War, in the midst of the Cold

War, the Gettysburg Address emerged as a testament to democracy and "government of the people, by the people, for the people." In the 1960s, Americans interpreted Lincoln's words as a challenge to eradicate racial discrimination and to fulfill the "dedication to the proposition that all men are created equal." Lincoln's tribute to the Union war dead and his articulation of "a new birth of freedom" for the nation became, to paraphrase Edwin Stanton, an address "for the ages."

Superintendent John Latschar's fifteen-year era brought stability and consistency to the battlefield's leadership. His resolution and leadership guided changes unprecedented among previous NPS superintendents. As illustrated, the influence of managers on the battlefield is significant. The superintendent holds considerable influence in developing and implementing management objectives. Subsequent change in leadership will continue to be a critical component in future battlefield operations. On January 8, 2010, Northeast Regional Director Dennis Reidenbach named James Robert (Bob) Kirby the new superintendent of Gettysburg National Military Park. Previously, Kirby served as the superintendent of Petersburg National Battlefield in Virginia and assistant superintendent at Delaware Water Gap National Recreation Area. Kirby assumed his duties as the eleventh NPS superintendent at Gettysburg on March 1, 2010.[3]

The change in the park's leadership paralleled a transition in the management of the Gettysburg Foundation. Upon the resignation of Robert Wilburn, on October 8, 2009, the Foundation named Richard Buchanan as its second president. His tenure with the Gettysburg Foundation proved short-lived, however, and on January 26, 2010, the Foundation announced his departure to "pursue other opportunities." After nearly a year-long search, the Foundation announced the selection of Joanne M. Hanley. Hanley, whose appointment began on February 1, 2011, arrived to Gettysburg with a career of management experience in the National Park Service, which included time as superintendent of National Parks of Western Pennsylvania, Flight 93 National Monument, and Fort Necessity National Battlefield.[4]

A little less than two years after the opening of the Gettysburg Museum and Visitor Center, the two leading figures behind the partnership, John Latschar and Robert Wilburn, assumed other positions. In his final annual report, Latschar declared the public-private partnership with the Gettysburg Foundation to be the "gold standard of partnerships" within the Park Service.[5] Certainly, for the National Park Service at Gettysburg, the partnership solved the agency's resource problems, provided a state-of-the-art museum, improved archival collections, and restored the Gettysburg Cyclorama, which otherwise simply would not have been possible. While the cost of the facility and the influence of private investments in the project generated considerable criticism, the Foundation readily raised millions of dollars. Philanthropists, businesses, and thousands of Americans contributed money to build a better visitor center at one of the nation's most treasured historic sites. But would the American people willingly donate money to a site of lesser national significance? Could a similar project succeed at Catoctin National Park in Thurmont, Maryland, or Effigy Mounds National Monument in Iowa? Though a lesser-known site would not need the fiscal resources obtained during the Gettysburg project, it seems unlikely that Americans would so generously donate money for a partnership at any other national park. Simply put, Gettysburg worked because the project was at Gettysburg.

Fallacies remain apparent in the "gold standard," however. Bob Kirby and Joanne Hanley are now charged with the responsibility of making the partnership viable and solvent. Indeed, improving the public-private partnership will be one of the key questions the new management team faces. Most critically, the Foundation must demonstrate improvements in its ability to operate the multi-million dollar facility. Former Foundation President Wilburn and staff proved adept at raising money for the project, but the Foundation, to date, has struggled to remain fiscally solvent. The near revolving door of Foundation management only exacerbates these challenges and undermines morale in the organization. Revenue challenges prevailed soon after the visitor center opened, which resulted in a $7.50 fee for admission to the museum, film, and cyclorama. After another fee increase in January 2012, the fee, as of January 2013, stands at $12.50. Other causes for public disappointment with the Foundation rest on seemingly poor judgment. For example, in March 2012 the visitor center bookstore began selling John Wilkes Booth bobble-head dolls. After national media attention and criticism from park visitors and historians, the dolls were pulled from the shelf. Certainly the decision to sell bobble-head dolls of the man who assassinated President Lincoln demonstrated a simple lack of taste and judgment. Harold Holzer, Lincoln scholar, summarized, "It's inappropriate to celebrate a criminal who took the life of a great American whose memory and words are celebrated at Gettysburg."[6]

Issues of the partnership aside, Gettysburg remains contested ground and interest groups continue to seek ways to capitalize on its popularity. Recent efforts to bring casino slots are a testament to local interests' ongoing attempts for economic gain. On April 14, 2011, the Pennsylvania Gaming Control Board rejected a proposal to install 500 slot machines and 50 gambling tables at the Eisenhower Resort and Conference Center, located along the Emmitsburg Road, less than a mile south of the battlefield. The rapid proliferation of ghost tours stands as a crass, commercializing enterprise, if not exploitation. Ghost touring companies arrived in Gettysburg in the mid-1990s. Initiated by local entrepreneur and former NPS ranger Mark Nesbitt, the "Ghosts of Gettysburg Candlelight Walking Tours" opened in 1994. Today, over a dozen ghost tours are available to visitors seeking the paranormal experience of Gettysburg. Locally owned museums are a long-held tradition in Gettysburg. Currently, approximately twelve for-profit museums operate outside the federal boundary. Ranging in theme from the American Civil War Wax Museum, to the Lincoln Train Museum, to the Hall of Presidents and First Ladies, or General Lee's Headquarters and Museum, these museums provide an alternative to the official narrative found in the Gettysburg Museum and Visitor Center.[7]

Commemorative activities of the Civil War Sesquicentennial crystallized on the Gettysburg battlefield. On June 30, 2013, the opening ceremonies, "Gettysburg: A New Birth of Freedom," held on the grounds near General Meade's Headquarters, featured country music artist Trace Adkins singing the National Anthem and presidential historian Doris Kearns Goodwin as the keynote speaker. Goodwin, who had delivered a keynote at the previous year's Remembrance Day event, emphasized a sweeping civil rights theme, providing scant attention to the cause of commemoration—the battle of Gettysburg itself. Instead, Goodwin addressed women's rights, equality for minorities, the recent Supreme Court decision over the Defense of Marriage Act, and spoke at length about Eleanor Roosevelt. Goodwin's keynote immediately drew a firestorm of condemnation from across the nation. Critics charged Goodwin with a seemingly dismissive attitude toward the battle of Gettysburg and the men who had fought and died on the fields and with politicizing the battle's anniversary. One critic summarized Goodwin's speech as "rambling, self-promoting, and borderline inappropriate," noting her speech to be more fitting for an "alumni weekend" or "Georgetown cocktail party." Few rushed to her defense. A columnist for Hanover's *Evening Sun* concluded that Goodwin "got it right" by emphasizing the ongoing struggle for human rights and equalities, themes that mirrored Lincoln's address 150 years earlier.[8]

The product of years of planning, the National Park Service and the Gettysburg Foundation hosted a myriad of ranger programs, battle walks, living-history encampments, lectures, and book signings. During the anniversary dates, park rangers presented "key moment" programs that occurred at the exact time and location of the battle's action in 1863. For instance, on July 1 at 9:30 A.M., visitors followed a park ranger in the footsteps of the 1,800 Union soldiers in the famed Iron Brigade as they arrived to the fields northwest of town. In addition to the "key moment" interpretive programs, rangers presented "battle overview hikes," lasting sixty to ninety minutes in length, which explored a deeper aspect of the battle. On the afternoon of July 2, for example, hundreds of enthusiasts gathered in the Peach Orchard to learn about the Confederate assault on General Daniel Sickles's Third Corps. Other interpretive opportunities included "battlefield experience programs" that explored a unique aspect of the battle, such as General Meade's Council of War. The National Park Service's herculean interpretive effort proved immensely popular with battlefield visitors. On July 2, 2013, for example, park staff presented forty-eight "key moment" programs for over 10,000 visitors, six "battle overview hikes" for nearly 4,000, and two "battle experience programs" for approximately 1,500 people. At the conclusion of the sesquicentennial, Gettysburg's staff had presented a total of 287 interpretive programs for an estimated 110,000 visitors.[9]

Since 1933, the National Park Service has strived to accomplish its dual mission of "providing for the enjoyment" of battlefield visitors while leaving the site "unimpaired for future generations." With each successive administration, the definition of a national military park and Americans' expectations of the Gettysburg experience evolved. For the Gettysburg Battlefield Memorial Association and the War Department, Gettysburg stood as a living memorial to the events of July 1–3, 1863, and a means to honor and remember the sacrifices of the men who gave "the last full measure of devotion." When David McConaughy spearheaded the preservation effort, he noted, "there could be no more fitting and expressive memorial of the heroic valor and signal triumphs of our Army . . . than the Battle-field itself." In 1895, when the federal government chartered Gettysburg National Military Park, the enabling legislation stated a similar mission, to "mark the boundaries of the said park" and to "mark the lines of battle of all troops engaged."[10]

When the National Park Service acquired Gettysburg in 1933, the Park Service struggled to maintain the battlefield consistent with the purpose of a national military park. Most significantly, the agency promoted a multiuse landscape that presented the battlefield more as a *park* and less a *national military park*. This management philosophy, however, reflected larger trends within the National Park Service. Since its establishment in 1916, the NPS has promoted itself as a protector of the nation's cultural and natural treasures, but also as an agent of tourism. At Gettysburg promotion of a tourist culture included advertising the battlefield as a site of scenic beauty. Park officials encouraged visitors to come to the battlefield to enjoy the redbuds and dogwoods that rejuvenated the springtime landscape. Other tourist amenities included the installation of scenic viewers on the battlefield, a service consistent with the western parks. As significant, the Park Service cultivated Gettysburg as a tourist destination. In 1941, then Superintendent James Coleman declared the Park Service to be in the "tourist business," noting an intent to attract "as great a number of visitors here as possible." Consideration for tourism continued in the postwar years. In 1964, the park superintendent squarely placed the agency's mission toward visitor entertainment, stating, "Let's really have concern for the visitor and let's really give him the 'time of his life.'"[11]

Throughout the twentieth century, the Park Service continued to offer the battlefield as a multiuse landscape, which often deemphasized the battlefield as a memorial to war and instead promoted the park as a recreational site. In part, this reflected larger trends within the national park system. The agency's "Parkscape U.S.A." movement of the 1970s encouraged a diversity of recreational and educational opportunities. As late as the 1970s, Gettysburg's staff encouraged visitors to use the battlefield for various recreational pursuits, including sleigh riding, ice skating, Easter egg hunts, and kite flying. Following prevalent trends of environmental awareness that gripped the nation in the 1960s and 1970s, park staff constructed an Environmental Study Area on Big Round Top to promote the battlefield's natural features. While par for the course of larger administrative trends within the agency, certainly these recreational activities stood at odds with the original purpose of preserving the battlefield and remained incongruent with the functions of a national military park. Recent Park Service philosophy combined with a pervasive perception of Gettysburg as a sacred landscape has curtailed these recreational pursuits. Efforts to reclaim the battlefield's "historic integrity" include preserving the landscape for its historical significance and the removal of non-historic structures that detract from the battlefield's "integrity."

Giving the visitor the "time of his life" took several forms. Most significantly, the National Park Service established an educational program and became proactive in shaping the understanding of the battle and the Civil War. Based on Freeman Tilden's theories of interpretation, park rangers sought not merely to inform visitors about the battle, but to provoke an emotional connection. Whereas the War Department relied upon the scores of static itinerary tablets to describe the campaign and fighting, the National Park Service installed wayside exhibits that not only recounted specific battle action, but also served to interpret the battlefield and help visitors "read" the landscape. Beginning in the 1960s, several audio-visual exhibits were installed to provide more engaging medium. In the 1970s, national parks across the country adopted a new, interactive form of interpretation termed living-history. At Gettysburg, rangers presented first-person narrations of the experience of Civil War soldiers or the civilian population. These immersive experiences allowed visitors to gain what David Glassberg defines as a "sense of history."[12]

Since 1863 the purpose and use of the Gettysburg battlefield have evolved, and each successive park manager has fashioned the battlefield in different ways. As important, Americans' expectations and connections to the battle and its landscape have likewise evolved. For much of its history, the battlefield has served as a site of patriotic display. Though veterans established Gettysburg as a site for sectional reconciliation, in an attempt to "bind the nation's wounds," in later years Americans journeyed to Gettysburg to reaffirm their American heritage and citizenship. Certainly the prevalence of civic tourism reaffirmed the "heritage syndrome." The simultaneous occasion of the Civil War Centennial and the Civil Rights Movement offered an opportunity for a reevaluation of the entrenched reconciliationist narrative told at Civil War battlefields. Though orators stood on the battlefield urging the realization of the "proposition that all men are created equal," the occasion did not bring any immediate and meaningful changes to the predominant narrative. For the time being, Civil War battlefields remained landscapes to champion the "heritage syndrome," a place to discuss tales of heroism, courage, and valor while selectively ignoring the war's social causes and consequences. In the wake of the Civil War Centennial, Americans dissociated Gettysburg and civic patriotism. The battlefield no longer served as a destination for civic expression, patriotic, flag-waving faith, or debating contemporary political issues. Instead, Gettysburg became a place to be experienced, where visitors could gain a "sense of history." The enthusiasm for Memorial Day celebrations, once the highlight of the annual calendar, is now replaced with scores of visitors descending on Gettysburg for the annual battle reenactment.[13]

More than any other battlefield, Gettysburg holds an exceptional place among America's public landscapes. A sense of collective ownership generates unprecedented interest in its management and fate. Fundamentally, the preservation of the battlefield owes itself to the interests and efforts of local citizens. The Gettysburg Battlefield Memorial Association, charted in 1864, consisted of residents who had the foresight to purchase lands affiliated with the battle. As the popularity of the battlefield increased, particularly in the mid-twentieth century, Americans scrutinized decisions made by the National Park Service, and in doing so, laid claim to its future. These interest groups vary from Licensed Battlefield Guides, to profiteering businessmen, to spiritually connected visitors. Policy decisions at Gettysburg have regularly played out in the national media. People from Adams County to California continue to express their opinions to management and their congressional representatives on how the battlefield should be interpreted, preserved, and promoted. The recent popularity of Civil War–related internet sites and blogs has only served to increase venues for debate.

The management of the Gettysburg battlefield between 1933 and 2013 proved to be as controversial as the battle itself, and possibly even more so. The National Park Service manages approximately seventy sites associated with the Civil War era; state parks or local preservation associations administer other battlefields and Civil War–era sites. None of these places engender the attention and power that Gettysburg does, however. Gettysburg is a field of battle far different in its meaning, symbolism, and power than Manassas or Fredericksburg or even Saratoga or Yorktown. For generations these once horrific slaughter fields define our nation's history and what it means to be an American. Gettysburg, without a doubt, will remain a place that "shall not perish from the earth."

NOTES

Preface

1. Gettysburg National Military Park, "The Gettysburg Sesquicentennial: 2013, a Year in Review," 3–4. (Anticipated future filecode A54.) Posted to Gettysburg National Military Park Website, https://www.nps.gov/gett/learn/management /index.htm, accessed July 21, 2022, via https://archive.org/web/. (All operational updates hereinafter will be cited as GNMP with the designated date and corresponding page number when available.)

2. "Holding the High Ground: A National Park Service Plan for the Sesquicentennial of the American Civil War," National Park Service, May 2008. Available at https://hst409509.files.wordpress.com/2011/01/holding-the-high-ground.pdf.

3. "Civil War to Civil Rights Commemoration, Summary Report," National Park Service, November 2016, 6–9; 25. Available at https://www.nps.gov/civilwar /upload/civil-war-to-civil-rights-summary-report-1-v2.pdf; Marty Blatt, "From Civil War to Civil Rights," *George Wright Forum* 31 (1) (2014): 5–9; Nick Sacco, "A Statistical Analysis of Visitation to National Park Service Civil War Sites During the Sesquicentennial," *Muster,* January 9, 2018. Available at https://www .journalofthecivilwarera.org/2018/01/statistical-analysis-visitation-national -park-service-civil-war-sites-sesquicentennial/. The establishment of Reconstruction Era National Historical Park (South Carolina) in January 2017 marks the first national park site charged with interpreting the Reconstruction Era.

4. Sacco, "A Statistical Analysis of Visitation to National Park Service Civil War Sites During the Sesquicentennial." Gallagher described the Civil War Sesquicentennial as "anemic" in an interview with the Civil War Trust in 2013. For a similar perspective, see Cameron McWhirter, "For Civil War Buffs, 150-Year Anniversary Has Been Disappointing So Far," *Wall Street Journal,* April 10, 2014.

5. GNMP, "Operational Update, 2013," 2.

6. GNMP, "Operational Update, Fall 2014," 1; Sacco, "A Statistical Analysis of Visitation to National Park Service Civil War Sites During the Sesquicentennial." Sacco found that thirty-three sites that participated in the 150th events

experienced an increase in visitation when compared to visitation trends between 2006 and 2010.

7. Timothy B. Smith used the term "golden age" to describe the battlefield preservation efforts at the end of the nineteenth century in *The Golden Age of Battlefield Preservation: The Decade of the 1890s and the Establishment of America's First Five Military Parks* (Knoxville: Univ. of Tennessee Press, 2008).

8. Bob Kirby, "On My Watch," Blog of Gettysburg National Military Park, December 26, 2013. Available at https://npsgnmp.wordpress.com/2013/12/26 /on-my-watch/.

9. Press Release, "Ed W. Clark Selected Park Superintendent for Gettysburg and Eisenhower," January 1, 2014.

10. Katie Lawhon, "Another Piece of the Puzzle on Cemetery Ridge," Blog of Gettysburg National Military Park, September 25, 2014. Available at https:// npsgnmp.wordpress.com/2014/09/25/another-piece-of-the-puzzle-on -cemetery-ridge/.

11. Katie Lawhon, "Rehabbing Cemetery Ridge," Blog of Gettysburg National Military Park, May 21, 2015. Available at https://npsgnmp.wordpress.com/2015 /05/21/gettysburg-details-rehabbing-cemetery-ridge/; GNMP, "Operational Update, Fall 2016," 1; GNMP, "Operational Update 2016: Year in Review," 2; GNMP, "Operational Update, Spring 2017," 1; GNMP, "Operational Update 2017: Year in Review," 3. The Hancock Avenue gate was one the main point of entry onto the Army of the Potomac's battle line. There were earlier versions of the historic entrance gate at Hancock Avenue (one built in 1889 and another in 1896), but the 1923 design was selected because of the availability of historic materials. In addition to Battery F, 5th U.S. Artillery, other monuments returned to their original location included the 12th Massachusetts, 88th Pennsylvania, 1st Massachusetts Sharpshooters, and Battery I, 1st U.S. Artillery. Cope was the last living member of the original 1893 park commission.

12. Linda Wheeler, "Lee's Gettysburg Headquarters Restored, Set to Open October 28," *Washington Post*, September 15, 2016; Jarrad Hedes, "Civil War Trust Plans to Purchase Lee's Headquarters," *Gettysburg Times*, July 1, 2014.

13. "Mulligan MacDuffer's Final Day Sunday," *Gettysburg Times*, September 29, 2017.

14. "Battlefield Trust Buys Six Acres Along Baltimore Pike," *Gettysburg Times*, May 25, 2021. It appears that the Trust is in discussions to purchase the Battlefield Military Museum, located along Baltimore Pike just south of Slocum Avenue.

15. Jim Hale, "Trust to Buy, Raze Pickett's Buffett," *Gettysburg Times*, November 17, 2022. It is anticipated that Pickett's Buffett will move into the abandoned Boyd's Bear facility further south along Business 15.

16. Mason Adams, "Dylann Roof's Rebel Yell: How the Persistence of the Confederacy Led to Charleston's Slaughter," *Politico*, June 20, 2015. Civil War historians have produced a plethora of works on Civil War memory and memorialization. Among the most recent works on Civil War monuments are the following:

Thomas J. Brown, *Civil War Monuments and the Militarization of America* (Chapel Hill: Univ. of North Carolina Press, 2019), and Karen Cox, *No Common Ground: Confederate Monuments and the Ongoing Fight for Racial Justice* (Chapel Hill: Univ. of North Carolina Press, 2021).

17. Press Release, "Statement Regarding the Confederate Flag," June 25, 2015; "Gettysburg Bookstore Pulls Confederate Flag Merchandise," *CBS News,* June 25, 2016. Gettysburg's bookstore is managed by a partner organization, Event Network.

18. Barbara Miller, "Confederate Flag Day Planned for Gettysburg 'Just Like We Have An American Flag Day,' Organizer Says," *PennLive,* February 18, 2016; Chris Cappella, "Tensions Run High at Gettysburg Confederate Flag Rally," *Evening Sun* (Hanover, PA), March 5, 2016; "Confederate Flag Disputes Prompts Verbal Clashes at Gettysburg," *The Guardian,* March 5, 2016; Daniel Simmons-Ritchie, "Hundreds Gather in Gettysburg in Heated Clash Over Confederate Flag," *PennLive,* March 6, 2016. Gary Casteel, a noted Civil War sculptor and commander of the Gettysburg chapter of the Sons of Confederate Veterans (SCV), organized the Confederate Flag Day event.

19. Debbie Elliot, "The Charlottesville Rally Five Years Later," NPR, August 12, 2022. Heather Heyer's killer and self-professed white supremacist, James Alex Fields, Jr., was convicted of hate crimes and sentenced to life in prison.

20. Debbie Elliot, "Charlottesville Plans to Melt Robert E. Lee Statue to Create Public Art Installation," NPR, August 11, 2022.

21. SPLC, "Over 160 Confederate Symbols Removed in 2020," February 23, 2021. Available at https://www.splcenter.org/presscenter/splc-reports-over-160 -confederate-symbols-removed-2020. By contrast, between 2015 and 2019, 58 Confederate monuments were removed from public spaces. Since the Charleston shooting in 2015, 312 Confederate symbols have been removed or relocated.

22. Ben Schreckinger, "Trump, in Gettysburg, Aims to Beat Back Assault Claims," *Politico,* October 22, 2016.

23. Glenn Kessler, "'The Very Fine People at Charlottesville': Who Were They?" *Washington Post,* May 8, 2020; Rosie Gray, "Trump Defends White Nationalist Protestors," *The Atlantic,* August 15, 2017; "Ku Klux Klan Holds Rally on Gettysburg Battlefield," *NBCPhiladelphia,* November 3, 2013; Allison Doughtery, "KKK Holds Protest in Gettysburg," *PennLive,* June 28, 2014; Christopher Mathias and Andy Campbell, "Guns and KKK Members at Gettysburg Confederate Rally, But No Foes to Fight," *Huffington Post,* July 2, 2017.

24. Information about each Confederate monument at Gettysburg can be found at https://www.nps.gov/gett/learn/historyculture/confederate-monuments.htm. The first Confederate monument to be placed on the battlefield was the 2nd Maryland Infantry. Located on Culp's Hill, this monument was dedicated in 1886. This regiment was known as the 1st Maryland at the time of the battle, but the park commissioners required that the marker be redesignated as the 2nd Maryland because there were 1st Maryland U.S. regiments present at the battle

(the First Maryland Eastern Shore and the First Maryland Potomac Home Brigade).

25. Shawn Boburg and Dalton Bennett, "Militias Flocked to Gettysburg to Foil a Supposed Antifa Flag Burning," *Washington Post,* July 4, 2020; Mike Argento, "Gettysburg Filled With Guns, Political Rhetoric on July 4, But No Antifa or Violence," *Evening Sun* (Hanover, PA), July 4, 2020; Christopher Mathias and Andy Campbell, "Guns and KKK Members at Gettysburg Confederate Rally, But No Foes to Fight," *Huffington Post,* July 2, 2017. Twenty-three-year-old Benjamin Hornberger, of Shippensburg, Pennsylvania, accidentally triggered his revolver inside his leg-holster and injured himself. Hornberger later ran for—and lost—the seat in the state's 13th congressional district. Antifa is the shorthand name for a loosely organized group of "anti-fascists" on the far left that oppose right-wing extremists, including fascists.

26. The 33rd district includes all of Adams County.

27. Jenna Wise, "Dozens, Some Armed, Come to Gettysburg to Guard Against Rumors of Violence," *PennLive,* July 4, 2020.

28. Peter S. Carmichael, "Gettysburg National Military Park and July 4, 2020: Personal Reflections," *Muster, JCWE,* July 20, 2020. Available at https://www.journalofthecivilwarera.org/2020/07/gettysburg-and-july-4–2020-four -historians-respond/.

29. The Superintendent's Compendium is available at https://www.nps.gov/gett /learn/management/superintendents-compendium.htm.

30. Peter S. Carmichael, "Gettysburg National Military Park and July 4, 2020: Personal Reflections"; Scott Hancock, "Fear of A Black Planet," *Muster, JCWE,* July 20, 2020. Available at https://www.journalofthecivilwarera.org/2020/07 /gettysburg-and-july-4–2020-four-historians-respond/.

31. As a matter of transparency, I spearheaded the counter-protest. To comply with the agency's regulations, I filed for and received a free speech permit, and our group conducted our event in the designated area adjacent to Meade's headquarters. We concluded this event, and then many of us walked into the cemetery to the site where Lincoln had delivered the Gettysburg Address. Within minutes, several law-enforcement patrol cars arrived at the cemetery and confronted our group, explaining that we had vacated the free-speech zone and that we were not allowed to carry signs (which were rolled up and folded) into the cemetery. To many in the counter-protest, myself included, this show of force seemed wildly incongruent with the impotent response shown by the Park Service on July 4, 2020. Unsatisfied with the park's reaction to the July 4, 2020, incident and disturbed by the treatment of my group just weeks later, I crafted a letter to the park superintendent. Approximately three hundred people signed this letter, including concerned citizens and prominent Civil War historians. Three members of the park's management met with me and three others who had been present at the counter-demonstration. This meeting offered a welcome opportunity to discuss the incident in the national cemetery, as well as our perceptions of the

July 4 incident. To date, but not unsurprisingly, the Park Service has never offered a public statement about its handling of the July 4, 2020, incident.

32. Jennifer M. Murray, "Ground Zero: Gettysburg National Military Park, July 4,
2020," *Muster, JCWE,* July 20, 2020. Available at https://www.journalofthecivil
warera.org/2020/07/3416/.

33. Christopher Gwinn, "Trials and Triumphs: A New Opportunity to Explore the
Abraham Brian Farm," Blog of Gettysburg National Military Park, May 15, 2015.
Available at https://npsgnmp.wordpress.com/2015/05/15/trials-and-triumphs-a
-new-opportunity-to-explore-the-abram-brian-farm/.

34. Press Release, "Selective Demolition of Modern Additions at Historic Warfield
House to Begin December 2," November 21, 2019, Available at https://www.nps
.gov/gett/learn/historyculture/warfield-house.htm.

35. Ta-Nehisi Coates, "Why Do So Few Blacks Study the Civil War?" *The Atlantic,
Special Commemorative Issue: The Civil War,* December 2011.

36. GNMP, "Summer Season Interpretive Programs, June 6–August 16, 2015";
GNMP, "Summer Season Interpretive Programs, June 10–August 13, 2017." For
example, "Key Moments" programs during the summer of 2015 included talks on
Little Round Top, Culp's Hill, Devil's Den, East Cavalry Field, and East Cemetery Hill. All of these programs were often offered daily and at various times
throughout the day. By 2017, the summer's interpretive programming dwindled
to sixteen different topical programs, with some of the more popular programs
(the afternoon battle walk and evening campfire) offered only on weekends.

37. GNMP, "Summer Season Interpretive Programs, Summer 2022."

38. Statistics in staffing drawn from "2015: A Year in Review" and "2018: A Year in
Review." The park archivist indicated that the archives could only accommodate
one researcher each month (on the first Wednesday of each month). Seasonal
rangers are often employed in the summer months (the battlefield's busiest time
of year) and the majority of them work in the interpretation division or on the
maintenance crew.

39. GNMP, "Operational Update: A Year in Review, 2015"; GNMP, "Operational
Update: A Year in Review, 2017"; GNMP, "Operational Update: A Year in
Review, 2018"; GNMP, "Operational Update: Summer 2018"; Murray, *On A
Great Battlefield,* 186–87. The 2023 winter lecture series, for instance, runs each
weekend from January 7 through February 26, 2023, and the schedule is available
at https://www.nps.gov/thingstodo/gettysburg-winter-programs.htm; Facebook
Post, GNMP, January 23, 2023; GNMP, "Wisler House." Available at: https://
www.nps.gov/gett/learn/historyculture/wisler-house.htm.

40. GNMP, "Operational Update: A Year in Review, 2017"; GNMP, "Operational
Update: Spring 2017"; National Trust for Historic Preservation, "Historic
Leasing in the National Park Service: Preserving History Through Effective
Partnerships," September 2013. Available at https://forum.savingplaces.org
/HigherLogic/System/DownloadDocumentFile.ashx?DocumentFileKey=98fd
09ff-b112-ec05-35ad-21eca5f99fc2; Press Release, "Unique Business Opportunity

Announced at Gettysburg National Military Park," January 23, 2023; Facebook Post, GNMP, January 25, 2023. The park solicited proposals from businesses interested in managing the historic homes as vacation rentals. Gettysburg is charged with the management of 147 historic structures.

41. Vanessa Pellechio, "Clark Reassigned to Harpers Ferry," May 26, 2017, *Gettysburg Times;* Miranda Green, "Watchdog: Gettysburg Park Chief Violated Ethics Rules, Accepted $23K in Vouchers," November 1, 2018, *The Hill.*

42. Office of the Inspector General, "Investigative Report of Allegations of Conflict of Interest at Gettysburg National Military Park," 1. In short, Clark violated government ethics rules by falsifying travel reports and failing to report over $23,000 in travel-related expenses that the Gettysburg Foundation had paid for. Full report available at https://www.oversight.gov/sites/default/files/oig-reports /WebRedacted_GettysburgConflictofInterest.pdf.

43. Press Release, "Steven Sims Named Permanent Superintendent of Gettysburg NMP, Eisenhower NHS," November 7, 2019. Sims also worked for the NPS at Hopewell Furnace National Historic Site and the Washington-Rochambeau Revolutionary Route National Historic Trail.

44. At this time, the park is considering designated volunteer work days on established national volunteer days, like Earth Day or National Public Lands Day. This was the approach that the park chose for the clearing of Devil's Den in the fall of 2022. Thus, rather than have organizations or communities invest in one specific part of the battlefield and take responsibility for up keeping their adopted positions, the plan currently under consideration would put all volunteer labor (including park staff and partners) on one specific project. For instance, the Greater Pittsburgh Civil War Round Table, for instance, has adopted the 155th Pennsylvania Infantry Monument on Little Round Top, the unit raised from their community.

45. Press Release, "Gettysburg National Military Park & Gettysburg Foundation Partnership Project: Culp's Hill Rehabilitation," January 28, 2021.

46. "Devil's Den Rehabilitation Project." Available at https://www.nps.gov/gett/learn /historyculture/devils-den.htm; Facebook Post, GNMP, September 30, 2022.

47. Little Round Top Rehabilitation Project. Available at https://www.nps.gov/gett /learn/historyculture/little-round-top.htm; Facebook Post, GNMP, February 8, 2023. On February 8, 2023, the park announced on social media the discovery of an unexploded artillery shell within the rehabilitation zone. An ordnance disposal team from Fort Belvoir, Virginia removed the shell and exploded it off park property.

48. Michael Cooper-White, "Gettysburg National Military Park Proposes Shorter Hours, Banning Race Events," *Gettysburg Times,* January 24, 2021. Races were relatively popular; in 2019 seven races were held on the battlefield, with over 2,300 participants. The Park Service found such events to be "inconsistent with the park purpose and has unacceptable impacts on park resources, visitor experience, and visitor safety."

49. Vanessa Pellechio Sanders, "No Ceremony, Wreath Laying This Year," *Gettysburg Times,* September 7, 2022; *Addressing Gettysburg,* "Special Edition: Superintendent Steven Sims," October 5, 2022, available at https://www.youtube.com/watch?v=qZA5Md1edrU; "College Students' Walk Altered," Gettysburg *Times,* August 25, 2022. The Sgt. Mac tradition was spawned as a means to honor Sgt. Eric McColley, a Gettysburg native killed when two Marines Corps helicopters collided off the coast of Africa on February 17, 2006. The Sgt. Mac Foundation appealed to local congressmen for help in getting its ceremony approved, and Congressman John Joyce and local media took up their cause. The National Park Service's Washington Office reviewed Gettysburg's policies (including the thirteen other national cemeteries in the national park system) and on August 15, 2022, confirmed the regulations as Gettysburg had outlined them in the Superintendent's Compendium. These dates include the following: Armed Forces Day, Flag Day, July 1–3, July 4, August 23 (Cemetery Annex Rededication Day), National POW/MIA Day, November 19 (Dedication Day), Remembrance Day, and December 7 (Pearl Harbor Day). The Sgt. Mac Foundation would have been permitted to place their wreaths as desired, and the National Park Service suggested that they move the ceremonial part of the event to one of the specific "First Amendment Zones." Stan Clark, director of Adams County Veterans Affairs, indicated that holding the ceremony outside of the national cemetery would detract from the significance of the event. In sum, Clark proved unwilling to compromise on the location of the short ceremony before the group placed its wreaths, resulting in the event being canceled.

50. Alex J. Hays, "Superintendent Updates Rotary Club on National Park," *Gettysburg Connection,* October 4, 2022; Sims, *Addressing Gettysburg,* October 5, 2022.

51. Press Release, "Park Deer Management Program Will Run October 2022 Through March 2023," September 22, 2022. The venison is donated to area food banks.

52. Press Release, "Kristina Heister Selected as the Permanent Deputy Superintendent of Gettysburg National Military Park and Eisenhower Historic Site," April 28, 2020. Before transferring to Gettysburg, Heister worked as the superintendent of the Upper Delaware Scenic and Recreational River.

53. William G. Gale and Darrell M. West, "Is the US Headed for Another Civil War," Brookings Institute, September 16, 2021. Available at https://www.brookings.edu/blog/fixgov/2021/09/16/is-the-us-headed-for-another-civil-war/.

54. Greg Jaffe and Jenna Johnson, "In America, Talk Turns To Something Not Spoken of for 150 Years: Civil War," *Washington Post,* March 2, 2019, available at https://www.washingtonpost.com/politics/in-america-talk-turns-to-something-unspoken-for-150-years-civil-war/2019/02/28/b3733af8–3ae4–11e9-a2cd-307b06d0257b_story.html; Emma Green, "The Conservatives Dreading—And Preparing For—Civil War," *The Atlantic,* October 1, 2021, available at https://www.theatlantic.com/politics/archive/2021/10/claremont-ryan-williams-trump/620252/; Charles M. Blow, "We're Edging Closer to Civil War," *New York Times,* December 12, 2021, available at https://www.nytimes.com/2021/12/12/opinion

/abortion-rights-america.html; Ron Elving, "Imagine Another Civil War, But This Time in Every State," *NPR*, available at January 11, 2022, https://www.npr .org/2022/01/11/1071082955/imagine-another-american-civil-war-but-this-time -in-every-state.

55. For a thoughtful analysis of invocations of a modern civil war, see Nina Silber, a leading historian of the nineteenth century: "BU Historian Answers: Are We Headed for Another Civil War," *BU Today*, March 27, 2019. Available at https:// www.bu.edu/articles/2019/are-we-headed-for-another-civil-war/.

56. Jared Peatman, *The Long Shadow of Lincoln's Gettysburg Address* (Carbondale: Southern Illinois University Press, 2013), 12, 19. A note on terminology: the name Soldiers' National Cemetery was formally changed to Gettysburg National Cemetery in 1872 when the administration of the cemetery was turned over to the U.S. War Department.

Introduction

1. Ultimately the Gettysburg landscape is significant beyond the events of July 1–3, 1863. The history of the Gettysburg battlefield from 1933 to the present underscores the complicated relationship between public and private interests, between preservation theories and utilitarian uses, between the National Park Service and the American people, and between fact and fiction. The history of the Gettysburg battlefield, and a prevailing belief that Americans own Gettysburg and its memory, is a positive indicator that national discourse on slavery and freedom will be heard on the Gettysburg battlefield. Absolutely no other piece of terrain on American soil can polarize and impassion as many people as the Gettysburg battlefield, recently referred to by one preservationist as "the most hallowed piece of earth." It is, without a doubt, through this "hallowed ground" that we, the American people, have chosen to define ourselves and come to understand our history. Dwight T. Pitcaithley, "'A Cosmic Threat': The National Park Service Addresses the Causes of the American Civil War," in *Slavery and Public History: The Tough Stuff of American Memory,* eds. James Oliver Horton and Lois E. Horton, (Chapel Hill: Univ. of North Carolina, 2006), 169–86; Scott Williams to Secretary of Interior Bruce Babbitt, undated, Folder 6, Box 5, A36, Park Main (Central) Files, 1987–present, Records of the National Park Service at Gettysburg National Military Park, Gettysburg National Military Park Archives [Files from this collection have not yet been processed and all notes hereafter will be cited by Box, File Code, (Unprocessed Central Files, 1987–present), GNMP Archives].

2. Timothy B. Smith, *The Golden Age of Battlefield Preservation: The Decade of the 1890s and the Establishment of America's First Five Military Parks* (Knoxville: Univ. of Tennessee Press, 2008); Michael Kammen, *Mystic Chords of Memory: The Transformation of Tradition in American Culture* (New York: Alfred A. Knopf, 1991), 626; Abraham Lincoln, "Second Inaugural," March 4, 1865. Available at The Avalon Project: Documents in Law, History, and Diplomacy, www.avalon .law.yale.edu/19th_century/lincoln2.asp.

3. Roy Appleman to Regional Director, November 4, 1946, Folder 833, Box 46, RG 79, Historic Shrines, Sites, Monuments, and Parks, Subject Files, 1937–1957, Northeast Regional Office, National Archives and Records Administration, Philadelphia, Pennsylvania (all notes hereafter cited by Box, SF, RG 79, NARA, Philadelphia).

4. For a listing of the seventy sites see: http://www.nps.gov/features/waso/cw15oth /civwarparks.html; Anne Masak to Superintendent John Latschar, February 20, 1998, Folder Public Comments During Scoping, General Comments, February 1998, Box 5, D18, (General Management Plan, Environmental Impact Assessment, 1996–1998), Records of the National Park Service at Gettysburg National Military Park, Gettysburg National Military Park Archives (all notes hereafter cited by Box, File Code, GMP, GNMP Archives).

5. Harlan D. Unrau, *Administrative History: Gettysburg National Military Park and Gettysburg National Cemetery* (United States Department of Interior: National Park Service, 1991); Barbara L. Platt, *"This is Holy Ground": A History of the Gettysburg Battlefield* (Harrisburg, Pa.: Huggins Printing, 2001); Karlton Smith, "The Changing Faces of Gettysburg: The National Park Service at Gettysburg," in "Gettysburg 1895-1995: the Shaping of an American Shrine, the Fourth Annual Gettysburg Seminar;" Gettysburg National Military Park 1995, 124-134; Amy Kinsel, "From Turning Point to Peace Memorial: A Cultural Legacy" in *The Gettysburg Nobody Knows*, ed. Gabor S. Boritt (New York: Oxford Univ. Press, 1997); Amy Kinsel, "'From These Honored Dead': Gettysburg in American Culture, 1863–1938," (PhD diss., Cornell Univ., 1992); Timothy B. Smith, *This Great Battlefield: History, Memory, and the Establishment of a Civil War National Military Park* (Knoxville: Univ. of Tennessee Press, 2006); Timothy B. Smith, *The Untold Story of Shiloh: The Battle and the Battlefield.* (Knoxville: Univ. of Tennessee Press, 2006); John Patterson, "A Patriotic Landscape: Gettysburg, 1863–1913," *Prospects* 7 (1982): 315–33; Jim Weeks, *Gettysburg: Memory, Market, and an American Shrine* (Princeton, N.J.: Princeton Univ. Press, 2003); Carol Reardon, *Pickett's Charge in History and Memory* (Chapel Hill: Univ. of North Carolina Press, 1997); Thomas Desjardin, *These Honored Dead: How The Story of Gettysburg Shaped American Memory* (Cambridge, Mass.: Da Capo Press, 2003). See also, Benjamin Y. Dixon, "Gettysburg, A Living Battlefield," (PhD diss., Oklahoma State Univ., 2000); Edward Tabor Linenthal, *Sacred Ground: Americans and Their Battlefields* (Urbana: Univ. of Illinois Press, 1991); and Paul Shackel, *Memory and Black in White: Race, Commemoration, and the Post-Bellum Landscape* (Landam, Md.: AltaMira Press, 2003).

6. Gaines Foster, *Ghosts of the Confederacy: Defeat, the Lost Cause, and the Emergence of the New South, 1865–1913* (New York: Oxford Univ. Press, 1988); Charles Reagan Wilson, *Baptized in Blood: The Religion of the Lost Cause, 1865–1920* (Athens: Univ. of Georgia Press, 1983); Nina Silber, *The Romance of Reunion: Northerners and the South, 1865—1900* (Chapel Hill: Univ. of North Carolina Press, 1993); Kirk Savage, *Standing Soldiers, Kneeling Slaves: Race, War, and Monument in Nineteenth-Century America* (Princeton: Princeton Univ. Press, 1997); David

Blight, *Race and Reunion: The Civil War in American Memory* (Cambridge, Mass.: Harvard Univ. Press, 2001); William Blair, *Cities of the Dead: Contesting the Memory of the Civil War in the South, 1865–1914* (Chapel Hill: Univ. of North Carolina Press, 2003); Barbara Gannon, *The Won Cause: Black and White Comradeship in the Grand Army of the Republic* (Chapel Hill: Univ. of North Carolina Press, 2011); Kevin Levin, *Remembering the Battle of the Crater: War as Murder* (Lexington: Univ. of Kentucky Press, 2012).

7. Ary J. Lamme III, *America's Historic Landscapes: Community Power and the Preservation of Four National Historic Sites* (Knoxville: Univ. of Tennessee Press, 1989), 182.

8. For additional reading on tourism, see Susan Sessions Rugh, *Are We There Yet? The Golden Age of American Family Vacations* (Lawrence: Univ. of Kansas Press, 2008); Kammen, "Mystic Chords of Memory," 626.

9. Rick Hampton, "150 Years after Civil War, Descendants Deal with Legacy," *USA Today,* April 7, 2011.

Chapter 1

1. "Victory! Waterloo Eclipsed!! The Desperate Battles Near Gettysburg!" *Philadelphia Inquirer,* July 6, 1863; William Calder to mother, July 8, 1863, William Calder Papers, no. 00125, Southern Historical Collections, University of North Carolina, Chapel Hill; Samuel Wilkeson, "Details from Our Special Correspondent," *New York Times,* July 6, 1863.

2. Drew Gilpin Faust, *This Republic of Suffering: Death and the American Civil War* (New York: Alfred A. Knopf, 2008).

3. The best work on the aftermath of the Battle of Gettysburg is Gregory A. Coco's *A Strange and Blighted Land: Gettysburg, the Aftermath of the Battle* (Gettysburg, Pa.: Thomas Publications, 1998); Mark Grimsley, *The Hard Hand of War: Union Military Policy Toward Southern Civilians, 1861–1865* (Cambridge: Cambridge University Press, 1995).

4. For additional reading on President Lincoln's Gettysburg Address, see Garry Wills, *Lincoln at Gettysburg: The Words That Remade America* (New York: Simon and Schuster, 1992). Abraham Lincoln, "The Gettysburg Address," November 19, 1863. Lincoln's words from the Gettysburg Address will be cited subsequently without citation.

5. David McConaughy to Hon. Jos. R. Ingersoll, August 19, 1863, Vertical Files, 11–29 B, Gettysburg National Military Park Library (hereafter cited as VF, GNMP Library); Harlan D. Unrau, *Administrative History: Gettysburg National Military Park and Gettysburg National Cemetery* (Denver, Colo.: Branch of Publications and Graphic Design, Denver Service Center, 1991), 41.

6. Address of the Gettysburg Battle-Field Memorial Association, April 24, 1866. VF, 11–30, GNMP Library; "Minutes of the Gettysburg Battlefield Memorial Association," 1872–1875, bound volume in the GNMP Library; John Vanderslice, *Gettysburg Then and Now: The Field of American Valor, Where and How the Regiments Fought, And the Troops They Encountered, An Account of the Battle, Giving*

Movements, Positions, and Losses of the Commands Engaged (New York: G.W. Dillingham, 1899); John Vanderslice, *Gettysburg: A History of the Gettysburg Battle-field Memorial Association With an Account of the Battle* (Philadelphia, Pa.: The Association, 1897).

7. Ronald F. Lee, "The Origin and Evolution of the National Military Park Idea" (Office of Historic Preservation, Washington, D.C.: Department of the Interior, National Park Service, 1973), 13; Timothy B. Smith, *The Golden Age of Battlefield Preservation: The Decade of the 1890s and the Establishment of America's First Five Military Parks* (Knoxville: Univ. of Tennessee Press, 2008), 241. *The Golden Age of Battlefield Preservation* currently stands as the leading work on the establishment of the Civil War parks. Smith's comparative approach allows readers to see how the battlefields developed in comparison to one another. Smith examines the establishment of the battlefields; their continual operation of the battlefields is beyond the scope of his scholarship. Much research remains to be done on how the park commissioners operated the battlefields through the late nineteenth century and early twentieth century. Considerably more research needs to be done on the era between the park commissioners' management and the acquisition of the National Park Service—the transition era—when the battlefields were managed by the Quartermaster Department.

8. Journal of William McKenna Robbins, Commissioner, Gettysburg National Park, 1898 to 1905, GNMP Archives; Thomas L. Schaefer, "If You See His Monument Look Around: E. B. Cope and the Gettysburg National Military Park," *Unsung Heroes of Gettysburg: Programs of the Fifth Annual Gettysburg Seminar* (National Park Service: Gettysburg National Military Park, 1996), 107–33; E. B. Cope, "Annual Report, 1893," Folder 1, Box 1, Engineer's Annual Reports, 1893—1921 (GETT 41121), Records of the Gettysburg National Park Commission, Office of the Commissioners, Gettysburg National Military Park Archives, page 1 [hereafter cited as (GETT 41121), GNMP Archives]. Colonel Nicholson served with the 28th Pennsylvania and Brigadier General Forney served with the 10th Alabama at the battle. John Bachelder traveled with the Army of the Potomac as a civilian reporter on the war's events. He was not present at the battle of Gettysburg, but arrived a few days after to begin writing the battle's first history. Forney and Bachelder died in 1894 and were replaced by William Robbins, veteran of the 4th Alabama, and Charles Richardson of the 126th New York. According to Major Robbins's journal, the commissioners received three hundred dollars a month for their services.

9. Unrau, *Administrative History,* 78; Elihu Root, Secretary of War, to the Gettysburg National Park Commission, n.d., Folder 1, Box 2, General Records, 1922–1933 (GETT 41155), U.S. War Department, Office of the Quartermaster General, Gettysburg National Military Park Archives [hereafter cited as (GETT 41155), GNMP Archives]; *An Act to Establish a National Military Park at Gettysburg, Pennsylvania,* 28 Stat. 651, approved February 11, Gettysburg National Park Commission, "Office of the Commissioners, Record Books of Legislation, 1873–1921," Box 6, Gettysburg National Park Commission, (GETT

41122), Records of the Gettysburg National Park Commission, Gettysburg National Military Park Archives [hereafter cited as (GETT 41122), GNMP Archives].

10. Blight, *Race and Reunion*, 1–5, 381.

11. Gettysburg National Military Park Commission, "Annual Report, 1896," in *Annual Reports to the Secretary of War, 1893–1901* (Washington, D.C.: Government Printing Office, 1902), 21–22 (hereafter cited as GNPC, "Annual Reports," including the year's report and page number); E. B. Cope "1894, Annual Report," 6; E. B. Cope, "1895, Annual Report." Folder 2, Box 1, (GETT 41121), GNMP Archives, 1–2; Colonel E. A. Garlington, "Gettysburg National Park Inspection Report, November 1904" (Washington, D.C.: Government Printing Office, 1904); GNPC, "Annual Report, 1895," GNMP Library, 16; GNPC, "Daily Journals, 1916," Box 25, Daily Journals, 1893–1921 (GETT 41144), Records of the Gettysburg National Park Commission, Office of the Commissioners, Gettysburg National Military Park Archives, 87 [hereafter cited as (GETT 41144), GNMP Archives]; GNPC, "Annual Report, 1896," 23.

12. GNPC, "Annual Report, 1895," 15; GNPC, "Annual Report, 1896," 21; GNPC, "Annual Report, 1898," 31; GNPC, "Annual Report, 1899," 37; GNPC, "Annual Report, 1901," 52. In 1896 and 1897, for example, commissioners proudly boasted that slightly over seven miles of roads had been built, including Seminary, Sickles, Hancock, Slocum, Sedgwick, Sykes, and Meade Avenues. Most of the initial roads constructed were on the second and third days' battlegrounds, but in 1898 and 1899 laborers laid telford roads on the first day's terrain, including Howard, Reynolds, Wadsworth, Doubleday, and Robinson Avenues. When these roads were constructed offers an insight into the popular locations of the battlefield. Often tourists flocked to the Soldiers' National Cemetery, Cemetery Hill, and the High Water Mark; few ventured out to the first day's field because of its distance from the center of town and the train station. For an additional discussion on the development of the battlefield roads as it influenced visitation and popular memory see, John Patterson, "From Battle Ground to Pleasure Ground: Gettysburg as a Historic Site," in *History Museums in the United States: A Critical Assessment*, eds. Warren Leon and Roy Rosenzweig (Urbana: Univ. of Illinois Press, 1989), 128–57; Jim Weeks, "Gettysburg: Display Window for Popular Memory," *Journal of American Culture* (Winter 1998), 41–56; Dixon, "Gettysburg, A Living Battlefield"; and Weeks, *Gettysburg*.

13. GNPC, "Annual Report, 1894," 9; Justice Peckham majority opinion, delivered January 27, 1896 in *United States v. Gettysburg Electric Railway Co.*, Box 8, Record Books of Testimony and Proceedings, 1893–1905 (GETT 41123), Gettysburg National Park Commission, Office of the Commissioners, Gettysburg National Military Park Archives [hereafter cited as (GETT 41123), GNMP Archives]. In April 1895, the case was heard before the U.S. Circuit Court, Eastern District of Pennsylvania, and the ruling favored the electric railroad company. The case was appealed to the U.S. Supreme Court.

14. GNPC, "Annual Report, 1894," 11; GNPC, "Annual Report, 1900," 46–47; E. B. Cope, "Annual Report, 1901," Folder 4, Box 2, (GETT 41121), GNMP Archives, 15; E. B. Cope, "Annual Report, 1905," Folder 3, Box 3, (GETT 41121), GNMP Archives, 5; GNPC, "Annual Report, 1898," Folder 1, Box 2, (GETT 41121), GNMP Archives, 5–8, 31–32.

15. GNPC, "Annual Report, 1897," 29; GNPC, "Annual Report, 1898," Folder 1, Box 2, (GETT 41121), GNMP Archives, 34; Cope, "Annual Report, 1898," Folder 1, Box 2, (GETT 41121), GNMP Archives, 8–9.

16. Gary W. Gallagher, *The Confederate War: How Popular Will, Nationalism, and Military Strategy Could Not Stave Off Defeat* (Cambridge, Mass.: Harvard Univ. Press, 1997); Frank Aretas Haskell, *The Battle of Gettysburg* (Commandery of the State of Massachusetts, Military Order of the Loyal Legion of the United States, Boston, 1908), 80.

17. *Fiftieth Anniversary of the Battle of Gettysburg, Report of the Pennsylvania Commission* (Harrisburg, Pa.: W. M. Stanley Ray, State Printer, 1914), 6; GNPC, "Annual Report, 1913," Folder 3, Box 5, Publications, Annual Reports, 1893–1921 (GETT 41148), Records of the Gettysburg National Park Commission, Office of the Commissioners, Gettysburg National Military Park Archives, 10 [hereafter cited as (GETT 41148), GNMP Archives]; GNPC, "Annual Report, 1914," Folder 4, Box 5, (GETT 41148), GNMP Archives, 4; Blight, *Race and Reunion*, 8, 383–91; Woodrow Wilson speech, reprinted in *Fiftieth Anniversary of the Battle of Gettysburg, Report of the Pennsylvania Commission*, 174–76.

18. Unrau, *Administrative History*, 119; E. B. Cope, "Gettysburg National Military Park," (c. 1925), (GETT 41155), GNMP Archives, 3. The following year, on April 1, 1923, the War Department shifted the five Civil War battlefields from the Secretary of War's jurisdiction to the Quartermaster Department. The sites then remained under control of the Quartermaster General until July 1, 1930, when they were transferred to the Commanding Generals of the Corps area under which the sites were geographically located. This transfer placed Gettysburg under the administration of the Commanding General in Baltimore, Maryland, where it remained until acquired by the National Park Service in 1933. Cope's influence on the battlefield was unparalleled. He was actively involved in the administration and daily operations of the battlefield for over three decades. Cope oversaw the construction and placement of the narrative tablets and the cannons. He also designed and positioned the five observation towers. Cope also assisted in the design and location of the road system and the restoration of the historic fences and stone walls. His *Gettysburg National Military Park, 1925* is an extensively written and visual report on the state of the battlefield near the end of his administration. This report is located in the park archives under General Records, 1922–1933 (GETT 41155), Records of the Office of the Quartermaster General, GNMP Archives. Upon Cope's death in 1927, Colonel E. E. Davis was appointed superintendent. Davis was the first non–Civil War veteran to manage the battlefield and served until August 1932. J. Frank Barber replaced him on August 24, 1932, and held the position until February 1933. In 1932, the

War Department announced the superintendent position under the civil service classification. James McConaghie was appointed superintendent on February 7, 1933.

19. William C. Everhart, *The National Park Service* (Boulder, Colo.: Westview Press, 1983), 8; *The National Parks: Shaping the System,* (Washington, D.C.: Division of Publications and the Employee Development Division, National Park Service, 1991), 13–30; Harlan D. Unrau and G. Frank Williss, "Administrative History: Expansion of the National Park Service in the 1930s" (Denver Service Center: National Park Service, 1983), available online at http://www.cr.nps.gov/history/online_books//unrau-williss/adhi.htm; "American Antiquities Act," June 8, 1906, available online at http://www.nps.gov/history/local-law/anti1906.htm.

20. Marguerite S. Shaffer, *See America First: Tourism and National Identity, 1880–1940* (Washington, D.C.: Smithsonian Books, 2001), 4–6; John F. Sears, *Sacred Places: American Tourist Attractions in the Nineteenth Century* (Amherst: Univ. of Massachusetts Press, 1989), 7.

21. Shaffer, *See America First,* 7–39; Georgie Boge and Margie Holder Boge, *Paving Over the Past: A History and Guide to Civil War Battlefield Preservation* (Washington, D.C.: Island Press, 1993), 25; *The National Parks: Shaping The System,* 19; Conrad L. Wirth, *Parks, Politics, and the People* (Norman: Univ. of Oklahoma Press, 1980), 1–39; John Ise, *Our National Park Policy: A Critical History* (Baltimore, Md.: The Johns Hopkins Univ. Press, 1961).

22. Richard West Sellars, *Preserving Nature in the National Parks: A History* (New Haven, Conn.: Yale Univ. Press, 1997), 181; Paul Sutter, *Driven Wild: How the Fight Against Automobiles Launched the Modern Wilderness Movement* (Seattle: Univ. of Washington Press, 2002), 48–49; Everhart, *The National Park Service,* 17–23.

23. Lee, "The Origin and Evolution of the National Military Park Idea." For additional information on Albright, see Horace Alright and Marian Albright Schenck, *Creating the National Park Service: The Missing Years* (Norman: Univ. of Oklahoma Press, 1999).

24. Everhart, *The National Park Service,* 23; *Final General Management Plan and Environmental Statement, Vol. I, Gettysburg National Military Park* (United States Department of the Interior: National Park Service, June 1999), xxvi (hereafter cited as *GMP*); James R. McConaghie, "Qualifications of James R. McConaghie for Park Superintendent," Folder 201, Box 2490, RG 79, Central Classified File, 1933–1949, National Parks, Gettysburg National Military Park, National Archives and Records Administration, College Park, Maryland.

Chapter 2

1. Everhart, *The National Park Service,* 23. Roosevelt signed the executive order on June 10, 1933, and it took effect on August 10. At this time, the National Park Service assumed control of twelve natural sites and fifty-seven historical sites.

2. Everhart, *The National Park Service,* 23–25; Harlan D. Unrau and G. Frank Williss, *Administrative History: Expansion of the National Park Service in the*

1930s (Denver Service Center: National Park Service, 1983), online publication, available at http://www.cr.nps.gov/history/online_books/unrau-williss/adhi. htm; Sutter, *Driven Wild*, 48–49. Unrau and Williss note that between 1933 and 1937, the Public Works Administration allocated $40.2 million, the Works Progress Administration allocated $24.2 million, the Civilian Conservation Corps allocated $82.2 million, and the Civil Works Administration allocated $2.4 million. Sutter's work explores the growth of the modern wilderness movement and the impact of widespread automobile ownership on the environment and the rise of a recreational culture. The nation's other federally preserved Civil War sites, including Antietam, Shiloh, Chickamauga and Chattanooga, and Vicksburg, also received federal money through New Deal projects. These Civil War sites benefited from infrastructure improvements, mainly in roads and trails, as well as advancements in research and educational opportunities. At Antietam, for example, Civil Works Administration money funded a "Historical Survey Project," which in addition to employing nine people, resulted in the first thorough and reasonably professional study done about the September 1862 battle since the early War Department studies. At Chickamauga and Chattanooga National Military Park, Civilian Conservation Corps workers improved road access and constructed restroom facilities on Lookout Mountain. For additional information on Antietam, see Charles W. Snell and Sharon A. Brown, *Antietam National Battlefield and National Cemetery: An Administrative History* (Washington, D.C.: U.S. Department of the Interior, National Park Service, 1986), 151–58; John C. Paige and Jerome A. Greene, *Administrative History of Chickamauga and Chattanooga National Military Park* (Denver, Colo.: Denver Service Center, National Park Service, Department of the Interior, February 1983), available online at www.nps.gov/archive/chch/adhi/adhi.htm.

3. Sutter, *Driven Wild*, 24.

4. Sutter, *Driven Wild*, 50.

5. Unrau, *Administrative History*, viii; Everhart, *The National Park Service*, 23; *Final General Management Plan and Environmental Impact Statement*, Gettysburg National Military Park, Pennsylvania, vols. 1 & 2 (U.S. Department of the Interior, National Park Service, June 1999), xxvi (hereafter cited as *GMP*, vol. 1 or vol. 2); James R. McConaghie, "Qualifications of James R. McConaghie for Park Superintendent," Folder 201, Box 2490, RG 79, Central Classified File, 1933–1949, National Parks, Gettysburg National Military Park, National Archives and Records Administration, College Park, Maryland (hereafter cited by Box, CCF, RG 79, NARA College Park). At this time, the Gettysburg superintendent also oversaw administration of Fort McHenry National Monument, Fort Necessity National Battlefield, Antietam National Battlefield, and Monocacy National Park. Fort McHenry and Fort Necessity became individual entities in January 1936. Antietam remained under Gettysburg's management until December 1935, when the NPS appointed Washington County native John Kyd Beckenbaugh as Antietam's superintendent. For additional reading on Antietam's history, see Susan B. Trail, "Remembering Antietam: Commemoration and Preservation

NOTES TO PAGE 21

of a Civil War Battlefield," (PhD diss., Univ. of Maryland, 2005). In July 1917, McConaghie enlisted with the First Iowa Infantry, U.S. Army, but in September accepted a commission with the 133rd Infantry in New Mexico, where he was promoted to First Lieutenant in December 1917. Deployed to France and Germany, he served with the 39th Infantry and was wounded in the Argonne. In September 1919, he was honorably discharged and granted vocational rehabilitation to study at the University of Minnesota, but he completed his academic studies at Harvard University. McConaghie served as the superintendent at GNMP until January 1941, when he was transferred to Vicksburg National Military Park. This resume found in the National Archives represents the only known source on McConaghie's background. Sections of this chapter previously appeared as Jennifer Murray, "'Far Above Our Poor Power to Add or Detract': National Park Service Administration of Gettysburg Battlefield, 1933–1938" *Civil War History* 55, March 2009, 56–81.

6. Superintendent James McConaghie, "Superintendent's Annual Report, 1936–1937," Box 2, Park Main (Central) Files, 1933–1954, (GETT 41113), Records of the National Park Service at Gettysburg National Military Park, Gettysburg National Military Park Archives, 47 [hereafter cited as (GETT 41113), GNMP Archives].

7. Christopher Waldrep, *Vicksburg's Long Shadow: The Civil War Legacy of Race and Remembrance* (Lanham, Md.: Rowman & Littlefield, 2005), 261; John C. Paige, *The Civilian Conservation Corps and the National Park Service, 1933–1942: An Administrative History* (Washington, D.C.: National Park Service, Department of the Interior, 1985), available online at www.nps.gov/history/history/online_books/ccc.index.htm. The 94 sites housed a total of 198 camps. In addition to performing valuable work in America's national parks, CCC enrollees also worked in 881 state, county, and local parks. The original name of this agency was the Emergency Conservation Works (ECW). Because most Americans, as well as the media, typically referred to the agency as the CCC, its name was officially changed to the Civilian Conservation Corps in 1937. For the sake of consistency, the term CCC will be used. The three other departments overseeing CCC work included the Departments of War, Labor, and Agriculture. The Department of War, specifically the Army, was responsible for the conditioning and transportation of the enrollees, as well as supervision of the camps/barracks. Though the camps were supervised by a military officer, the daily activity in the parks was supervised by NPS personnel.

8. Joseph Speakman, *At Work in Penn's Woods: The Civilian Conservation Corps in Pennsylvania* (University Park: Pennsylvania State Univ. Press, 2006), 149; Frederick Tilberg, "Historians' Narrative Reports, March 1942," written on April 4, 1942, Folder 3, Box 7, (GETT 41113), GNMP Archives, 3; R. L. Jones, "CCC Files," undated report, Folder 6, Box 9, Historians' Files, 1933–1965 (GETT 41151), Records of the National Park Service at Gettysburg National Military Park, Gettysburg National Military Park Archives [hereafter cited by (GETT 41151), GNMP Archives]. Speakman notes that Pennsylvania served as a prime

location for the CCC camps because of the high numbers of unemployed men and the abundance of conservation work.

9. Timothy B. Smith, "Black Soldiers and the CCC at Shiloh National Military Park," *CRM: The Journal of Heritage Stewardship,* 3 (Summer 2006): 73–84; Paige, *The Civilian Conservation Corps and the National Park Service, 1933–1942,* online publication; Waldrep, *Vicksburg's Long Shadow,* 257–88; Speakman, *At Work in Penn's Woods,* 135, 148–50. Over 400 black World War I veterans worked at two camps on the Tennessee battlefield from 1934 until the camps closed in 1942.

10. Unrau, *Administrative History,* 156–62; Superintendent James McConaghie, "Superintendent's Annual Report, 1936–1937," Box 2, (GETT 41113), GNMP Archives, 34; Superintendent James McConaghie, "Superintendent's Monthly Report, April 1937," written on May 19, 1937, Folder 1, Box 6, (GETT 41113), GNMP Archives; Olen Cole, Jr., *The African American Experience in the Civilian Conservation Corps* (Gainesville: Univ. of Florida Press, 1999), 16–17; Speakman, *At Work in Penn's Woods,* 143–50. Cole's work stands as a definitive work on the black experience in the CCC, and a detailed picture of the camps in California.

11. "History of CCC Camp No. 2 at Gettysburg," June 22, 1936, reproduced in Unrau's *Administrative History,* appendix S, 418–19; Memo from Superintendent James McConaghie to Region 1 Director, September 14, 1939, ID 24444, Folder NMP, CCC, Gettysburg, Part 12 [2], 1939–1940, Box 35, Records of the National Park Service, Northeast Regional Office, Historic Shrines, Sites, Monuments, and Parks, Subject Files, RG, 79, Box 35, Philadelphia Regional Archives (hereafter cited by Box, SF, RG 79, NARA Philadelphia); Smith "Black Soldiers and the CCC at Shiloh National Military Park," 82–84; Kathy Harrison, Senior Historian, interview by author, 15 February 2009. According to Kathy Harrison, Senior Historian at Gettysburg National Military Park, King rented a home on South Washington Street. To date, no documented source on King's living arrangements has been found.

12. Frederick Tilberg, "Historians' Narrative Reports, March 1942," written on April 4, 1942, Folder 3, Box 7, (GETT 41113), GNMP Archives, 3; Superintendent James McConaghie, "Superintendent's Annual Report, 1936–1937," Box 2, (GETT 41113), GNMP Archives, 34; Memo from Superintendent James McConaghie to Region 1 Director, September 14, 1939, ID 24444, Folder NMP, CCC, Gettysburg, Part 12 [2], 1939–1940, Box 35, SF, RG 79, NARA Philadelphia.

13. Barry Mackintosh, "Interpretation in the National Park Service: A Historical Perspective," (Department of the Interior, National Park Service, 1986), NPS publication available online at http://www.cr.nps.gov/history/online_books /mackintosh2/index.htm.

14. Frederick Tilberg, "Historians' Narrative Reports, March 1942," written on April 4, 1942, Folder 3, Box 7, (GETT 41113), GNMP Archives, 3; Superintendent James McConaghie, "Superintendent's Annual Report, 1936–1937," Box 2,

(GETT 41113), GNMP Archives, 29, 36–37; Paul L. Roy, *Last Reunion of the Blue and Gray*, (Gettysburg: Paul Roy, 1950), 29-33.

15. "Museum and Visual Education, CWA Educational Program, 1933," Folder 8, Box 9, (GETT 41151), GNMP Archives.

16. R. L. Jones to Verne Chatelain, February 5, 1934, Folder 9, Box 9, (GETT 41151), GNMP Archives. New Deal monies did provide, however, for a new administrative facility at Shiloh National Military Park. Smith, "Black Soldiers and the CCC at Shiloh National Military Park," 73–75. See also Charles E. Shedd, Jr., "A History of Shiloh National Military Park, Tennessee" (National Park Service, 1954), available online at http://www.nps.gov/history/history/online_books/shil/adhi.pdf.

17. Lawrence Eckert, Jr., to Mrs. Douglas Poage, April 26, 1977, Vertical Files 14–23 (Rosensteel Collection), Gettysburg National Military Park Library (hereafter cited as VF, GNMP Library); "National Museum Will Be Enlarged," April 1938, Folder 0–31, Box 2489, RG 79, CCF, NARA College Park; Superintendent James McConaghie, "Superintendent's Monthly Report, July 1939," written on August 5, 1939, Folder 2, Box 4, (GETT 41113), GNMP Archives, 1; Superintendent James McConaghie, "Superintendent's Monthly Report, December 1940," written on January 8, 1941, Folder 1, Box 4, (GETT 41113), GNMP Archives, 4–5; George Rosensteel to Congressmen Harry Haines, June 29, 1938, Folder 0–31, Box 2489, CCF, RG 79, NARA College Park.

18. Unrau, *Administrative History*, 168–69; Superintendent James McConaghie, "Superintendent's Annual Report, 1934–1935," Box 2, (GETT 41113), GNMP Archives; R. L. Jones to Verne Chatelain, February 5, 1934; R. L. Jones, "Report of the Historical Technician, Gettysburg National Military Park, December 1933," written on January 2, 1934, Folder 9, Box 9, (GETT 41151), GNMP Archives; Superintendent James McConaghie, "Superintendent's Annual Report, 1936–1937," Box 2, (GETT 41113), GNMP Archives, 25; National Park Service, Gettysburg National Military Park Brochure, 1938, GNMP Library; Superintendent James McConaghie, "Superintendent's Monthly Report, May 1939," written on June 13, 1939, Folder 2, Box 4, (GETT 41113), GNMP Archives, 4. Tilberg received his doctoral degree from the University of Iowa in 1928. In July 1937, the National Park Service director instructed its historians to devote the majority of their off-season time to research and during the tourist season to educational programs. Gettysburg quickly took advantage of this directive to increase interpretation. The park also hired two seasonal ranger/historians, whose primary duties were to present educational programs, assist with visitor services, and conduct historical research.

19. "Report on Roads and Trails, National Parks, Emergency Construction Act June 19, 1934," Folder 8, Box 8, (GETT 41113), GNMP Archives; Superintendent James McConaghie, "Superintendent's Monthly Report, November 1939," written on December 8, 1939, Folder 2, Box 4, (GETT 41113), GNMP Archives, 5; Superintendent James McConaghie, "Superintendent's Annual Report, 1934–

1935"; Superintendent James McConaghie, "Superintendent's Annual Report, 1936–1937," Box 2 (GETT 41113), GNMP Archives, 36, 43–45.

20. Superintendent James McConaghie, "Superintendent's Monthly Report, May 1937," Box 5, (GETT 41113), GNMP Archives; Frederick Tilberg, "Historians' Narrative Reports, September 1936," Folder 3, Box 8, (GETT 41113), GNMP Archives; Superintendent James McConaghie, "Superintendent's Annual Report, 1934–1935"; Superintendent James McConaghie, "Superintendent's Annual Report, 1936–1937," Box 2, (GETT 41113), GNMP Archives, 1, 47. Using the Weikert house as a makeshift visitor center necessitated the construction of a driveway and parking lot to accommodate vehicles.

21. Superintendent James McConaghie, "Circular No. 1," May 3, 1934, Folder 12, Box, 18, (GETT 41113), GNMP Archives, 1; Superintendent James McConaghie, "Circular No. 1," January 24, 1935, Folder 10, Box 18, (GETT 41113), GNMP Archives, 4.

22. Superintendent James McConaghie, "Circular No. 1," January 24, 1935, Folder 10, Box 18, (GETT 41113), GNMP Archives, 4.

23. Lamme, *America's Historic Landscapes*, 181–82.

24. Superintendent James McConaghie, "Superintendent's Annual Report, 1934–1935," Box 2, (GETT 41113), GNMP Archives; Lamme, "America's Historic Landscapes," 181–82..

25. Superintendent James McConaghie to Director, NPS, October 5, 1937 and attached Press Release October 5, 1937, Folder 10, Box 11, (GETT 41113), GNMP Archives; Frederick Tilberg, "Historians' Narrative Reports, May 1940," written on June 6, 1940, Folder 4, Box 7, (GETT 41113), GNMP Archives.

26. Superintendent James McConaghie, "Superintendent's Annual Report, 1936–1937," Box 2, (GETT 41113), GNMP Archives, 46; R. L. Jones to Verne Chatelain, March 7, 1934. In one instance, for example, New Dealers cleaned up twenty-six acres along Culp's Hill as noted in J. Howard Diehl, narrative report to Superintendent James McConaghie, July 17, 1934, Folder 10, Box 9, (GETT 41151), GNMP Archives.

27. R. L. Jones to Verne Chatelain, November 1, 1934, Folder 1, Box 1, (GETT 41113), GNMP Archives; R. L. Jones to James McConaghie, February 9, 1934, Folder 2, Box 1, (GETT 41151), GNMP Archives; Senior Historian Kathy Harrison, interview by author, 15 February 2009. As reflected in his comment, Jones became disillusioned and discouraged by McConaghie's efforts to change the battlefield's historic landscape and, as a result, left Gettysburg in 1937. This assertion comes from Harrison's personal interview with Jones conducted in 1994. There is no record of the interview in the GNMP Archives or Library.

28. "The Gettysburg National Cemetery: An Exposition of Emergency Conservation Work Projects, September 1935," Folder 10, Box 1, (GETT 41113), Gettysburg National Military Park Archives, 1 (hereafter cited as "The Gettysburg National Cemetery," GNMP Archives).

29. "The Gettysburg National Cemetery," (GETT 41113), GNMP Archives, 10; "Friends of the National Parks at Gettysburg" Newsletter, Fall 1996, 1. When

the CCC laborers reset the headstones, they only altered the identified dead, leaving the two sections of unknown (979 soldiers) at their original height. Furthermore, the Park Service discontinued the War Department's policy of maintaining the etched names on the stones. As early as 1866, loved ones coming to Gettysburg to pay respects and mourn their fallen sons, brothers, husbands, and friends, were dismayed by the etching of the names on the granite stones. The stone selected for the headstones did not adequately provide contrast when incised, thus limiting its readability. After numerous complaints cemetery administrators began the practice of using black paint to fill the etching on the stones, providing greater visibility of the soldiers' names. When the National Park Service assumed management of the cemetery, it argued that there was insufficient historic evidence of this practice, and the painting ended. In the 1970s and 1980s visitor complaints caused the park historians to research the practice of painting the names on the granite headstones. Research confirmed the War Department's practice, and the park resumed this practice in 1996.

30. "The Gettysburg National Cemetery," (GETT 41113), GNMP Archives, 6; R. L. Jones, "Report of the Historical Technician, Gettysburg National Military Park, December 1933," written on January 2, 1934, Folder 9, Box 9, (GETT 41151), GNMP Archives. This was done as part of an 1863 agreement with Evergreen Cemetery to erect the boundary fence at an ordinary height of the battle-era picket and rail fence it replaced. See also Reed Engle, "Cultural Landscape Report: The Soldiers' National Cemetery Gettysburg, Pennsylvania 1994," uncataloged report, Gettysburg National Military Park Archives, 18 (hereafter cited as CLR). The fence from East Cemetery Hill originally surrounded Lafayette Square and was placed on the battlefield in 1888 by a congressional order.

31. Gettysburg National Military Park National Register Documentation, Adams County, PA, (NRIS 66000642), National Register of Historic Places, Washington, DC, 1/23/2004, 251–52 (hereafter cited as "National Register"); CLR, 116; Ronald F. Lee, "The Origin and Evolution of the National Military Park Idea" (Office of Historic Preservation, Washington, D.C.: Department of the Interior, National Park Service, 1973), 18; Superintendent James McConaghie to NPS Director, July 11, 1938; "S. of V. Protest Removing of Gate Pillars," *Gettysburg Times,* February 4, 1939, Folder 0–1, Box 2489, RG 79, CCF, NARA College Park; Superintendent James McConaghie, "Superintendent's Monthly Report, April 1939," written on May 15, 1939, Folder 2, Box 4, (GETT 41113), GNMP Archives. CCC laborers were used for this work. Only the gates along the Baltimore Street entrance were removed and reset; the ones along the Taneytown Road remained in place. The present Baltimore Street gates are neither originals nor replicas, but are entirely of non-historic design and size.

32. William L. Meals to Hon. Joseph Guffey, February 9, 1939, Folder 0–31, Box 2489, CCF, RG 79, NARA, College Park.

33. Superintendent James McConaghie to the Director of the National Park Service, November 20, 1937, Box 5, unprocessed collection (GETT 41161), Records of the National Park Service at Gettysburg National Military Park, Gettysburg

National Military Park Archives [hereafter cited as (GETT 41161), GNMP Archives]. For additional reading on the dedication of the Peace Light, see Kinsel, "From Turning Point to Peace Memorial," 203–22. The National Park Service acquired the Forney buildings from the Pennsylvania Commission.

34. Superintendent James McConaghie to Director of the National Park Service, November 20, 1937, Box 5, (GETT 41161), GNMP Archives; Memo from Arno B. Cammerer, NPS Director, June 20, 1938, Box 18, (GETT 41113), GNMP Archives.

35. Franklin D. Roosevelt's speech reproduced in Roy, *The Last Reunion of the Blue and Gray*, 113.

36. R. L. Jones to Verne Chatelain, March 7, 1934, Folder 10, Box 9, (GETT 41151), GNMP Archives. For additional information on the agency's policy for managing historic farmlands, see John G. Wilson, "Brief summary of survey study of battlefield farms to date, January 30, 1934," Folder 10, Box 9 (GETT 41151), GNMP Archives; "Series of Farm Maps," Park Maps and Drawings, 1933–1960 (GETT 41107), GNMP Archives; "Materials Pertaining to the Proposed Redistribution of Lands, Gettysburg National Military park, Gettysburg Pennsylvania," November 1938, Folder 3, Box 7 (GETT 41151), GNMP Archives; Louis E. King, "Farm Policy: Farm Areas in the Gettysburg National Military Park, May 1937," Folder 9, Box 1, (GETT 41113), GNMP Archives. In short, the agency's philosophy to manage the battlefield farms involved consolidating the farm lands that allowed the agency to extract maximum profit; Charles E. Shedd, Jr. "A History of Shiloh National Military Park, Tennessee" (National Park Service, 1954), 59–60, 62, available online at http://www.nps.gov/history/history/online_books/shil/adhi.pdf.

37. Shedd, Jr., "A History of Shiloh National Military Park, Tennessee," 64–65; Frederick Tilberg, "Vista Cutting Project: Area of Little Round Top, Devil's Den, the Wheatfield, and Peach Orchard," December 28, 1939, Folder 30, Box 7, (GETT 41151), GNMP Archives. The main sources used to obtain an understanding of the historic landscape were the Warren Map and Brady and Tipton photographs. Today, the NPS defines rehabilitation as making possible "compatible uses for properties through repair, alterations and additions while preserving those historic features that remain and that are significant and convey historical values." The agency defines restoration as "accurately depicting the form, features and character of a property as it appeared at a particular period of time." For a more detailed description of these methods of preservation, see *Final General Management Plan and Environmental Impact Statement*, Gettysburg National Military Park, Pennsylvania, vol. 1 (U.S. Department of the Interior, National Park Service, June 1999), 61–62. For the sake of clarity and consistency to the spirit of the terms, rehabilitation will be used when referring to landscape alterations and restoration when referring to changes of physical structures.

38. Frederick Tilberg, "Research Program Report," December 28, 1939, Box 7, (GETT 41113), GNMP Archives. Tilberg's report notes that as many as 80 CCC laborers worked on the vista cutting during the winter of 1940–1941;

Superintendent James McConaghie, "Superintendent's Monthly Reports, October 1940," written on November 14, 1940, 4; Superintendent James McConaghie, "Superintendent's Monthly Reports, November 1940," written on December 12, 1940, Folder 1, Box 4, (GETT 41113), GNMP Archives, 4.

39. Superintendent James McConaghie, "Superintendent's Annual Report, 1936–1937," Box 2, (GETT 41113), GNMP Archives.

40. Superintendent James McConaghie, "Superintendent's Annual Report, 1936–1937," Box 2, (GETT 41113), GNMP Archives. As of this writing, the only post and pipe fence that still stands on the battlefield is along Wainwright Avenue. In the summer of 2011, this fencing was repaired.

41. H. L. Garrett memorandum to Mr. Chatelain, May 26, 1936, included in Louis E. King's "Information and Historical Notes Concerning the Swope Property, Known in 1863 as Warfield Property," written on April 21, 1936, Folder 30, Box 6 (GETT 41151), GNMP Archives. Also located along West Confederate Avenue was a small building that, according to popular legend, was used by General Longstreet for his headquarters. Though no credible historic evidence indicated that Longstreet used the building for his headquarters, the Park Service recommended securing this building and identifying it as Longstreet's headquarters.

42. Superintendent James McConaghie, "Superintendent's Monthly Reports, September 1940," written on October 24, 1940, Folder 1, Box 4, (GETT 41113), GNMP Archives, 3.

43. *Gettysburg Times,* November 30, 1940, Folder 9, Box 11, (GETT 41113), GNMP Archives; Superintendent James McConaghie, "Superintendent's Monthly Reports, December 1940," written on January 8, 1941, Folder 1, Box 4, (GETT 41113), GNMP Archives, 1; Superintendent James McConaghie, "Superintendent's Annual Report, 1934–1935," Box 2 (GETT 41113), GNMP Archives, 40.

Chapter 3

1. Arno B. Cammerer, "And New World Idealism," *The Regional View,* Vol. IV, No. 6, June 1940, available online at http://www.cr.nps.gov/history/online_books/regional_review/vol4-6b.htm.

2. Superintendent James McConaghie, "Superintendent's Monthly Reports, December 1940," written on January 8, 1941, Folder 1, Box 4, Park Main (Central) Files, 1933–1954, (GETT 41113), Records of the National Park Service at Gettysburg National Military Park, Gettysburg National Military Park Archives, 1 [hereafter cited as (GETT 41113), GNMP Archives]; "Dr. Coleman To Take Over Park Duty On Saturday," *Gettysburg Times,* January 31, 1941, Folder 2, Box 35, Newspaper Clippings (Unbound), 1940–1945, (GETT 43663), Records of the National Park Service at Gettysburg National Military Park, Gettysburg National Military Park Archives [hereafter cited as (GETT 43663), GNMP Archives].

3. Sellers, *Preserving Nature in the National Parks*, 151, 181.

4. "Coleman Tells Broad Policy on Battlefield," *Gettysburg Times*, April 9, 1941, Folder 2, Box 35, (GETT 43663), GNMP Archives.

5. Frederick Tilberg, "Research Program Report," December 28, 1939, Box 7, (GETT 41113), GNMP Archives; Superintendent James McConaghie, "Superintendent's Monthly Reports, October 1940," written on November 14, 1940, 4; Superintendent James McConaghie, "Superintendent's Monthly Reports, November 1940," written on December 12, 1940, Folder 1, Box 4, (GETT 41113), GNMP Archives, 4; Superintendent J. Walter Coleman, "Superintendent's Monthly Report, December 1941," written on January 10, 1942, Folder 4, Box 3, (GETT 41113), GNMP Archives, 1; Superintendent J. Walter Coleman, "Superintendent's Monthly Report, January 1942," written on February 11, 1942, Folder 3, Box 3, (GETT 41113), GNMP Archives, 3; Frederick Tilberg, "Historians' Monthly Report, January 1945," written on February 5, 1945, Folder 3, Box 7 (GETT 41113).

6. Frederick Tilberg, "Historians' Monthly Report, December 1941," written on January 10, 1942, Folder 3, Box 7, (GETT 41113), GNMP Archives; Superintendent J. Walter Coleman to Region One Director, September 6, 1944, Folder 1, Box 8, Historians' Files, 1933–1965, Records of the National Park Service at Gettysburg National Military Park, (GETT 41151), GNMP Archives [hereafter cited as (GETT 41151), GNMP Archives]. Harold Steiner of Pennsylvania State College Experimental Laboratory oversaw the planting and care of the peach trees, which were planted on December 19. According to Tilberg's monthly report, Steiner planted 270 trees for "experimental purposes on the peach borer."

7. Letter from Hillory Tolson to the Regional Director, January 5, 1944, Folder 15, Box 17, (GETT 41113), GNMP Archives; Frederick Tilberg, "Historians' Monthly Report, July 1943," written on August 5, 1943, 1–2; Frederick Tilberg, "Historians' Monthly Report, March 1943," written on April 5, 1943, Folder 3, Box 7, (GETT 41113), GNMP Archives, 2; Benjamin Y. Dixon, "Gettysburg, A Living Battlefield" (PhD dissertation, Oklahoma Univ., 2002), 188. Dixon notes that eight American flags flew on the battlefield—from the five observation towers, Meade's headquarters, the Soldiers' National Cemetery, and the Angle. All of these flags, however, except the one at the Angle, had been placed at these locations by the War Department. As tourists concentrated in the sector of the Soldiers' National Cemetery, Cemetery Ridge, and the southern end of the battlefield, other portions of the battlefield remained neglected by the Park Service and visitors. These areas the agency delegated for practical usage. During World War II, the Park Service allocated grounds at East Cemetery Hill, Oak Ridge, and Culp's Hill for Victory Gardens.

8. Frederick Tilberg, "Report on the Proposed Restoration of the Bryan House," November 20, 1943, Folder 15, Box 17, (GETT 41113), GNMP Archives; Letter from Hillory Tolson to the Regional Director, January 5, 1944, Folder 15, Box 17, (GETT 41113), GNMP Archives; Frederick Tilberg, "Historians' Monthly

Report, April 1951," written on May 4, 1951, 2; Frederick Tilberg, "Historians'
Monthly Report, May 1951," written on June 5, 1951, Folder 1, Box 7, (GETT
41113), GNMP Archives, 2.

9. Oliver Taylor memorandum to Region One Superintendents, October 30, 1943,
Folder 4, Box 12, (GETT 41113), GNMP Archives.

10. "Coleman Tells Broad Policy on Battlefield," *Gettysburg Times*, April 9, 1941,
Folder 2, Box 35 (GETT 43663), GNMP Archives; Superintendent James
McConaghie, "Superintendent's Monthly Report, December 1940," written on
January 8, 1941, Folder 1, Box 4, (GETT 41113), GNMP Archives, 3; Superin-
tendent J. Walter Coleman, "Superintendent's Monthly Report, April 1941,"
written on May 13, 1941, Folder 4, Box 3, (GETT 41113), GNMP Archives, 4;
Superintendent J. Walter Coleman, "Superintendent's Monthly Report, July
1943," written on August 14, 1943, Folder 2, Box 3, (GETT 41113), GNMP
Archives, 2; Superintendent C. S. Dunn, "Superintendent's Monthly Report,
April 1943," written on May 10, 1943, Box 2443, RG 79, Central Classified File,
1933–1949, National Parks, Chickamauga and Chattanooga National Military
Park, National Archives and Records Administration, College Park, Maryland,
5 (hereafter cited as Folder, Box, CCF, RG 79, NARA College Park). Superintendent Dunn reported a total profit to the viewers, to date, at $2,590.20.

11. Superintendent J. Walter Coleman to NPS Director, May 27, 1941, Folder 201–
06, Box 2490, CCF, RG 79, NARA College Park; Superintendent J. Walter
Coleman, "Superintendent's Monthly Report, July, 1941," written on August 12,
1941, Folder 4, Box 3, (GETT 41113), GNMP Archives, 2–3; "250 Hear Talk on
U.S. Parks Here on Sunday," *Gettysburg Times,* July 14, 1941, Folder 6, Box 35,
(GETT 43663), GNMP Archives; Superintendent J. Walter Coleman, "Superin-
tendent's Monthly Report, August 1941," written on September 9, 1941,
Folder 4, Box 3, (GETT 41113), GNMP Archives, 2; Superintendent J. Walter
Coleman, "Superintendent's Monthly Report, June 1942," written on July 9, 1942,
Folder 3, Box 3, (GETT 41113), GNMP Archives, 2; "Sutton Jett To Discuss
Canal Along Potomac," *Gettysburg Times,* July 18, 1941, Folder 6, Box 35, (GETT
43663), GNMP Archives; Superintendent J. Walter Coleman, "Superintendent's
Monthly Report, July 1942," written on August 12, 1942, Folder 3, Box 3, (GETT
41113), GNMP Archives 2; "Color Slides To Illustrate Talk On Field," *Gettysburg
Times,* July 25, 1942, Folder 6, Box 35, (GETT 43663), GNMP Archives; Superintendent J. Walter Coleman to Associate Director, November 23,
1942, Folder 201, Box, 2490, CCF, RG 79, NARA, College Park; Unrau, *Administrative History*, 222.

12. Superintendent J. Walter Coleman to NPS Director, May 27, 1941, Folder
201–06, Box 2490, CCF, RG 79, NARA College Park.

13. Abraham Lincoln, "Inaugural Address," March 4, 1861. Avaliable at www.ava-
lon.law.yale/19th_century/lincoln1.asp.

14. Superintendent J. Walter Coleman, "Superintendent's Monthly Report, May
1942," written on June 10, 1942, Folder 3, Box 3, (GETT 41113), GNMP
Archives, 1; "Sunday Travel Curtailed by Gas Rationing," *Gettysburg Times,*

May 18, 1942, Folder 8, Box 35, (GETT 43663), GNMP Archives; Sellars, *Preserving Nature in the National Parks,* 150–51; Superintendent J. Walter Coleman, "Superintendent's Monthly Report, January 1943," written on February 10, 1943, Folder 2, Box 3, (GETT 41113), GNMP Archives, 1–2. As a point of comparison, in January 1942, the park recorded 3,858 visitors.

15. Superintendent J. Walter Coleman, "Superintendent's Monthly Report, April 1942," written on May 12, 1942, Folder 3, Box 3, (GETT 41113), GNMP Archives, 1; Earl H. Brown, "Audit Report," to NPS Director, April 20, 1942, Folder 204–20, Box 2491, CCF, RG 79, NARA College Park. For additional reading on the Gettysburg Cyclorama see, Sue Boardman and Kathryn Porch, *The Battle of Gettysburg Cyclorama: A History and Guide* (Gettysburg, Pa.: Thomas Publications, 2008). When Philippoteaux came to the United States in 1879, business entrepreneurs commissioned him to paint a battle scene for display in Chicago. The artist travelled to Gettysburg in 1882 and began to study the terrain, interview battle veterans, and make scene sketches for the cyclorama. "The Cyclorama of the Battle of Gettysburg" premiered in Chicago in 1883, complete with the three dimensional foreground objects. Based on its popularity, Philippoteaux was asked to paint a second cyclorama for display in Boston, which premiered in 1884. After its heyday of display, the "Chicago Cyclorama" fell into private hands and was eventually donated to Wake Forest University in North Carolina. "The Battle of Gettysburg," as his painting was called, remained in Boston for nearly twenty years, at which time Americans lost interest in cycloramas. Thereafter, a local entrepreneur, Jeremiah Hoover, purchased the painting and moved it to Gettysburg in time for display for the 50th anniversary in 1913. The cyclorama painting was housed on Baltimore Street in a building owned by the Gettysburg Water Company. As early as 1936, the Park Service recommended acquiring the painting from Jeremiah Hoover. After years of negotiations, Hoover finally signed an agreement, on April 1, 1942, and transferred it to the National Park Service. The negotiations stipulated that the Park Service retain the services of Charles Cobean, the long time interpreter of the painting. He received $600 a year for his services, which came from cyclorama ticket sales. After the NPS acquired the cyclorama and the building, the service continued to display the painting in the building on Cemetery Hill until it relocated the cyclorama to its new visitor center in 1962.

16. Roy Appleman to Regional Director, November 4, 1946, Folder 833, Box 46, Subject Files, 1937–1957, NARA Philadelphia.

17. "Museum Prospectus: Gettysburg National Military Park," January 23, 1947, Folder 4, Box 17, (GETT 41113), GNMP Archives, 16–22; Frederick Tilberg, "Historians' Narrative Reports, June 1942," written on July 3, 1942. Folder 3, Box 7, (GETT 41113), GNMP Archives, 1; Memo from Frederick Tilberg to Superintendent J. Walter Coleman, October 19, 1942, Folder: Gettysburg 620–46: Administration, Museum Building, 1942–1947, Box 44, RG 79, Historic Shrines, Sites, Monuments, and Parks, Subject Files, 1937–1957, Northeast Regional Office, Philadelphia, Pennsylvania (hereafter cited by Folder, Box, SF, RG 79,

NARA Philadelphia); Superintendent J. Walter Coleman to the Regional Director, February 19, 1945, Folder 9, Box 7, (GETT 41151), GNMP Archives; Memo from Thomas Allen to Director, February 26, 1945, Folder: Gettysburg 620–46: Administration, Museum Building, 1942–1947, Box 44, SF, RG 79, NARA Philadelphia.

18. Superintendent J. Walter Coleman to the Regional Director, October 16, 1942, Folder 9, Box 7, (GETT 41151), GNMP Archives; Roy Appleman to Regional Director, November 6, 1946, Folder: Gettysburg 620–46, Box 44, SF, RG 79, Philadelphia NARA.

19. Fredrick Tilberg to Superintendent Coleman, February 19, 1945, Folder 4, Box 9, (GETT 41151), GNMP Archives; Superintendent Walter Coleman to the Regional Director, February 19, 1945, Folder 9, Box 7, (GETT 41151), GNMP Archives; Roy Appleman to the Regional Director, November 6, 1946, Folder: Gettysburg 620–46, Box 44, SF, RG 79, NARA Philadelphia; Sellars, *Preserving Nature in the National Parks*, 58.

20. Sutter, *Driven Wild*, 24; Superintendent J. Walter Coleman to the Regional Director, October 16, 1942, Folder 9, Box 7, (GETT 41151), GNMP Archives, 2.

21. Superintendent J. Walter Coleman to the Regional Director, October 16, 1942, Folder 9, Box 7, (GETT 41151), GNMP Archives, 4.

22. Superintendent J. Walter Coleman to Regional Director, October 16, 1942, Folder 9, Box 7, (GETT41151), GNMP Archives, 1.

23. Frederick Tilberg, "Historians' Monthly Report, November 1950," written on December 4, 1950, Folder 1, Box 7, (GETT 41113), GNMP Archives, 2; Superintendent J. Walter Coleman, "Superintendent's Monthly Report, May 1944," written on June 14, 1944, Folder 1, Box 3, (GETT 41113), GNMP Archives, 2–3; Dixon, "Gettysburg, A Living Battlefield," 174–91. See also Douglas Southall Freeman, *R. E. Lee: A Biography,* 4 vols. (New York: Scribner Sons, 1934); Douglas Southall Freeman, *Lee's Lieutenants: A Study in Command,* 3 vols. (New York: Scribner Sons, 1942–1944).

24. Frederick Tilberg, "Historians' Monthly Report, March 1939," written on April 3, 1939, Folder 4, Box 7, (GETT 41113), GNMP Archives, 2; Frederick Tilberg, "Historians' Monthly Report, May 1942," written on June 3, 1942, Folder 3, Box 7, (GETT 41113), GNMP Archives, 2. For additional reading on Lincoln's growing popularity, see Merrill Peterson, *Lincoln in American Memory* (New York: Oxford Univ. Press, 1994).

25. Superintendent J. Walter Coleman, "Superintendent's Monthly Report, April 1941," written on May 13, 1941, Folder 4, Box 3, (GETT 41113), GNMP Archives, 5; Superintendent J. Walter Coleman to NPS Director, August 13, 1941, Folder 201, Box 2490, CCF, RG 79, NARA College Park.

26. Superintendent J. Walter Coleman to NPS Director, August 13, 1941, Folder 201, Box 2490, CCF, RG 79, NARA College Park; Oliver Taylor, Herbert Evison, and J. Walter Coleman, "Recommendations for Gettysburg Guide System Prepared Jointly By the Regional Director, the Associate Director, and the

Park Superintendent," March 17, 1944, Folder 201, Box 2490, RG 79, NARA College Park, 3–5.

27. Oliver Taylor, Herbert Evison, and J. Walter Coleman, "Recommendations for Gettysburg Guide System," 4–8, Folder 201, Box 2490, CCF, RG 79, NARA College Park; Newton Drury to the Secretary of the Interior, December 10, 1945, Folder 201, Box 2490, CCF, RG 79, NARA College Park; Unrau, *Administrative History*, 240. Initially licensed by the War Department and then the National Park Service, guides were not federal employees, and the park had little control over their behavior. Guides were self-employed; they were able to dictate their own hours and rates for battlefield tours. Management believed that making guides federal employees, with a consistent salary, would at least eliminate their aggressive solicitation. It was also determined that guides would be eligible for sick leave and annual leave and that the guides would be required to wear the standard green and gray NPS uniform.

28. Acting Regional Director Fred T. Johnson to Superintendent Coleman, October 14, 1942, Folder 9, Box 7 (GETT 41151), GNMP Archives; Unrau, *Administrative History*, 223.

29. "February Tops January Scrap Mark, 135 Tons," *Gettysburg Times*, March 6, 1943, Folder 9, Box 35, (GETT 43663), GNMP Archives. Gettysburg and Adams County residents also donated a significant amount of material to the war drive. Superintendent Coleman served as the local salvage chairman. The *Gettysburg Times* frequently reported on the area's contribution to the war effort. The March 6, 1943, paper reported 278.5 tons of scrap materials collected during February; Sellers, *Preserving Nature in the National Parks*, 150–53. Secretary of the Interior Harold Ickes approved the mining of salt in Death Valley, and his successor, Newton Drury, acquiesced to the cutting of the Sitka trees in Olympic, after much debate.

30. Frederick Tilberg, "Historians' Monthly Report, July 1942," written on August 4, 1942, Folder 3, Box 7, (GETT 41113), GNMP Archives, 2; "Other Parks To Get Local Surplus Metal," *Gettysburg Times*, July 28, 1942, Folder 9, Box 35, (GETT 43663), GNMP Archives; Acting Assistant Historian Bernard Levine, "Historians' Reports, August 1942," written on September 3, 1942, 3; Frederick Tilberg, "Historians' Monthly Report, September 1942," written on October 3, 1942, Folder 3, Box 7, (GETT 41113), GNMP Archives, 3. The surplus cannon went via rail to Antietam and the National Capital Parks; Superintendent J. Walter Coleman to Regional Director, June 30, 1942, Cultural Resource Management Files, GNMP; "May Release Field Shells to War Effort," *Gettysburg Times*, July 11, 1942, Folder 9, Box 35, (GETT 43663), GNMP Archives. The iron fence panels had been removed from the Soldiers' National Monument in the cemetery several years earlier. The cautionary signs included "Keep Off This Mound" and "Do Not Drive on this Ground" signage. The guns included twenty-six bronze siege guns, thirty-eight bronze guns, eight bronze howitzers, and fourteen iron guns.

31. Superintendent J. Walter Coleman to the Director, NPS, October 13, 1942, Vertical Files, 17–3, GNMP Library; Superintendent J. Walter Coleman, "Superintendent's Monthly Report, October 1942," written on November 17, 1942, Folder 3, Box 3, (GETT 41113), GNMP Archives; Newton Drury to Superintendent J. Walter Coleman, October 30, 1942, Vertical Files, 17–3, GNMP Library.

32. "Preliminary Report on Non-Ferrous Metals, Gettysburg National Military Park," December 31, 1942, Vertical Files, 17–3, GNMP Library.

33. Newton Drury to Thorton Smith, War Production Board, February 10, 1943, Vertical Files, 17–3, GNMP Library.

34. Superintendent Chas. S. Dunn, "Superintendent's Monthly Report, December 1944," written on January 11, 1945, Box 2443, CCF, RG 79, NARA College Park, 1–2; Superintendent Blair Ross, "Superintendent's Monthly Report, July 1942," written on August 10, 1942, Box 2546, CCF, RG 79, NARA College Park, 1.

35. Superintendent James McConaghie, "Superintendent's Annual Report, 1943," written in September 1943, Folder 207–01, Box 2560, CCF, RG 79, NARA College Park, 14.

36. Superintendent Chas. S. Dunn, "Superintendent's Monthly Report, November 1942," written on December 11, 1942, Box 2443, CCF, RG 79, NARA College Park, 1–2.

37. A considerable amount of literature exists regarding prisoner of war camps in America during World War II. For additional reading, see John Hammond Moore, *The Faustball Tunnel: German POWs in America and Their Great Escape* (New York: Random House, 1978) or Arnold Krammer, *Nazi Prisoners of War in America* (New York: Stein and Day, 1979).

38. Superintendent J. Walter Coleman, "Superintendent's Monthly Report, May 1944," written on June 14, 1944, Folder 1, Box 3, (GETT 41113), GNMP Archives, 4; Unrau, *Administrative History*, 219; Frederick Tilberg, "Historians' Monthly Report, October 1944," written on November 3, 1944, Folder 3, Box 7, (GETT 41113), GNMP Archives, 2; "War Prisoner Camp Nearly Ready For Use," *Gettysburg Complier*, June 22, 1944, Vertical Files, 11- 40, GNMP Library; Superintendent J. Walter Coleman, "Superintendent's Monthly Report, June 1944," written on July 10, 1944, Folder 1, Box 3, (GETT 41113), GNMP Archives, 1.

39. Superintendent J. Walter Coleman, "Superintendent's Monthly Report, May 1944," written on June 14, 1944, Folder 1, Box 3, (GETT 41113), GNMP Archives, 4–5; Untitled article, *Gettysburg Compiler*, April 13, 1946; "Work Camp Is Being Built By Prisoners," *Gettysburg Compiler*, June 17, 1944; "War Prisoner Camp Nearly Ready For Use," *Gettysburg Compiler*, July 15, 1944; "Nazi Prisoners From Camp Here Cutting Wood," *Gettysburg Compiler*, February 10, 1945.

40. "Site For $200,000 Longstreet Statue Is Dedicated; 71st Coast Artillery Re-Enacts '63 Battle Scene," *Gettysburg Times*, July 2, 1941, Folder 5, Box 35, (GETT

43663), GNMP Archives. Assistant Secretary of State H. Breckenridge Long delivered these comments at the dedicated site for a planned monument to Confederate General James Longstreet.

41. "Preservation of U.S. Ideals Best Memorial—Gen. Martin," *Gettysburg Times*, May 30, 1941, Folder 3, Box 35, (GETT 43663), GNMP Archives.

42. Superintendent J. Walter Coleman, "Superintendent's Monthly Report, May 1943," written on June 12, 1943, Folder 2, Box 3, (GETT 41113), GNMP Archives, 1; "Governor's Address," *Gettysburg Times*, May 31, 1943, Vertical Files 10–32, GNMP Library.

43. Governor J. Melville Broughton, "Address Delivered at Gettysburg Memorial Day Exercises, May 30, 1944," Folder 502, Box 2500, CCF, RG 79, NARA College Park.

44. Governor Leverett Saltonstall, "Address Delivered at Gettysburg Memorial Day Exercises, May 30, 1944," Folder 502, Box 2500, CCF, RG 79, NARA College Park.

45. Wills, *Lincoln at Gettysburg*, 146, 175; Barry Schwartz, "Rereading the Gettysburg Address: Social Change and Collective Memory," *Qualitative Sociology* 19 (1996): 395–422; Barry Schwartz, "Memory as a Cultural System: Abraham Lincoln in World War II," *American Sociological Review* 61 (October 1996): 908–27. Schwartz, too, finds the power of the Gettysburg Address to lay in the ways successive generations have interpreted it to their circumstances. In this article, Schwartz traces the ways in which Americans have interpreted the address, using the Progressive era, the Second World War, and the civil rights movement as eras of reengagement with the speech.

46 Governor J. Melville Broughton, "Address Delivered at Gettysburg Memorial Day Exercises, May 30, 1944," Folder 502, Box 2500, CCF, RG 79, NARA College Park.

Chapter 4

1. John A. Jakle, *The Tourist: Travel in the Twentieth-Century* (Lincoln: Univ. of Nebraska Press, 1985), 185–99; Susan Sessions Rugh, *Are We There Yet? The Golden Age of American Family Vacations* (Lawrence, University of Kansas Press, 2008), 2, 12, 20. Jakle notes that an average work week in 1940 was 44 hours, but by 1950 the average work week had fallen to a standard 40 hours. Given the importance of tourism in the postwar period, surprisingly little scholarship has been devoted to the topic, and Rugh and Jakle's books stand among the most complete. Rugh examines family vacations in the thirty-year period after 1945. She defines this period as the "golden age of family vacations" because "unprecedented prosperity and widespread vacation benefits at work meant most middle-class families could afford to vacation" (2–15). Jakle, on the other hand, offers a discussion of tourist trends in the twentieth century, by exploring the influence of the automobile and the rise of commercial strips.

2. Jakle, *The Tourist*, 185–99; Rugh, *Are We There Yet?*, 13, 41–54, 69–70; Shaffer, *See America First*, 4.

3. Kammen, *Mystic Chords of Memory*, 533, 537–40, 626.

4. Kammen, *Mystic Chords of Memory*, 539, 551, 626; Sellars, *Preserving Nature in the National Parks*, 151, 173; Rugh, *Are We There Yet?*, 131–32.

5. Superintendent J. Walter Coleman, "Superintendent's Monthly Report, August 1945," written on September 13, 1945, Box 2497, RG 79, Central Classified File, 1933–1949, National Parks, Gettysburg National Military Park, National Archives and Records Administration, College Park, Maryland, 2 (hereafter this collection will be cited by Folder, Box, CCF, RG 79, NARA College Park); Superintendent J. Walter Coleman "Superintendent's Monthly Report, September 1945," written on October 5, 1945, Box 2497, RG 79 NARA College Park, 2; Frederick Tilberg, "Museum Prospectus: Gettysburg National Military Park and Cemetery," written on November 27, 1956, Folder 10, Box 8, Historians' Files, 1933–1965, Records of the National Park Service at Gettysburg National Military Park, (GETT 41151), Gettysburg National Military Park Archives, 16 [hereafter cited by (GETT 41151), GNMP Archives]; Historians' Files, "Monthly Statistical Report of Interpretive Services, 1939–1953," Folder 15, Box 9, (GETT 41151), GNMP Archives; Frederick Tilberg, "Historians' Monthly Report, September 1949," written on October 5, 1949, Folder 2, Box 7, Park Main (Central) Files, 1933—1954, (GETT 41113), Records of the National Park Service at Gettysburg National Military Park, Gettysburg National Military Park Archives, 2 [hereafter cited as (GETT 41113), GNMP Archives]; Sellars, *Preserving Nature in the National Parks*, 181. Annual visitation is calculated from October 1 through September 30 of the following year. According to Tilberg's September 1949 monthly, the 659,222 reached for the 1948–1949 fiscal year was the third busiest season, following 1929 and 1938.

6. Superintendent James McConaghie, "Superintendent's Annual, Report 1946," 10; Superintendent James McConaghie, "Superintendent's Annual Report, 1948," written on June 1, 1948, Folder 207–01.4, Box 2560, CCF, RG 79, NARA College Park, 5; Unidentified author, "Superintendent's Annual Report, Fiscal Year 1948," undated, Folder 201–01, Box 2439, CCF, RG 79, NARA College Park, 3. McConaghie reported visitation from forty-six states and six foreign countries.

7. "For a Bigger and Better Gettysburg," *Gettysburg Times*, October 26, 1946, Folder 501–Publicity, 1945–1952, Box 41, RG 79, Historic Shrines, Sites, Monuments, and Parks, Subject Files, 1937–1957, Northeast Regional Office, Philadelphia, Pennsylvania [hereafter cited by Folder, Box, SF, RG 79, NARA Philadelphia].

8. Frederick Tilberg, "Annual Report on Information and Interpretive Services, 1955," written on January 31, 1956, Folder Y2623, Box 16, RG 79, Historic Shrines, Sites, Monuments, and Parks, General Correspondence, 1952–1966, Northeast

Regional Office, Philadelphia, Pennsylvania, 8 (hereafter cited by Folder, Box, GC, NARA Philadelphia); Superintendent J. Walter Coleman, "Superintendent's Monthly Report, July 1946," written on August 5, 1946, 2; Superintendent J. Walter Coleman "Superintendent's Monthly Report, August 1946," written on September 12, 1946, 2; Superintendent J. Walter Coleman "Superintendent's Monthly Report, August 1947," written on September 11, 1947, Box 2497, CCF, RG 79, NARA College Park, 3; Frederick Tilberg, "Historians' Monthly Report, July 1947," written on August 4, 1947, Folder 207–03, Box 2498, CCF, RG 79, NARA College Park, 2; Frederick Tilberg, "Historians' Monthly Report, June 1948," written on July 2, 1948, Box 2498, CCF, RG 79, NARA College Park; Superintendent J. Walter Coleman, "Superintendent's Monthly Report, July 1953," written on August 6, 1953, 2; Superintendent J. Walter Coleman, "Superintendent's Monthly Report, August 1952," written on September 11, 1952, Box 191, CCF, RG 79, NARA College Park, 2.

9. Superintendent J. Walter Coleman, "Superintendent's Monthly Report, May 1945," written on June 6, 1945, Box 2497, CCF, RG 79, NARA College Park, 1; Senator Robert Taft, "Compulsory Military Training in Peace Time: Against Fundamental Policy of America," address delivered on May 30, 1945 at Gettysburg National Military Park, *Vital Speeches,* vol. XI, 554–57, accessed online at www.ibiblio.org/pha/policy/1945/1945-05-30a.html; Superintendent J. Coleman, "Superintendent's Monthly Report, May 1946," written on June 11, 1946, Box 2497, CCF, RG 79, NARA College Park, 1, 2; "Bricker Appeals for End of 'Ineptitudes' in U.S. Direction of Economics," *Gettysburg Times,* May 30, 1946, Vertical Files, 10–32, Gettysburg National Military Park Library (all notes hereafter cited as VF, GNMP Library). For additional reading on Senator Robert Taft, see Russell Kirk, *The Political Principles of Robert A. Taft* (New York: Fleet Press Corp, 1967) or James T. Patterson, *Mr. Republican: A Biography of Robert Taft* (Boston: Houghton Mifflin, 1972). A conservative Republican, Taft, along with conservative southern Democrats, had been a regular critic of President Franklin Roosevelt's New Deal programs. During World War II, Taft maintained an isolationist perspective and argued that America should not become involved in European affairs. Taft had sought the Republican nomination for president three times, 1940, 1948, and 1952, but was unsuccessful. He is probably best known for his labor relations policies, authoring the famed Taft-Hartley Act in 1947. As indicated by the title of Patterson's work, Taft became the leading Republican figure and earned the nickname "Mr. Republican." Taft was also an ally of fellow conservative Republican John Bricker, also of Ohio. Taft supported Bricker's nomination for the 1944 presidential bid, but New York governor Thomas Dewey, who led the more moderate Republican faction, received the Republican nomination and selected Bricker as his running mate. The ticket lost to incumbent President Roosevelt. To date the best biography on John Bricker is Richard Davies, *Defender of the Old Guard: John Bricker and American Politics* (Columbus: Ohio State Univ. Press, 1993). The National Park Service had no association with or influence on individuals invited to be the Memorial Day (or

later Dedication Day) speakers. The local chapter of the Sons of Union Veterans, the Lincoln Fellowship, and the borough council coordinated these celebrations. For a complete discussion of the social and cultural currents of the Cold War era see, Stephen J. Whitfield, *The Culture of the Cold War* (Baltimore, Md.: The Johns Hopkins Univ. Press, 1991).

10. Superintendent J. Walter Coleman, "Superintendent's Monthly Report, May 1946," written on June 11, 1946, Box 2497, CCF, RG 97, NARA College Park, 2; Elbert Cox to Superintendent James Coleman, June 14, 1946, Folder 501–Publicity, 1945–1952, Box 41, SF, RG 79, NARA Philadelphia; Superintendent J. Walter Coleman, "Superintendent's Monthly Report, May 1947," written on June 13, 1947, Box 2497, CCF, RG 79, NARA College Park, 1; "Governor Duff's Address," *Gettysburg Times*, May 30, 1947, VF, 10–32, GNMP Library.

11. Congressman Joseph Martin's Memorial Day speech, reprinted in "Congressman Martin Asserts United States Seeking Peace," *Gettysburg Times*, May 31, 1948; "Governor of Maryland Says America Must 'Set Example' For Government Of People In Memorial Day Address Here," *Gettysburg Times*, May 31, 1951, VF, 10–32, GNMP Library. Similar to Taft and Bricker, Martin was a conservative Republican and an outspoken critic of the New Deal. He did, however, become more moderate toward the end of his political career and served as Speaker of the House between 1947 and 1949 and again from 1953 to 1955. McKeldin served as a two-term Maryland governor, from 1951 to 1959.

12. Barry Schwartz, "Rereading the Gettysburg Address: Social Change and Collective Memory," in *Qualitative Sociology*, 19 (1996): 395–422; 79th Congress, Joint Resolution, "Designating November 19, 1946, the Anniversary of Lincoln's Gettysburg Address as Dedication Day," Approved August 7, 1946, Folder Gettysburg Legislation 1948, Box 37, SF, RG 79, NARA Philadelphia. For additional reading on Lincoln and memory, see Wills, *Lincoln at Gettysburg*; Peterson, *Lincoln in American Memory*; and Gabor Boritt, *The Gettysburg Gospel: The Lincoln Speech That Nobody Knows* (New York: Simon & Schuster, 2006). To date, Peterson's work offers the best analysis on Lincoln within popular culture and memory. He explores Lincoln's image in literature, biography, history, art, and politics and identifies five prevailing themes to the Lincoln image: Savior of the Union; Emancipationist; Man of the People; First America; and Self Made Man. Peterson also identifies two periods critical to the making of the Lincoln image. The first era, 1870s and 1880s, produced the first Lincoln memories and collections. In the second period, the 1920s and 1930s, scholars (namely Carl Sandburg and James G. Randall) tried to separate the Lincoln folk-image from Lincoln the politician and statesman. He concludes that the diversity in the Lincoln image makes him appeal to all Americans.

13. Superintendent J. Walter Coleman, "Superintendent's Monthly Report, October 1946," written on November 13, 1946, Box 2497, CCF, RG 79, NARA College Park, 2; *Gettysburg Times*, November 19, 1951; Waldo Warder Braden, ed., *Building the Myth: Selected Speeches Memorializing Abraham Lincoln* (Chicago: Univ.

of Illinois Press, 1990), 218–19; James Holland to Regional Director, November 20, 1951, Box 675, CCF, RG 79, NARA College Park. Stevenson received the Democratic nomination for president in 1952 and again in 1956, but lost both times to Republican nominee Dwight D. Eisenhower. For additional reading on Stevenson, see John Bartlow Martin, *Adlai Stevenson and the World: The Life of Adlai Stevenson* (New York: Doubleday, 1977); Porter McKeever, *Adlai Stevenson: His Life and Legacy* (New York: Morrow, 1989); and Jeff Broadwater, *Adlai Stevenson and American Politics: The Odyssey of a Cold War Liberal* (New York: Twayne, 1994).

14. Superintendent J. Walter Coleman, "Superintendent's Monthly Report, February 1949," written on March 8, 1949, Box 2497, CCF, RG 79, NARA College Park, 1–2; Superintendent J. Walter Coleman, "Superintendent's Monthly Report, February 1950," written on March 10, 1950, Box 191, CCF, RG 79, NARA College Park, 1–2; "More than 4,000 Boy Scouts Participate in Annual Lincoln Pilgrimage Here Saturday," *Gettysburg Times*, February 12, 1951; Superintendent J. Walter Coleman, "Superintendent's Monthly Report, October 1952," written on November 7, 1952, Box 191, CCF, RG, 79, NARA College Park, 2–3.

15. Frederick Tilberg, "Annual Report on Information and Interpretive Services, 1955," written on January 31, 1956, Folder Y2623, Box 16, GC, RG 79, NARA Philadelphia, 6–7; Albert Cox to J. Coleman, March 17, 1947, Folder Gettysburg National Military Park, Exhibits, General From September 1941, Box 46, SF, RG 79, NARA Philadelphia; Frederick Tilberg, "Historians' Monthly Report, May 1947," written on June 5, 1947, 2; Frederick Tilberg, "Historians' Monthly Report, June 1947," written on July 2, 1947, 2; Frederick Tilberg, "Historians' Monthly Report, November 1947," written on December 2, 1947, all in Folder 2, Box 7, (GETT 41113), GNMP Archives, 1; Director Drury to Regional Director, March 11, 1947, Folder Exhibits, Box 46, SF, RG 79, NARA Philadelphia; Frederick Tilberg, "Historians' Monthly Report, August 1948," written on September 3, 1948, 1; Frederick Tilberg, "Historians' Monthly Report, October 1948," written on November 2, 1948, both in Folder 2, Box 7, (GETT 41113), GNMP Archives, 1; Director Drury to Regional Director, March 11, 1947, Folder Exhibits, Box 46, SF, RG 79, NARA Philadelphia.

16. Frederick Tilberg, "Historians' Monthly Report, October 1948," written on November 2, 1948, Folder 2, Box 7, (GETT 41113), GNMP Archives, 1; Frederick Tilberg, "Annual Report on Information and Interpretive Services, 1955," written on January 31, 1956, Folder Y2623, Box 16, GC, RG 79, NARA Philadelphia, 6–7; Frederick Tilberg, "Historians' Monthly Report, August 1948," written on September 3, 1948, 1; Frederick Tilberg, "Historians' Monthly Report, July 1948," Folder 2, Box 7, (GETT 41113), GNMP Archives.

17. Frederick Tilberg, "Historians' Monthly Report, August 1947," written on September 3, 1947, Folder 2, Box 7, (GETT 41113), GNMP Archives, 2; Frederick Tilberg, "Annual Report on Information and Interpretive Services, 1955," written on January 31, 1956, 7; Frederick Tilberg, "Annual Report on Information and

Visitor Services, 1956," written on February 6, 1957, Folder Y2623, Box 16, GC, RG 79, NARA Philadelphia, 1; Frederick Tilberg, "Historians' Monthly Report, July 1948," Folder 2, Box 7, (GETT 41113), GNMP Archives. The rangers also sold the park's informational booklets from their stations at Devil's Den and Little Round Top. Interested visitors could purchase a copy of *The Gettysburg Handbook* for twenty-five cents or a copy of *Abraham Lincoln From His Own Words* for thirty-five cents. The sale items were operated by the park historian, who acted as an agent of Eastern National Park and Monument Association. Eastern National was Gettysburg's non-profit partner organization, but also operated in over 100 other national park sites, namely on the east coast. Congress authorized the creation of such non-profit partner associations to enhance visitor experience to America's national parks in 1946. A year later, in May 1947, several NPS rangers met at Gettysburg National Military Park to establish such a non-profit called Eastern National Park and Monument Association (or Eastern National, for short). Gettysburg was Eastern National's first sales outlet and partner park. For additional reading on Eastern National and its role in the NPS system, see www .easternnational.org.

18. Weeks, *Gettysburg*, 115–44; Superintendent J. Walter Coleman to the Regional Director, March 8, 1949; Newton Drury to Regional Director, June 2, 1949; Thomas Allen to J. Coleman, May 11, 1949, all in Folder 900-Concessions, 1944–1951, Box 46, SF, RG 79, NARA Philadelphia.

19. Frederick Tilberg, "Annual Report on Information and Interpretive Services, 1955," written on January 31, 1956, Folder Y2623, Box 16, GC, RG 79, NARA Philadelphia, 3–6; Frederick Tilberg, "Museum Prospectus: Gettysburg National Military Park and Cemetery," written on November 27, 1956, Folder 10, Box 8, (GETT 41151), GNMP Archives, 1 (hereafter cited as Tilberg, "Museum Prospectus, 1956"); Unrau, *Administrative History*, 246; Charles D. Drew to Director, August 4, 1951, Folder Gettysburg 833-Exhibits, 1942–1952, Box 46, SF, RG 79, NARA Philadelphia; Thomas Allen to Director, May 26, 1942, "Gettysburg National Military Park, Exhibits, General From September 1941," Box 46, SF, RG 79, NARA Philadelphia; Ned Burns to Director, May 21, 1948, Folder Exhibits, Box 46, SF, RG 79, NARA Philadelphia, 3; Frederick Tilberg, "Historians' Monthly Report, June 1948," written on July 2, 1948, Box 2498, RG 79, NARA College Park, 2. Visitors could view the painting from April through November; the facility closed for four months during the winter season because the building lacked heat. The National Park Service awarded the contract to New York conservationist E. Richard Panzironi, and by late June 1948 Panzironi and crew had completed the painting's restoration. Workers stabilized the cyclorama's canvas, retouched the painting, and painted the wooden beams supporting the canvas. The cyclorama building remained open during the restoration process.

20. Frederick Tilberg, "Annual Report on Operation of Gettysburg Cyclorama, 1951," Folder 833-Exhibits, 1942–1952, Box 46, SF, RG 79, NARA Philadelphia; Frederick Tilberg, "Museum Prospectus, 1956," Folder 10, Box 8, (GETT 41151),

GNMP Archives, 17; Frederick Tilberg, "Annual Report on Information and Interpretive Services, 1955," written on January 31, 1956, Folder Y2623, Box 16, GC, RG 79, NARA Philadelphia, 4–5, 8; "Gettysburg Cyclorama" flyer, n.d., Folder 503-Pictures, General, 1934–1949, Box 2500, CCF, RG 79, NARA College Park.

21. Roy Appleman to Regional Director, November 4, 1946, Folder 833, Box 46, SF, RG 79, NARA Philadelphia; Newton Drury to Regional Director, January 28, 1946; Roy Appleman to Regional Director, November 6, 1946; Frederick Tilberg to Superintendent J. Walter Coleman, October 19, 1942, all in Folder Gettysburg 620–46, Box 44, CCF, RG 79, NARA Philadelphia; "Museum Prospectus: Gettysburg National Military Park," January 23, 1947, Folder 4, Box 17, (GETT 41113), GNMP Archives, 1–45 (hereafter cited as Tilberg, "Museum Prospectus, 1947," to distinguish it from Tilberg's 1956 Museum Prospectus); Sellars, *Preserving Nature in the National Parks*, 58.

22. Albert Cox to Superintendent J. Walter Coleman, March 24, 1949; E. M. Lisle to Superintendent J. Walter Coleman, May 4, 1949, both in Folder: Gettysburg 501-01, Box 41, SF, RG 79, NARA Philadelphia; Superintendent J. Walter Coleman, "Superintendent's Monthly Report, November 1950," written on December 11, 1950, Box 191, CCF, RG 79, NARA College Park, 2; Frederick Tilberg, "Annual Report on Information and Interpretive Services, 1955," written on January 31, 1956, Folder Y2623, Box 16, GC, RG 79, NARA Philadelphia, 7; "Put New Signs on Battlefield," *Gettysburg Times*, May 24, 1951.

23. "7 Chamber Directors Ask Probe of Local National Park Office; Say Coleman Did Not Cooperate," *Gettysburg Times*, March 13, 1951; "Coleman Declares Battlefield Guides Requested Civil Service; Denies Chamber of Commerce Directors' Charges," *Gettysburg Times*, March 14, 1951; "3 Park Service Officials Will Hear Charges," *Gettysburg Times*, March 29, 1951; "Park Service Officials Deny Charges That Guides Will Be Placed Under U.S. Civil Service," *Gettysburg Times*, March 31, 1951. In late March 1951, Lind presided over an informal meeting between the parties. For over two hours, in a crowded, smoke-filled room, Superintendent Coleman, Regional Director Thomas Allen, and historians Ronald Lee and Herbert Kahler addressed concerns before the battlefield guides.

24. "Dr. Tilberg Is Author of New Book On Park," *Gettysburg Times*, March 24, 1951; "7 Chamber Directors Ask Probe of Local National Park Office; Say Coleman Did Not Cooperate," *Gettysburg Times*, March 13, 1951. Fred Tilberg authored the historical book, simply titled *Gettysburg*. The final five pages of the booklet outlined the fourteen stops of the self-guided tour. The booklet did inform visitors of the availability of the licensed guides.

25. "Coleman Declares Battlefield Guides Requested Civil Service; Denies Chamber of Commerce Directors' Charges," *Gettysburg Times*, March 14, 1951.

26. Superintendent J. Walter Coleman to Regional Director, December 7, 1951, Folder Gettysburg, 504, Leaflets, 1942–1952, Box 42, SF, RG 79, NARA

Philadelphia; "Guides Voice Opposition to Tourist Booth," *Gettysburg Times*,
June 30, 1953; "Complaining Guides Met With Counter Charges At Meeting Of
Retail Merchants Tuesday," *Gettysburg Times*, July 1, 1953.

27. Winnie Langley to Newton Drury, April 4, 1947, Folder 201, Box 2490, CCF,
RG 79, NARA College Park; Unidentified letter to the editor, *Gettysburg Times*,
July 21, 1953, Folder 6, Box 11, (GETT 41113), GNMP Archives.

28. "Dr. Tilberg Is Author of New Book on Park," *Gettysburg Times*, March 24, 1951;
"7 Chamber Directors Ask Probe of Local National Park Office; Say Coleman
Did Not Cooperate," *Gettysburg Times*, March 13, 1951; "Park Ser-
vice Officials Deny Charges That Guides Will Be Placed Under U.S. Civil
Service," *Gettysburg Times*, March 31, 1951; "Complaining Guides Met With
Counter Charges At Meeting Of Retail Merchants Tuesday," *Gettysburg Times*,
July 1, 1953.

29. Frederick Tilberg, "Annual Report on Information and Interpretive Services,
1955," written on January 31, 1956, 1–2; Frederick Tilberg, "Annual Report on
Information and Interpretive Services, 1956," written on February 6, 1957, Folder
Y2623, Box 16, GC, RG 79, NARA Philadelphia, 1–2; "Park Service Officials
Deny Charges That Guides Will Be Placed Under U.S. Civil Service," *Gettysburg
Times*, March 31, 1951.

30. Weeks, *Gettysburg*, 115; "General 'Ike' Goes To Europe Instead of Moving to
His Farm Here; Uncertainty Clouds Plans," *Gettysburg Times*, January 1, 1951.
Eisenhower purchased the property in 1950, but did not immediately move to
Gettysburg because he left for Europe to assume command of NATO. The
Eisenhowers retired to the farm in 1952 and used the occasion to kick off his
presidential bid. For additional reading on Eisenhower's time at Gettysburg,
visit the Eisenhower National Historic Site website at http://www.nps.gov/eise/
historyculture/eisenhower-at-gettysburg.htm.

31. Superintendent J. Walter Coleman to Regional Director, April 20, 1951, Folder
620, Bryan House, 1951, Box 43, SF, RG 79, NARA Philadelphia; Frederick
Tilberg, "Historians' Monthly Report, February 1949," written on March 2, 1949,
Folder 2, Box 7, (GETT 41113), GNMP Archives, 1; Superintendent
J. Walter Coleman, "Superintendent's Monthly Report, June 1950," written on
July 12, 1950, Box 191, CCF, RG 79, NARA College Park, 2; Frederick Tilberg,
"Historians' Monthly Report, February 1950," written on March 6, 1950, 2; Fred-
erick Tilberg, "Historians' Monthly Report, March 1950," written on
April 3, 1950, 2; Frederick Tilberg, "Historians' Monthly Report, January 1953,"
written on February 4, 1953, 2; Frederick Tilberg, "Historians' Monthly Report,
March 1952," written on April 3, 1952, 2, all in Folder 1, Box 7, (GETT 41113),
GNMP Archives.

32. "Master Plan Development Outline, Gettysburg National Military Park,
Land Status," April 1952, Folder 3, Box 12, (GETT 41113), GNMP Archives,
2–3; Frederick Tilberg, "Museum Prospectus, 1956," Folder 10, Box 8, (GETT
41151), GNMP Archives, 1; Frederick Tilberg, "Historians' Monthly Report,

April 1949," written on May 5, 1949, Folder 2, Box 7, (GETT 41113), GNMP Archives, 3.

33. "Master Plan Development Outline, Gettysburg National Military Park, Land Status," April 1952, Folder 3, Box 12, (GETT 41113), GNMP Archives, 2–3; Superintendent J. Coleman, "Superintendent's Monthly Report, September 1952," written on October 13, 1952, Box 191, RG 79, NARA College Park, 3; Jackson Price to Chief Counsel to GNMP, October 5, 1953; Appraisal sheet signed by John Bream; Hillory Tolson to Regional Director, February 1953, all in Folder 9, Box 14, (GETT 41113), GNMP Archives; "Park Buying Tract West of Lee-Meade Inn for $18,000," *Gettysburg Times*, February 19, 1953.

34. Frederick Tilberg, "Historians' Monthly Report, January 1946," written on February 4, 1946, Box 7, (GETT 41113), GNMP Archives, 2–3. Luther Sachs purchased the property from Ada Leister in 1945. See Frederick Tilberg to J. Walter Coleman, "Acquisition of Luther Sachs Property," October 18, 1950, Folder 9, Box 13, (GETT 41113), GNMP Archives; "Congress Gets Bills To Sell 20 Acres Of Park Land As Site For New School Building Here," *Gettysburg Times*, January 27, 1953; Senator Edward Martin to John Basehore, Chairman of the Adams County Republican Committee, September 10, 1952, Folder 3, Box 12, (GETT 41113), GNMP Archives.

35. Senator Edward Martin to John Basehore, Chairman of the Adams County Republican Committee, September 10, 1952, Folder 3, Box 12, (GETT 41113), GNMP Archives; Unrau, *Administrative History*, 265–66; Regional Director to NPS Director, October 10, 1952, Folder 3, Box 12, (GETT 41113), GNMP Archives.

36. Conrad Wirth to Senator Edward Martin, October 1952; Regional Director to NPS Director, October 10, 1952, both in Folder 3, Box 12, (GETT 41113), GNMP Archives; "School Land Bill Passes House Monday," *Gettysburg Times*, July 21, 1953, Folder 6, Box 11, (GETT 41113), GNMP Archives; Superintendent J. Walter Coleman, "Superintendent's Monthly Report, July 1953," written on August 6, 1953, Box 191, CCF, RG 79, NARA College Park, 2; NPS Director to Superintendent J. Walter Coleman, October 1953, Folder 12, Box 13, (GETT 41113), GNMP Archives; Superintendent J. Walter Coleman, "Superintendent's Monthly Report, November 1953," written on December 9, 1953, Box 191, CCF, RG 79, NARA College Park, 2; "Completion Report for the Sach's Property," Folder 5, Box 29, Park Central Files (1954–1987), Records of the National Park Service at Gettysburg National Military Park, (GETT 41160), Gettysburg National Military Park Archives [hereafter cited as (GETT 41160), GNMP Archives]; "Soil and Moisture Control: Removal of Trees and Brush on Sachs Land," November 1957–January 1958, Folder 6, Box 29, (GETT 41160), GNMP Archives. The government's tract appraised at $12,500, and the Sachs property appraised at $10,000.

37. "Congress Gets Bills To Sell 20 Acres Of Park Land As Site For New School Building Here," *Gettysburg Times*, January 27, 1953; Unrau, *Administrative History*, 266.

Chapter 5

1. Rugh, *Are We There Yet?*, 2; Frederick Tilberg, "Museum Prospectus: Gettysburg National Military Park and Cemetery," written on November 27, 1956, Folder 10, Box 8, Historians' Files, 1933–1965, (GETT 41151), Records of the National Park Service at Gettysburg National Military Park, Gettysburg National Military Park Archives, 3 [hereafter cited as (GETT 41151), GNMP Archives]. In all subsequent citations, this report will be noted as "Museum Prospectus, 1956."

2. Jakle, *The Tourist*, 120–21, 125–27; Weeks, *Gettysburg*, 116; Elaine Tyler May, *Homeward Bound: American Families in the Cold War Era* (New York: Basic Books, 1988), 169.

3. Wirth, *Parks, Politics, and the People*, 238.

4. Ethan Carr, *Mission 66: Modernism and the National Park Dilemma* (Amherst: Univ. of Massachusetts Press, 2007), 6–7; Wirth, *Parks, Politics, and the People*, 237–38, 285.

5. Carr, *Mission 66*, 34; Wirth, *Parks, Politics, and the People*, 237.

6. Wolfgang Saxon, "Conrad L. Wirth, 93; Led National Parks Service," *New York Times*, July 28, 1993. Massachusetts Agricultural College is now the University of Massachusetts.

7. Wirth, *Parks, Politics, and the People*, 237–40, 253–85; Carr, *Mission 66*, 8–10, 254–56. Wirth's first day in the office was Monday, December 10, 1951; he replaced Arthur Demaray as NPS Director. "MISSION 66: Gettysburg National Military Park," Box 733, Administrative Files, 1949–1971, RG 79, National Archives Records Administration College Park (hereafter material from the Administrative Files, 1949–1971, will be cited by Folder, Box, AF, RG 79, NARA College Park); Sellars, *Preserving Nature in the National Parks*, 180–83. Of the $1,035,225,000, a total of $412,392,000 was allocated for operation expenses and $622,833,000 for improvements. During this time, the National Park Service also made a concerted effort to improve its image with the American public. Included in this new identity was the agency's adoption, in 1951, of the arrowhead logo, which figured prominently at national park entrances, buildings, publications, and on service employees' uniforms.

8. Wirth, *Parks, Politics, and the People*, 262–270; Sarah Allaback, "MISSION 66 Visitor Centers: The History of a Building Type," (Washington, D.C.: U.S. Department of the Interior, National Park Service, Park Historic Structures & Cultural Landscape Program, 2000), available through NPS online books at www.nps.gov/history/history/online_books/allaback.; Remarks by Conrad Wirth, Dedication of the Visitor Center, Gettysburg National Military Park, November 19, 1962, Folder 5, Box 5, Park Main (Central) Files, 1954–1987, (GETT 41160), Records of the National Park Service at Gettysburg National Military Park, GNMP Archives [all sources from Park Main (Central) Files, 1954–1987, (GETT 41160), will hereafter be cited as (GETT 41160), GNMP Archives]; "MISSION 66: Gettysburg National Military Park," Box 733, AF, RG 79, NARA College Park. Aside from the New Deal programs of the 1930s,

MISSION 66 marked the most important period in the development of the National Park Service. Yet, for all its significance, surprisingly little scholarship has been written about the era. To date, only two works have been produced on MISSION 66 and both focus primarily on its architecture. In an online Department of Interior (DOI) publication, Sarah Allaback examines the history of the program's visitor centers in "MISSION 66 Visitor Centers: The History of a Building Type." Allaback explores the planning, design, and construction of several visitor centers, including Gettysburg's. In *Mission 66: Modernism and the National Park Dilemma*, Ethan Carr also looks at the architecture of these facilities. Unlike Allaback, Carr provides a better contextual understanding of the purpose, process of planning, and significance of MISSION 66. Carr's work is well-researched, offers a plethora of photographs, and consequently stands as the definitive work on the project to date.

9. Sellers, *Preserving Nature in the National Parks*, 185–89, 203–5; Weldon F. Heald, "Urbanization of the National Parks," *National Parks Magazine* 35 (January 1961), 8.

10. "MISSION 66 For Antietam National Battlefield Site and Cemetery," n.d., Box 731, AF, RF 79, NARA College Park, 2; Susan W. Trail, "Remembering Antietam: Commemoration and Preservation of a Civil War Battlefield" (PhD diss., Univ. of Maryland, 2005), 373–75. See Trail's dissertation for a complete discussion of the impact of MISSION 66 at Antietam and subsequent land acquisition.

11. NPS Press Release, "MISSION 66 Program for Chickamauga and Chattanooga Military Park Announced," July 23, 1956, Folder 904, Box 80, AF, RG 79, NARA College Park; "MISSION 66 For Chickamauga and Chattanooga National Military Park," n.d., Box 80, AF, RG 79, NARA College Park, 5–7; "MISSION 66 for Vicksburg National Military Park," n.d., Box 735, AF, RG 79, NARA College Park, 5–7; "MISSION 66 For Antietam National Battlefield Site and Cemetery," n.d., Box 731, AF, RG 79, NARA College Park, 2; Trail, "Remembering Antietam, 373–75; "MISSION 66 For Shiloh National Military Park," n.d., Box 735, AF, RG 79, NARA College Park, 1–10.

12. Wirth, *Parks, Politics, and the People*, 249; Carr, *Mission 66*, 10; "MISSION 66: Gettysburg National Military Park," Box 733, AF, RG 79, NARA College Park, 4. This included $665,050 for building and utilities expenses and $349,700 in roads and trails; Tilberg, "Museum Prospectus, 1956,"(GETT 41151), GNMP Archives, 1–7; Unrau, *Administrative History*, 254; "James Myers Is Promoted to Hatteras," *Gettysburg Times*, n.d., Box 5, Newspaper Clipping (Unbound), 1958–1961, (GETT 43663), Records of the National Park Service at Gettysburg National Military Park, Gettysburg National Military Park Archives [hereafter cited as (GETT 43663), GNMP Archives]. Myers began working with the National Park Service in 1937 as a clerk in the regional office in Richmond, Virginia. In 1948, he transferred to Manassas National Battlefield Park to become its custodian and was eventually named site superintendent. In 1955, he became superintendent of Roosevelt-Vanderbilt National Historic Site in Hyde

Park, New York, a position Myers held until June 1958, when he transferred to Gettysburg.

13. Freeman Tilden, *Interpreting Our Heritage* (Chapel Hill: Univ. of North Carolina Press, 1957), 1–10.

14. "Master Plan For the Preservation and Use of Gettysburg National Military Park, Mission 66 Edition," August 1960, Folder 3, Box 10, (GETT 41160), GNMP Archives, 1–8. No authors are listed, however, given that Frederick Tilberg authored most of Gettysburg's reports, it is not unreasonable to assume that he participated in the development of this plan, as well.

15. Tilberg, "Museum Prospectus, 1956," (GETT 41151), GNMP Archives, 3.

16. "Master Plan For the Preservation and Use of Gettysburg National Military Park, Mission 66 Edition," August 1960, Folder 3, Box 10, (GETT 41160), GNMP Archives, 4; "MISSION 66: Gettysburg National Military Park," Box 733, AF, RG 79, NARA College Park.

17. Newton Drury to Regional Director, January 28, 1946, Folder Gettysburg, 620–46, Box 44, Subject Files, 1937–1957, RG 79, NARA Philadelphia (hereafter cited as Folder, Box, SF, RG 79, NARA Philadelphia); Richard Neutra, *Life and Shape* (New York: Appleton-Century-Crofts, 1962), 303. For additional reading on the life and architecture of Richard Neutra, see Thomas S. Hines, *Richard Neutra and the Search for Modern Architecture* (New York: Oxford Univ. Press, 1982) and Arthur Drexler and Thomas S. Hines, *The Architecture of Richard Neutra: From International Style to California Modern* (New York: Museum of Modern Art, 1982), 1–15. Hines explores Neutra's six-decade career and his buildings that dominated the California landscape. According to Hines, Neutra believed that designing community buildings, schools, stores, theaters, and museums was his most important work. Neutra was well known for the design of residential homes. He also constructed schools and hospitals in Puerto Rico. In the late 1940s, Neutra met Robert Alexander, a recent graduate from Cornell University. Impressed with the young architect's enthusiasm and intellect, Neutra formed a partnership with Alexander that resulted in one of the country's leading architectural firms.

18. Allaback, "MISSION 66 Visitor Centers," chapter 3; Edward Zimmer to Superintendent James Myers, November 17, 1958, Folder 1, Box 5, Series II, Cyclorama Building Records, 1957–1967, (GETT 41097), Records of the National Park Service at Gettysburg National Military Park, Gettysburg National Military Park Archives [hereafter cited by Series and (GETT 41097), GNMP Archives]. Neutra's original design included a nine-story tower located between the rotunda and the office wing. The tower was to be equipped with an elevator to offer visitors a bird's eye view of the battlefield. He also recommended an elaborate rooftop promenade. The Park Service removed both the rooftop promenade and the nine-story viewing tower.

19. Superintendent James Myers, "Accomplishments, 1959," Folder Park Service Area & Regional Accomplishments, Box 11, RG 79, Historic Shrines, Sites,

Monuments, and Parks, Historical Studies Files, 1952–1967, Northeast Regional Office, Philadelphia, Pennsylvania (hereafter cited as Folder, Box, HSF, RG 79, NARA Philadelphia); "Bids For New Cyclorama Top Be Opened on September 29," *Gettysburg Times,* September 2, 1959; Summary Notes, Gettysburg Meeting, February 1–2, 1960, Folder 1, Box 3, Series II, (GETT 41097), GNMP Archives, 6; "Cultural Landscape Report: Defense of Cemetery Hill," (Department of the Interior, National Park Service, June 2004), 180–181; Superintendent James Myers, "Superintendent's Monthly Report, April 1961," written on May 12, 1961, Box 192, AF, RG 79, NARA College Park, 3; Superintendent James Myers, "Superintendent's Monthly Report, June 1960," written on July 13, 1960, Box 192, AF, RG 79, NARA College Park, 1; "Steel Tower at Zeigler's Grove Razed," *Gettysburg Times,* July 25, 1961, Box 4, (GETT 43663), GNMP Archives; Board of Contract Appeals, Department of the Interior, May 29, 1963, Folder 7, Box 3, Series II, (GETT 41097), GNMP Archives; Addendum, 1959, Folder 1, Box 1, Series I, (GETT 41097), GNMP Archives. Though the NPS removed the tower in Ziegler's Grove, four other War Department observation towers remained (Oak Ridge, Culp's Hill, West Confederate Avenue, and Big Round Top). The road bed of Hancock Avenue ran near where the third parking bay of the visitor center was developed. The agency also moved the Hancock Avenue sign from its original location at the intersection of Taneytown Road and Hancock Avenue to the west side of the avenue at Ziegler's Grove, as well as the Gettysburg National Military Park designation marker from its original location near the northern section of Ziegler's Grove to the intersection of the realigned Hancock Avenue and Steinwehr Avenue. The relocated monuments included the 88th Pennsylvania, the 90th Pennsylvania, the 1st Company Massachusetts Sharpshooters, the Battery G, 2nd U.S. Artillery Marker, and the Battery F, 5th U.S. Artillery Marker. Work on the new visitor center was plagued with construction delays and complications. For additional information on the sources for the construction and delay of the building and subsequent deficiencies, see files in Series I and II (GETT 41097), GNMP Archives.

20. "Will Begin Restoration of Painting," *Gettysburg Times,* October 29, 1959, Folder Gettysburg 1957–1961, Box 6, AF, RG 79, NARA Philadelphia; Superintendent James Myers, "Superintendent's Monthly Report, July 1960," written on August 12, 1960, Box 192, AF, RG 79, NARA College Park, 5; Superintendent James Myers to Jeremiah Hoover, September 29, 1960, Folder Gettysburg 1957–1961, Box 6, HSF, RG 79, NARA Philadelphia. A detailed history of Gettysburg Cyclorama, as well as the restoration work performed on the cyclorama painting, is viewable at http://memory.loc.gov/pnp/habshaer/pa/pa3900/pa3988/data/pa3988.pdf. This is a report produced by the Historic America Buildings Survey on the Gettysburg Cyclorama Building, project number HABS-PA-6709; Superintendent James Myers, "Superintendent's Monthly Report, September 1960," written on October 14, 1960, Box 192, AF, RG 79, NARA College Park, 3.

21. Superintendent James Myers to Regional Director, October 11, 1960; Assistant Superintendent Sollenberg to Superintendent James Myers, October 10, 1960;

Frederick Tilberg to Superintendent James Myers on October 10, 1960, Box
13, K1815, General Correspondence, 1952–1966, RG 79, Historic Shrines, Sites,
Monuments, and Parks, Northeast Regional Office, Philadelphia, Pennsylvania
(hereafter cited by Folder, Box, GC, RG 79, NARA Philadelphia); "Two Battlefield Avenues Will Be Removed," *Gettysburg Times*, July 28, 1960, Box 4, (GETT
43663), GNMP Archives; Individual Building Data File, Building Reports, A-V
Files, Folder 1, Box 23, (GETT 41160), GNMP Archives. Hancock Avenue runs
from the southern slope of Little Round Top northward along the spine of the
Union line at Cemetery Ridge. The park did eliminate Chamberlain Avenue,
which ran along Vincent's Spur on Little Round Top toward the 20th Maine
monument.

22. "Coleman Tells Broad Policy on Battlefield," *Gettysburg Times*, April 9, 1941,
Folder 2, Box 35, (GETT 43663), GNMP Archives.

23. Hans Knight, "Commercialism Launches 2nd Battle of Gettysburg," *Gettysburg
Times*, April 5, 1959; Jean White, "The 2nd Battle of Gettysburg," *Gettysburg
Times*, April 8, 1959; Editorial, "Custard's Last Stand?" *Reading* [Pennsylvania]
Eagle, April 12, 1959, Box 4, (GETT 43663), GNMP Archives.

24. Whitfield, *Culture of the Cold War*, 53; Editorial, "How To Mess Up A U.S.
Shrine," *Rochester* [New York] *Democrat Chronicle*, n.d.; Ashley Hasley, Jr., "Let's
Not Surrender Our Battlefields," *Saturday Evening Post*, September 19, 1959, both
in Box 4, (GETT 43663), GNMP Archives.

25. "Now or Never to Buy 'Field, Says Wirth; Ask $2,415,185," *Gettysburg Times*,
March 17, 1959. Kirwan served as a Democratic congressman from Ohio from
1937 to 1970. Interestingly, he supported conservation projects in his home state,
namely a canal from Lake Erie to the Ohio River via rivers in his district of
Youngstown. Wirth requested a total of $5,368,585 for land acquisition to be
distributed across the agency. Of this, Gettysburg would receive slightly over $2
million. When the Department of Interior's budget reached Congress, however,
the House eliminated $1,250,000 of the requested funds.

26. Speech delivered in the House of Representatives by Congressman James
Quigley, April 20, 1959, Folder L1417, Box 1630, AF, RG 79, NARA College
Park (hereafter cited as "Quigley, April 1959," NARA College Park); "Clark To
Ask Hearings on Acquiring Battlefield Land," *Gettysburg Times*, March 24, 1959.
Portions of Quigley's speech were reprinted in this article on March 24, 1959.

27. "Many Protests Registered Against Commercialization of Gettysburg Battlefield," *Gettysburg Times*, October 15, 1959; Jess Gorkin's essay reprinted in "Editor
of Parade Magazine Appeals to U.S. Senators To Preserve Gettysburg Shrine,"
Gettysburg Times, May 18, 1959.

28. "Scharf Tells Committee Importance of Providing Funds To Preserve Shrine,"
Gettysburg Times, May 19, 1959; "Two Senators Favor Saving Battlefield," *Gettys-
burg Times*, May 20, 1959; "Scott Urges More Funds to Save 'Field," *Gettysburg
Times*, May 21, 1959; "Senate Committee Votes $650,000 To Acquire Land For
Gettysburg, Manassas," *Gettysburg Times*, June 6, 1959; Unrau, *Administrative*

History, 267–72; Joan Zenzen, *Battling for Manassas: The Fifty-Year Preservation Struggle at Manassas National Battlefield Park* (University Park: Pennsylvania State Univ. Press, 1998), 60–65. Manassas received appropriation from the 1959 budget of $500,000. Prince William Board of County Supervisors had already enacted zoning laws surrounding the Manassas battlefield.

29. "Form Group To Preserve Battlefield," *Gettysburg Times*, September 14, 1959; "Distinguished Men Helping to Save Field," *Gettysburg Times*, January 11, 1960; "Over $6,000 Received By Group to Save Battlefield," *Gettysburg Times*, December 21, 1959, Box 4, (GETT 43663), GNMP Archives; Superintendent James Myers, "Superintendent's Monthly Report, March 1960," written on April 14, 1960, Box 192, AF, RG 79, NARA College Park, 3. The GBPA opened their headquarters in the Weaver Building at the Lincoln Square.

30. Rugh, *Are We There Yet?*; Superintendent James Myers to Regional Director, July 27, 1959; Superintendent James Myers to Regional Director, July 21, 1959; James Myers to Carroll Voss, July 22, 1959, all in Folder W4618, Box 11, GC, RG 79, NARA Philadelphia. In the July 27 letter, Myers included a time chart of the helicopters' landings and take offs, showing an entry or departure every five to six minutes. Voss used the Henry Wright property as his headquarters, which today is used by the Park Service for law enforcement headquarters.

31. "Fantasyland Opens in July," *Gettysburg Times*, June 16, 1959; "Fantasyland, Wonderland of Make Believe Open on Taneytown Road Saturday or Old and Young," *Gettysburg Times*, July 17, 1959; "Letters: View on Gettysburg," *New York Times*, June 14, 1959, Box 4, (GETT 43663), GNMP Archives.

32. Weeks, *Gettysburg*, 161–63; Rugh, *Are We There Yet?*, 41–67.

33. John Fried, *The Russians Are Coming! The Russians Are Coming! Pageantry and Patriotism in Cold-War America* (New York: Oxford Univ. Press, 1998), 86–117; Stephen Whitfield, *The Culture of the Cold War* (Baltimore: The John Hopkins Univ. Press, 1991), 53; Kammen, *Mystic Chords of Memory*, 626.

34. Superintendent James Myers, "Superintendent's Monthly Report, July 1959," written on August 13, 1959, Folder 192, AF, RG 79, NARA College Park, 2; "Re-enactment of Pickett's Charge July 5 Will Climax Battle Anniversary Events," *Gettysburg Times*, June 25, 1959; "Several Hundred Uniformed Men to Take Part in Re-enactment of Pickett's Charge on Saturday," *Gettysburg Times*, July 3, 1959; "Special Battle Anniversary Ceremonies Today; Pickett's Charge and Service Sunday," *Gettysburg Times*, July 2, 1960, Box 4, (GETT 43663), GNMP Archives; Superintendent James Myers, "Superintendent's Monthly Report, July 1960," written on August 12, 1960, Box 192, RG 79, NARA College Park, 2.

35. "Many Salutes To A. Lincoln Are Broadcast Around The World," *Gettysburg Times*, November 19, 1959; "Carl Sandburg, World Famous Authority on Lincoln, Will Speak at Exercises Here November 19 Closing Lincoln Sesquicentennial Year," *Gettysburg Times*, November 12, 1959, Box 4, (GETT 43663), GNMP Archives. The North-South Skirmish Association was established in 1950 to

commemorate the Civil War and particularly focused their commemorative and educational efforts on firing demonstrations and weapon displays. By the end of the decade, the NSSA had attracted enough interest in Civil War reenacting that they were able to perform a reenactment of Pickett's Charge.

Chapter 6

1. Jon Wiener, "Civil War, Cold War, Civil Rights: The Civil War Centennial in Context, 1960–1965," in *The Memory of the Civil War in American Culture*, edited by Alice Fahs and Joan Waugh (Chapel Hill: Univ. of North Carolina Press, 2004), 237–57.

2. Blight, *Race and Reunion*, 2–4, 361.

3. Blight, *Race and Reunion*, 2, 383–91; Governor William Hodges Mann, July 3, 1913, printed in *Fiftieth Anniversary of the Battle of Gettysburg: Report of the Pennsylvania Commission* (Harrisburg, Pa.: December 31, 1913), 143–46.

4. Wirth, *Parks, Politics, and the People*, 249–62; "MISSION 66: Gettysburg National Military Park," Box 733, Administrative Files, 1949–1971, RG 79, National Archives and Records Administration College Park, Maryland, 1–4 (hereafter cited as Folder, Box, AF, RG 79, NARA College Park). As discussed, this included $665,050 for building and utilities expenses and $349,700 in roads and trails; Superintendent James Myers to Joseph Campbell, Comptroller General, November 28, 1961, Folder 11, Box 4, Series I, (GETT 41097), GNMP Archives; Superintendent James Myers to Regional Director, July 24, 1961, Folder 4, Box 3, Series II, (GETT 41097), Cyclorama Building Records, 1957–1967, Series I and II, (GETT 41097), Records of the National Park Service at Gettysburg National Military Park, Gettysburg National Military Park Archives [hereafter cited by Series (GETT 41097), GNMP Archives]. For additional information on the construction problems with the building, refer to the records in Series I and II of GETT 41097; "Gettysburg Visitor Center Opening Set," *Hanover Evening Sun*, March 11, 1962, Box 5, Newspaper Clipping (Unbound), 1962–1963, (GETT 43663), Records of the National Park Service at Gettysburg National Military Park, Gettysburg National Military Park Archives [hereafter cited as (GETT 43663), GNMP Archives]; Superintendent James Myers to Regional Director, March 20, 1962, Folder 4, Box 7, Park Main (Central) Files, 1954–1987, (GETT 41160), Records of the National Park Service at Gettysburg National Military Park, Gettysburg National Military Park Archives [hereafter cited as (GETT 41160), GNMP Archives]; Superintendent James Myers to Mrs. Dion Neutra, May 25, 1962. Folder 5, Box 3, Series II, (GETT 41097), GNMP Archives; Superintendent James Myers, "Superintendent's Monthly Report, June 1962," written on July 12, 1962, Box 192, AF, RG 79, NARA College Park, 1; Superintendent James Myers, "Superintendent's Monthly Report, July 1962," written on August 15, 1962, Box 192, AF, RG 79, NARA College Park, 1. Though the visitor center's 80,000 people seems small when compared to the nearly 404,800 battlefield visitors for July 1962, this

represented a sizable increase when compared to how few people stopped in the headquarters building.

5. "Gettysburg Visitor Center Opening Set," *Hanover Evening Sun*, March 11, 1962; John Stepp, "A New Look for Gettysburg," *Star Magazine*, February 11, 1962, Box 5, (GETT 43663), GNMP Archives; James Myers, "Auditorium Interim Script," December 21, 1961, Folder K1815, Box 13, General Correspondence, 1952–1966, RG 79, Historic Shrines, Sites, Monuments, and Parks, Northeast Regional Office, Philadelphia, Pennsylvania [hereafter cited by Folder, Box, GC, RG 79, NARA Philadelphia]; Allaback, "MISSION 66 Visitor Centers," available online at www.nps.gov/history/history/online_books /allaback; Superintendent James Myers to Mrs. Dion Neutra, August 22, 1962, Folder 6, Box 3, Series II, (GETT 41097), GNMP Archives; Superintendent James Myers, "Superintendent's Monthly Report, July 1962," written on August 15, 1962, 2–3; Superintendent James Myers, "Superintendent's Monthly Report, January 1963," written on February 14, 1963, Box 192, AF, RG 79, NARA College Park, 4.

6. Superintendent James Myers, "Auditorium Interim Script," December 21, 1961; Harry Pfanz Memorandum, November 3, 1961, Folder K1815, Box 13, GC, RG 79, NARA Philadelphia.

7. Press Release from Bethlehem Steel Company, n.d., received at GNMP on July 28, 1961, Folder 4, Box 3, Series II, (GETT 41097), GNMP Archives; Richard Neutra, *Life and Shape* (New York: Appleton-Century-Crofts, 1962), 303; Superintendent James Myers to Mrs. Dion Neutra, May 25, 1962, Folder 5, Box 3, Series II, (GETT 41097), GNMP Archives; Superintendent James Myers, "Superintendent's Monthly Report, November 1962," written on December 13, 1962, Box 192, AF, RG 79, NARA College Park, 1–2.

8. Superintendent Kittridge Wing, "Superintendent's Monthly Report, May 1964," written on June 15, 1964, Box 192, AF, RG 79, NARA College Park, 2; Individual Building Data File, Building Reports, February 1955–August 1969, Folder 1, Box 23, (GETT 41160), GNMP Archives.

9. John Hope Franklin, "A Century of Civil War Observance," *Journal of Negro History*, 47 (April 1962): 103. For all the planning, activities, and media attention it received beginning in the late 1950s until its conclusion in 1965, the Civil War Centennial has received surprisingly little attention from scholars. Indeed, historian Robert Cook authored the only inclusive book to date on the centennial. He places the centennial celebrations into the larger, more turbulent events of the 1960s. Cook examines the origins of the commemoration, racial undercurrents, and the divisiveness of the memory of the Civil War. He further explores issues of civil rights within the celebrations of the Civil War. For additional reading, see Robert Cook, *Troubled Commemoration: The American Civil War Centennial, 1961–1965* (Baton Rouge: Louisiana State Univ. Press, 2007); Robert Cook "(Un)Furl That Banner: The Response of White Southerners to the Civil War Centennial of 1961–1965," *Journal of Southern History*, 68

(November 2002): 879–912; Robert Cook, "Unfinished Business: African Americans and the Civil War Centennial," in *Legacy of Disunion: The Enduring Significance of the American Civil War,* eds. Susan-Mary Grant and Peter J. Parish (Baton Rouge: Louisiana State Univ. Press, 2003). For additional reading on the display of patriotism within the larger Cold War context, see Fried, *The Russians Are Coming!.*

10. Linenthal, *Sacred Ground,* 97–98; Cook, *Troubled Commemoration,* 19. Catton's trilogy included: *Mr. Lincoln's Army* (1951), *Glory Road* (1952), and *A Stillness at Appomattox,* published in 1953. Capitalizing on Americans' insatiable appetite for anything Civil War, Catton authored another trilogy that included *The Coming Fury* (1961), *Terrible Swift Sword* (1963), and *Never Call Retreat* (1965). Beginning in 1955, other contemporary professional Civil War historians, including Bell Wiley and Allan Nevins, engaged in academic debates in the newly inaugurated journal, *Civil War History.* In 1961, Robert Penn Warren, the renowned American poet, novelist, and historian, wrote *The Legacy of the Civil War: Mediations on the Centennial* (New York: Random House, 1961).

11. Cook, "(Un)Furl That Banner," 882–85; Cook, *Troubled Commemoration,* 31–36, 44–45; Cook, "Unfinished Business," 51. President Eisenhower announced the members from his home in Gettysburg. It is worth noting that the twenty-five member commission was comprised entirely of white men. Most of the members were from northern states. For a complete listing of the twenty-five members, see Cook's *Troubled Commemoration,* 31. "Re-enactment of 8 Civil War Battles Planned for Centennial Celebration," *Gettysburg Times,* March 18, 1959; Franklin, "A Century of Civil War Observance," 97–107. At the same time, the CWCC was planning its first annual meeting to be held in Charleston, South Carolina, in April 1961. In early February, the New Jersey Civil War Centennial Commission expressed concern to the national organization that one of its members, Madeline Williams, an African American, would probably not be well received in the Jim Crow South. As expected, the conference hotel refused to accommodate Williams. Northern state commissions boycotted the national convention and criticized the executive board for its ambivalent stance on racial issues. Eager not to lose southern support for the centennial activities, and unwilling to take a stand against Jim Crow laws, the CWCC transferred its national meeting to a naval base in Charleston. In the wake of the racial crisis in South Carolina, and the controversy that followed, Betts and Grant resigned from the executive board. Two historians, Allan Nevins and James I. Robertson, replaced them. For a more detailed discussion of the Charleston crisis, see Cook, *Troubled Commemoration,* 88–119 and Cook, "(Un)Furl That Banner," 879–912. Aside from being the descendent of the commander who accepted General Robert E. Lee's surrender at Appomattox in April 1865, Grant had proven himself worthy of the family name. Like his grandfather, he was a graduate of the United States Military Academy. He saw extensive combat in Cuba, the Philippine-America War, World War I, and World War II. Commissioners

appointed Karl Betts as executive director. Betts, a Kansas native and World War I veteran, had served as chairman of the Civil War Round Table of the District of Columbia. By May 1961, forty-four states had established Civil War Centennial Commissions. For additional reading on Karl Betts, see Victor Gondos, Jr., "Karl Betts and the Civil War Centennial Commission," *Military Affairs*, 27 (1963): 51–57.

12. Official Program, "A Nation United on the 100th Anniversary of the Battle of Gettysburg, July 1–3,1963," Folder 6, Box 8, (GETT 41160), GNMP Archives, 2; Superintendent James Myers, "Superintendent's Monthly Report, April 1961," written on May 12, 1961, Box 192, AF, RG 79, NARA College Park, 2. The Independent Blues were organized into Company E of the 2nd Pennsylvania Regiment.

13. Superintendent James Myers, "Superintendent's Monthly Report, March 1961," written on April 14, 1961, 2–3; Superintendent James Myers, "Superintendent's Monthly Report, April 1961," written on May 12, 1961, 1; Superintendent Kittridge Wing, "Superintendent's Monthly Report, March, 1963," written on April 17, 1963, 2, all in Box 192, AF, RG 79, NARA College Park, 2; "President And Family Visit 'Field Sunday,'" *Gettysburg Times*, April 1, 1963, Box 5, (GETT 43663), GNMP Archives. The presidential party had made prior arrangements for Jacob Melchior Sheads, Gettysburg High School history teacher and NPS seasonal ranger, to be their tour guide.

14. Zenzen, *Battling for Manassas*, 65–71; McCandlish Phillips, "Two Sides Leave Field At Bull Run," *New York Times*, July 24, 1961, 8; "Manassas Gun Boom Again As Colorful Show Begins," *Gettysburg Times*, July 21, 1961; "Civil War Battle Reenacted," *Gettysburg Times*, July 25, 1961, Box 4, (GETT 43663), GNMP Archives; McCandlish Phillips, "Confederates Carry Day Again at Bull Run," *New York Times*, July 23, 1961, 1.

15. Zenzen, *Battling For Manassas*, 69–71; McCandlish Phillips, "Two Sides Leave Field at Bull Run," *New York Times*, July 24, 1961, 8; "A Strange Spectacle at Bull Run," *Gettysburg Times*, July 25, 1961, Box 4, (GETT 43663), GNMP Archives. The total cost of the Manassas reenactment was $170,000.

16. Zenzen, *Battling For Manassas*, 71; Trail, "Remembering Antietam," 400–18; "Antietam Marked By Reenactment," *New York Times*, September 16, 1962, 86. Trail attributes the low turnout to the poor weather and suggests that the logistical complications of parking deterred visitors from attending.

17. "Successor to James Myers Is Announced," *Gettysburg Times*, April 2, 1963, Box 5, (GETT 43663), GNMP Archives; Superintendent Kittridge Wing, "Superintendent's Monthly Report, March 1963," written on April 17, 1963, Box 192, AF, RG 79, NARA College Park, 1–2. Wing officially entered on duty on the 11th.

18. "Vice President Pleads For End Of Hate Among Men in May 30 Address," *Gettysburg Times*, May 31, 1963, Box 5, (GETT 43663), GNMP Archives; Remarks

of Vice President Lyndon B. Johnson, May 30, 1963, Statements File, Box 80, Lyndon Baines Johnson Presidential Library, available online at http://www.lbjlib.utexas.edu/johnson/archives.hom/speeches.hom/630530.asp.

19. "Eisenhower Tells Audience Of 6,000 That Lincoln Gave True Meaning Of Battle Here," *Gettysburg Times*, July 1, 1963, Box 5, (GETT 43663), GNMP Archives; Edith Evans Asbury, "Eisenhower Cites Perils to Liberty: Risks as Great as in 1863, He Asserts at Gettysburg 'A Certain Uneasiness'," *New York Times*, July 1, 1963, 17. President John F. Kennedy had been invited to deliver a speech at the battle's centennial, but a previously arranged trip abroad prevented him from attending.

20. Weeks, *Gettysburg*, 138–39; "An Account of the Centennial Commemoration, Report of the Commission to the General Assembly," edited by Louis M. Simon (Harrisburg: Commonwealth of Pennsylvania, 1964), GNMP Vertical Files, 11–63, GNMP Library. This publication includes all of the speeches offered during the centennial ceremonies, as well as several pictures of the celebrations; Official Program, "A Nation United on the 100th Anniversary of the Battle of Gettysburg, July 1–3, 1963," Folder 6, Box 8, (GETT 41160), GNMP Archives; "Place Wreaths at N.Y. Monuments," *Gettysburg Times*, July 2, 1963, Box 5 (GETT 43663), GNMP Archives; Superintendent James Myers, "Superintendent's Monthly Report, March 1960," written on April 14, 1960, Box 192, AF, RG 79, NARA College Park, 2–3; "Loyal Legion Plans 12-Acre Gift to Park," *Gettysburg Times*, October 27, 1960, Folder K3827, Box 24, GC, RG 79, NARA Philadelphia; Superintendent James Myers, "Superintendent's Monthly Report, September 1961," written on October 13, 1961, Box 192, AF, RG 79, NARA College Park, 4; "Will Present Land to U.S.," *Gettysburg Times*, May 16, 1962, Box 4, (GETT 43663), GNMP Archives; Harry Pfanz to Superintendent Kittridge Wing, April 22, 1963, Folder 1, Box 8, (GETT 41160), GNMP Archives. The Military Order of the Loyal Legion of the United States (MOLLUS) and the Gettysburg Battlefield Preservation Association (GBPA) purchased endangered tracts, which they then donated to the federal government. Between 1960 and 1961, MOLLUS purchased two key properties along the first day's fields, near Reynolds and Buford Avenues, and members formally presented the tracts to the federal government during the centennial celebrations. Meanwhile, in the spring of 1962, the GBPA donated fifty-five acres of the historic Wolf farm, located near Devil's Den.

21. Official Program, "A Nation United on the 100th Anniversary of the Battle of Gettysburg, July 1–3, 1963," Folder 6, Box 8, (GETT 41160), GNMP Archives; "Rebel Yells and Dixie Bells Are Part of Spectacle at Gettysburg," *Chattanooga Daily Times*, July 3, 1963, Box 5, (GETT 43663), GNMP Archives; Edith Evans Asbury, "Gettysburg Fete Depicts 2 Armies: Parade Recalls Events in Battle 100 Years Ago Confusion Like That in Battle Many Units Depicted," *New York Times*, July 3, 1963, 28.

22. The Virginia monument was the first to be erected on June 8, 1917. North Carolina's monument was dedicated on July 3, 1929, and Alabama's on November 12, 1933.

23. Superintendent James Myers, "Superintendent's Monthly Report, September 1961," written on October 13, 1961, Box 192, AF, RG 79, NARA College Park, 2; Official Program, "A Nation United on the 100th Anniversary of the Battle of Gettysburg, July 1–3, 1963," Folder 6, Box 8, (GETT 41160), GNMP Archives; Trail, "Remembering Antietam," 396; Speech by Ronald F. Lee, September 21, 1961; speech by James Myers, September 21, 1961, both in GNMP Vertical Files, GNMP Library.

24. Speech by Ronald F. Lee, September 21, 1961; speech by James Myers, September 21, 1961, both in GNMP Vertical Files, GNMP Library.

25. Speech by James Myers, September 21, 1961; speech by Ernest Vandiver, September 21, 1961, both in GNMP Vertical Files, GNMP Library; Kammen, *Mystic Chords of Memory*, 626.

26. Speech by Ernest Vandiver, September 21, 1961, GNMP Vertical Files, GNMP Library.

27. Speech by Samuel Gibbons, July 3, 1963, GNMP Vertical Files, GNMP Library.

28. Speech by Samuel Gibbons, July 3, 1963, GNMP Vertical Files, GNMP Library.

29. Edith Evans Asbury, "Hughes Charges Moral Failure To Aid Negroes Since Civil War," *New York Times*, July 2, 1963, 14; Unrau, *Administrative History*, 263. For additional reading on George Wallace, see Dan T. Carter, *Politics of Rage: George Wallace, the Origins of the New Conservatism, and the Transformation of American Politics* (Baton Rouge: Louisiana State Univ. Press, 2000); Dan T. Carter, *From George Wallace to Newt Gingrich: Race and the Conservative Counter-revolution, 1963–1994* (Baton Rouge: Louisiana State Univ. Press, 1996); Stephan Lesher, *George Wallace: American Populist* (New York: Da Capo Press, 1995).

30. "Negroes' Liberty Held 'Unfinished'": Notre Dame's Head Urges Action in Gettysburg Talk," *New York Times*, June 30, 1963, 39; Edith Evans Asbury, "Hughes Charges Moral Failure To Aid Negroes Since Civil War," *New York Times*, July 2, 1963, 14. Hesburgh was born in New York in 1917, graduated from Notre Dame, and earned his doctorate degree from Catholic University in Washington, D.C., in 1945. Upon graduation, Hesburgh served as a faculty member at Notre Dame before being appointed president in 1952. Hughes spoke at Gettysburg as a recently elected governor, having served in the state's supreme court before entering the gubernatorial race. He also served as a charter member to the U.S. Commission on Civil Rights. For additional reading on Richard Hughes, see John Wefing, *The Life and Times of Richard H. Hughes* (New Brunswick, N.J.: Rutgers Univ. Press, 2009).

31. Martin Luther King, Jr., "I Have A Dream Speech," August 28, 1963, accessed online at www.archives.gov/press/exhibits/dream-speech.pdf.

32. Official Program, "A Nation United on the 100th Anniversary of the Battle of Gettysburg, July 1–3, 1963," Folder 6, Box 8, (GETT 41160), GNMP Archives,

5; "Nation Eyes Gettysburg As Centennial Re-creation Of Battle Draws Near," *Gettysburg Times*, June 26, 1963, Box 5, (GETT 43663), GNMP Archives; Edith Evans Asbury, "Battle of Gettysburg Relived at Centennial: Pickett's Charge Is Re-enacted, Then Amity Prevails," *New York Times*, July 4, 1963, 1.

33. Don Robertson, "Vulgar Show at Gettysburg," *The Plain Dealer*, July 14, 1963, Box 5, (GETT 43663), GNMP Archives.

34. Weeks, *Gettysburg*, 137–40. Cliff Arquette was a popular television and radio personality. In 1948, Arquette developed a comic character named "Charley Weaver." In the mid-1950s, he purchased Gettysburg's Orphan Home, near the Soldiers' National Cemetery on Baltimore Pike, and opened his museum on March 2, 1959. Several years later, Arquette renamed the museum Charley Weaver's American Museum of the Civil War.

35. Superintendent James Myers to Louis Simon, February 6, 1963, Folder 1, Box 8, (GETT 41160), GNMP Archives; Harry Pfanz to Superintendent Kittridge Wing, "Report on Campfire Programs, Gettysburg," July 22, 1963, Folder K1815, Box 13, GC, RG 79, NARA Philadelphia, 1; Superintendent James Myers, "Report On Proposed Campfire Program," n.d., Folder 3, Box 7, (GETT 41160), GNMP Archives; "Gettysburg Centennial Campfire Program," January 17–18, 1963, Box 675, AF, RG 79, NARA College Park, 1.

36. Harry Pfanz to Superintendent Kittridge Wing, "Report on Campfire Programs, Gettysburg," July 22, 1963, Folder K1815, Box 13, GC, NARA Philadelphia, 1–4. The four-page scripted narration is attached to Pfanz's report. "Gettysburg Centennial Campfire Program," January 17–18, 1963, Box 675, AF, RG 79, NARA College Park, 1–5; Individual Building Data File, Building Reports, Park Amphitheater, Folder 1, Box 23, (GETT 41160), GNMP Archives; Superintendent Kittridge Wing, "Superintendent's Monthly Report, July 1963," written on August 14, 1963, Box 192, AF, RG 79, NARA College Park, 4; "2,000 Initiate Amphitheater Here For NPS," *Gettysburg Times*, July 2, 1963, Box 5, (GETT 43663), GNMP Archives. The superintendent estimated that approximately 1,000 people attended each program on July 1–3, nearly 400 people on July 4, and approximately 200 people each night for the remainder of the month.

37. "Remarks by the Honorable Dean Rusk, Secretary of State, Commemorating the One Hundredth Anniversary of President Lincoln's Gettysburg Address," GNMP Vertical Files, GNMP Library.

38. Superintendent Kittridge Wing, "Superintendent's Monthly Report, July 1963," written on August 14, 1963, Box 192, AF, RG 79, NARA College Park, 1; Official Program of the 100th Anniversary of Lincoln's Gettysburg Address, November 17–19, 1963; "Address Delivered by H.E.M. Herve Alphand, French Ambassador to the United States, on the Occasion of the Centennial Anniversary of the Gettysburg Address"; and "Remarks by the Honorable Dean Rusk, Secretary of State, Commemorating the One Hundredth Anniversary of President Lincoln's Gettysburg Address," all in GNMP Vertical Files, GNMP Library.

39. Superintendent Kittridge Wing, "Superintendent's Monthly Report, July 1963," written on August 14, 1963, Box 192, AF, RG 79, NARA College Park, 1; Superintendent Kittridge Wing, "Superintendent's Monthly Report, December 1963," written on January 14, 1964, Box 192, AF, RG 79, NARA College Park, 1; "An Account of the Centennial Commemoration, Report of the Commission to the General Assembly," ed. Simon. GNMP Vertical Files 11-63, GNMP Library. Wing recorded a total of 2,041,378 visitors, not including December's total.

40. Superintendent Jack Anderson, "Superintendent's Monthly Report, July 1963," written on August 5, 1963, Box 307, AF, RG 79, NARA College Park, 1–3; "Generals' Grandsons Meet," *New York Times*, July 4, 1863, 7; Acting Superintendent John Fisher, "Superintendent's Monthly Report, September 1963," written on October 7, 1963, Box 150, RG 79, NARA College Park, 1–3. By this time, Grant had been removed as the chairman of the CWCC.

41. Trail, "Remembering Antietam," 410; Superintendent Kittridge Wing, "Superintendent's Monthly Report, November 1964," written on December 14, 1964, 1; Superintendent Kittridge Wing, "Superintendent's Monthly Report, March 1964," written on April 11, 1964, 2; Superintendent Kittridge Wing, "Superintendent's Monthly Report, July 1964," written on August 14, 1964, 2, all in Box 192, AF, RG 79, NARA College Park; "Issue New Park Folder," *Gettysburg Times*, August 28, 1964, Box 6, (GETT 43663), GNMP Archives; Superintendent Kittridge Wing, "Superintendent's Monthly Report, April 1965," written on May 14, 1965, 2; Superintendent Kittridge Wing, "Superintendent's Monthly Report, November 1965," written on December 15, 1965, 3, all in Box 192, AF, RG 79, NARA College Park; "Battlefield is Presented in 100-Year-Ago Appearance by Tree, Brush Removal Work," *Gettysburg Times*, February 12, 1964, Box 6, (GETT 43663), GNMP Archives. The NPS purchased the one-acre tract from the Evergreen Cemetery. The tract was adjacent to the Taneytown Road. On April 14, 1965, the GBPA deeded the one-hundred acre Meals farm to the federal government and officially presented it to the National Park Service on November 19, 1965. The brochure included four battle maps (one for the campaign and one for each of the three days of battle) and the text of the Gettysburg Address. The Park Service distributed this brochure at the new visitor center, the guide stations along Route 15 and 30, and the information/guide booth in the Soldiers' National Cemetery. Much of Gettysburg's interpretive programming had been developed and conceptualized by park historian, Frederick Tilberg, who, after twenty-eight years of service at Gettysburg National Military Park, retired November 30, 1965. Harry Pfanz remained as the park's senior historian.

42. Franklin, "A Century of Civil War Observance," 107; "Negroes' Liberty Held 'Unfinished'": Notre Dame's Head Urges Action in Gettysburg Talk," *New York Times*, June 30, 1963, 39; David Blight, *American Oracle: The Civil War in the Civil Rights Era* (Cambridge, Mass.: Harvard Univ. Press, 2011), 3.

Chapter 7

1. Sellars, *Preserving Nature in the National Parks*, 204–8; George B. Hartzog Jr., Biographical Vignettes, available at http://www.nps.gov/history/history/online_books/sontag/hartzog.htm. Other urban recreational areas added to the NPS during this era included Cuyahoga Valley, Cleveland; Chattahoochee River, near Atlanta; and Santa Monica Mountains, Los Angeles.

2. Kammen, *Mystic Chords of Memory*, 533, 537–39, 626.

3. Linenthal, *Sacred Ground*, 10; Superintendent Kittridge Wing, "Superintendent's Monthly Report, December 1963," written on January 14, 1964, 1; Superintendent Kittridge Wing, "Superintendent's Monthly Report, November 1964," written on December 14, 1964, Box 192, Administrative Files, 1949–1971, RG 79, National Archives and Records Administration, College Park, Maryland, 1 (hereafter cited as Folder, Box, AF, RG 79, NARA College Park). The 1963 visitation was 2,041,378. "Master Plan, 1969," rev. ed., July 1969, Folder 3, Box 1, Gettysburg National Military Park, General Management Plan Records, 1968–1983, (GETT 41105), Records of the National Park Service at Gettysburg National Military Park, Gettysburg National Military Park Archives, 81 [hereafter cited as (GETT 41105), GNMP Archives]; "Coleman Tells Broad Policy on the Battlefield," *Gettysburg Times*, April 9, 1941, Folder 2, Box 35, Newspaper Clipping (Unbound), (GETT 43663), Records of the National Park Service at Gettysburg National Military Park, Gettysburg National Military Park Archives [hereafter cited as (GETT 43663), GNMP Archives].

4. Lamme, *America's Historic Landscapes*, 182; Unrau, *Administrative History*, 254–55, 291; Harry W. Pfanz, "Master Plan for the Preservation and Use of Gettysburg National Military Park," February 1962, Folder 3, Box 10, Park Main (Central) Files, 1954–1987, (GETT 41160), Records of the National Park Service at Gettysburg National Military Park, Gettysburg National Military Park Archives, 9 [hereafter cited as (GETT 41160), GNMP Archives]; Harry W. Pfanz, "Master Plan of Gettysburg National Military Park," February 18, 1965, Folder 2, Box 11, (GETT 41160), GNMP Archives, 1–37; "Master Plan, 1969," Folder 3, Box 1, (GETT 41105), GNMP Archives, 81. [All notes hereafter will be cited by "Master Plan" and the corresponding year.] Kittridge Wing served as superintendent until January 16, 1966, when George F. Emery replaced him. Emery's previous management experience included appointments as superintendent at Andrew Johnson National Historic Site and Petersburg National Battlefield. In November 1970, the Park Service transferred Emery to the Washington office and appointed Jerry Schober as superintendent. Schober had previously served as superintendent of Abraham Lincoln Birthplace National Historic Site. John Earnst replaced Schober after serving as park superintendent for four years. Arriving at Gettysburg, Earnst had nearly a decade of upper-management experience, serving as superintendent at Perry's Victory & International Peace Memorial National Monument (Ohio) and Badlands National Monument (South Dakota). Previously Earnst served as Chief of Operations Evaluation in the Pacific Northwest

Regional Office in Seattle. In addition to managing the Civil War battlefield, in 1967 Congress created Eisenhower National Historic Site, which was placed directly under Gettysburg's management authority. The government permitted Mamie Eisenhower to continue to live in the house until her death; the site opened in 1980.

5. Sellars, *Preserving Nature in the National Parks*, 204–5; "Master Plan, 1969," n.d., Folder 3, Box 1, (GETT 41105), GNMP Archives, 3.

6. "Master Plan, 1966," n.d., Folder 2, Box 11, (GETT 41160), GNMP Archives, 6–18.

7. "Master Plan, 1962"; "Master Plan, 1969," Folder 3, Box 1, (GETT 41105), GNMP Archives, 53–54; Big Round Top Loop Trail Brochure, 1977, Folder 12, Box 20, (GETT 43970), GNMP Archives; Harrison, et al., "A Master Plan Report, 1972," March 1972, Folder 1, Box 2, (GETT 41105), GNMP Archives, 84; Superintendent Jerry Schober, "Superintendent's Annual Report, 1973," written on January 25, 1974, Folder 2, Box 1, (GETT 41160), GNMP Archives, 8, 11; "Master Plan, 1965," Folder 2, Box 11, (GETT 41160), GNMP Archives, 1–37.

8. Sellars, *Preserving Nature in the National Parks*, 210.

9. "Master Plan, 1969," n.d., Folder 3, Box 1, (GETT 41105), GNMP Archives, 53–54; Superintendent Jerry Schober, "Superintendent's Annual Report, 1972," written on January 22, 1973, Folder 2, Box 1, (GETT 41160), GNMP Archives, 3; Thomas Harrison to Dr. Jacob Wentzel, Superintendent Waynesboro School District, December 5, 1972, Folder 2, Box 24, Interpretive Program Files, 1930–present, Records of the National Park Service at Gettysburg National Military Park, (GETT 43970), Gettysburg National Military Park Archives [hereafter cited as (GETT 43970), GNMP Archives]. In the 1972 annual, Schober reported that fifteen of the seventy-five schools contacted to use the ESA expressed interest in future use.

10. Weeks, *Gettysburg*, 126.

11. Eric Foner, *Who Owns History: Rethinking the Past in a Changing World* (New York: Hill and Wang, 2002), 11; Kevin M. Levin, *Remembering the Battle of the Crater: War as Murder* (Lexington: Univ. Press of Kentucky, 2012), 125–26. In 1974, for example, the Park Service erected a marker at Battery Nine to indicate its capture by the USCT. That summer, the Park Service employed two black students in the living-history program. As Levin recounts, the discussion of the role of the USCT units at Petersburg had largely been absent from the predominant narrative.

12. "Gettysburg: Summer Programs, 1974," (Eastern National in Cooperation with Gettysburg National Military Park), Folder 7, Box 21, (GETT 43970), GNMP Archives; "Critique 1973 Summer Seasonal Programs: Gettysburg National Military Park," Folder 7, Box 19, (GETT 43970), 4. The 1974 Summer Program brochure notes the Peace Memorial talk was presented only on Saturday and Sunday and at three times in the afternoon (2:00, 3:00, and 4:00 p.m.).

13. Sellars, *Preserving Nature in the National Parks,* 209–10; Thomas Harrison to Superintendent George Emery, September 17, 1969, Folder 10, Box 37, (GETT 41160), GNMP Archives; Superintendent Jerry Schober, "Superintendent's Annual Report, 1972," written on January 22, 1973, Folder 2, Box 1, (GETT 41160), GNMP Archives, 2–3; "Gettysburg: Summer Programs, 1974," (Eastern National in Cooperation with Gettysburg National Military Park), Folder 7, Box 21, (GETT 43970), GNMP Archives; Thomas Harrison, "Operational Programs, 1969 Summer Season," November 18, 1969, Folder 1, Box 21, (GETT 43970), GNMP Archives; "Critique 1973 Summer Seasonal Programs, Gettysburg National Military Park," Folder 7, Box 19, (GETT 43970), GNMP Archives, 1–11. After visitors saw the cyclorama program, they were escorted with a park ranger outside to the overlook where the ranger pointed out significant landmarks associated with Pickett's Charge.

14. Superintendent Jerry Schober, "Superintendent's Annual Report, 1972," written on January 22, 1973, Folder 2, Box 1, (GETT 41160), GNMP Archives, 2–3; "Gettysburg: Summer Programs, 1974," (Eastern National in Cooperation with Gettysburg National Military Park), Folder 7, Box 21, (GETT 43970), GNMP Archives; Thomas Harrison to Superintendent George Emery, September 17, 1969, Folder 10, Box 37, (GETT 41160), GNMP Archives; Superintendent Jerry Schober, "Superintendent's Annual Report, 1973," written on January 25, 1974, 3, 8–9; Superintendent John Earnst, "Superintendent's Annual Report, 1976," written on March 9, 1977, Folder 2, Box 1, (GETT 41160), GNMP Archives, 2. Eastern National, the park's non-profit partner, gave the park a $5,141 donation for the farming tools.

15. "Critique 1973 Summer Seasonal Programs, Gettysburg National Military Park," Folder 7, Box 19, (GETT 43970), GNMP Archives, 1–3.

16. "Earth Day, A History of the Movement, " available online at http://www. earthday.org/earth-day-history-movement.

17. Sellars, *Preserving Nature in the National Parks,* 209–10; Thomas J. Harrison to Superintendent George Emery, November 18, 1969, Box 21, (GETT 43970), GNMP Archives; Thomas Harrison, "Experiment in Awareness: Amphitheater Report for July 21 through August 30, 1969," Box 20, K18, (GETT 43970), GNMP Archives, 1–11. In years past, the campfire's film ("Gettysburg") was the main attraction. During the environmental programs, however, the film was shown in the cyclorama center. Environmental films included, "A Matter of Time," "For All To Enjoy," "Living Heritage," and "This Land." The park rangers also led an open question and answer session and talked informally with the attendees about various conservation issues in their home towns. Park staff, as well as the public, expressed some resistance to environmental conservation programs. Harrison reported some "apathy and downright hostility" among the staff, which may have stifled the enthusiasm of potential visitors.

18. Superintendent John Earnst, "Superintendent's Annual Report, 1972," Folder 2, Box 1, (GETT 41160), GNMP Archives, 12.

19. "Master Plan, 1966," Folder 2, Box 11, (GETT 41160), GNMP Archives, 9; "Information Relating to Alternate Tour Center Sites," n.d., Folder 3, Box 49, (GETT 41160), GNMP Archives; "Master Plan, 1969," Folder 3, Box 1, (GETT 41105), GNMP Archives, 44–57, 82. The proposal to close the battlefield to automobile traffic was first discussed in 1969.

20. "Master Plan, 1969," Folder 3, Box 1, (GETT 41105), GNMP Archives, 41–43; Superintendent George Emery to Chairman, Master Plan Team, Gettysburg NMP, November 7, 1969, Folder 2, Box 1, (GETT 41105), GNMP Archives; "Completion of Route 30 Bypass Urged Immediately at NPS Session This Morning," *Gettysburg Times*, July 29, 1971; George Hartzog to Shane Creamer, November 11, 1971, Folder 5, Box 1, (GETT 41105), GNMP Archives; "Master Plan, 1966," Folder 2, Box 11 (GETT 41160), GNMP Archives, 6–18; Ronald Lee to Chief EODC, July 1965, Folder 2, Box 11, (GETT 41160), GNMP Archives; "History of Planning at Gettysburg," n.d., Folder 6, Box 4, (GETT 41105), GNMP Archives; Meeting minutes on Route 30 Bypass, May 5, 1972, Folder 7, Box 1, (GETT 41105), GNMP Archives; "A Master Plan Report, 1972," Folder 1, Box 2, (GETT 41105), GNMP Archives, 42–47; Thomas J. Harrison, Memorandum For the Master Plan Files, March 1, 1974, Folder 11, Box 2, (GETT 41105), GNMP Archives; Superintendent Jerry Schober, "Superintendent's Annual Report, 1974," written on January 25, 1973, Folder 2, Box 1, (GETT 41160), GNMP Archives, 7; "Local Groups Have Until January 30 To Comment On Park Service Master Plan," *Gettysburg Times*, December 11, 1974; Richard Schweiker, Senator, to John Volpe, Secretary of Transportation, February 24, 1972, Folder 6, Box 1, (GETT 41105), GNMP Archives; "Gettysburg, Preliminary Environmental Impact Statement, 1972," Box 4, Thomas J. Harrison Files, Records of the National Park Service at Gettysburg National Military Park, Gettysburg National Military Park Archives (hereafter cited as TH Files, GNMP Archives); "Information Relating to Alternate Tour Center Sites," n.d., Folder 3, Box 49, (GETT 41105), GNMP Archives; "A New Tour Center For the Gettysburg National Park," n.d., Folder 3, Box 3, (GETT 41105), GNMP Archives; Superintendent Jerry Schober to Northeast Regional Director, May 24, 1973, Folder 5, Box 2, (GETT 41105), GNMP Archives. A component of the proposed visitor center included a revised, chronological tour route. The 1972 Master Plan, for example, outlined a twelve-stop tour beginning at the information center, then proceeding to the Eternal Light Peace Memorial, the Railroad Cut, the Virginia Memorial, the Wheatfield, Devil's Den, Little Round Top, the Pennsylvania Memorial, and Culp's Hill. After visiting Culp's Hill, visitors would be directed to the cyclorama center to see the Gettysburg Cyclorama, before proceeding to the Soldiers' National Cemetery. The tour would then direct visitors downtown before returning them to the information center.

21. "GNMP Museum Collection Background," n.d., Box 71, W32, Park Main (Central) Files, 1987–present, Records of the National Park Service at Gettysburg National Military Park, Gettysburg National Military Park Archives

[Files from this collection have not yet been processed and all notes hereafter will be cited by Box, File Code, (Unprocessed Central Files, 1987–present), GNMP Archives]; Thomas J. Harrison to Superintendent Jerry Schober, January 5, 1971, Folder 9, Box 1, (GETT 41105), GNMP Archives. A clarification on terminology: after the NPS acquired the Gettysburg National Museum building it was referred to as the park's visitor center, while the Neutra building situated in Ziegler's Grove would be called the cyclorama center. Just ten years after the opening of the Park Service's visitor center in Ziegler's Grove, the acquisition of the Rosensteel museum brought new operational challenges. In addition to maintaining the daily operations of the cyclorama center, park staff was also responsible for the operations of the Rosensteel building, including the Electric Map, sales and museum operations, as well as providing basic visitor information. Lacking adequate ranger staff to operate both buildings, the Park Service entered into a concession contract with Eastern National Park and Monument Association to operate the Electric Map, the bookstore, as well as daily maintenance and cleaning of the building.

22. Alan E. Kent, Senior Interpretive Planner, Denver Service Center, to Superintendent John Earnst, April 3, 1972, Folder 9, Box 1, (GETT 41105), GNMP Archives.

23. Thomas Harrison, "Operational Programs, 1969 Summer Season," November 18, 1969, Folder 1, Box 21, (GETT 43970), GNMP Archives; Alan E. Kent, Senior Interpretive Planner, Denver Service Center, to Superintendent John Earnst, April 3, 1972, Folder 9, Box 1, (GETT 41105), GNMP Archives.

24. Paul Armstead to Gary Everhardt, January 30, 1975. Folder 5, Box 11, (GETT 41160), GNMP Archives; "Earnst Says Master Plan To Be Flexible To Fit Needs," *Gettysburg Times*, January 17, 1975; James Reaver to Superintendent John Earnst, January 29, 1975; Ruth Detwiler to Superintendent John Earnst, February 1975, both in Folder 5, Box 11, (GETT 41160), GNMP Archives. This survey reports that 7 percent of those surveyed favored the proposed Cobean farm site.

25. "County Alleges Farm Sale To NPS Would Cause Area 'Environmental Damage,'" *Gettysburg Times*, December 27, 1974; "U.S. Buys Tract in Gettysburg," *Philadelphia Inquirer*, February 1, 1975. Albert Butterfield, a retired professor at Gettysburg College, purchased the land in 1949 for $13,000; *Biesecker v. Morton*, Civil Action No. 74–1244, Filed December 24, 1972, Folder 7, Box 7 (GETT 41105), GNMP Archives; "Local Groups Have Until January 30 To Comment On Park Service Master Plan," *Gettysburg Times*, December 11, 1974; "Earnst Says Master Plan To Be Flexible To Fit Needs," *Gettysburg Times*, January 17, 1975. Harry Biesecker, Robert Klunk, and Kenneth Guise filed the claim individually and as commissioners of Adams County. The defendants were listed as Secretary of the Interior Rogers Morton; Ronald Walker, Director of the NPS; Chester Brooks, Northeast Regional Director; and Gettysburg Superintendent John Earnst. The commissioners asserted that the Park Service's acquisition of the site and subsequent development of a visitor center would violate the

National Environmental Policy Act of 1969. Construction would generate excessive dirt, noise, and air pollution that would cause irreparable damage to the environment.

26. Weeks, *Gettysburg*, 8.

27. Thomas Ottenstein, from Bethesda, Maryland, was a successful and wealthy businessman. He established the National Gettysburg Battlefield Tower, Inc., in 1969 and became president of the organization. Ottenstein had received a bachelor's degree from Syracuse University and a law degree from Georgetown University Law School. He also served as a Special Agent in the Counterintelligence Corps of the U.S. Army between 1954 and 1956. Prior to founding NGBT, Ottenstein had served as Director of State National Bank in Bethesda from 1961–1970. For a complete resume on Thomas Ottenstein see, Thomas Ottenstein resume in "Tower For One Nation," Box 1, Gettysburg National Tower, Gettysburg National Military Park Library (hereafter cited as GNT, GNMP Library); "Gettysburg: Local Planning Adjacent to a Federal Park," n.d., Folder 1, Box 1, (GETT 41105), GNMP Archives; "History of Planning at Gettysburg," n.d., Folder 6, Box 4, (GETT 41105), GNMP Archives; Ben A. Franklin, "Tower Plan Stirs Battle at Gettysburg," *New York Times*, December 20, 1970, 64.

28. "Gettysburg: Local Planning Adjacent to a Federal Park," n.d., Folder 1, Box 1, (GETT 41105), GNMP Archives; "History of Planning at Gettysburg," n.d., Folder 6, Box 4, (GETT 41105), GNMP Archives; Ben A. Franklin, "Tower Plan Stirs Battle at Gettysburg," *New York Times*, 20 December 1970, 64. In addition to the regular newspaper coverage on the events surrounding the Gettysburg Tower, several other pieces have been written on the history of the tower. For additional reading on the National Tower, see John Oyler, "Pickett Charges; Everyone Else Pays: The Story of the Gettysburg Tower Controversy" (Senior Thesis, Princeton Univ., April 17, 1972); Charles R. Roe, "The Second Battle of Gettysburg: Conflict of Public and Private Interests in Land Use Policies," *Environmental Affairs* 2 (Spring 1972): 16–64; Dorn C. McGrath, Jr., "A Proposed Observation Tower Overlooking The Gettysburg National Military Park, Review of the Proposed Undertakings and Evaluation of Its Probable Effects, A Report to the Advisory Council on Historic Preservation," April 1972; Secretary of Interior Rogers Morton to Pennsylvania Governor Milton Shapp, June 14, 1971, both in Folder 8, Box 1, (GETT 41105), GNMP Archives; Secretary of Interior Rogers Morton to Pennsylvania Governor Milton Shapp, June 14, 1971, Folder 6, Box 52, (GETT 41160), GNMP Archives. Oyler's Thesis is the most comprehensive on the early history of the tower, but since it was written in the spring of 1972, it does not cover the later years of the tower's history, including its opening.

29. Frank Masland, "Letter to the Editor, " *New York Times*, February 20, 1971; Ben A. Franklin, "Tower Plan Stirs Battle at Gettysburg," *New York Times*, December 20, 1970, 64; Ben A. Franklin, "Disputed Gettysburg Tower Going Up," *New York Times*, May 16, 1971, 38; Charles Roe, "Second Battle of Gettysburg: Conflict of Public and Private Interests in Land Use Policies," (master's thesis,

Indiana Univ., 1971); Bill Richards, "Tower Power: Battlefield Vista Facility
Rises Despite Pa. Officials' Opposition," *Washington Post*, October 28, 1973.

30. "Give Option On Colt Park Tower Site," *Gettysburg Times*, November 18, 1970.
Ottenstein initially purchased land (for $42,900) for the tower in Colt Park,
a residential area bordering Steinwehr Avenue. This property was located
immediately behind the Home Sweet Home Hotel, at the intersection of Johns
Avenue and Long Lane. On May 8, 1971, residents of Colt Park filed a class-ac-
tion suit to prevent the construction of the tower within their community. On
July 20, 1970, Nelson J. Groft, Building Official, issued Ottenstein a permit
(No. G-378) to begin construction on the tower. A copy of the permit can be
found in "Tower For One Nation," Box 1, GNT, GNMP Library; Director
George B. Hartzog, Jr., to Secretary of the Interior, May 17, 1971, Folder 6, Box
52, (GETT 41160), GNMP Archives; Frank E. Masland, Jr., to Henry Scharf,
September 14, 1970, Folder 1, Box 54, (GETT 41160), GNMP Archives; Log
of events on the tower's construction, Box 1, GNT, GNMP Library. In June
1971, Park Service officials from Washington, D.C., along with Gettysburg's
staff, explored potential sites which would be agreeable to all parties. The
Department of Interior sent J. C. Herbert Bryant, Jr., a twenty-nine-year-old
special assistant, to negotiate an agreement between Ottenstein and the Park
Service. Officials who participated in this June 18, 1971, site inspection included
William Everhart of the Washington Office; Richard Giamberdine of the
Northeast Region; Superintendent Schober; and park historian Tom Harrison.
Richard Giamberdine to Northeast Regional Director, June 23, 1971, Folder 5,
Box 1, (GETT 41105), GNMP Archives; "Court Upholds Proposal for Tower
at Gettysburg," *New York Times*, October 27, 1971, 28; "Work Begins On New
Site Of Ottenstein Tower Today," *Gettysburg Times*, July 12, 1971; "Say Gov.
Shapp Will Come Here Monday To File Court Action To Stop 'Field Tower,'"
Gettysburg Times, July 17, 1971; Agreement between the National Park Service
and National Gettysburg Battlefield Tower, Inc., July 2, 1971, Folder 2, Box 51,
(GETT 41160), GNMP Archives. One year after the tower opened, on June 30,
1975, Ottenstein and the National Park Service revised the original 1971 land
exchange agreement. This revision specified that the 5 percent taxable income
would be donated to the National Park Foundation, a nonprofit preservation
organization chartered by Congress in 1967 to raise money for the national
park system. The agreement stipulated that the donation would be earmarked
for land acquisition or improvements at Gettysburg National Military Park.
John Maitland, president of Apple County Lodge, owned the desired property,
but leased it to Hans Enggren and George and Elizabeth Moose, who operated
the Stonehenge Hotel and Restaurant on the tract. Oyler, "Pickett Charges;
Everyone Else Pays," 140–46; Bill Richards, "Tower Power: Battlefield Vista
Facility Rises Despite Pa. Officials' Opposition," *Washington Post*, October 28,
1973; "Commissioners Pleased Over Tower Switch," *Gettysburg Times*, July 13,
1971; Superintendent Jerry Schober to Regional Director, December 14, 1971,
Folder 2, Box 53, (GETT 41160), GNMP Archives. In an interview with the

Washington Post, Director Hartzog said that, while he had discussed the terms of the agreement with Bryant, the special assistant had negotiated the right-of-way exchange without his approval. Pennsylvania governor Milton Shapp continued the fight with suits in both Adams County court and the Pennsylvania State Supreme Court. On October 3, 1973, the state supreme court ruled to allow construction of the tower to continue. On July 13, eleven days after the agreement was signed, Schober told the *Gettysburg Times* that he did not know of the agreement until a week after the national office signed it. In a letter to the regional director, Schober blasted the breakdown in communication and informed the regional director that he only found out about the agreement from a July 11 news release, which he had to request from the Washington office. Schober did not obtain a copy of the agreement until a month after the signing, when he received one from a local county commissioner. Nearly six weeks after the agreement was signed, the national office finally provided Schober with a copy.

31. National Gettysburg Battlefield Tower Brochure, n.d., Folder 4, Box 45, (GETT 41160), GNMP Archives; "Gettysburg Tower Opens 'For The People' and Profit," *New York Times,* July 28, 1974, 28; "Ottenstein Dedicates His Tower To 'Our Nation and Free Enterprise,'" *Gettysburg Times,* August 19, 1974; "Tourists High on Gettysburg Tower," *Philadelphia Inquirer,* August 4, 1971; Benjamin Zerbey to Acting Regional Director, James Gowen; William Doherty to Ronald Walker, NPS Director, November 23, 1973, both in Folder 3, Box 53, (GETT 41160), GNMP Archives; "Bryant Denies Allegations In New Tower Court Action," *Gettysburg Times,* December 21, 1973; Bill Richards, "Tower Power: Battlefield Vista Facility Rises Despite Pa. Officials' Opposition," *Washington Post,* October 28, 1973.

32. Kent Frizzell, Solicitor, to Carla Hills, Assistant Attorney General, July 1974; William Everhart, NPS Director, to Honorable William Ford, House of Representatives, July 1974, both in Folder 2, Box 54, (GETT 41160), GNMP Archives; "U.S. Buys Fantasyland For $1,382,650; Mother Goose Will Move Within 10 Years," *Gettysburg Times,* April 8, 1974; Chester Brooks, Regional Director, to Honorable Herman Schneebeli, September 1974, Folder 2, Box 49, (GETT 41160), GNMP Archives; "H. Biesecker Praises NPS For Tax Plan," *Gettysburg Times,* April 10, 1974; "Offer To Sell Real Property" agreement between Gettysburg National Military Park and the Peace Light Inn, September 26, 1975, Folder 3, Box 49, (GETT 41160), GNMP Archives. The Park Service purchased the 22.15 acres for $630,000.

33. Superintendent Jerry Schober, "Superintendent's Annual Report, 1972," written on January 22, 1973, Folder 2, Box 1, (GETT 41160), GNMP Archives, 4; "Master Plan, 1972," Folder 1, Box 3, (GETT 41105), GNMP Archives; Superintendent Jerry Schober, "Superintendent's Annual Report, 1973," written on January 25, 1974, Folder 2, Box 1, (GETT 41160), GNMP Archives, 5; Superintendent John Earnst, Request For Grant from the National Park Foundation, December

14, 1976, Folder 5, Box 11, (GETT 41160), GNMP Archives; Kenneth E. Foote, *Shadowed Ground: America's Landscapes of Violence and Tragedy* (Austin: Univ. of Texas Press, 1997), 9. Foote notes that one component of sanctification is the clear delineation of the site from its surrounding environment.

34. Unrau, *Administrative History,* 312–13; Superintendent John Earnst, "Superintendent's Annual Report, 1976," March 9, 1977, Folder 2, Box 1, (GETT 41160), GNMP Archives, 19; *General Management Plan,* Gettysburg National Military Park and National Cemetery, (Prepared by Mid-Atlantic Regional Office, December 1982), 13–16 (hereafter cited by *GMP,* 1982); *Land Protection Plan,* October 1993, (Gettysburg: Gettysburg National Military Park, 1993), 1–92. Since the 1880s, the War Department and subsequently the National Park Service based their practice of land acquisition on the Sickles Map and the 1895 enabling legislation, which provided for 15,360 acres. The GBHD includes the acreage of Gettysburg National Military Park, as well as battle action land outside of the park boundary and the surrounding townships of Cumberland, Straban, Mount Joy, and Mount Pleasant. The National Register of Historic Places was authorized under the National Historic Preservation Act of 1966 and is officially administered by the National Park Service. This register lists cultural and historic resources, including buildings, sites significant to American history, that are worthy of preserving. To date, over 80,000 properties are listed on the register. For more information on the National Register of Historic Places, see www.nps.gov/history/nr or www.nationalregisterof historicplaces.com.

35. Zenzen, *Battling for Manassas,* 86–98.

36. "The Hucksters Close in on Gettysburg's Grandeur," *Detroit Free Press,* May 12, 1974.

Chapter 8

1. The final decades of the twentieth century underscored the developing nature of the battlefield and Americans' relationship to the historic landscape. Park management continued to struggle with the seemingly irreconcilable tensions between preservation and visitor accessibility. Decisions made by the superintendents, in this instance John Earnst and Daniel Kuehn, called attention to the considerable autonomy one individual had in administering the battlefield. Lacking uniform directives and guidelines, superintendents held considerable authority over the protection and management of the battlefield. For decades Gettysburg had served as a landscape of patriotic expression and hosted thousands of visitors on civic pilgrimages. By the late 1970s, this patriotic desire had diminished. A new generation of visitors engaged Gettysburg in a different manner. "While the World War II generation wrapped family bonding experiences in a cloak of patriotism," Jim Weeks argues, "postwar sons and daughters generally sought a personal experience with the original event

shorn of associations to national purpose or cross-generational bonding." Civic disengagement from Gettysburg, however, in no way lessened interest in the battle. In subsequent years, change in park leadership further defined the Park Service's role in creating a unique visitor experience. In the final decades of the twentieth century, Gettysburg once again became a battleground for interpretive and symbolic control over the battle and its landscape. Rugh, *Are We There Yet?*, 41–67; Weeks, *Gettysburg*, 173–74, 195; *General Management Plan for Gettysburg National Military Park and Gettysburg National Cemetery* (Mid-Atlantic Regional Office, National Park Service, United States Department of the Interior, approved on December 1, 1982), 37. All citations hereafter will be noted as *GMP, 1982*. Weeks classifies the "Heritage Gettysburg" phase emerging around 1970.

2. Chester Brooks to Park Superintendents, January 30, 1976, Folder 3, Box 6, A8215, Park Main (Central) Files, 1954–1987, (GETT 41160), Records of the National Park Service at Gettysburg National Military Park, Gettysburg National Military Park Archives [hereafter cited as (GETT 41160), GNMP Archives]; Superintendent John Earnst, "Superintendent's Annual Report, 1976," written on March 9, 1977, Folder 2, Box 1, (GETT 41160), GNMP Archives, 2. The Mid-Atlantic Region's allocation of $563,000 was the largest sum received by any region with the National Park Service. The "What You Can Do: A Bicentennial Idea Book" included suggestions on how to develop cookbooks, art displays, anti-pollution campaigns, or folk culture displays.

3. Kammen, *Mystic Chords of Memory*, 626; Superintendent John Earnst, "Superintendent's Annual Report, 1976," written on March 9, 1977, 2–3; Superintendent John Earnst, "Superintendent's Annual Report, 1975," written on February 11, 1976, Folder 2, Box 1, (GETT 41160), GNMP Archives, 2; Barry Mackintosh, "Interpretation in the National Park Service: A Historical Perspective," History Division, National Park Service, Department of Interior, Washington, D.C., 1986, available online at http://www.nps.gov/history/history/online_books/mackintosh3/index.htm. These plays were produced by the National Park Service's Harper's Ferry Center. This center had been established in 1970 to design various interpretive media, exhibits, and pamphlets for the National Park Service. The center also provides conservation and restoration assistance. For more information on Harper's Ferry Center see http://www.nps.gov/hfc; Gettysburg Administrative Officer to John Shreve, President of Footlight Ranch, February 27, 1976, Folder 3, Box 6, A8215, (GETT 41160), GNMP Archives; Superintendent John Earnst to Regional Director, September 24, 1976, Folder 3, Box 6, A8215, (GETT 41160), GNMP Archives; *GMP, 1982*, 37.

4. J. P. Cessna to Superintendent John Earnst, July 13, 1977, Folder 2, Box 12 (GETT 41160), GNMP Archives; Traci A. Lower, "Farewell After 14," *Gettysburg Times*, August 27, 1988. After earning a Bachelor of Science degree in Education and Biology, Earnst began his career with the National Park Service in 1966 as superintendent at Perry's Victory and International Peace Memorial in Ohio. Between 1967 and 1970, Earnst worked at Badlands National Monument

in South Dakota, before he was transferred to the Pacific Northwest Regional Office in Seattle, where he worked until his appointment as Gettysburg's superintendent. For detailed reading on the series of management plans, see *Draft General Management Plan, Gettysburg National Military Park and National Cemetery,* May 1977, Box 3, Thomas J. Harrison Files, Records of the National Park Service at Gettysburg National Military Park, Gettysburg National Military Park Archives, D-5-D-7 [hereafter cited as *Draft GMP,* 1977; notes from this collection will be cited as TH Files, GNMP Archives]; *GMP,* 1982; *Draft Development Concept Plan/ Environment Assessment, Little Round Top/Devil's Den, Gettysburg National Military Park, Pennsylvania* (United States Department of the Interior: National Park Service, May 1985), 1–72 (all notes hereafter cited as *Draft DCP*); *Draft Development Concept Plan/Environmental Assessment Supplement, Little Round Top/Devil's Den, Gettysburg National Military Park, Pennsylvania* (United States Department of Interior: National Park Service, May 1986), 1–18 (hereafter cited as *Draft DCP, Supplement*); *Development Concept Plan: Little Round Top, Devil's Den, Gettysburg National Military Park, Pennsylvania,* (United States Department of the Interior, National Park Service, 1986), approved by Regional Director James Coleman, Jr., on November 25, 1986 (hereafter cited as *DCP,* 1986).

5. Sandra Hauptman to Regional Director, April 3, 1979, Folder 3, Box 5, Gettysburg National Military Park, General Management Plan Records, 1968–1983, (GETT 41105), Records of the National Park Service at Gettysburg National Military Park, Gettysburg National Military Park Archives [hereafter cited as (GETT 41105), GNMP Archives]. Hauptman served as the Outdoor Recreation Planner, Division of Planning. James Cole to Superintendent John Earnst, July 29, 1977, Folder 7, Box 4, (GETT 41105), GNMP Archives; Louise Hartzell to Superintendent John Earnst, July 28, 1977, Folder 10, Box 4 (GETT 41105), GNMP Archives; Richard Michael, Sr., to Superintendent John Earnst, August 3, 1977; W. G Weaver to Superintendent John Earnst, July 29, 1977, both in Folder 9, Box 4 (GETT 41105), GNMP Archives; J. P. Cessna to Superintendent John Earnst, July 13, 1977, Folder 2, Box 12 (GETT 41160), GNMP Archives.

6. Quoted in *Historic Roads in the National Park System,* National Park Service online publication, available at http://www.cr.nps.gov/history/online_books/roads/ shst.htm; "Coleman Tells Broad Policy on Battlefield," *Gettysburg Times,* April 9, 1941, Folder 2, Box 35, Newspaper Clippings (Unbound), 1940–1945, (GETT 43663), Records of the National Park Service at Gettysburg National Military Park, Gettysburg National Military Park Archives [hereafter cited as (GETT 43663), GNMP Archives].

7. Superintendent Kittridge Wing, "Superintendent's Monthly Report, November 1964," written on December 14, 1964, Box 192, AF, RG 79, NARA College Park, 1; *GMP,* 1982, 37; Superintendent J. Walter Coleman to Regional Director, October 16, 1942, Folder 9, Box 7, Historians' Files, 1933–1965, Records of the National Park Service at Gettysburg National Military Park, (GETT 41151), GNMP Archives [hereafter cited as (GETT 41151), GNMP Archives]; Superintendent

John Earnst, "Letter to the Editor," *Gettysburg Times*, June 3, 1977, Folder 2, Box 12, (GETT 41160), GNMP Archives.

8. *GMP*, 1982, 77, 130–31; Superintendent John Earnst, "Letter to the Editor," *Gettysburg Times*, June 3, 1977, Folder 2, Box 12 (GETT 41160), GNMP Archives.

9. Harry W. Pfanz, "Master Plan of Gettysburg National Military Park," February 2, 1965, 12; "Master Plan, 1966," n.d., Folder 2, Box 11, (GETT 41160), GNMP Archives, 9; "Master Plan, 1969," rev. ed., July 1969, Folder 3, Box 1, (GETT 41105), GNMP Archives, 44–52; "Information Relating to Alternate Tour Center Sites," n.d., Folder 3, Box 49, (GETT 41160), GNMP Archives.

10. *Draft GMP*, 1977, Box 3, TH, GNMP Archives, D5–D28; Superintendent John Earnst, "Letter to the Editor," *Gettysburg Times*, June 3, 1977, Folder 2, Box 12 (GETT 41160), GNMP Archives. The Park Service first proposed the Devil's Den bypass in the 1977 *Draft General Management Plan* and, though it caused immediate debate, the agency retained this in the 1982 *GMP*.

11. *Draft GMP*, 1977, Box 3, TH, GNMP Archives, D6–D12. For additional information on the various proposals for the Devil's Den bypass, see the agency's three reports: *Draft DCP*; *Draft DCP, Supplement*; and *DCP, 1986*.

12. *GMP*, 1982, 67–68. Crawford Avenue services visitors traveling from the Wheatfield Road into Devil's Den. Park officials also listed vegetation management as an objective. If vehicle traffic was eliminated from the area, the park proposed introducing livestock as a cost effective method to manage vegetation.

13. J. P. Cessna to Superintendent John Earnst, July 13, 1977, Folder 2, Box 12 (GETT 41160), GNMP Archives; "Devil's Den Group Plans to Present Goodling Petitions," *Gettysburg Times*, August 19, 1988; "Devil's Den Petition To Be Presented Sept. 12," *Gettysburg Times*, September 8, 1988; "Goodling To Receive Devil's Den Petitions," *Gettysburg Times*, September 9, 1988; "Park Service Stands By Its Plans For Battlefield Change," *Gettysburg Times*, September 12, 1988; "Message to Washington: No Dollars for Devil's Den," *Gettysburg Times*, September 13, 1988; "Devil's Den Access Committee Is Optimistic After Meeting in D.C.," *Gettysburg Times*, September 17, 1988; "Mott Plans to Visit Military Park," *York Dispatch*, September 22, 1988; "Mott Supporting Road Elimination," *York Dispatch*, October 25, 1988.

14. William Marvel to Regional Director James Coleman, November 23, 1985; James McLean, Jr., to Regional Director James Coleman, July 12, 1985, both in Folder 5, Box 13 (GETT 41160), GNMP Archives; "Petition From Gettysburg Civil War Round Table," July 18, 1985; "Petition From Baltimore Civil War Round Table," July 31, 1985, both in Folder 6, Box 13 (GETT 41160), GNMP Archives; Kathy Georg to Superintendent John Earnst, September 3, 1982, Folder 1, Box 13 (GETT 41160), GNMP Archives; Kathy Georg to Regional Director James Coleman, July 19, 1985, Folder "Development Concept Plan, 1985–1989," Box 6, TH files, GNMP; Senior Historian Kathy Harrison, interview by author, December 11, 2009, GNMP. Janet Licate, president of the

CWRT, challenged Earnst to advertise the park's *GMP* to the nation, arguing that many Americans were unaware of the park's management changes.

15. "Farewell After 14," *Gettysburg Times*, August 27, 1988; "Earnst Transferring to North Cascade Park," *Evening Sun* (Hanover), August 30, 1988; "Gettysburg National Military Park," *Record Harold* (Waynesboro), October 4, 1988; Bobbie Platt "Superintendent Daniel Kuehn Looks Forward to New Job at Historic Park," *Gettysburg Times*, November 3, 1988; "Mott Supporting Road Elimination," *York Dispatch*, October 25, 1988; David Perlis, "Devil's Den Road Will Stay Open," *Evening Sun* (Hanover), February 9, 1989; Martin Sipkoff, "Devil's Den Plan Ok'd," *York Dispatch*, February 9, 1989, Box 27, (GETT 43663), GNMP Archives; David Perlist, "New Park Chief Keeps Open Mind on Devil's Den," *Gettysburg Times*, November 26, 1988. Kuehn received his bachelor's degree in history from the University of Minnesota. Prior to his appointment, Kuehn had served as superintendent at Santa Monica Mountains National Recreation Area near Los Angeles. He had also worked at Salem Maritime National Historic Site, Manassas National Battlefield Park, Chickamauga & Chattanooga National Military Park, Sitka National Historical Park, and Mount McKinley National Park. The new plan for Devil's Den retained the chronological tour route and used South Confederate Avenue as access to Little Round Top. After visiting the Federal left flank, visitors would travel west along the Wheatfield Road to visit the Wheatfield and the Peach Orchard. Visitors interested at stopping at Devil's Den could do so by accessing Sickles and Warren Avenue.

16. J. P. Cessna to Superintendent John Earnst, July 13, 1977, Folder 2, Box 12 (GETT 41160), GNMP Archives.

17. Superintendent James McConaghie, "Superintendent's Annual Report, 1934–1935," Box 2, Park Main (Central) Files, 1933–1954, (GETT 41113), Records of the National Park Service at Gettysburg National Military Park, Gettysburg National Military Park Archives, unnumbered page 40 [hereafter cited as (GETT 41113), GNMP Archives]; "Natural Resources Management Plan," October 29, 1981, Folder 6, Box 5 (GETT 41105), GNMP Archives, 1.

18. "Natural Resources Management Plan," October 29, 1981, Folder 6, Box 5 (GETT 41105), GNMP Archives, 10–13.

19. "Natural Resources Management Plan," October 29, 1981, Folder 6, Box 5 (GETT 41105), GNMP Archives, 13–14.

20. Memo, NPS Director to all superintendents, October 25, 1979, Folder 2, Box 24, (GETT 43970), GNMP Archives; Big Round Top Trail Brochure, 1977, Folder 12, Box 20 (GETT 43970), GNMP Archives.

21. "Interpretive Media Inventory," n.d., Folder 8, Box 24, (GETT 43970), GNMP Archives. These ten stations included: "Council of War" at General Meade's Headquarters; "Third Corps, Second Day" at Little Round Top; "Reminiscence of Alabama Soldier," at Devil's Den; "Barksdales Brigade" at the Mississippi Memorial; "Third Day" at the Virginia Memorial; "Retreat of Pickett's Division" at the Point of Woods; "11th Corps, First Day" at Oak Ridge; "Welcome to the

Park" at Oak Hill; "First Day" at Oak Hill; and "Spangler's Spring," Culp's Hill at Spangler's Spring. In 1984, the park opened two audio stations in the visitor center, the "Council of War" and "Civil War Music." Granite Farm House Brochure, Folder 6, Box 20 (GETT 43970), GNMP Archives.

22. University of Idaho, Park Studies Unit, available online at http://www.psu.uidaho.edu/vsp.htm.

23. "Visitor Services Project: Gettysburg National Military Park," Cooperative Park Studies Unit, University of Idaho, 1986, Folder 3, Box 18, (GETT 43970), GNMP Archives, iii–18. Nearly half of the park's visitors toured during the summer season. The authors also estimated that approximately 44 percent of the visitors stayed more than one day. The visitor surveys were distributed between July 22 and July 26 at eleven different battlefield sites. Questionnaires were administered to 1,093 visitors, and 454 returned the survey.

24. "Visitor Services Project: Gettysburg National Military Park," Cooperative Park Studies Unit, University of Idaho, 1986, Folder 3, Box 18, (GETT 43970), GNMP Archives, iii–18.

25. "Visitor Services Project: Gettysburg National Military Park," Cooperative Park Studies Unit, University of Idaho, 1986, Folder 3, Box 18, (GETT 43970), GNMP Archives, iii–18; James Coates, "Visitors Prefer to Set Sights on Amenities," *Chicago Tribune*, April 21, 1991.

26. Dick Sage, "125th: Tourist Barrage Expected for Gettysburg Battle Anniversary," *The Patriot* (Harrisburg), February 19, 1988; David Perlis, "Record Crowd Relieve 3-Day Battle," *Evening Sun* (Hanover), June 27, 1988, Box 24, (GETT 43663), GNMP Archives; "Commemorative Battle Re-enactment Announced For 125th Anniversary," *Gettysburg Times*, January 4, 1988; "Coordinating Commission For '88 Battle Anniversary Meets," *Gettysburg Times*, January 6, 1988.

27. "Anniversary Events," *Gettysburg Times*, June 24, 1988; Jerry Price, "Events Mark Anniversary On First Day," *Evening Sun* (Hanover), July 2, 1988, Box 25, (GETT 43663), GNMP Archives.

28. "Coordinating Commission For '88 Battle Anniversary Meets," *Gettysburg Times*, January 6, 1988; "Lincoln Coming To Gettysburg!" *Gettysburg Times*, November 19, 1988; Martin Sipkoff, "Gettysburg Celebration Today," *York Dispatch*, November 19, 1988; Traci A. Lower, "Gettysburg Address Events Draw 15,000," *Gettysburg Times*, November 21, 1988.

Chapter 9

1. For additional reading on this issue, see James Davison Hunter, *Culture Wars: The Struggle to Define America* (New York: Basic Books, 1991).

2. Lynne Cheney, "The End of History," *Wall Street Journal*, October 20, 1994; Richard H. Kohn, "History at Risk: The Case of the *Enola Gay*," in *History Wars: The Enola Gay and Other Battles for the American Past*, eds. Edward T.

Linenthal and Tom Engelhardt (New York: Henry Holt, 1996), 140–70; Kammen, *Mystic Chords of Memory*, 626.

3. Zenzen, *Battling for Manassas*, 166–83.

4. Linenthal, *Sacred Ground*, 97–98; Robert Brent Toplin, *Ken Burns's The Civil War: Historians Respond* (New York: Oxford Univ. Press, 1996), xv.

5. Matthew McAvoy, "Gettysburg National Military Park and Eisenhower National Historic Site: Economic Impact on Gettysburg and Adams County, 1994," prepared and distributed by Gettysburg-Adams County Area Chamber of Commerce, 27.

6. Martin Sipkoff, "Park Chief Quits Post Out Of Anger," *York Sunday News*, September 17, 1989; Bobbie Platt, "Frustrated Park Superintendent Decides To Retire," *Gettysburg Times*, September 6, 1989; "Slaughter Pen Cleared As Farewell Gift To Park Superintendent," *Gettysburg Times*, November 1, 1989; Bill Neil, "Park Superintendent Retires: Daniel Kuehn Bids Farewell," *Gettysburg Times*, November 4, 1989; Management Team Meeting Minutes, October 31, 1989, and Management Team Meeting Minutes, February 27, 1990, both in Folder Copies of Meeting Minutes, 6/27/89–12/20/89, Box 8, A40, Park Main (Central) Files, 1987–present, Records of the National Park Service at Gettysburg National Military Park, Gettysburg National Military Park Archives [Files from this collection have not yet been processed and all notes hereafter will be cited by Box, File Code, (Unprocessed Central Files, 1987–present), GNMP Archives]; Bobbie Platt, "New Park Superintendent Arrives," *Gettysburg Times*, March 30, 1990; "New Park Service Superintendent Ready," *Gettysburg Times*, March 13, 1990; Martin Sipkoff, "Military Park Gets New Chief," *York Sunday News*, February 11, 1990. Officially Gettysburg NMP also had two interim superintendents between Kuehn's departure and Cisneros's arrival: Frank Deckert, whose regular position was superintendent of Petersburg National Battlefield, and Robert Davidson, who served as Gettysburg's assistant superintendent. Cisneros received his Bachelor of Science degree from Texas A&I in Kingville. He worked at the Office of Personnel Management (OPM) between 1970 and 1973 and then at the Southwest Regional office as a personnel officer (stationed in Santa Fe, New Mexico) from 1973 to 1978. In 1978, Cisneros assumed his first superintendent duties at the newly established San Antonio Missions National Park, where he served until 1988, when he transferred to Bandelier National Historic Monument.

7. Superintendent James McConaghie, "Superintendent's Annual Report, 1936–1937," Box 2, Park Main (Central) Files, 1933–1954, (GETT 41113), Records of the National Park Service at Gettysburg National Military Park, Gettysburg National Military Park Archives, 46 [hereafter cited as (GETT 41113), GNMP Archives].

8. J. P. Cessna to Superintendent John Earnst, July 13, 1977, Folder 2, Box 12, Park Main (Central) Files, 1954–1987, (GETT 41160), Records of the National Park Service at Gettysburg National Military Park, Gettysburg National Military

Park Archives [hereafter cited as (GETT 41160), GNMP Archives]; *General Management Plan,* Gettysburg National Military Park and National Cemetery, (Prepared by Mid-Atlantic Regional Office, National Park Service, United States Department of the Interior, December 1982), 53–60, approved on December 1, 1982 (hereafter cited as *GMP,* 1982); Superintendent Jose Cisneros, "Superintendent's Annual Report, 1993," written on March 11, 1994, Box 3, A26, (Unprocessed Central Files, 1987–present), GNMP Archives, 6.

9. "Statement For Management: Outline of Planning Requirements, May 1991," Gettysburg National Military Park, approved by Regional Director James W. Coleman, Jr., on July 3, 1991, Folder 32, Box 24, D18, (Unprocessed Central Files, 1987–present), GNMP Archives (hereafter cited as "Statement For Management, 1991"); Superintendent Jose Cisneros to Division Chiefs, April 13, 1992, Folder 26, Box 24, D18, (Unprocessed Central Files, 1987–present), GNMP Archives; Director Roger Kennedy to Congressman James A. Traficant, Jr., November 23, 1994, Folder 30, Box 44, H30, (Unprocessed Central Files, 1987–present), GNMP Archives; Regional Director B. J. Griffin to R. Michael Kaar, December 21, 1993, Folder 28, Box 24, D18, (Unprocessed Central Files, 1987–present), GNMP Archives. An example of ornamental fencing is the iron fence around the Copse of Trees at the High Water Mark.

10. Regional Director B. J. Griffin to R. Michael Kaar, December 21, 1993, Folder 28, Box 24, D18, (Unprocessed Central Files, 1987–present), GNMP Archives; Superintendent Jose Cisneros to Stephen Killian, January 22, 1991; Acting Superintendent Frank Deckert to Terry Fox, January 29, 1990, both in Folder 27, Box 24, D18, (Unprocessed Central Files, 1987–Present), GNMP Archives.

11. R. Michael Kaar to Regional Director B.J. Griffin, December 9, 1993, Folder 28, Box 24, D18, (Unprocessed Central Files, 1987–Present), GNMP Archives; Congressman James A. Traficant, Jr., to Director Roger Kennedy, November 4, 1994, Folder 30, Box 44, H30, (Unprocessed Central Files, 1987–present), GNMP Archives; Congressman Tim Holden to Superintendent Jose Cisneros, October 12, 1993, Folder 29, Box 44, H30, (Unprocessed Central Files, 1987–present), GNMP Archives.

12. Deborah Fitts, "Gettysburg Battlefield Is Being Taken Back To 1890s," *Civil War News,* May 1990; Lamme, *America's Historic Landscapes,* 182.

13. Acting Superintendent Frank Deckert to Terry Fox, January 29, 1990, Folder 27, Box 24, D18, (Unprocessed Central Files, 1987–present), GNMP Archives; "Statement For Management, 1991," Folder 32, Box 24, D18, (Unprocessed Central Files, 1987–present), GNMP Archives, 65; Regional Director B. J. Griffin to R. Michael Kaar, December 21, 1993, Folder 28, Box 24, D18, (Unprocessed Central Files, 1987–present), GNMP Archives; John Andrews and D. Scott Hartwig, "Cultural Landscape Management and Interpretation: A Dilemma," *Ranger: The Journal of the Association of National Park Rangers,* 10 (Spring 1994): 14–16.

14. Fitts, "Gettysburg Battlefield Is Being Taken Back To 1890s," *Civil War News,* May 1990.

15. *Boundary Study, Gettysburg National Military Park: Draft Report To Congress, Environmental Assessment,* August 1988 (hereafter cited as *Boundary Study, Draft*); Martin Sipkoff, "Historian Answers Call to Arms in Latest Battle Over Battlefield," *Gettysburg Times,* June 2, 1986; Traci A. Lower, "Park Service Accepts Taney Farm," *Gettysburg Times,* September 16, 1988; Jeffrey B. Roth, "Boundary Study Draft Report For Battlefield Now Complete," *Gettysburg Times,* September 7, 1988, Box 26, Newspaper Clipping (Unbound), (GETT 43663), Records of the National Park Service at Gettysburg National Military Park, Gettysburg National Military Park Archives [hereafter cited as (GETT 43663), GNMP Archives]; "Battle Grows as Politicians Trade Votes," *Hanover Evening Sun,* June 2, 1986; Gerald Jordan, "Expansion at Gettysburg is Rejected by House vote," *Philadelphia Inquirer,* June 17, 1986; Shelley Jones, "'Second Battle of Gettysburg' Over: 31-Acre Taney Farm to enter Park," *Gettysburg Times,* July 17, 1986, Box 22, (GETT 43663), GNMP Archives; Congressman William Goodling Testimony, House Committee on Government Operations, *Land Exchange Between National Park Service/Gettysburg National Park and Gettysburg College,* 103rd Cong., 2d sess., May 9, 1994, 7–8; "Boundary Study: Gettysburg National Military Park" Newsletter, (Gettysburg: National Park Service, 1987), July 1987, No.1; and "Boundary Study: Gettysburg National Military Park" Newsletter, (Gettysburg: National Park Service, 1987), March 1988, No. 2, both in Folder 1987, Box 76, W32, (Unprocessed Central Files, 1987–present), GNMP Archives. The catalyst for the executive order that required the park to complete a boundary study resulted from a land donation made by the Gettysburg Battlefield Preservation Association (GBPA) in 1986. Two years earlier, in 1984, the GBPA had purchased the thirty-one acre Taney farm, located near Spangler's Spring and used as a Confederate hospital during the battle, with the intention of donating it to the national park. The thirty-one acre donation, however, surpassed the battlefield's 3,874-acre limit. In October 1987, President Ronald Reagan signed Public Law 100–132, which directed the National Park Service to conduct a boundary study and submit the findings to Congress within one year. Meanwhile, Congress authorized Gettysburg National Military Park to accept the donation of the Taney farm. Congressman William Goodling (Adams County) only conceded his support to the bill after two provisions. First, the government froze any future land acquisitions until the Park Service completed a boundary study, and, second, local officials had to consult in any future boundary study process. The tracts included: 65 acres along General Jubal Early's line of battle on the first day's fields; 65 acres along the Union army's 11th Corps line, also on the first day's fields; 208 acres at Herr's Ridge; 4 acres at the First Shot Marker along the Chambersburg Pike; 17 acres along the Union army's 1st Corps line, along Seminary Ridge; 227 acres at Pitzer Farm; 210 acres at South Cavalry Field; 210 acres at Howe and Wright Avenues, which included the 20th Maine Monument; 85 acres at the George Spangler Farm; 121 acres along Neill Avenue; 55 acres of the Baltimore Pike corridor; 11 acres at Hospital Woods; and 630 acres at East Cavalry Field. Officially, these tracts total 1,849 acres.

16. Superintendent Jose Cisneros, "Superintendent's Annual Report, 1990," written on April 10, 1991, Box 1, Thomas J. Harrison Files, Records of the National Park Service at Gettysburg National Military Park, Gettysburg National Military Park Archives, 5 (hereafter cited as TH, GNMP Archives); Congressman William Goodling Testimony, House Committee on Government Operations, *Land Exchange Between National Park Service/Gettysburg National Park and Gettysburg College*, 103rd Cong., 2d sess., May 9, 1994, 9–11; Management Team Meeting Minutes, October 24, 1991, Folder October 24, 1991, Box 78, A1619, (Unprocessed Central Files 1989–present), GNMP Archives, 4–18; "President Signs Gettysburg Boundary Bill," *Gettysburg Times*, August 20, 1990, Box 28, Newspaper Clipping, 1990, (GETT 43663), GNMP Archives; Bill Walker, Public Relations Official at Gettysburg College, to Faculty, Administrators, and Staff, February 1, 1991, Exhibit 20, House Committee on Government Operations, *Land Exchange Between National Park Service/Gettysburg National Park and Gettysburg College*, 103rd Cong., 2d sess., May 9, 1994, 284–85. Eight sites recommended for removal included: the Washington Street Garage; Seminary Avenue; Jones Battalion Avenue; West Confederate Avenue/Reynolds Road Connector; Taneytown Road bypass; Colt Park tracts; the Cemetery Annex driveway along Baltimore Pike; and the boundary between the battlefield and Gettysburg College. For additional reading on this aspect of the battle, see Harry Pfanz, *Gettysburg: The First Day* (Chapel Hill: Univ. of North Carolina Press, 2001), 297–307, or Noah Andre Trudeau, *Gettysburg: A Testing of Courage* (New York: Harper Collins, 2002), 567.

17. Bill Walker, Public Relations Official at Gettysburg College, to Faculty, Administrators, and Staff, February 1, 1991, Exhibit 20, House Committee on Government Operations, *Land Exchange Between National Park Service/Gettysburg National Park and Gettysburg College*, 103rd Cong., 2d sess., 9 May 1994, 284–85; Regional Director Lorraine Mintzmyer to Charles J. McHugh, March 16, 1992, Folder 1992, January–April, Box 75, W32, (Unprocessed Central Files, 1987–present), GNMP Archives; Gerald Kirwan, Chief, Land Resources Division, to William VanArsdale, Treasurer, Gettysburg College, September 7, 1990, Folder 21, Box 56, L1425, (Unprocessed Central Files, 1987–present), GNMP Archives; Robin Lepore, Office of the Solicitor, to Fred Herling, Outdoor Recreation Planner, December 8, 1993, Binder I, Box 73, W32, (Unprocessed Central Files, 1987–present), GNMP Archives; Briefing Statement, Gettysburg Railroad Re-routing/Synar Subcommittee Oversight, March 9, 1994, Folder January–May 1994, Box 74, W32, (Unprocessed Central Files 1987–present), GNMP Archives; Congressman William Goodling Testimony, House Committee on Government Operations, *Land Exchange Between National Park Service/Gettysburg National Park and Gettysburg College*, 103rd Cong., 2d sess., May 9, 1994, 10–12; *Phase I Archeological Survey of the Proposed Land Offer from Gettysburg National Military Park to Gettysburg College, Gettysburg, Pennsylvania*, prepared by R. Christopher Goodwin & Associates, Frederick, Maryland, October 25, 1990, Folder Archeological Survey Materials, Box 75, W32 (Unprocessed Central Files, 1987–present), GNMP Archives.

18. Robin Lepore, Office of the Solicitor, to Fred Herling, Outdoor Recreation Planner, December 8, 1993, Exhibit 22, House Committee on Government Operations, *Land Exchange Between National Park Service/Gettysburg National Park and Gettysburg College,* 103rd Cong., 2d sess., May 9, 1994, 296–306; Martin Sipkoff, "Where Did Seminary Ridge Go?" *Civil War Times Illustrated* (March/April 1992): 42–64; *Final Report: Gettysburg College-National Park Service Land Exchange, Study of Alternatives/Environmental Assessment* (Gettysburg: National Park Service, Gettysburg National Military Park, May 1995), 3 (hereafter cited as *Land Exchange, Study of Alternatives*); Chairman Mike Synar, Opening Statement, House Committee on Government Operations, *Land Exchange Between National Park Service/Gettysburg National Park and Gettysburg College,* 103rd Cong., 2d sess., May 9, 1994, 1–3; Gettysburg Battlefield Preservation Association to Inland Empire Civil War Round Table (California), May 30, 1991, Folder November–December 1991, Box 75, W32, (Unprocessed Central Files, 1987–present), GNMP Archives; GBPA Press Release, "GBPA Files 12 Million Dollar Lawsuit Against Gettysburg College and The National Park Service For Destruction of Battlefield," November 18, 1991, Folder January–April 1992, Box 75, W32, (Unprocessed Central Files, 1987–present), GNMP Archives; Briefing Statement, Gettysburg Railroad Re-routing/Synar Subcommittee Oversight, March 9, 1994, Folder January–May 1994, Box 74, W32, (Unprocessed Central Files, 1987–present), GNMP Archives; Superintendent Jose Cisneros, "Superintendent's Annual Report, 1993," written on March 11, 1994, Box 1, (TH Files), GNMP Archives; Rudolf Jager to Director James Ridenour, April 25, 1992; R. Lincoln Morris to Director James Ridenour, April 22, 1992, both in Folder May–June 1992, Box 75, W32, (Unprocessed Central Files, 1987–present), GNMP Archives.

19. Statements by Chairman Mike Synar, William Frassanito, Director Roger Kennedy, and Gordon A. Haaland, House Committee on Government Operations, *Land Exchange Between National Park Service/Gettysburg National Park and Gettysburg College,* 103rd Cong., 2d sess., May 9, 1994; *Land Exchange, Study of Alternatives,* 3, 9, 26–54. Director Roger Kennedy to "Friends," May 2, 1995, Folder 22, Box 56, L1425, (Unprocessed Central Files, 1987–present), GNMP Archives; Superintendent John Latschar, "Superintendent's Annual Report, 1995," Box 1, (TH Files), GNMP Archives, 13; President Gordon A. Haaland to Dr. John Latschar, September 28, 1994, Folder September–December 1994, Box 74, W32, (Unprocessed Central Files, 1987–present), GNMP Archives; Chairman Mike Synar to Director Roger Kennedy, June 9, 1994, Folder June–August 1994, Box 74, W32, (Unprocessed Central Files, 1987–present), GNMP Archives; *Land Exchange, Study of Alternatives,* 32–38; Mary Lou Kranias to Dr. John Latschar, October 10, 1994; Steven L. Cassel to Dr. John Latschar, October 19, 1994; Harry Gaul, Friends of the National Parks at Gettysburg Questionnaire, n.d., all in Folder Public Comments, Box 74, W32, (Unprocessed Central Files, 1987–present), GNMP Archives; Scott Newkirk, Friends of the National Parks at Gettysburg Questionnaire, n.d.; Robert Clark, Jr., to Dr. John Latschar, September 27, 1994, all in Folder Public Comments, Box 74, W32, (Unprocessed Central Files, 1987–present), GNMP Archives.

20. Barbara J. Finfrock, *Twenty Years On Six Thousand Acres: The History of the Friends of the National Parks at Gettysburg* (Harrisburg, Pa.: Huggins Printing, 2009), 106–37. The appendix of this work includes the correspondence establishing the association, the Articles of Incorporation, signed on June 16, 1989 and approved by the Commonwealth of Pennsylvania on June 22, 1989, and the Memorandum of Agreement between the NPS and FNPG signed on May 25, 1990. Officially the FNPG is an association dedicated to the preservation and education of both Gettysburg NMP and Eisenhower NHS, thus the name The Friends of the National Parks at Gettysburg. The Friends is a non-profit organization managed by a Board of Directors. The land exchange controversy and the GBPA's subsequent lawsuit created notably weakened relations between the Park Service and the Gettysburg Battlefield Preservation Association.

21. Finfrock, *Twenty Years On Six Thousand Acres*, 6, 26–27; Superintendent Jose Cisneros, "Superintendent's Annual Report, 1990," written on April 10, 1991, Box 1, (TH Files), GNMP Archives, 12; "FNPG Accomplishments, June 1989–June 1994," n.d., Folder 1, Box 11, A42, (Unprocessed Central Files, 1987–present), GNMP Archives; Superintendent James McConaghie, "Superintendent's Annual Report, 1936–1937," Box 2, (GETT 41113), GNMP Archives; Victoria Greenlee to Superintendent John Latschar, August 9, 1994, Folder 1, Box 11, A42, (Unprocessed Central Files, 1987–present), GNMP Archives. TNT donated $50,000 to the park, and this money was then earmarked for the power line project.

22. Matthew McAvoy, "Gettysburg National Military Park and Eisenhower National Historic Site: Economic Impact on Gettysburg and Adams County, 1994," prepared and distributed by Gettysburg-Adams County Area Chamber of Commerce, 27; Weeks, *Gettysburg*, 190; "Friends of the National Parks at Gettysburg Annual Report, 1995," Folder 2, Box 11, A42, (Unprocessed Central Files, 1987–present), GNMP Archives; Superintendent John Latschar, "Superintendent's Annual Report, 2000," Folder 4, Box 3, A26, (Unprocessed Central Files, 1987–present), GNMP Archives, 12.

23. "Site For $200,000 Longstreet Statue Is Dedicated: 71st Coast Artillery Re-Enacts '63 Battle Scene," *Gettysburg Times*, July 2, 1941; General James Longstreet Memorial Fund Fact Sheet, Folder 19, Box 41, D66 (Unprocessed Central Files, 1987–present), GNMP Archives; Superintendent John Latschar, "Superintendent's Annual Report, 1998," Box 3, A26, (Unprocessed Central Files, 1987–present), GNMP Archives, 9. The North Carolina Division of the Sons of Confederate Veterans (SCV) established a Longstreet Memorial Fund in 1991 with a specific goal to raise the necessary funding. For additional reading on Longstreet see, William Garrett Piston, *Lee's Tarnished Lieutenant: James Longstreet and His Place In Southern History* (Athens: Univ. of Georgia Press, 1987) and Jeffery Wert, *General James Longstreet: The Confederacy's Most Controversial Soldier* (New York: Simon & Schuster, 1993).

24. McAvoy, "Gettysburg National Military Park and Eisenhower National Historic Site," 4; Weeks, *Gettysburg*, 190; Superintendent John Latschar,

"Superintendent's Annual Report, 1996," Folder 25, Box 3, A26, (Unprocessed Central Files, 1987–present), GNMP Archives, 10; Wendy Becker, "Gettysburg National Military Park and Eisenhower National Historic Site: Economic Impact on Gettysburg and Adams County," prepared and distributed by Gettysburg-Adams County Area Chamber of Commerce, 1995. The Economic Impact Study relied upon the results of the University of Idaho's National Park Service Cooperative Park Studies Unit, conducted in the late 1980s. Excepting the University of Idaho survey, park management did not have a comprehensive understanding of their visitors, their expectations from their battlefield experience, or the impact of the tourism industry on the community. Percentages do not equal 100 because visitors may have responded to more than one reason for visiting Gettysburg.

25. "Coleman Tells Broad Policy on Battlefield," *Gettysburg Times*, April 9, 1941, Folder 2, Box 35, (GETT 43663), GNMP Archives; Economic Impact Study, 1995, 8–10.

26. Prior to obtaining his doctorate, Latschar served as an Army officer, including a tour in Vietnam in 1970 and 1971. He retired from the U.S. Army Reserve as a Lieutenant Colonel in 1994. While completing his dissertation, Latschar worked as a Research Historian for the Western Team of the Denver Service Center (DSC) in July 1977 and subsequently became the Cultural Resource Compliance Specialist for the Western Team in 1981, and later the Chief of Cultural Resources for the Western Team in 1984. As mentioned, J. Walter Coleman, superintendent from 1941 through 1958, had also earned a Ph.D. in American History.

27. Superintendent John Latschar, interview by author, January 4, 2010; Superintendent John Latschar, "Gettysburg: The Next 100 Years," presented at the 4th Annual Gettysburg Seminar, March 4, 1995. This speech is reproduced in the park's seminar proceedings, *The Fourth Annual Gettysburg Seminar, Gettysburg 1895–1995: The Making of an American Shrine* (Gettysburg, Pa.: Eastern National, 1995), 112–23.

28. Superintendent John Latschar, "Superintendent's Annual Report, 1996," 10, 18–19; Economic Impact Study, 1995, 29. GNMP visitation for 1994 totaled 1,748,932 and for 1995 totaled 1,717,382; *Draft Development Concept Plan, Environmental Assessment: Collections Storage, Visitor and Museum Facilities,* April 1996 (Gettysburg: Gettysburg National Military Park, April 1996), 6 (hereafter cited as *Draft DCP, Collections Storage,* 1996); Latschar, "Gettysburg: The Next 100 Years," 118; Superintendent John Latschar, "Superintendent's Annual Report, 1997," Box 23, A26, Unprocessed Central Files 1987-present, GNMP Archives, 15–17. According to Latschar's calculations, for every $100,000 paid in taxes, Gettysburg battlefield received a mere 20 cents. Some of the National Park Service and Department of Interior's fiscal constraints can be traced back to President Ronald Reagan's administration and specifically his Secretary of the Interior, James G. Watt. Watt served as Secretary of the Interior between 1981 and 1983 before resigning his post in the fall of 1983. The leader of a department

charged to oversee the nation's environmental issues, Watt was famously hostile to environmentalism and conservation policies. Instead of advocating for the preservation of National Parks and undisturbed lands, he favored drilling and mining and urged such lands be used for utilitarian practices. In short, Watt's hostility toward preservation issues, which trickled down to the National Park Service, can help explain fiscal constraints faced by the agency in the 1990s.

29. Superintendent John Latschar to Ed Bearss, March 29, 1995, Folder Development of Draft, Box 1, D18, (General Management Plan, Environmental Impact Assessment, 1996–1998), Records of the National Park Service at Gettysburg National Military Park, Gettysburg National Military Park Archives [hereafter cited as (GMP, 1996–1998), GNMP Archives]; *Draft Development Concept Plan, Environmental Assessment: Gettysburg Museum of the Civil War,* April 1995 (Gettysburg: Gettysburg National Military Park, April 1995), 9–16 (hereafter cited as *Draft, DCP, Gettysburg Museum,* 1995); Superintendent John Latschar to Associate Director, Cultural Resources, March 29, 1995, Folder Development of Draft, Box 1, D18, (GMP, 1996–1998), GNMP Archives; NPS Press Release, "Gettysburg National Military Park Plans New Museum," March 27, 1995, Folder Public Meetings, Box 1, D18, (GMP, 1996–1998), GNMP Archives; Superintendent John Latschar to Brenda Barrett, SHPO, February 21, 1995, Folder 106 Compliance, Box 1, D18, (GMP, 1996–1998), GNMP Archives; Pauline and Dick Peterson to Director Roger Kennedy, August 28, 1995; Edward Linenthal to Superintendent John Latschar, August 22, 1995; Richard Moe, President, National Trust of Historic Preservation, to Superintendent John Latschar, July 15, 1995, all in Folder Public Comments on Draft, Box 1, D18, (GMP, 1996–1998), GNMP Archives; NPS Press Release, "NPS Will Defer Pursuing Museum Proposal," August 31, 1995, Folder Public Meetings Information, Box 1, D18, 1996–1998, GNMP Archives. The new facility would have been constructed located along the Taneytown Road near General George Meade's Headquarters, the site where Kenneth Dick built Fantasyland in 1959. In 1974, the Park Service purchased the amusement park, and, in 1980, Fantasyland closed. Robert Monahan, Jr., a lifelong Gettysburg resident, founded the Monahan Group, a business and real estate company, in 1987. Between 1981 and 1986, Monahan worked as Special Assistant to President Ronald Reagan and Special Assistant to the Secretary of Transportation.

30. NPS Press Release, "NPS Will Defer Pursuing Museum Proposal," August 31, 1995, Folder Public Meetings Information, Box 1, D18, (GMP, 1996–1998), GNMP Archives; Superintendent John Latschar to "Friend," October 17, 1995, Folder Public Comments Received During Scoping, Box 1, D18, (GMP, 1996–1998), GNMP Archives; *Draft, DCP, Collections Storage,* 1996, 8. Deputy Director, Denis P. Galvin, "Statement of Denis P. Galvin, Before the Subcommittee on National Parks, Historic Preservation and Recreation, Senate Committee on Energy and Natural Resources, Concerning the Visitor Center and Museum Facilities Project at Gettysburg National Military Park," February 24, 1998, Folder "Senate Hearing," Box 6, D18, (GMP, 1996–1998), GNMP

Archives. For additional information on the planning for the new museum, see *Draft, Development Concept Plan, Gettysburg Museum, Environmental Assessment: Gettysburg Museum of the Civil War,* (Gettysburg, Pa.: Gettysburg National Military Park, 1995); *Draft Development Concept Plan, Environmental Assessment: Collections Storage, Visitor and Museum Facilities,* April 1996 (Gettysburg, Pa.: Gettysburg National Military Park, April 1996); *Request For Proposals: Visitor Center & Museum Facilities, Gettysburg National Military Park* (Gettysburg, Pa.: United States Department of Interior, National Park Service, Northeast Field Area, December 11, 1996).

31. Michael Alderstein to Director Robert Stanton, October 13, 1997, in *Final General Management Plan and Environmental Impact Statement,* Gettysburg National Military Park, Pennsylvania, vol. 1 (U.S. Department of the Interior, National Park Service, June 1999), 363–76; Director Robert Stanton to Randy Harper, February 6, 1998, in *GMP,* vol. 1, 393–405; Director Roger Stanton to Robert Kinsley, November 6, 1997, Folder RFP Selection, Box 2, D18, (GMP, 1996–1998), GNMP Archives; NPS Press Release, "Proposal Selected for Gettysburg Museum Project," November 7, 1997, Folder Announcement of Selection, Box 2, D18, (GMP, 1996–1998), GNMP Archives; "Visitor Center, Gettysburg National Military Park, Visitor Center & Museum Facilities, Request for Proposals," submitted by Kinsley Equities, May 9, 1997, Folder 17, Box 18, A7221, (Unprocessed Central Files, 1987–present), GNMP Archives, 1–140.

Chapter 10

1. Dwight Pitcaithley, "'A Cosmic Threat': The National Park Service Addresses the Causes of the American Civil War," in *Slavery and Public History: The Tough Stuff of American Memory,* eds. James Oliver Horton and Lois E. Horton (Chapel Hill: Univ. of North Carolina Press, 2006), 172; Public Law, Fredericksburg/Spotsylvania National Military Park Boundary, December 11, 1989, Public Law 101-214, 101st Congress; *Draft Development Concept Plan, Environmental Assessment: Collections Storage, Visitor and Museum Facilities,* April 1996 (Gettysburg: Gettysburg National Military Park, April 1996), 6 (hereafter cited as *Draft DCP, Collections Storage,* 1996); Kammen, *Mystic Chords of Memory,* 626.

2. Pitcaithley, "A Cosmic Threat," 172.

3. "Secretary of the Interior's Standards for the Treatment of Historic Properties With Guidelines for the Treatment of Cultural Landscapes" (1992), available at http://www.nps.gov/tps/standards/four-treatments/landscape-guidelines/index.htm. These standards became effective on August 11, 1995. *Final General Management Plan and Environmental Impact Statement,* Gettysburg National Military Park, Pennsylvania, vol. 1 (U.S. Department of the Interior, National Park Service, June 1999), 61–62 (hereafter cited as *GMP* or *GMP,* vol. 2). An example of restoration would be the fabrication of a new bronze sword on a monument where the original sword has been stolen or vandalized. Rehabilitation, on the other hand, allows for improvements to historic features that had deteriorated

or changed. This could include regrading a historic swale, reclaiming a field that has become overgrown, or replacing missing historic features. To keep the terms consistent and accurate to the Park Service's effort, the term rehabilitation will be used when referring to improvement of landscape features. Restoration will be used to describe improvements to historic structures.

4. "Secretary of the Interior's Standards for the Treatment of Historic Properties With Guidelines for the Treatment of Cultural Landscapes" (1992), available at http://www.nps.gov/tps/standards/four-treatments/landscape-guidelines/ terminology.htm.

5. Charles Birnbaum, "Preservation Brief 36: Protecting Cultural Landscapes, Planning, Treatment, and Management of Historic Landscapes" (Washington, D.C: National Park Service, 1994), available at http://www.nps.gov/hps/tps/ briefs/brief36.htm.

6. "Visitor Center, Gettysburg National Military Park, Visitor Center & Museum Facilities, Request for Proposals," submitted by Kinsley Equities, May 9, 1997, 1–140, Folder 17, Box 18, A7221, Park Main (Central) Files, 1987–present, Records of the National Park Service at Gettysburg National Military Park, Gettysburg National Military Park Archives [Files from this collection have not yet been processed and all notes hereafter will be cited by Box, File Code, (Unprocessed Central Files, 1987–present), GNMP Archives]; Michael Alderstein to Director Roger Stanton, October 13, 1997; Director Roger Stanton to Robert Kinsley, November 6, 1997, all in Folder RFP Selection, Box 2, D18, (General Management Plan, Environmental Impact Assessment, 1996–1998), Records of the National Park Service at Gettysburg National Military Park, Gettysburg National Military Park Archives [hereafter cited as (GMP, 1996–1998), GNMP Archives]; NPS Press Release, "Proposal Selected for Gettysburg Museum Project," November 7, 1997, Folder Announcement of Selection, Box 2, D18, (General Management Plan, Environmental Impact Assessment, 1996–1998), GNMP Archives.

7. *Draft, DCP, Collections Storage,* 1996, 8; *Draft General Management Plan and Environmental Impact Statement,* Gettysburg National Military Park, Pennsylvania (U.S. Department of the Interior, National Park Service, August 1998) (hereafter cited as *Draft, GMP*); Superintendent John Latschar, "Superintendent's Annual Report, 1998," 2–3. Superintendent John Latschar's annual reports from 1995 through 2003 can be found in Box 3, A26, (Unprocessed Central Files, 1987–present), GNMP Archives, while reports from 2004 to 2009 are filed in the Contemporary Administrative Files, GNMP. All references hereafter to Latschar's annual will only be cited by the year's report and page number. During 1998, the NPS received over 3,700 written comments, which led to several changes on the Kinsley proposal, namely a reduction in commercial facilities. Approximately 85 percent of the comments supported efforts to restore the battlefield's historic landscapes and called for proceeding with the implementation of the proposed partnership with the Gettysburg National Battlefield Museum Foundation.

8. Superintendent John Latschar, interview by author, January 4, 2010.

9. *GMP,* vol. 1, 61–62.

10. *Draft, GMP,* i–vi, 59–150; *GMP,* vol. 1, 124.

11. *Draft, GMP,* 43, 122–38; *GMP,* vol. 1, 124, 130.

12. Carol Shull, Keeper of the National Register of Historic Places, to Associate Director, Cultural Resource Stewardship, May 12, 1998; Superintendent John Latschar to Carol Shull, March 25, 1998; Brent Glass, Pennsylvania Historical Museum Commission, to Carol Shull, Keeper of the National Register of Historic Places, June 29, 1998, all in Folder Cyclorama Center Consultation, Box 4, D18, (GMP, 1996–1998), GNMP Archives; "Determination of Eligibility Notification," National Register of Historic Places, Cyclorama Building, Gettysburg National Military Park, by Cathy Shull, September 24, 1998, in *GMP,* vol. 2, 5–7. The NHPA can be viewed at http://www.achp.gov/NHPA.pdf; Richard Longstreth, President, Society of Architectural Historians, to Superintendent John Latschar, January 6, 1999; Eileen Woodford, Northeast Regional Director of the National Parks and Conservation Association, to Superintendent John Latschar, January 11, 1999, both in Folder Cyclorama Center Consultation, Comments on Draft, Box 4, D18, (GMP, 1996–1998), GNMP Archives; "Meeting Notes, Cyclorama Consultation," April 20, 1999, Folder Cyclorama Consultation Meeting, Box 4, D18, (GMP, 1996–1998), GNMP Archives; Superintendent John Latschar, "Superintendent's Annual Report, 1999," 2–4; "Draft Memorandum of Agreement," National Park Service, the Pennsylvania State Historic Preservation Office, and the Advisory Council on Historic Preservation, June 16, 1999, Folder Cyclorama, MOA Draft, Box 4, D18, (GMP, 1996–1998), GNMP Archives; Superintendent John Latschar, "Timeline," Superintendent's personal files, in author's possession; "Holding the High Ground: Principles and Strategies for Managing and Interpreting Civil War Battlefield Landscapes," Proceedings of a Conference of Battlefield Managers, Nashville, Tennessee, August 24–27, 1998, (hereafter cited as "Holding the High Ground, 1998"). The ACHP report, "A Problem of Common Ground," explored the preservation problems of three historic objects in question—the cyclorama building, the Gettysburg Cyclorama painting, and the historic battlefield landscape. In fact, the report recognized management's tendency to preserve and maintain non-historic structures that were incompatible with the historic landscape and declared, "Battlefield managers remain committed to preserving all significant historic resources when they do not constitute a significant degradation of the primary battlefield landscape. When post-war resources adversely affect the primary battlefield landscape, the NPS will develop solutions in close consultation with the SHPO and ACHP, in accordance with NEPA and 106."

13. "Holding the High Ground," 1998, 1–14.

14. *GMP,* vol. 1, iii; *Draft, GMP,* 43. Staff classified the intensity of the fighting at three levels: minor action with light casualties; moderate action with medium casualties; and major action that resulted in heavy casualties.

15. Petition to Oppose the Removal of 576 Acres of Trees, presented to the Advisory Commission, February 15, 2001, Folder 15, Box 25, D18, (Unprocessed Central Files, 1987–present), GNMP Archives; Aurelia S. Lutton to Bruce Babbitt, Secretary of the Interior, May 17, 1999, Folder 16, Box 25, D18, (Unprocessed Central Files, 1987–present), GNMP Archives; Gene Albright, "Letter to the Editor, " *Hanover Sun,* September 27, 1998, Folder Congressional Correspondence Related to *Final GMP,* Box 6, D18, (GMP, 1996–1998), GNMP Archives; C.K. Roulette comment, "Transcript of Proceedings of Public Hearings," October 3, 1998, Folder Public Meetings, Hearings, Box 6, D18, (GMP, 1996–1998), GNMP Archives; Elaine and Bill Jones to Superintendent John Latschar, September 25, 1998; William Wilkinson to Congressman William Goodling, October 9, 1998, both in Folder Congressional Correspondence Related to *Final GMP,* Box 6, D18, (GMP, 1996–1998), GNMP Archives.

16. Todd Jones to Superintendent John Latschar, n.d., Folder Congressional Correspondence Related to *Final GMP,* Box 6, D18, (GMP, 1996–1998), GNMP Archives.

17. Christine Riker to Superintendent John Latschar, January 18, 1998; Nathaniel Reed to Superintendent John Latschar, January 27, 1998, both in Folder Public Comments During Scoping, General Comments, January 1998, Box 5, D18, (GMP, 1996–1998), GNMP Archives; Richard Rogers to Superintendent John Latschar, February 5, 1998, Folder Public Comments During Scoping, General Comments, February 1998, Box 5, D18, (GMP, 1996–1998), GNMP Archives; Rudolph Kosits to Superintendent John Latschar, March 25, 1998, Folder Public Comments During Scoping, General Comments, March 1998, Box 5, D18, (GMP, 1996–1998), GNMP Archives; Anne Masak to Superintendent John Latschar, February 20, 1998, Folder Public Comments During Scoping, General Comments, February 1998, Box 5, D18, (GMP, 1996–1998), GNMP Archives.

18. Thomas Connell to Bruce Babbitt, Secretary of the Interior, n.d., Folder 17, Box 25, D18, (Unprocessed Central Files, 1987–present), GNMP Archives; Dennis Matthews, Public Comment, "Transcript of Proceedings of Public Hearings," October 3, 1998, Folder Public Meetings, Box 6, D18, (GMP, 1996–1998), GNMP Archives, 16–19.

19. Holly Giles to John Eline, October 13, 1998, *GMP,* vol. 2, 41; "Statement of Eric Uberman Before the Gettysburg Military Park Advisory Commission," April 15, 1998; Joyce Jackson, President of the Gettysburg Area Retail Merchant Association, to Director Robert Stanton, June 2, 1998, both in Folder Public Meetings, May 1997–August 1998, Box 4, D18, (GMP, 1996–1998), GNMP Archives; Paul Witt, President, Gettysburg Convention and Visitor's Bureau, to Superintendent John Latschar, June 12, 1998, Folder Comments, Survey Gettysburg Visitors Bureau, Box 5, D18, (GMP, 1996–1998), GNMP Archives; "Resolution," Gettysburg Area Retail Merchants Association, May 27, 1998, Folder Public Relations, October 1997–August 1998, Box 5, A38, (Unprocessed Central Files, 1987–present), GNMP Archives; Eric Uberman, Peter Bienstock, and Frank Silbey memo,

n.d., Folder FOIA, July 1999–August 1999, Box 16, A7221, (Unprocessed Central Files, 1987–present), GNMP Archives.

20. Comment on a Gettysburg Visitors Bureau Survey, unidentified author, Folder Comments, Survey Gettysburg Visitors Bureau, Box 5, D18, (GMP, 1996–1998), GNMP Archives; Larry Defuge, Comment, *GMP* Meeting, Folder Comments Received on Draft, Box 6, D18, (GMP, 1996–1998), GNMP Archives; Superintendent John Latschar, "Superintendent's Annual Report, 1999," 2.

21. "Coleman Tells Broad Policy on Battlefield," *Gettysburg Times*, April 9, 1941, Folder 2, Box 35, (GETT 43663), GNMP Archives; James Hansen to NPS Director Robert Stanton, May 7, 1999, Folder "House Hearing," Box 6, D18, (GMP, 1996–1998), GNMP Archives.

22. Robert Monahan, "Transcript of Proceedings of Public Hearing," October 1, 1998, Folder Public Meetings, Hearings, Box 6, D18, (GMP, 1996–1998), GNMP Archives, 57.

23. Superintendent John Latschar, "Superintendent's Annual Report, 1998," 1; NPS Press Release, "National Park Service Holds Public Workshops on Museum and Visitor Center Plans," March 3, 1998; "Gettysburg National Military Park, Proposed Collections Storage, Museum and Visitor Center," June 17, 1998, both in Folder Public Meetings, Box 4, D18, (GMP, 1996–1998), GNMP Archives; Michael Alderstein to Director Stanton, October 13, 1997, *GMP*, vol. 1, 363–76; Statement of Paul Hoffman, Deputy Director, U.S. Fish and Wildlife, House Subcommittee on National Parks and Public Lands, *The Future Visitor's Center at Gettysburg National Military Park and the Associated Fundraising Efforts*, 107th Cong., 2d sess., March 21, 2002, 10–21; Marie Rust, Northeast Regional Director, to Robert Kinsley, July 10, 1998, Folder Letter of Intent, Box 2, D18, (GMP, 1996–1998), GNMP Archives. The original proposal included a National Geographic bookstore, the Civil War Arts & Crafts Gallery, and the tour center gift shop. Kinsley signed the agreement on July 16, which created a non-profit partnership, the Gettysburg National Battlefield Museum Foundation, with a goal to raise the necessary money to build and operate the Gettysburg Visitor Center and Museum.

24. Superintendent John Latschar, "Superintendent's Annual Report, 1998," 1–3; Senator Dale Bumpers to Secretary Interior Bruce Babbit, November 24, 1997, Folder Congressional Correspondence, Box 2, D18, (GMP, 1996–1998), GNMP Archives; Craig Thomas, "Statement by Chairman Craig Thomas, Subcommittee on National Parks, Historic Preservation and Recreation, Oversight Hearing on the issues relating to the visitor center and museum facilities at Gettysburg National Military Park"; Deputy Director Denis P. Galvin, "Statement of Denis P. Galvin, Before the Subcommittee on National Parks, Historic Preservation and Recreation, Senate Committee on Energy and Natural Resources, Concerning the Visitor Center and Museum Facilities Project at Gettysburg National Military Park," February 24, 1998; Dennis Frye, "Testimony, Association for the Preservation of Civil War Sites, Before the Subcommittee on National Parks, Historic Preservation and Recreation, Senate Committee on Energy

and Natural Resources, Regarding Visitor Center and Museum at Gettysburg National Military Park," February 24, 1998, all in Folder Senate Hearing, Box 6, D18, (GMP 1996–1998), GNMP Archives; Superintendent John Latschar, "Superintendent's Annual Report, 1999," 1; James V. Hansen, Chairman, "Opening Statement, Subcommittee on National Parks and Public Lands, Oversight Hearing, Gettysburg National Military Park," February 11, 1999, Folder House Hearing, Box 6, D18, (GMP, 1996–1998), GNMP Archives; Eileen Woodford, "Testimony of Eileen Woodford, Northeast Regional Director, National Parks and Conservation Association Before the Subcommittee on National Parks and Public Lands, United States House of Representatives on the Proposed Museum Complex and *General Management Plan* at Gettysburg National Military Park," February 11, 1999; Robert Kinsley, "Statement of Robert Kinsley, Managing Partner, Kinsley Equities, House Subcommittee on National Parks and Public Lands, Oversight Hearing on Gettysburg National Military Park and *General Management Plan* and Proposed Visitor Center," February 11, 1999; Franklin R. Silbey, "The National Park Service Should Not Be Allowed To Promote Commercial Development Within Gettysburg National Military Park," all in Folder House Hearing, Box 6, D18, (GMP, 1996–1998), GNMP Archives; Dr. Walter Powell, "Testimony of Walter Powell, President, Gettysburg Battlefield Preservation Association, for House Subcommittee on National Parks and Public Lands," February 11, 1999; Chairman James Hansen to NPS Director Robert Stanton, February 17, 1999; James Hansen and George Miller to Director Robert Stanton, March 29, 1999; James Hansen to NPS Director Robert Stanton, May 7, 1999, all in Folder House Hearing, Box 6, D18, (GMP, 1996–1998), GNMP Archives; House Subcommittee on National Parks and Public Lands of the Committee on Resources, *Oversight Hearing On Gettysburg National Military Park General Management Plan And Proposed Visitors Center,* 106th Cong., 1st sess., February 11, 1999, Washington, D.C.; This transcript is available online at http://commdocs.house.gov/committees/resources/hii55029.000/hii55029_of. htm; Superintendent John Latschar, "Timeline," December 11, 2007, Superintendent's personal files, possession of the author. The full text of the endorsement reads: "The committees, through previous appropriations, have supported the preparation of a new *General Management Plan* for Gettysburg NMP to enable the NPS to more adequately interpret the Battle of Gettysburg and to preserve the artifacts and landscapes that help tell the story of this great conflict of the Civil War. Accordingly, the managers acknowledge the need for a new visitor facility and support the proposed public-private partnership as a unique approach to the interpretive needs of our National Parks."

25. Daniel Kuehn to Superintendent John Latschar, September 20, 1998 in *GMP,* vol. 2, 459–62; Philip Stewart, "GMP Survey Response Form," Folder Public Comments During Scoping, Response to Newsletter 4, Box 5, D18, (GMP, 1996–1998), GNMP Archives; Bart Fordham to Superintendent John Latschar, February 9, 1998, Folder Public Comments During Scoping, General Comments, March 1998, Box 5, D18, (GMP, 1996–1998), GNMP Archives; Gabor Boritt to Director Robert Stanton, December 10, 1998 in *GMP,* vol. 2, 228–29;

Margaret Blough to Senator Murkowski, March 1, 1998, Folder Public Meetings, Constituent Comment, Box 6, D18, (GMP, 1996–1998), GNMP Archives, 57; Superintendent John Latschar, "Superintendent's Annual Report, 1999," 1. The park recorded over 500 comments during the 60-day public review period for the *Draft GMP* (September–October 1998). The park reported over 75 percent of the comments supported the plan and noted that 85 percent of the comments from within the Civil War community expressed approval. On a more local level, the park reported that roughly half of the writers from south-central Pennsylvania supported the proposal, while half opposed it.

26. Kammen, *Mystic Chords of Memory*, 626.

27. Blight, *Race and Reunion*, 2–4; Governor William Hodges Mann, July 3, 1913, printed in *Fiftieth Anniversary of the Battle of Gettysburg: Report of the Pennsylvania Commission* (Harrisburg, Pa.: Wm. Stanley Ray, State Printer, December 31, 1913), 143–46.

28. Eric Foner, "Gettysburg National Military Park Evaluation"; James McPherson, "Gettysburg National Military Park Evaluation"; Nina Silber, "Report for the Organization of American Historians (OAH) and the National Park Service (NPS) on Gettysburg National Military Park," August 1998, all in possession of the author (hereafter cited as "OAH Evaluation, 1998")

29. Quoted in Pitcaithley, "'A Cosmic Threat'," 171.

30. Superintendent John Latschar, "Gettysburg: The Next 100 Years," presented at the 4th Annual Gettysburg Seminar, March 4, 1995. This speech is reproduced in the park's seminar proceedings, *The Fourth Annual Gettysburg Seminar, Gettysburg 1895–1995: The Making of an American Shrine* (Gettysburg: Eastern National, 1995), 112–23.

31. Scott Williams to Secretary of Interior Bruce Babbitt, n.d.; Sons of Confederate Veterans' Heritage Committee Comment Card, to Secretary of Interior Bruce Babbitt, both in Folder 6, Box 5, A36, (Unprocessed Central Files, 1987–present), GNMP Archives; David Ensor, FNPG Mailing Survey, Folder FNPG Comments, Box 5, D18 (GNMP, 1996–1998), GNMP Archives; G. Elliott Cummings, Commander, Maryland Division, Sons of Confederate Veterans, to Alan Hoeweler, President, FNPG, September 28, 1995, Folder 5, Box 5, A36, (Unprocessed Central Files, 1987–present), GNMP Archives. Each card had a prepared, typed statement, and the individuals signed their name and address.

32. Superintendent John Latschar to Andy Sterlen, n.d., Folder 6, Box 5, A36, (Unprocessed Central Files, 1987–present), GNMP Archives; David Ensor, FNPG Mailing Survey, Folder FNPG Comments, Box 5, D18, (GMP, 1996–1998), GNMP Archives; *Arkansas Democrat Gazette*, October 20, 2002; Pitcaithley, "A Cosmic Threat," 178–79.

33. Rick Hampton, "150 Years after Civil War, Descendants Deal with Legacy," *USA Today*, April 7, 2011.

34. NPS Press Release, "Leading Historians Pledge Support for Gettysburg Plan," September 29, 1998. This press release is available at http://www.nps.gov/archive/gett/gettplan/gmp99archive/press1098.htm, "OAH Evaluation, 1998."

35. "Holding the High Ground, 1998."

36. "Holding the High Ground, 1998."

37. Pitcaithley, "'A Cosmic Threat'," 175–76.

38. Robert Sutton, "Introduction," *Rally On The High Ground: The National Park Service Symposium on the Civil War,* ed. Robert K. Sutton (Fort Washington, Pa.: Eastern National, 2001), xvi; Jesse Jackson, Jr., "A More Perfect Union," *Rally On The High Ground,* ed. Sutton, v–vii, 1–10.

39. *Department of the Interior FY 2000 Appropriations: Joint Explanatory Statement of the Committee of the Conference,* Title I, U.S. Congress 1999, 96. The full text of this appropriation reads, "The managers recognize that Civil War battlefields throughout the country hold great significance and provide vital historic educational opportunities for millions of Americans. The managers are concerned, however, about the isolated existence of these Civil War battle sites in that they are often not placed in the proper historical context. The Service does an outstanding job of documenting and describing the particular battle at any given site, but in the public displays and multi-media presentations, it does not always do a similarly good job of documenting and describing the historical social, economic, legal, cultural and political forces and events that originally led to the larger war which eventually manifested themselves in specific battles. In particular, the Civil War battlefields are often weak or missing vital information about the role that the institution of slavery played in causing the American Civil War. The managers direct the Secretary of the Interior to encourage Civil War battle sites to recognize and include in all of their public displays and multi-media educational presentations the unique role that the institution of slavery played in causing the Civil War and its role, if any, at the individual battle sites. The managers further direct the Secretary to prepare a report by January 15, 2000, on the status of the educational information currently included at Civil War sites that are consistent with and reflect this concern."

40. Superintendent John Latschar to James McPherson, February 28, 2000, Folder 12, Box 21, A82, (Unprocessed Central Files, 1987–present), GNMP Archives; Memo, undated, Folder Holt, Box 16, A7221, (Unprocessed Central Files, 1987–present), GNMP Archives; "OAH Evaluation, 1998." This commission consisted of eight renowned Civil War historians selected to provide a broad knowledge of the war. They included: James McPherson, Princeton University; Eric Foner, Columbia University; Gary Gallagher, University of Virginia; Nina Silber, Boston University; Gabor Boritt, Gettysburg College; Dwight Pitcaithley, Chief Historian, National Park Service; Robin Reed, Museum of the Confederacy; and Olivia Mahoney, Chicago Historical Society. The Museum Advisory Commission held its first meeting on July 27, 2000. For additional reading on the *Enola Gay* incident see, Edward Linenthal and Tom Engelhardt, *History Wars: The Enola Gay and Other Battles for the American Past* (New York: Metropolitan Books, 1996).

41. "Record of Decision, *Final General Management Plan/Environmental Impact Statement,* Gettysburg National Military Park," signed on November 23, 1999

by Regional Director Marie Rust, Folder Record of Decision, Box 6, D18, (GMP, 1996–1998), GNMP Archives; Superintendent John Latschar, "Superintendent's Annual Report, 2000," 19. Superintendent Latschar signed the "ROD" on November 11. Wilburn arrived as the Museum Foundation's first president with a wealth of experience. A graduate of the United States Air Force Academy, Wilburn earned a Ph.D. in economics and public affairs from Princeton University. He served as president of the University of Indiana at Pennsylvania from 1976 to 1978. Wilburn also held positions in the Department of Defense, the White House, and cabinet posts in Pennsylvania governor Richard Thornburg's administration. He worked as CEO of the Carnegie Institute in Pennsylvania before accepting the position as president of the Colonial Williamsburg Foundation.

42. "Gone!" *Friends of the National Parks at Gettysburg* Newsletter, Fall 2000, 1–3; Edward T. Pound, "Tower Gives Gettysburg Little In Returns," *USA Today,* February 16, 1998. Box 1, Gettysburg National Tower, Gettysburg National Military Park Library (hereafter cited as GNT, GNMP Library); John Latschar, "The Taking of the Gettysburg Tower," *The George Wright Society,* 18 (2001): 24–33; *Boundary Study: Gettysburg National Military Park: Draft Report to Con-gress, Environmental Assessment,* August 1998; *Land Protection Plan,* October 1993 (Gettysburg: Gettysburg National Military Park, 1993), 1–92; NPS Press Release, "Demolishing the Gettysburg Tower," June 27, 2000, Box 72, W32, (Unprocessed Central Files, 1987–present), GNMP Archives; Superintendent John Latschar, "Superintendent's Annual Report, 2000," 9–11; *National Tower Demolition and Removal Environmental Assessment, Draft* (Gettysburg, Pa.: Gettysburg National Military Park, May 2000), Box 2, GNT, GNMP Library.

43. Stephanie Dudley to Superintendent John Latschar, n.d.; Chris Bowling to Secretary of the Interior Bruce Babbitt, July 1, 2000, both in Folder Tower Comments, FY 2000, Box 72, W32, (Unprocessed Central Files, 1987–present), GNMP Archives; John Vockroth email to John Heiser, May 25, 2000; Email from an unidentified author to John Heiser, July 3, 2000, both in Folder 16–21B, Vertical Files, GNMP Library; Matthew Taylor email comment to Superintendent John Latschar, July 3, 2000, Folder Tower Comments, FY 2000, Box 72, W32, (Unprocessed Central Files, 1987–present), GNMP Archives; NPS Press Release, "Gettysburg Tower Demolition," June 27, 2000; John Albright to Superintendent John Latschar, September 11, 2000; Barbara Finfrock, "Remarks," all in Folder National Tower, FY 2000, Box 72, W32, (Unprocessed Central Files, 1987–present), GNMP Archives.

44. Kammen, *Mystic Chords of Memory,* 626.

Chapter 11

1. "The Hucksters Close in on Gettysburg's Grandeur," *Detroit Free Press,* May 12, 1974.

2. Pitcaithley, "'A Cosmic Threat,'" 169–86; Kammen, *Mystic Chords of Memory*, 626; *Draft Development Concept Plan, Environmental Assessment: Collections Storage, Visitor and Museum Facilities*, April 1996 (Gettysburg: Gettysburg National Military Park, April 1995), 6 (hereafter cited as *Draft DCP, Collections Storage*, 1996); Public Law, Fredericksburg/Spotsylvania National Military Park Boundary, December 11, 1989.

3. National Park Service Sesquicentennial Commemoration, "The Civil War: 150 Years," available online at http://www.nps.gov/features/waso/cw150th/civwar parks.html; Zenzen, *Battling for Manassas*, xix; Blight, *Race and Reunion*, 361; "Holding the High Ground, 1998, 1–14; "Department of the Interior FY 2000 Appropriations: Joint Explanatory Statement of the Committee of the Conference," 96.

4. Superintendent John Latschar, "Battlefield Rehabilitation Goals," FNPG Newsletter, Winter 2000, 3; Charles Birnbaum, "Preservation Brief 36: Protecting Cultural Landscapes, Planning, Treatment, and Management of Historic Landscapes" (Washington, D.C: National Park Service, 1994), available at http://www.nps.gov/hps/tps/briefs/brief36.htm; *Final General Management Plan and Environmental Impact Statement*, Gettysburg National Military Park, Pennsylvania, vol. 1 (U.S. Department of the Interior, National Park Service, June 1999), 281 (hereafter cited as *GMP* or *GMP*, vol. 2).

5. David McConaughy to Hon. Jos. R. Ingersoll, August 19, 1863, Vertical Files, 11–29 B, Gettysburg National Military Park Library (hereafter cited as VF, GNMP Library); Unrau, *Administrative History*, 41; *An Act to Establish a National Military Park at Gettysburg, Pennsylvania*, 28 Stat. 651, approved February 11, 1895 Gettysburg National Park Commission, "Office of the Commissioners, Record Books of Legislation, 1873–1921," Box 6, Gettysburg National Park Commission, (GETT 41122), Records of the Gettysburg National Park Commission, Gettysburg National Military Park Archives [hereafter cited as (GETT 41122), GNMP Archives]; Weeks, *Gettysburg*, 194.

6. Superintendent John Latschar, "Superintendent's Annual Report, 2001," 3–4; Superintendent John Latschar, "Superintendent's Annual Report, 2002," 5 [Superintendent John Latschar's annual reports from 1995 through 2003 can be found in Box 3, A26, (Unprocessed Central Files, 1987–present), GNMP Archives, while reports from 2004 to 2009 are filed in the Contemporary Administrative Files, GNMP. All references hereafter to Latschar's annual will only be cited by the year's report and page number]; FNPG, "Annual Report, 2001–2002." Folder 5, Box 12, A42, (Unprocessed Central Files, 1987–present), Records of the National Park Service at Gettysburg National Military Park, Gettysburg National Military Park Archives [Files from this collection have not yet been processed and all notes hereafter will be cited by Box, File Code, (Unprocessed Central Files, 1987–present), GNMP Archives].

7. Eric Campbell, "An Interpreter's View of the Codori-Trostle Thicket Project," FNPG Newsletter, Spring 2002, 3.

8. Barry Dusel email to Superintendent John Latschar, March 22, 2002, Folder 43, Box 26, (Unprocessed Central Files, 1987–present), GNMP Archives; Arthur House, "Letter to the Editor," *Gettysburg Times*, June 22, 2005. These appropriations include: $300,000 in 2003; $300,000 in 2004; $300,000 in 2005; $200,000 in 2006; nothing in 2007; $200,000 in 2008; and $200,000 in 2009. These figures are obtained from Latschar's annual reports.

9. Superintendent John Latschar, "Superintendent's Annual Report, 2003," 3; Superintendent John Latschar, "Superintendent's Annual Report, 2004," 4; Superintendent John Latschar, "Superintendent's Annual Report, 2007," 3.

10. Superintendent John Latschar, "Superintendent's Annual Report, 2004," 4–6; Superintendent John Latschar, "Superintendent's Annual Report, 2005," 4–5; Superintendent John Latschar, "Superintendent's Annual Report, 2006," 3; Superintendent John Latschar, "Superintendent's Annual Report, 2007," 3.

11. Superintendent John Latschar, "Superintendent's Annual Report, 2009," 8–10.

12. Superintendent John Latschar, "Superintendent's Annual Report, 2007," 3; *Chickamauga Battlefield: Chickamauga and Chattanooga National Military Park, Cultural Landscape Report*, September 2004, prepared by John Milner Associates. This publication is available online at http://www.nps.gov/history/history/online_books/chch1/clr.pdf; James Ogden, Senior Historian, Chickamauga & Chattanooga NMP, interview by author, 25 February 2010; *Vicksburg National Military Park, Environmental Assessment for Landscape Rehabilitation, Statement of Findings for Executive Order 11990, (Protection of Wetlands)*, prepared for the National Park Service by MACTEC Engineering and Consulting, August 3, 2009, available online at http://www.nps.gov/vick/parkmgmt/upload/CLR-EA%20Wetlands%20Statement-of-Findings%20-%20Final.pdf.

13. Martha Temkin, "Freeze-Frame, September 17, 1862: A Preservation Battle at Antietam National Battlefield Park," in *Myth, Memory, and the Making of the American Landscape*, ed. Paul A. Shackel (Gainesville: Univ. Press of Florida, 2001), 123–39.

14. Superintendent John Latschar, "Superintendent's Annual Report, 2001," 7–8; Superintendent John Latschar, "Superintendent's Annual Report, 2005," 9; Superintendent John Latschar, "Superintendent's Annual Report, 2006," 6; FNPG, Board of Directors Meeting Minutes, January 18–19, 2002, Folder FNPG, October 2001–September 2002, Box 12, A42, (Unprocessed Central Files, 1987–present), GNMP Archives; FNPG, Newsletter, Spring 2002; "FNPG and Park Complete First Shot Property Acquisition," FNPG, Newsletter, Fall 2002, 4; Superintendent John Latschar, "Superintendent's Annual Report, 2003," 7.

15. Superintendent John Latschar, "Superintendent's Annual Report, 2005," 11. Approximately 10 percent of park visitors (1,779,999 during the 2005 calendar year) attended a ranger program. The "real-time" programs, generally lasting forty minutes, were set up so that visitors could follow their progression throughout the day. For example, at 7:30 AM on July 1 a ranger (at the West End Guide Station) presented a discussion of the opening shots of the battle. Visitors then drove to the Peace Light for a discussion of the morning phase of the battle.

16. David Glassberg, *Sense of History: The Place of the Past in the American Life* (Amherst: Univ. of Massachusetts Press, 2001), 6–7; John B. Gatewood and Catherine M. Cameron, "Battlefield Pilgrims at Gettysburg National Military Park," *Ethnology*, 43 (Summer 2004): 193–216; NPS Press Release, "The Battle of Little Round Top: Free Podcast Available From Gettysburg National Military Park," 21 February 2007, Folder 2007, K34, Contemporary Administrative Files, Gettysburg National Military Park (hereafter cited as Contemporary Administrative Files, GNMP). Park Ranger Eric Campbell, for example, developed the fifty-three minute podcast for Little Round Top.

17. *GMP*, vol. 1, 93–94; Superintendent John Latschar, "Superintendent's Annual Report, 2004," 5; Superintendent John Latschar, "Superintendent's Annual Report, 2005," 6; Superintendent John Latschar, "Superintendent's Annual Report, 2008," 6, 11. Senator Rick Santorum offered the opening remarks. FNPG, Board of Directors Meeting Minutes, May 17–18, 2002, Folder FNPG October 2001–September 2002, Box 12, A42, (Unprocessed Central Files, 1987–present), GNMP Archives.

18. Superintendent John Latschar, "Superintendent's Annual Report, 2008," 1–2.

19. Superintendent John Latschar to James McPherson, February 28, 2000, Folder 12, Box 21, A82, (Unprocessed Central Files, 1987–present), GNMP Archives; Memo, n.d., Folder Holt, Box 16, A7221, (Unprocessed Central Files, 1987–present), GNMP Archives; Superintendent John Latschar, "Superintendent's Annual Report, 2001," 1–2. These eleven galleries include: 1) Impact of War: In a Larger Sense; 2) Causes of War, 1776–1861: Conceived in Liberty?; 3) Approach to War: A New Nation; 4) Civil War, 1861–1863: Now We Are Engaged in a Great Civil War; 5) Campaign to Gettysburg: Testing Whether That Nation Can Long Endure; 6) Battle of Gettysburg: Now We Are Met on a Great Battlefield of That War; 7) Aftermath: The Brave Men, Living and Dead; 8) Gettysburg Address: A New Birth of Freedom; 9) Civil War, 1863–1865: A Great Task Remaining Before Us; 10) Results of War: That These Dead Shall Not Have Died in Vain; and 11) Preservation of the Battlefield: Never Forget What They Did Here. In addition to the eleven galleries, park planners added a twelfth for special exhibits from the Gilder Lehrman Institute.

20. Peter Jorgensen, "Paging Thru: The New Gettysburg Museum and Visitor Center," *Civil War News*, July 2008; Bill Hallet comment, March 7, 2009, on "Ratings of a Civil War Historian" blog (Eric Wittenburg), accessible at www.civilwarcavalary.com, accessed March 2010.

21. Pitcaithley, "'A Cosmic Threat,'" 175; *GMP*, vol. 1, 90. More information on this organization can be found at www.savetheelectricmap.com, accessed March 1, 2010. The top layer of the map is infested with asbestos.

22. Jeffery Bender to Superintendent John Latschar, email, September 11, 2008, Folder 2, Public Comments on the Fee Proposal, A22, Contemporary Administrative Records, GNMP; Conrad Richter to Superintendent John Latschar, email, September 27, 2008, Folder 5, Public Comments on the Fee Proposal, A22,

Contemporary Administrative Records, GNMP; Terry Klima to Superintendent
John Latschar, email, August 31, 2008, Folder 1, Public Comments on the Fee
Proposal, A22, Contemporary Administrative Records, GNMP.

23. Superintendent John Latschar, "Superintendent's Annual Report, 2009," 1; F.
Zech to Superintendent John Latschar, August 31, 2008 Folder 1, A22, Con-
temporary Administrative Records, GNMP; Superintendent John Latschar,
"Superintendent's Annual Report, 2006," 3; NPS Press Release, "Gettysburg
Museum Fee Proposal Released for Public Comment," August 28, 2008, Folder
Public Comments on the Fee Proposal, A22, Contemporary Administrative
Records, GNMP; Superintendent John Latschar, "Superintendent's Annual
Report, 2007," 14–15. Using the 33 percent projections, this meant that the theater
fell $1,784,780 short of projections on an annual basis. Partners believed that the
pro forma budget could be obtained if 33 percent of the visitors paid for the film,
but evidently the majority of visitors entering the building were not interested in
viewing the film or believed that the $7.00 admission fee too high for twenty-
two-minute introductory film.

24. NPS Press Release, "Gettysburg Museum Fee Proposal Released for Public
Comment," August 28, 2008; "National Park Service and Gettysburg Founda-
tion Proposal to Amend the Fee Structure at the Gettysburg National Military
Park Museum and Visitor Center, Gettysburg, Pennsylvania," both in Folder
Public Comments on the Fee Proposal, A22, Contemporary Administrative
Records, GNMP; Rebecca Yost to Superintendent John Latschar, email, Sep-
tember 29, 2008, Folder 6, Public Comments on the Fee Proposal, A22, Contem-
porary Administrative Records, GNMP; *GMP*, vol. 1, 90; Michael Alderstein to
Director Robert Stanton, October 13, 1997, *GMP*, vol. 1, 363–76; Director Robert
Stanton to Randy Harper, February 6, 1998, *GMP*, vol. 1, 393–405.

25. Robert Blama to Superintendent John Latschar, September 19, 2008, Folder 4;
Tom Vossler to Superintendent John Latschar, email, September 11, 2008, Folder
3; Michael Vice to Superintendent John Latschar, email, September 16, 2008,
Folder 4; Joe Wurzer to Superintendent John Latschar, email, Septem-
ber 29, 2008, Folder 1; Kathy Harrison to Superintendent John Latschar, Sep-
tember 25, 2008, Folder 5, all in Public Comments on the Fee Proposal, A22,
Contemporary Administrative Records, GNMP; Superintendent John Latschar,
"Superintendent's Annual Report, 2008," 3; Scot Andrew Pitzer, "It's Official:
Museum Fee Takes Effect Today," *Gettysburg Times*, October 2, 2008; Rebecca
Yost to Superintendent John Latschar, email, September 29, 2008, Folder 6;
Carol Hegeman to Superintendent John Latschar, email, September 25, 2008;
Karla Flook to Superintendent John Latschar, email, September 22, 2008, all
in Public Comments on the Fee Proposal, A22, Contemporary Administrative
Records, GNMP.

26. Scot Andrew Pitzer, "Civil War Celebration," *Gettysburg Times*, September 27,
2008; "Gettysburg National Military Park Museum and Visitor Center: Grand
Opening Celebration Event Schedule," September 26–28, 2008, in possession of

the author; Edward Rothstein, "Renewed Vantage at Center of Battle," *New York Times*, September 25, 2008, B1.

27. Superintendent John Latschar, "Superintendent's Annual Report, 2004," 2–3; Superintendent John Latschar, "Superintendent's Annual Report, 2005," 1; "Cyclorama Center Will Close in November," *Hanover Evening Sun*, September 28, 2005; Superintendent John Latschar, "Superintendent's Annual Report, 2006," 1; "The Gettysburg Cyclorama," GNMP, available online at http://www.nps.gov/gett/historyculture/gettysburg-cyclorama.htm; Gettysburg Foundation, "About the Conservation of the Gettysburg Cyclorama Painting," in author's possession; Gettysburg Foundation, "David Olin," in author's possession; Statement of Robert Wilburn, President, Gettysburg National Battlefield Museum Foundation, House Subcommittee on National Parks and Public Lands, *The Future Visitor's Center at Gettysburg National Military Park and the Associated Fundraising Efforts*, 107th Cong., 2d sess., March 21, 2002, 23; Superintendent John Latschar, "Superintendent's Annual Report, 2002," 2–3; Superintendent John Latschar, "Superintendent's Annual Report, 2003," 1–2. After its hey-day of display, the painting was shuffled from owner to owner and survived several fires, water damage, and improper display, all of which resulted in a damaging effect. Moreover, while in storage during the early twentieth century, the top section, termed the sky section, had been removed. As noted, the NPS performed limited conservation on the painting in 1962. In June 2002, the Foundation selected the consortium team of Perry Huston & Associates, of Fort Worth, Texas, and Olin Conservation, Inc., of Great Falls, Virginia. Both firms brought a wealth of experience and qualifications. Huston's firm notably had assisted in the restoration of the Atlanta Cyclorama. David Olin, Chief Conservator of Olin Conservation, had worked on murals in the U.S. National Archives, the U.S. Capitol, and the Department of Justice.

28. Scot Andrew Pitzer, "Restoration Contract Awarded for Ziegler's Grove Project," *Gettysburg Times*, February 27, 2009; Superintendent John Latschar, "Superintendent's Annual Report, 2009," 7. After the Recent Past Preservation Network sued the NPS, both agencies filed motions and countermotions before the case was heard before the U.S. District Court in Washington, D.C., on October 20, 2008. On March 23, 2008, a magistrate judge submitted his recommendations to the district judge for final ruling. The magistrate judge found that the NPS complied with the National Historic Preservation Act, but ruled in favor of the plaintiff that the agency had not adequately explored environmental impacts of the demolition of the cyclorama building. On April 23, 2008, on behalf of the NPS, the Department of Justice filed an objection to the magistrate's ruling, and thereafter the plaintiff also filed objections. The Park Service proceeded to prepare an Environmental Assessment plan to review four alternatives for the building. The four alternatives include: keeping the cyclorama building in its current, unoccupied state in Ziegler's Grove and "mothballing" it; allowing another group to reuse the building on its current location; allowing another

group to remove the building to another location; or demolishing the building and rehabilitating the area to its 1863 condition.

29. Superintendent John Latschar, "Superintendent's Annual Report, 2009," 2–3.

30. Superintendent John Latschar, "Superintendent's Annual Report, 2009," 30–32. In December 2008, Latschar received the Stephen Mather award from the National Parks Conservation Association, awarded annually for superior work in the stewardship of National Park resources. That same year, he also received the National Park Service Preservationist of the Year Award from the Civil War Preservation Trust and the Honor Award from the National Trust for Historic Preservation. In 2008, Latschar also received the Stephen Mather award and, in 2005, he received the Man of the Year Award from the New Jersey Civil War Round Table. The Northeast Region named Latschar Superintendent of the Year for Natural Resource Stewardship in 2004 for his work in landscape rehabilitation. In 2001, Latschar received the Northeast Region Superintendent of the Year Award (he also won his award in 1991 for his work at Steamtown National Historic Site). Regional Director Marie Rust lauded Latschar's work in landscape rehabilitation and forming the partnership with the Foundation to provide for a new museum. In 2000, he received the Northeast Regional award for Outstanding Performance by a Superintendent in Planning, for his work in developing the *General Management Plan*. The NPS Director also awarded Latschar the Cultural Resources award in 2000.

31. Glassberg, "Sense of History," 6–7.

Conclusion

1. Superintendent John Latschar, "Superintendent's Annual Report, 2009," 8–10.

2. "Department of the Interior FY 2000 Appropriations: Joint Explanatory Statement of the Committee of the Conference," Title I, U.S. Congress 1999, 96; Pitcaithley, "'A Cosmic Threat'," 175.

3. Other prior assignments include: Chief of Interpretation at Lowell National Historical Park, Lowell, Mass., 1990–1995; Environmental Protection Specialist, Defense Logistics Agency, Ogden, Utah, 1986–1990; and Outdoor Recreation Director for the Department of the Army in West Germany, 1983–1986. He also worked as an interpretative ranger at Golden Gate National Recreation Area in San Francisco from 1974–1983. Kirby has a Bachelor of Arts degree in recreation and leisure studies and a Master of Science degree in recreation and park management from San Francisco State University.

4. Gettysburg Foundation Press Release, "The Gettysburg Foundation Announces the Departure of its President," January 26, 2010; Gettysburg Foundation Press Release, "The Gettysburg Foundation Names New President," November 29, 2010, all in Contemporary Administrative Files, Gettysburg National Military Park (hereafter cited as CF, GNMP). A rear admiral, Buchanan served as vice president of corporate services for First National Bank of Omaha and as president of the Midlands Venture Forum in Nebraska and Iowa.

5. Superintendent John Latschar, "Superintendent's Annual Report, 2009," 29.

6. Superintendent John Latschar, "Superintendent's Annual Report, 2009," 29–30; "Lincoln Scholar: 'Wiser Bobble Heads Prevailed,'" *Gettysburg Times*, March 12, 2012.

7. James Campi, et al., to David LeVan, January 26, 2010. Letter available online at http://www.civilwar.org/aboutus/news/news-releases/2010-news/assets/le-van-casino-letter.pdf (accessed on March 5, 2010). For more information on "No Casino" visit www.nocasinogettysburg.org. At this time LeVan does not own the Eisenhower Conference Center, but has secured an option to purchase the property. He maintains that he will not purchase the property unless he can obtain the gaming license.

8. Doris Kearns Goodwin, 30 June 2013. Keynote address available at http://www. c-spanvideo.org/program/Commemorativ; Tony Lee, "Doris Kearns Goodwin at Gettysburg: A Few Inappropriate Remarks," 1 July 2013. Available online at http://www.breitbart.com/Big-Journalism/2013/07/01/Doris-Kearns-Goodwin-A-Few-Inappropriate-Remarks-At-Gettysburg; Marc Charisse, "Historian Goodwin Got It Right," *The Evening Sun*, 2 July 2013.

9. "Gettysburg: 150th Anniversary, Commemorative Events Guide," Gettysburg Foundation and the National Park Service; D. Scott Hartwig, "Interpretive Operations Gettysburg 150th Statistics Report," July 5, 2013. Possession of the author.

10. David McConaughy to Hon. Jos. R. Ingersoll, August 19, 1863, Vertical Files, 11–29B, Gettysburg National Military Park Library; An Act To Establish A National Military Park at Gettysburg, Pennsylvania, Approved February 11, 1895 (28 Stat. 651); "Circular No. 1," January 24, 1935, by James McConaghie, Folder 10, Box 18, Park Main (Central) Files, 1933–1954, (GETT 41113), Records of the National Park Service at Gettysburg National Military Park, Gettysburg National Military Park Archives.

11. "Coleman Tells Broad Policy on Battlefield," *Gettysburg Times*, April 9, 1941, Folder 2, Box 35, (GETT 43663), GNMP Archives; Quoted in Weeks, *Gettysburg*, 126.

12. Glassberg, *Sense of History*, 6–7.

13. Abraham Lincoln, "Second Inaugural," March 4, 1864, available at www.avalon. law.yale.edu/19thcentury/lincoln2.asp; Kammen, "Mystic Chords of Memory," 626; Glassberg, "Sense of History," 6–7.

BIBLIOGRAPHY

Unpublished Primary Sources

Gettysburg National Military Park Archives:

Annual Reports, 1893–1921, (GETT 41148), Records of the National Park Commission.

Cyclorama Building Records, Series I and II, (GETT 41097), Records of the National Park Service at Gettysburg National Military Park.

Daily Journals, 1893–1921, (GETT 41144), Records of the National Park Commission.

General Management Plan Records, 1968–1983, (GETT 41105), Records of the National Park Service at Gettysburg National Military Park.

General Management Plan, Environmental Impact Assessment, 1996–1998. Records of the National Park Service at Gettysburg National Military Park.

General Records, 1922–1933, (GETT 41155), U.S. War Department, Office of the Quartermaster General.

Engineer's Annual Reports, 1893–1921, (GETT 41121), Records of the National Park Commission.

Historians' Files, 1933–1965, (GETT 41151), Records of the National Park Service at Gettysburg National Military Park.

Interpretive Program Files, 1930–present, (GETT 43970), Records of the National Park Service at Gettysburg National Military Park.

Newspaper Clippings, Unbound, (GETT 43663), Records of the National Park Service at Gettysburg National Military Park.

Park Main (Central) Files, 1933–1954, (GETT 41113), Records of the National Park Service at Gettysburg National Military Park.

Park Main (Central) Files, 1954–1987, (GETT 41160), Records of the National Park Service at Gettysburg National Military Park.

Park Main (Central) Files, 1987–present (Unprocessed), Records of the National Park Service at Gettysburg National Military Park.

Park Maps and Drawings, 1933–1960, (GETT 41107), Records of the National Park Service at Gettysburg National Military Park.

Record Books of Legislation, 1873–1921, (GETT 41122), Records of the National Park Commission.

Record Books of Testimony and Proceedings, 1893–1905, (GETT 41123), Records of the National Park Commission.

Thomas Harrison Files, Records of the National Park Service at Gettysburg National Military Park.

Unprocessed Collection, (GETT 41161), Records of the National Park Service at Gettysburg National Military Park.

Gettysburg National Military Park, Contemporary Files:
Cultural Resource Management Files
Friends of the National Parks at Gettysburg Newsletters
Gettysburg Foundation Newsletters
Public Comments on the Fee Proposal
Superintendent John Latschar's Annual Reports

Gettysburg National Military Park Library:
Vertical Files
Gettysburg National Tower Boxes

National Archives and Records Administration, College Park, Maryland:
Record Group 79, Records of the National Park Service, Central Classified File, 1933–1949.
Record Group 79, Records of the National Park Service, Administrative Files, 1949–1971.

National Archives and Records Administration, Northeast Region, Philadelphia, Pennsylvania:
Record Group 79, Records of the National Park Service, Northeast Regional Office, Historic Shrines, Sites, Monuments, and Parks, General Correspondence, 1952–1966.
Record Group 79, Records of the National Park Service, Northeast Regional Office, Historic Shrines, Sites, Monuments, and Parks, Historical Studies Files, 1952–1967.
Record Group 79, Records of the National Park Service, Northeast Regional Office, Historic Shrines, Sites, Monuments, and Parks, Subject Files, 1937–1957.

Documents in author's possession:
"About the Conservation of the Gettysburg Cyclorama Painting." Gettysburg Foundation.
"David Olin." Biography. Gettysburg Foundation.
"General Agreement Between Gettysburg National Military Park, National Park Service, and the Gettysburg National Battlefield Museum Foundation." Revised September 30, 2002.

"Gettysburg: 150th Anniversary, Commemorative Events Guide," Gettysburg Foundation and National Park Service.

"Grand Opening Celebration Event Schedule." September 26–28, 2008.

"Holding the High Ground: Principles and Strategies for Managing and Interpreting Civil War Battlefield Landscapes," Proceedings of a Conference of Battlefield Managers, Nashville, Tennessee, August 24–17, 1998.

"Interpretive Operations Gettysburg 150th Statistics Report," July 5, 2013, by D. Scott Hartwig.

"Report for the Organization of American Historians (OAH) and the National Park Service (NPS) on Gettysburg National Military Park. August 1998.

Published Primary Sources

Bachelder, John. *Gettysburg: What To See, And How To See It.* Boston: John B. Bachelder, 1873.

Beach, Warren. "Record of Decision on the White-Tailed Deer Management Plan Final Environmental Impact Statement for Gettysburg National Military Park/ Eisenhower National Historic Site, Pennsylvania." July 5, 1995. www.epa.gov/ EPA-IMPACT/1995/July/Day-13/pr-1083.html.

Fiftieth Anniversary of the Battle of Gettysburg, Report of the Pennsylvania Commission. Harrisburg: W. M. Stanley Ray, 1914.

Gettysburg-Adams County Area Chamber of Commerce. *Economic Impact Studies.*

Gettysburg Cyclorama Building, Historic American Buildings Survey, HABS-PA-6709. www.memory/loc/gov/habshaer/pa/pa3900/pa3988/data/pa3988.pdf.

Gettysburg National Military Park Commission, *Annual Reports to the Secretary of War, 1893–1901.* Washington: Government Printing Office, 1902.

Gettysburg National Military Park National Register Documentation, Adams County, PA, (NRIS 66000642), National Register of Historic Places, Washington, DC, January 23, 2004.

Minnigh, Luther W. *Gettysburg: What They Did Here.* Tipton and Blocher, 1924.

Roy, Paul L. *Last Reunion of the Blue and Gray.* Gettysburg: Paul Roy, 1950.

U.S. Congress. House. Committee on Government Operations. *Land Exchange Between National Park Service/Gettysburg National Military Park and Gettysburg College.* 103rd Cong., 2d sess., May 9, 1994.

U.S. Congress. House. Subcommittee on National Parks and Public Lands of the Committee on Resources. *Oversight Hearing on Gettysburg National Military Park General Management Plan and Proposed Visitors Center.* 106th Cong., 1st sess., February 11, 1999.

U.S. Congress. House. Subcommittee on National Parks and Public Lands. *The Future Visitor's Center at Gettysburg National Military Park and the Associated Fundraising Efforts.* 107th Cong., 2d sess., March 21, 2002.

United States Department of the Interior. *Boundary Study, Gettysburg National Military Park: Draft Report to Congress, Environmental Assessment.* United States Department of the Interior: National Park Service, August 1988.

United States Department of the Interior. *Draft Development Concept Plan, Environmental Assessment: Collections Storage, Visitor and Museum Facilities.* Gettysburg: National Park Service, Gettysburg National Military Park, April 1996.

United States Department of the Interior. *Draft Development Concept Plan, Environmental Assessment: Gettysburg Museum of the Civil War.* Gettysburg: National Park Service, Gettysburg National Military Park, April 1995.

United States Department of the Interior. *Development Concept Plan, Little Round Top/Devil's Den, Gettysburg National Military Park, Pennsylvania.* United States Department of the Interior: National Park Service, 1986.

United States Department of the Interior. *Draft Development Concept Plan/Environmental Assessment, Little Round Top/Devil's Den, Gettysburg National Military Park, Pennsylvania.* United States Department of the Interior: National Park Service, May 1985.

United States Department of the Interior. *Draft Development Concept Plan/Environmental Assessment Supplement, Little Round Top/Devil's Den, Gettysburg National Military Park, Pennsylvania.* United States Department of the Interior: National Park Service, May 1986.

United States Department of the Interior. *Draft Environmental Impact Statement, White-Tailed Deer Management Plan.* Gettysburg: National Park Service, Gettysburg National Military Park, November 1994.

United States Department of the Interior. *Draft General Management Plan, Gettysburg National Military Park and National Cemetery.* United States Department of the Interior: National Park Service, May 1977.

United States Department of the Interior. *Draft General Management Plan and Environmental Impact Statement, Gettysburg National Military Park and National Cemetery.* United States Department of the Interior: National Park Service, August 1998.

United States Department of the Interior. *Final Environmental Impact Statement, White-Tailed Deer Management Plan.* Gettysburg: National Park Service, Gettysburg National Military Park, May 1995.

United States Department of the Interior. *Final General Management Plan and Environmental Statement, Gettysburg National Military Park.* 2 vols. United States Department of the Interior: National Park Service, June 1999.

United States Department of the Interior. *Final Report: Gettysburg College-National Park Service Land Exchange, Study of Alternatives/Environmental Assessment.* Gettysburg: National Park Service, Gettysburg National Military Park, May 1995.

United States Department of the Interior. *General Management Plan, Gettysburg National Military Park and National Cemetery.* United States Department of the Interior: Mid-Atlantic Regional Office, December 1982.

United States Department of the Interior. *Land Protection Plan.* Gettysburg: National Park Service, Gettysburg National Military Park, October 1993.

United States Department of the Interior. *National Tower Demolition and Removal Environmental Assessment, Draft.* Gettysburg: National Park Service, Gettysburg National Military Park, May 2000.

United States Department of the Interior. *Request for Proposals: Visitor Center &*
Museum Facilities, Gettysburg National Military Park. Gettysburg: National Park
Service, Gettysburg National Military Park, December 1996.

United States Department of the Interior. Secretary of the Interior's Standards for
the Treatment of Historic Properties With Guidelines for the Treatment of
Cultural Landscapes. 1992.

Vanderslice, John. *Gettysburg: A History of the Gettysburg Battle-Field Memorial Associ-*
ation With An Account of the Battle. Philadelphia: The Association, 1897.

————. *Gettysburg Then and Now: The Field of American Valor, Where and How The*
Regiments Fought, And The Troops They Encountered, An Account of the Battle, Giv-
ing Movements, Positions, and Losses of the Commands Engaged. New York: G.W.
Dillingham, 1899.

Newspapers and Magazines

Chattanooga (Tenn.) Daily Times
Civil War Courier
Civil War News
Civil War Times Illustrated
Chicago Tribune
Detroit (Mich.)Free Press
Gettysburg (Pa.) Compiler
Gettysburg (Pa.) Times
Hanover (Pa.) Evening Sun
Harrisburg (Pa.) Patriot News
New York Times
Philadelphia (Pa.) Inquirer
Reading (Pa.) Eagle
Record Harold (Waynesboro, Pa.)
Regional View, National Park Service publication
Rochester (N.Y.) Democrat
Saturday Evening Post
Sunday News (Lancaster, Pa.)
Star Magazine
Star & Sentinel (Gettysburg, Pa.)
Patriot (Harrisburg, Pa.)
Plain Dealer (Cleveland, Ohio)
USA Today
Wall Street Journal
Washington Post
York (Pa.) Daily Record
York (Pa.) Dispatch
York (Pa.) Sunday News

Interviews by Author

Latschar, John. Interview by author, January 4, 2010.
Harrison, Kathy. Interview by author, February 15, 2009.
Marks, Jeff. Interview by author, February 16, 2010.
Nyeste, John. Interview by author, February 16, 2010.

Unpublished Secondary Sources

Engle, Reed. *Cultural Landscape Report: The Soldiers' National Cemetery Gettysburg, Pennsylvania, 1994.* Uncataloged report, Gettysburg National Military Park, GNMP Archives.
LaFantasie, Glenn W. "Terrain and the Battlefield as Artifacts: History and Preservation at Gettysburg National Battlefield Park." Presented at AHA.
Lee, Ronald F. "The Origin and Evolution of the National Military Park Idea." Office of Historic Preservation, Washington, D.C.: Department of the Interior, National Park Service, 1973, Gettysburg National Military Park Library.

Published Secondary Sources

Books:
Allaback, Sara. "Mission 66 Visitor Centers: The History of a Building Type," 2000. www.nps.gov/history/history/online_books/allaback.
Badger, Anthony. *The New Deal: The Depression Years, 1933–1940.* Chicago: Ivan R. Dee, 1980.
Belasco, Warren James. *Americans on the Road: From Autocamp to Motel, 1910–1945.* Cambridge, Mass.: MIT Press, 1979.
Billinger, Robert. *Hitler's Soldiers in the Sunshine State.* Gainesville: University of Florida Press, 2000.
———. *Nazi Prisoners of War in the Tar Heel State.* Gainesville: University of Florida Press, 2008.
Blair, William. *Cities of the Dead: Contesting the Memory of the Civil War in the South, 1865–1914.* Chapel Hill: University of North Carolina Press, 2003.
Blight, David. *American Oracle: The Civil War in the Civil Rights Era.* Cambridge, Mass.: Harvard University Press, 2011.
———. *Race and Reunion: The Civil War in American Memory.* Cambridge, Mass.: Belknap Press, 2001.
Boardman, Sue, and Kathryn Porch. *The Battle of Gettysburg Cyclorama: A History and Guide.* Gettysburg: Thomas Publications, 2008.
Bodnar, John. *Remaking America: Public Memory, Commemoration, and Patriotism in the Twentieth Century.* Princeton, N.J.: Princeton University Press, 1992.
Boge, Georgie, and Margie Holder Boge. *Paving Over the Past: A History and Guide to Civil War Battlefield Preservation.* Washington, D.C.: Island Press, 1993.
Boritt, Gabor. *The Gettysburg Gospel: The Lincoln Speech That Nobody Knows.* New York: Simon & Schuster, 2006.

Branch, Taylor. *Parting The Waters: America in the King Years, 1954–1963.* New York: Simon & Schuster, 1988.

———. *Pillar of Fire: America in the King Years, 1963–1965.* New York: Simon & Schuster, 1998.

Brewer, Susan. *Why America Fights: Patriotism and Propaganda from the Philippines to Iraq.* New York: Oxford University Press, 2009.

Broadwater, Jeff. *Adlai Stevenson and American Politics: The Odyssey of a Cold War Liberal.* New York: Twayne, 1994.

Carr, Ethan. *Mission 66: Modernism and the National Park Dilemma.* Amherst: University of Massachusetts Press, 2007.

Carter, Dan T. *From George Wallace to Newt Gingrich: Race and the Conservative Counterrevolution, 1963–1994.* Baton Rouge: Louisiana State University Press, 1996.

———. *Politics of Rage: George Wallace, the Origins of the New Conservatism, and the Transformation of American Politics.* Baton Rouge: Louisiana State University Press, 2000.

Coco, Gregory A. *A Strange and Blighted Land: Gettysburg, the Aftermath of the Battle.* Gettysburg: Thomas Publications, 1998.

Cole, Olen, Jr. *The African American Experience in the Civilian Conservation Corps.* Gainesville: University of Florida Press, 1999.

Connally, Eugenia Horstman, ed. *National Parks in Crisis.* Washington, D.C.: National Parks & Conservation Association, 1982.

Cook, Robert. *Troubled Commemoration: The American Civil War Centennial, 1961–1965.* Baton Rouge: Louisiana State University Press, 2007.

Davies, Richard. *Defender of the Old Guard: John Bricker and American Politics.* Columbus: Ohio State University Press, 1993.

Desjardin, Thomas A. *These Honored Dead: How The Story of Gettysburg Shaped American Memory.* Cambridge, Mass.: Da Capo Press, 2003.

Drexler, Arthur, and Thomas S. Hines. *The Architecture of Richard Neutra: From International Style to California Modern.* New York: Museum of Modern Art, 1982.

Everhart, William C. *The National Park Service.* Boulder, Colo.: Westview Press, 1983.

Faust, Drew Gilpin. *This Republic of Suffering: Death and the American Civil War.* New York: Alfred A. Knopf, 2008

Fiedler, David. *The Enemy Among Us: POWs in Missouri During World War II.* St. Louis: University of Missouri Press, 2003.

Finfrock, Barbara J. *Twenty Years On Six Thousand Acres: The History of the Friends of the National Parks at Gettysburg.* Harrisburg, Pa.: Huggins Printing, 2009.

Foner, Eric. *Who Owns History: Rethinking the Past in a Changing World.* New York: Hill and Wang, 2002.

Foote, Kenneth E. *Shadowed Ground: America's Landscapes of Violence and Tragedy.* Austin: University of Texas Press, 2003.

Foresta, Ronald A. *America's National Parks and Their Keepers.* Washington, D.C.: Resources For The Future, 1984.

Foster, Gaines. *Ghosts of the Confederacy: Defeat, the Lost Cause, and the Emergence of the New South, 1865–1913.* New York: Oxford University Press, 1988.

Fried, John. *The Russians Are Coming! The Russians Are Coming! Pageantry and Patriotism In Cold-War America*. New York: Oxford University Press, 1998.

Freeman, Douglas Southall. *Lee's Lieutenants: A Study in Command*. 3 vols. New York: Scribner Sons, 1942–44.

———. *R. E. Lee: A Biography*. 4 vols. New York: Scribner Sons, 1934.

Fussell, Paul. *The Great War and Modern Memory*. New York: Oxford University Press, 1975.

Gannon, Barbara. *The Won Cause: Black and White Comradeship in the Grand Army of the Republic*. Chapel Hill: University of North Carolina Press, 2011.

Glassberg, David. *Sense of History: The Place of the Past in American Life*. Amherst: University of Massachusetts Press, 2001.

Grant, Susan Mary, and Peter J. Parish, eds. *Legacy of Disunion: The Enduring Significance of the American Civil War*. Baton Rouge: Louisiana State University Press, 2003.

Grimsley, Mark C. *The Hard Hand of War: Union Military Policy toward Souther Civilians*. New York: Cambridge University Press, 1995.

Grover, Kathyrn. *Hard at Play: Leisure in America, 1840–1940*. Amherst: University of Massachusetts Press, 1992.

Handler, Richard, and Eric Gable. *The New History in an Old Museum: Creating the Past at Colonial Williamsburg*. Durham, N.C.: Duke University Press, 1997.

Harrison, Blake. *The View From Vermont: Tourism and the Making of an American Rural Landscape*. Burlington: University of Vermont Press, 2006.

Hattaway, Herman. *Gettysburg to Vicksburg: The Five Original Civil War Battlefield Parks*. Kansas City: University of Missouri Press, 2001.

Hines, Thomas S. *Richard Neutra and the Search for Modern Architecture*. New York: Oxford University Press, 1982.

Horton, James Oliver, and Lois E. Horton, eds. *Slavery and Public History: The Tough Stuff of American Memory*. Chapel Hill: University of North Carolina Press, 2006.

Hosmer, Charles, Jr. *Preservation Comes of Age: From Williamsburg to the National Trust*. Vol. 1. Charlottesville: University of Virginia Press, 1981.

Ise, John. *Our National Park Policy: A Critical History*. Baltimore: John Hopkins Press, 1961.

Jakle, John A. *The Tourist: Travel in the Twentieth-Century*. Lincoln: University of Nebraska Press, 1985.

Kammen, Michael. *Mystic Chords of Memory: The Transformation of Tradition in American Culture*. New York: Alfred A. Knopf, 1991.

Kennedy, David M. *Freedom From Fear: The American People in the Depression and War, 1929–1945*. New York: Oxford University Press, 1999.

Kirk, Russell. *The Political Principles of Robert A. Taft*. New York: Fleet Press Corp, 1967.

Krammer, Arnold. *Nazi Prisoners of War in America*. New York: Stein and Day, 1979.

Lamme, Ary J., III. *America's Historic Landscapes: Community Power and the Preservation of Four Historic Sites*. Knoxville: University of Tennessee, 1990.

Leuchtenburg, William E. *Franklin D. Roosevelt and the New Deal*. New York: Harper & Row, 1963.

Lesher, Stephan. *George Wallace: American Populist.* New York: Da Capo Press, 1995.

Levin, Kevin. *Remembering the Battle of the Crater: War As Murder.* Lexington: University of Kentucky Press, 2012.

Linenthal, Edward Tabor. *Preserving Memory: The Struggle to Create America's Holocaust Museum.* New York: Viking Press, 1995.

———. *Sacred Ground: Americans and Their Battlefields.* Urbana: University of Illinois Press, 1991.

———. *The Unfinished Bombing: Oklahoma City in American Memory.* Oxford: Oxford University Press, 2001.

Linenthal, Edward, and Tom Engelhardt. *Enola Gay and Other Battles for the American Past.* New York: Metropolitan Books, 1996.

MACTEC Engineering and Consulting. *Vicksburg National Military Park, Environmental Assessment for Landscape Rehabilitation, Statement of Findings for Executive Order 119900 (Protection of Wetlands).* August 3, 2009. www.nps.gov/vick/parkmgmt/upload/CRL-EA%20Wetlands%20Statement-of-Findings%20-%20-Final.pdf.

MacCannell, Dean. *The Tourist: A New Theory of the Leisure Class.* Berkley: University of Carolina Press, 1999.

Mackintosh, Barry. "Interpretation in the National Park Service: A Historical Perspective." Washington, D.C.: National Park Service, Department of the Interior, 1986. www.nps.gov/history/history/online_books/mackintosh3/index.htm.

May, Elaine Tyler. *Homeward Bound: American Families in the Cold War.* New York: Basic Books, 1998.

McKeever, Porter. *Adlai Stevenson: His Life and Legacy.* New York: Morrow, 1989.

Martin, Edward. *Always Be On Time: An Autobiography.* Harrisburg: Telegraph Press, 1959.

Mayo, James M. *War Memorials as Political Landscape: The American Experience and Beyond.* New York: Praeger Press, 1988.

Miles, John C. *Guardians of the Parks: A History of the National Parks and Conservation Association.* Washington, D.C.: Taylor and Francis, 1995.

Milner, John, and Associates. *Chickamauga Battlefield: Chickamauga and Chattanooga National Military Park, Cultural Landscape Report.* September 2004. www.nps.gov/history/history/online_books/chch1/clr.pdf.

Moore, John Hammond. *The Faustball Tunnel: German POWs in America and Their Great Escape.* New York: Random House, 1978.

Moyer, Teresa S., and Paul A. Shackel. *The Making of Harper's Ferry National Historical Park: A Devil, Two Rivers, and a Dream.* Lanham, Md.: AltaMira Press, 2008.

Neutra, Richard. *Life and Shape.* New York: Appleton-Century-Crofts, 1962.

Paige, John C. *The Civilian Conservation Corps and the National Park Service, 1933–1942: An Administrative History.* Department of the Interior, National Park Service, 1985. www.nps.gov/history/history/online_books/ccc.index.htm.

Paige, John C., and Jerome A. Greene. *Administrative History of Chickamauga and Chattanooga National Military Park.* Denver: Denver Service Center, National Park Service. February 1983. www.nps.gov/archive/chch/adhi/adhi.htm.

Patterson, James T. *Mr. Republican: A Biography of Robert Taft.* Boston: Houghton Mifflin, 1972.

Patterson, John S. "From Battle Ground to Pleasure Ground: Gettysburg as a Historic Site." In *History Museums in the United States: A Critical Assessment,* edited by Warren Leon and Roy Rosenzweig, 128-157. Urbana: University of Illinois Press, 1989.

Peatman, Jared. *The Long Shadow of Lincoln's Gettysburg Address.* Carbondale: Southern Illinois Press, 2013.

Peterson, Merrill. *Lincoln in American Memory.* New York: Oxford University Press, 1994.

Pfanz, Harry W. *Gettysburg: The First Day.* Chapel Hill: University of North Carolina Press, 2001.

Piehler, G. Kurt. *Remembering War the American Way.* Washington: Smithsonian Institution Press, 1995.

Piston, William Garrett. *Lee's Tarnished Lieutenant: James Longstreet and His Place In Southern History.* Athens: University of Georgia Press, 1987.

Platt, Barbara L. *"This is Holy Ground": A History of the Gettysburg Battlefield.* Harrisburg: Huggins Printing, 2001.

Purcell, Sarah J. *Sealed With Blood: War, Sacrifice, and Memory in Revolutionary America.* Philadelphia: University of Pennsylvania Press, 2002.

Reardon, Carol. *Pickett's Charge in History and Memory.* Chapel Hill: University of North Carolina Press, 1997.

Richard King Mellon Foundation. *National Parks For A New Generation: Visions, Realities, Prospects.* Washington, D.C.: The Conservation Fund, 1985.

Rothman, Hal. *Devil's Bargains: Tourism and the Twentieth-Century American West.* Lawrence: University Press of Kansas, 1998.

———. *Preserving Different Pasts: The American National Monuments.* Urbana: University of Illinois Press, 1989.

Rugh, Susan Sessions. *Are We There Yet? The Golden Age of Family Vacations.* Lawrence: University of Kansas Press, 2008.

Runte, Alfred. *National Parks: The American Experience.* Lincoln: University of Nebraska Press, 1979.

Savage, Kirk. *Standing Soldiers, Kneeling Slaves: Race, War, and Monument in Nineteenth-Century America.* Princeton, N.J.: Princeton University Press, 1997.

Schmid, Walter. *A German POW in New Mexico.* Albuquerque: University of New Mexico Press, 2005.

Sellers, Richard West. *Preserving Nature in the National Parks.* New Haven, Conn.: Yale University Press, 1997.

Shackel, Paul A. *Memory in Black and White: Race, Commemoration, and the Post-Bellum Landscape.* Landam, Md.: AltaMira Press, 2003.

Shaffer, Marguerite S. *See America First: Tourism and National Identity, 1880–1940.* Washington, D.C.: Smithsonian Books, 2001.

Silber, Nina. *The Romance of Reunion: Northerners and the South, 1865–1900.* Chapel Hill: University of North Carolina Press, 1993.

Smith, Timothy. *The Untold Story of Shiloh: The Battle and the Battlefield.* Knoxville: University of Tennessee Press, 2006.

———. *The Golden Age of Battlefield Preservation: The Decade of the 1890s and the Establishment of America's First Give Military Parks.* Knoxville: University of Tennessee Press, 2008.

———. *This Great Battlefield of Shiloh: History, Memory, and the Establishment of a Civil War National Military Park.* Knoxville: University of Tennessee Press, 2006.

Snell, Charles W., and Sharon A. Brown. *Antietam National Battlefield and National Cemetery: An Administrative History.* Washington, D.C.: U.S. Department of the Interior, National Park Service, 1986.

Speakman, Joseph. *At Work in Penn's Woods: The Civilian Conservation Corps in Pennsylvania.* University Park: Pennsylvania State University Press, 2006.

Spielvogel, Christian. *Interpreting Sacred Ground: The Rhetoric of National Civil War Parks and Battlefields.* Tuscaloosa: University of Alabama Press, 2013.

Sutter, Paul. *Driven Wild: How The Fight Against Automobiles Launched the Modern Wilderness Movement.* Seattle: University of Washington Press, 2002.

Sutton, Robert K., ed. *Rally on the High Ground: The National Park Service Symposium on the Civil War.* Fort Washington, Pa.: Eastern National, 2001.

Tilden, Freedman. *Interpreting Our Heritage.* Chapel Hill: University of North Carolina Press, 1957.

———. *The National Parks.* New York: Alfred A. Knopf, 1976.

Trudeau, Noah Andre. *Gettysburg: A Testing of Courage.* New York: Harper Collins, 2002.

Toplin, Robert Brent, ed. *Ken Burns's The Civil War: Historians Respond.* Oxford: Oxford University Press, 1996.

Tyler, Norman. *Historic Preservation: An Introduction to Its History, Principles, and Practice* New York: W.W. Norton, 2000.

Unrau, Harlan D. *Administrative History: Gettysburg National Military Park and Gettysburg National Cemetery.* United States Department of Interior: National Park Service, 1991.

Waldrep, Christopher. *Vicksburg's Long Shadow: The Civil War Legacy of Race and Remembrance.* Lanham, Md.: Rowman & Littlefield Publishers, 2005.

Warren, Robert Penn. *The Legacy of the Civil War: Meditations on the Centennial.* New York: Random House, 1961.

Waters, Michael. *Lone Star Stalag: German Prisoners of War at Camp Hearne.* College Station: Texas A&M Press, 2004.

Wefing, John. *The Life and Times of Richard H. Hughes.* New Brunswick, N.J.: Rutgers University Press, 2009.

Weeks, Jim. *Gettysburg: Memory, Market, and an American Shrine.* Princeton, N.J.: Princeton University Press, 2003.

Westbrook, Robert B. *Why We Fought: Forging American Obligations in World War II.* Washington: Smithsonian Books, 2004.

Wert, Jeffery. *General James Longstreet: The Confederacy's Most Controversial Soldier.* New York: Simon & Schuster, 1993.

Whitfield, Stephen J. *The Culture of the Cold War.* Baltimore, Md.: The Johns Hopkins University Press, 1991.

Wills, Garry. *Lincoln at Gettysburg: The Words That Remade America.* New York: Simon & Schuster, 1992.

Wilson, Charles Reagan. *Baptized in Blood: The Religion of the Lost Cause, 1865–1920.* Athens: University of Georgia Press, 1983.

Winter, Jay. *Remembering War: The Great War Between Memory and History in the Twentieth Century.* New Haven, Conn.: Yale University Press, 2006.

———. *Sites of Memory, Sites of Mourning: The Great War in European Cultural History.* New Haven, Conn.: Yale University Press, 1998.

———. *The Experience of World War I.* New York: Oxford University Press, 1989.

———. *The Great War and the British People.* Cambridge, Mass.: Harvard University Press, 1986.

Winter, Jay, and Antoine Prost. *The Great War in History: Debates and Controversies, 1914 To the Present.* New York: Cambridge University Press, 2005.

Wirth, Conrad. *Parks, Politics, and the People.* Norman: University of Oklahoma Press, 1980.

Zenzen, Joan. *Battling for Manassas: The Fifty Year Preservation Struggle at Manassas National Battlefield Park.* State College: Pennsylvania State University Press, 1998.

Articles and Essays:

Andrews, John, and D. Scott Hartwig. "Cultural Landscape Management and Interpretation: A Dilemma." *Ranger: The Journal of the Association of National Park Rangers* 10 (Spring 1994): 14–16.

Bearss, Edwin C. "The National Park Service and Its History Program: 1864–1986, An Overview." *The Public Historian* 9 (Spring 1987): 10–18.

Birnbaum, Charles. "Preservation Brief 36: Protecting Cultural Landscapes, Planning, Treatment, and Management of Historic Landscapes." Washington, DC: NPS, 1994.

Cook, Robert. "Unfinished Business: African Americans and the Civil War Centennial." In *Legacy of Disunion: The Enduring Significance of the American Civil War,* edited by Susan Mary Grant and Peter J. Parish, 48-64. Baton Rouge: Louisiana State University Press, 2003.

———. "(Un)Furl That Banner: The Response of White Southerners to the Civil War Centennial of 1961–1965." *Journal of Southern History,* 68 (Nov. 2002): 879–912.

Franklin, John Hope. "A Century of Civil War Observance." *Journal of Negro History* 47 (April 1962): 97–107.

Gondos, Victor, Jr. "Karl Betts and the Civil War Centennial Commission." *Military Affairs* 27 (1963): 49–70.

Kinsel, Amy J. "From Turning Point to Peace Memorial: A Cultural Legacy." In *The Gettysburg Nobody Knows,* edited by Gabor S. Boritt, 203–22. New York: Oxford University Press, 1997.

Kohn, Richard H. "History at Risk: The Case of the *Enola Gay*." In *History Wars: The Enola Gay and Other Battles for the American Past*, edited by Edward Linenthal and Tom Englehardt, 140-170. New York: Henry Holt, 1996.

Latschar, John. "Gettysburg: The Next 100 Years." In *The Fourth Annual Seminar, Gettysburg 1895–1995: The Making of an American Shrine*. Gettysburg: Eastern National, 1995: 112–23.

———. "The Taking of the Gettysburg Tower." *George Wright Society* 18 (2001): 24–33.

Makintosh, Barry. "The National Park Service Moves into Historical Interpretation." *The Public Historian* 9 (Spring 1987): 51–63.

Murray, Jennifer. "'Far Above Our Poor Power to Add or Detract': National Park Service Administration of Gettysburg Battlefield, 1933–1938." *Civil War History* 55 (March 2009): 56–81.

Patterson, John S. "A Patriotic Landscape: Gettysburg, 1863–1913." *Prospects: An Annual of American Cultural Studies* 7 (1982): 315–33.

Pitcaithley, Dwight T. "'A Cosmic Threat': The National Park Service Addresses the Causes of the American Civil War." In *Slavery and Public History: The Tough Stuff of American Memory*, edited by James Oliver Horton and Lois. E. Horton, 169–86. Chapel Hill: University of North Carolina Press, 2006.

Pound, Edward T. "Battle Ground!" *National Journal* 21 (February 2009): 26–33.

Roe, Charles R. "The Second Battle of Gettysburg: Conflict of Public and Private Interests In Land Use Policies." *Environmental Affairs* 2 (Spring 1972): 16–64.

Rogers, Jerry R. "Fulfilling Its Mandate: The National Park Service and Historic Preservation." *The Public Historian* 9 (Spring 1987): 143–46.

Roth, Jeffery B. "Gettysburg National Military—Deer—Park." *Pennsylvania Wildlife* XI: 27–29.

Schaefer, Thomas. "If You Seek His Monument- Look Around: E. B. Cope and the Gettysburg National Military Park." In *Unsung Heroes of Gettysburg: Programs of the Fifth Annual Gettysburg Seminar*, 107–33. Gettysburg National Military Park, 1996.

Schwartz, Barry. "Memory as a Cultural System: Abraham Lincoln in World War II." *American Sociological Review* 61 (October 1996): 908–27.

———. "Rereading the Gettysburg Address: Social Change and Collective Memory." *Qualitative Sociology* 19 (1996): 395–422.

Smith, Karlton. "The Changing Faces of Gettysburg: The National Park Service at Gettysburg." In *Gettysburg 1895–1995: The Shaping of an American Shrine, The Fourth Annual Gettysburg Seminar*, 124–34. Gettysburg National Military Park, 1995.

Smith, Timothy B. "Black Soldiers and the CCC at Shiloh National Military Park." *CRM: The Journal of Heritage Stewardship* 3 (Summer 2006): 73–84.

———. "Civil War Battlefield Preservation in Tennessee: A Nashville National Military Park Case Study." *Tennessee Historical Quarterly* 63 (2005): 236–47.

Stokes, Melvyn. "The Civil War in Movies." In *Legacy of Disunion: The Enduring Significance of the American Civil War*, edited by Susan Mary Grant and Peter J. Parish, 65-78. Baton Rouge: Louisiana State University Press, 2003.

Summers, John. "Gettysburg Regress: How the Government is Ruining America's Most Famous Battlefield." *The New Republic* (March 18, 2009): 22–24.

Temkin, Martha. "Freeze-Frame, September 17, 1862: A Preservation Battle at Antietam National Battlefield Park." In *Myth, Memory, and the Making of the American Landscape,* edited by Paul A. Shackel, 123-139. Gainesville: University Press of Florida, 2001.

Unrau, Harlan D., and G. Frank Williss. "To Preserve the Nation's Past: The Growth of Historic Preservation in the National Park Service during the 1930s." *The Public Historian* 9 (Spring 1987): 19–49.

Weeks, Jim. "Gettysburg: Display Window for Popular Memory." *Journal of American Culture* 21 (Winter 1998): 41–56.

Weiner, Jon. "Civil War, Cold War, Civil Rights: The Civil War Centennial in Context, 1960–1965." In *The Memory of the Civil War in American Culture,* edited by Alice Fahs and Joan Waugh, 237-257. Chapel Hill: University of North Carolina Press, 2004.

Theses and Dissertations:

Abroe, Mary Munsell. "All the Profound Scenes: Federal Preservation of Civil War Battlefields, 1861–1990." PhD diss., Loyola University, 1992.

Dixon, Benjamin Y. "Gettysburg, a Living Battlefield." PhD diss., Oklahoma University, 2000.

Kinsel, Amy J. "'From These Honored Dead': Gettysburg in American Culture, 1863–1938." PhD diss., Cornell University, 1992.

Oyler, John. "Pickett Charges; Everyone Else Pays: The Story of the Gettysburg Tower Controversy." Undergraduate thesis, Princeton University, 1972.

Roe, Charles. "Second Battle of Gettysburg: Conflict and Public and Private Interests in Land Use Policies." Master's thesis, Indiana University, 1971.

Spielvogel, John Christian. "Interpreting Sacred Ground: The Rhetoric of National Park Service Civil War Historical Battlefields and Parks." PhD diss., The Pennsylvania State University, 2003.

Trail, Susan W. "Remembering Antietam: Commemoration and Preservation of a Civil War Battlefield." PhD diss., University of Maryland, 2005.

Videos:

Griffith, Jeff. *Legacy at Gettysburg.* Produced and directed by Jeff Griffith. 10 min. nocasinogettysburg, 2010. http://nocasinogettysburg.org/legacyatgettysburg.

INDEX